GOD

The Contemporary Discussion
edited by
Frederick Sontag
& M. Darrol Bryant

DONATION

AEQUALIS OMNIBUS CARITAS

ARCHBISHOP

REMBERT G. WEAKLAND

GOD

The Contemporary Discussion

edited by

Frederick Sontag

& M. Darrol Bryant

The Rose of Sharon Press, Inc.

Conference series no. 12
First Edition
©1982
by
The Unification Theological Seminary
Barrytown, New York 12507

Cover by Jack Kiburz, Gil Roschuni and David Bruner

Printed in the United States of America
Library of Congress Catalog Number 82-70771
ISBN 0-932894-12-7

Distributed by
The Rose of Sharon Press, Inc.
G.P.O. Box 2432
New York, New York 10116

CONTENTS

INTRODUCTION

This volume of essays does not need a long introduction. Either its quality speaks for itself or else no explanation will do. However, the reader may be interested in the circumstances of the composition and selection of these collected papers.

The New Ecumenical Research Association (New ERA) is an ecumenical project of the Unification Theological Seminary. Its aim is to promote dialogue among the various religious and theological perspectives of the world. Its governing board develops and sponsors seminars on a variety of topics held in many locations.

For a world in religious turmoil, as ours is, the notion of 'God' must be the center of dialogue. Recognizing this, New ERA has inaugurated a series of conferences, to be held annually, on the topic of God. The first of these, "God: The Contemporary Discussion," was held on December 26-31, 1981, at Maui, Hawaii, and involved one hundred and sixty-four philosophers, religionists, and theologians. The participants represented most of the world's major religious, philosophical, and cultural perspectives. We hope that the high quality of ecumenical discussion begun there can be continued into the future.

The editors have sought to make this volume representative of the variety of approaches to the contemporary discussion of God. Out of the seventy-three papers submitted, we have chosen papers by theologians who stand in Buddhist, Christian, Hindu, Jewish, Muslim, and other traditions and by philosophers from traditions both East and West. Some papers simply present the perspective of a given religious or philosophical tradition; some address themselves to critical issues arising within a particular tradition or between traditions; some present an analysis of an issue that cuts across different religious and philosophical perspectives; and still others seek to cross over from one tradition to another.

All the papers presented at the conference were distributed to the participants in advance, along with prepared critiques. This left the conference time free for extended exchange on the differing viewpoints presented. In preparing this volume we wanted to give the reader a sense of the diversity, breadth, and scope of the topics discussed. We have also included the *Opening Remarks* of Huston Smith and the *Closing Remarks* of Arabinda Basu in the hope that these might set a tone for our readers in the same way that they served to set a tone for the conference.

Several people have contributed to the preparation of this volume and deserve to be mentioned here. Gil Roschuni designed the text of the book. Jack Kiburz, Jolanda Smalls and Margot Kindler cheerfully typed and retyped these essays; Judith Miller provided valuable editorial assistance; and Lynn Musgrave turned her careful attention to eliminating our editorial oversights.

Frederick Sontag
M. Darrol Bryant
January, 1982

Opening Remarks

Huston Smith

For some of us today (Sunday) is the week's holy day. For others that day was yesterday (Saturday), and for still others, *bismillah*, it was the day before (Friday). But crossing time zones as we all have to reach this island paradise—this after-image of Eden as it appears to those of us who have arrived from wintry ice—reminds us that on the sun itself time zones don't exist, any more than do days in the plural. There has never *been* a Friday, Saturday, or Sunday on the sun, for on the sun there has never been a *night* to factor out those days. And if our thoughts have travelled as far from our planet with its manifold divisions as the sun, we need not let them stop there. We can continue on to that which stands behind the sun, in keeping with Rumi's injunction: "Knowest thou not that the sun thou seest is but a reflection of the sun that stands behind the veil."

It is appropriate that at the start of this conference we raise our sights in this way to the One we have gathered to ponder, the God we have flown these many miles to (as we say) discuss. Before the discussions begin, it is appropriate to let our attention dwell for a moment on their object. Before we bring our *minds* into play on that object, perhaps we can center our *hearts* on it for a moment. Before the cascade of words breaks over us, perhaps we can sense in inner stillness the Reality "before whom all words recoil," as Shankara put the matter. Before our differences begin to surface—as surface they surely will, that being part of the purpose of our assembling here—perhaps we can celebrate the fields of shared discernment that we have in common.

Begin with our sense of the sacred, with its connotations of dignity, incorruptibility, generosity, and patience, without which there is no faith. As referent of this faith stands the reality to which it points: a reality (empty or full, depending on whether we approach it from East or West) that is wonderful, perfect, and the source of all that is; a reality that exceeds in majesty everything our minds can think or even dream. This reality is immanent *and* transcendent, at once both completely beyond us and at the same time foundational *to* us, in Eckhart's formulation, "God's is-ness is my is-ness." And being immanent, it is ever accessible in the depths of our being. Unconsciously dwelling at our inmost center; beneath the surface shuttlings of our sensations, percepts and thoughts; wrapped in the envelope of soul (which too is finally porous) is the eternal and the divine, the final Reality: not soul, not personality, but All-Self beyond all selfishness; spirit enwombed in matter and wrapped round with psychic traces. Within every phantom-self dwells this divine; within all creatures incarnate sleeps the Infinite Sentience—unevolved, hidden, unfelt, unknown, yet destined from all eternity to waken at last and, tearing away the web of sensuous mind, break forever its chrysalis of flesh and pass beyond all space and time.

But lest this inward turning leave us cloistered in cells of subjective privacy, let us remember that we are united, too, in belief that the reality that resides in the depths of ourselves is (in some starkly mysterious way) attuned to justice and order in the affairs of peoples and nations. So for a few moments let us turn our thoughts to the people of Poland, and to the oppressed on every continent as well. In bonds of shared silence, let us unite our spirits with theirs in this time of their ordeal and need.

Shanti. Sholom. Salām. Amen.

Does The Notion Of "Mystery"—As Another Name For God— Provide A Basis For A Dialogical Encounter Between The Religions?

Heinrich Ott

Let me start from the well-known fact that human-ity has grown together into a unity. We are united today among other things by fast transportation and mass-communication. And in such a unified human world the world's religions—of all sorts, those founded by individuals as well as traditional tribal religions —have all moved very near to one another, certainly nearer than ever before. Dialogue between them began unavoidably: they had to get to know each other, they had to live together. But in many parts of the world today the encounter of the religions has already moved far beyond this modest state of affairs. In any case the situation of encounter will more and more affect the course of all religious thought.

If we take this dialogical situation seriously, we have to take it as an open situation. Dialogue is essentially creative; it cannot be programmed in advance. Dialogical encounter among the religions requires a maximum of openness, of risk—it opens into the unpre-dictable. This means that the encounter also requires a minimum of formulated presuppositions. A Christian, for example, may not enter into such dialogue with any prefixed judgements about the truth of the other religion.

In the same way, a Buddhist, for example, may not judge in advance of the dialogue, what perception of truth is possible for a theistic Christian. The Buddhist prejudice about Christianity's belief in God as enormously anthropomorphic must be reexamined, just as the Christian prejudice that Buddhism is basically atheistic and even nihilistic must be reexamined.

But not only do we have to avoid such theological prejudice, we also have to avoid the prejudice of comparative religious studies. Certainly comparative religious studies is necessary, especially as preparation for the dialogue. But, as it objectifies and compares the forms of religion, it does not, out of its own religious attitude, expose this attitude to the integral claims to truth of another religion.

In fact no general concept of religion can be made the basis of dialogue. It would be wrong to assert a sort of anthropology as a basic framework that would include, for example, a religious dimension, a "religious a priori" in human being. In view of the really powerful event of real encounter, all such generalizations are far too premature. For purposes of the dialogue they are just as prejudiced and therefore just as wrong as the disqualification of all non-Christians as "heathens", that is so deeply rooted in traditional Christian thought.

Does that mean that we can say nothing at all about the basis, about the "condition of the possibility", of this dialogue that is so characteristic of our epoch? Is the dialogue like the boundless open sea, into which one must simply plunge and in which one must then swim without support or direction? In a certain sense it is like that. If this seems too risky and too adventurous, one must consider that in today's situation this risk is the only alternative to dogmatic proselytism on the one hand and to relativistic indifference or agnosticism on the other. But as soon as one postulates any sort of preconditions or obligatory basis of the dialogue, it cannot be carried on in creative freedom.

Thus dialogical encounter in the field of religion, as in other fields, certainly contains an element of paradox. On the one hand, the idea of dialogue requires that its participants allow any and every dogmatic formulation to be put in question. (That may seem an impossible requirement, but even where we find it unfulfilled we must rather assume—for the sake of the dialogue—that the other has allowed his beliefs to be put in question.) And yet, on the other hand, the dialogue can never be a life and death conflict in which each participant is pitted against the other or puts his religious convictions at stake with the conscious risk of finally losing them. Rather, faithfulness towards one's own religious convictions is something just as much required as openness. This point has been made in most of the recent discussions about the problem as one sees, for example, in the document "Dialogue in Community" from the World Council of Churches' conference of 1977 in Chiang Mai.

The apparent paradox, I think, can only be solved by a mode of thought that does not think in terms of positions or propositions, but rather one that understands itself as a way, a path. I have dealt with this subject several times before, as for example recently in the periodical *Japanese Religions* (September 1980) in which I spoke about the fruitfulness of Heideggerian thought for the encounter of Christianity and Buddhism. In this paper I sketched the project of a new style of "*dialogical theology*". Dialogical theology is a theology which does not concentrate upon defending one's own or attacking the others' positions like fortresses, but which knows that every position is essentially an open one, since the truth is always greater than any position or standpoint, and that therefore even seemingly contradictory positions can have their right and must not necessarily exclude each other. But today I should like to make one step further and to deal with another aspect of the problem. On the basis of what I have already said about the global dialogical situation and about the requirement that dialogue proceeds essentially without presuppositions, I would like to point out three things. First, in the rejection of presuppositions, or, stated positively, in the assumption of an unbounded openness, there *is* something like a theological self-understanding of the dialogical event as such. Second, this self-understanding has to do with the presence of God Himself. Third, the recognition of this connection has practical existential consequences.

✳✳✳

In what we call religious experience (in Christianity it is called faith, *pistis*) we experience an inexhaustible and fundamentally inexpressible mystery—whether we call this mystery "God", "Dhamma", "Brahman", or whatever. The more familiar one becomes with this mystery, the deeper and more astonishing becomes one's experience of it. That belongs to its essence! Biblically expressed, what we shall see face to face in the *eschaton* is indeed not less, but more of a mystery than what we see "as in a mirror dimly" today (I Cor. 13:12). God does not give up his quality of mystery when He is seen face to face. The mystery is not a riddle that at some future time can be solved and, therefore, can lose its quality of enigma. Because of this mysterious character of religious experience and because of the mysterious character of *what* we experience which transcends all forms and doctrinal formulations, the believer of a given religion can at least think it possible that the adherent of another religion is actually confronted with the same inexpressible reality. Considered again in relation to the Bible, the structure of this notion of mystery corresponds exactly to what one says about its "living God". For if God were not inexpressible mystery, He would not be God. To use Anselm's expression: He would not be that than which nothing greater can be thought.

If we search in the history of theology for our leading notion of mystery, we come upon *Rudolf Otto* (among the Protestants), who in his book *The Holy* (1917) described the numinous as the actual object of religious experience. The numinous is "*mysterium tremendum et fascinosum*": it effects both awe and fascination. According to Otto such experience falls into a category qualitatively different from all others. Otto advises one who has never experienced such awe to put down his book, to read no further, and he says that with such a person, if he exists, he could never discuss religion. Otto compares him to one who reduces the experience of beauty to the feeling of mere sensual pleasure. Furthermore, Otto can say that religiosity is first stirred by a feeling of the "uncanny". This is the beginning of religion, and in it, in the early dawn of humankind's history, both "demons" and "gods" have their roots. The "Holy" is the "totally-other", therefore it effects holy awe. It is the totally foreign, the completely un-understood, the essentially inexpressible, the *arrheton*. That accounts for its quality of mystery. In the Bible we constantly find events that inspired awe. Consider these several examples: Moses' encounter with God in the burning bush, Elijah's experience of God on Mount Horeb as a soft breeze passed by, Isaiah's calling to be a prophet; or from the New Testament: the narrative of the transfiguration and the authentic abrupt ending of the Gospel of Mark. One could give many more such examples. In emphasizing the qualitative peculiarity of the experience of the Holy, Otto distinguishes it from all other experiences, from the experiences of rational truth or moral good or aesthetic beauty. In doing so he rejects every attempt to reduce religion to something else—for example, the attempt of some sociologists to explain religion as a factor of social integration or as a mere function of basic needs.

But Otto's thought moves within a subjective psychological

framework, for he gives his attention solely to subjective religious experience, to the quality of feeling. It is important to recognize the "objective" situation as well. This brings me to the notion of mystery that I find in Karl Rahner. Human life is directed towards Being and exists within Being's horizon, and Rahner calls this Being inexpressible mystery. In the last analysis it is God himself. Human being experiences itself as encompassed by this inexpressible mystery even before it explicitly thinks, hears and addresses God. Rahner has drawn his notion from conventional Catholic classroom theology: what cannot be perceived by natural reason, but must be revealed by God if we are to perceive it, is "mysterium", a mystery of faith. Traditionally, this meant, for instance, the trinity, the incarnation, supernatural grace. One cannot see through this; one must accept it in humble belief. But Rahner makes two important changes in this traditional scheme.[1] The first change has to do with the statements revealed by God that we must accept in the obedience of faith. Rahner argues that it is not these statements as such that are mysterious, but God. What we do not comprehend is not the statements but God. God, who reveals himself to us, who is near to us—He is the mystery. In this way the traditional notion of mystery becomes to a certain degree "de-intellectualized". Secondly, traditional Catholic thinking implied that God could, if He wanted, communicate any number of mysterious statements. But Rahner sees rather only one mystery, God himself.

Rahner thinks that these changes and all they imply are important for the apologetic task. This distinguishes Rahner from Rudolf Otto, for apologetics (taken not in the traditional but in the more modern sense of communication and existential verification) always tries to attain agreement among the greatest possible number of persons, and that is apparently completely opposed to Otto's curt remark that anyone without religious feeling should not read his book. Rahner can even say that the mystery of God is *quasi* something self-evident:

> In the last depths a person knows nothing more exactly than that his knowledge is only a small island in an infinite and unexplored sea, than that the existential question is whether he loves more the island of his so-called knowledge or the infinite sea of mystery. Is

the mystery the only self-evident thing for him, or is the small lamp with which he explores his island (one calls it "science") to be his eternal light? (That would be hell itself!) ... The mystery is what is actually self-evident. ... Epistemologically and existentially it is both the threat to and the blessed peace of human being. It ... forces him to abandon the confines of an apparently reasonable self-evidence of himself and to step out into a space where there are not paths, "even when it is night"; it seems to challenge him ... far too much, far more than he can fulfill. ... And yet the mystery is for him who entrusts himself to it, who loves it humbly and yields himself completely to it without fear ... the only peace.[2]

Thus Rudolf Otto's two elements of the numinous as *mysterium tremendum* and *mysterium fascinosum*, are also to be found in Rahner's reflection on the inexpressible mystery.

***

In German theology of our century, then, we have thus found two related starting points. While Rudolf Otto refers us to the irreducible quality of the religious experience of the Holy, to the numinous as mystery, Karl Rahner refers us to the character of this mystery as something self-evident that constitutes the basic situation of every person; therefore—this is Rahner's intention also and according to him is especially crucial for modern humanity—it must be something existentially understandable for everyone. If it is difficult to present to modern humanity belief in God in its traditional theistic form as something self-evident, it may well be suggested that today's humanity can be shown as existing before, and surrounded by, the inexpressible mystery.

I assume now that this notion of mystery—as on the one hand "wholly-other" and on the other "self-evident"—is helpful and illuminating when we understand and continue our thinking about the religious situation I described in the beginning. I mean the dialogical situation that has developed and that has no fixed preconceptions.

"Mystery" does have a theo-logical and an anthropo-logical component. The theo-logical component lies in the fact that "mystery" is just another name for "God". It would be useless to search through the whole Bible for some sort of proof of that, since every doxological motive of the Bible—and it is full of them—witnesses to the mystery of God. That God is to be worshipped and in fact is worshipped certainly implies the kind of sovereignty that is inexhaustible and inscrutable, an absolute mystery that no creaturely spirit can ever penetrate, but toward which creaturely spirit can turn in worshipful perception. As free spirit, human being can defy (*trotz*) a "sovereignty" based simply on power and possessing a certain paternal character. Human freedom would give one a certain right to defy such a "sovereignty". In Buddhism, we should remember, the Buddha or Enlightened-One who is always human, has left the Gods far behind. According to a legend, Brahma, who rules the world, must earnestly plead with Buddha Shakyamuni not to remain silent about the highest enlightenment he had attained but to communicate it to the gods and to people.

On the other hand, defiance would not be a legitimate attitude toward a sovereignty of God that is based on inexhaustible mystery, because here creaturely spirit encounters not only the limits of its *power* but also the limits of its *essence* as well. In other words, here it hits not only on the outer but also on the inner limits of its freedom. The mystery is not only *one* of the attributes of God but it is the very structure of divine being, of the living God. As soon as we think of God as infinite Spirit in his relation to created or finite spirit—and otherwise he cannot become a subject at all for our finite thought!—he appears as mystery. Mystery is in fact another name for God.

There can be no other inexhaustible mystery than God himself. If we say that the human heart is inscrutable, unfathomably deep, we are already in process of thinking humanity in the light, or perspective, of the inexhaustible mystery of God. God is so near to the human heart that he alone fathoms its impenetrable depths, and through such being known by God, the essence of human being participates in the mystery of God.

We now already have in view the second, the anthropological component of the notion "mystery". Human being is neither a mechanism nor an organism, nor an inwardness or mere subjectivity that could be content with itself. Rather, human being is *essentially* being near the mystery that transcends it—which mystery is the truth that is always more, always greater than any human knowledge. Human being is *essentially* being encompassed by and being opened into mystery, or, as I earlier tried to express it in my book, *God*, "Human being is more than what it is".

As we give the notion "mystery" this dominating position, we make thereby both a theo-logical and an anthropo-logical decision. Because we decide at the same time against both a naturalistic understanding of human being and an anthropomorphic understanding of God, which, while it attributes to God special qualities such as omniscience and omnipotence, nevertheless places him, in principle, on the same level as human being. Yet we do *not* decide against the Bible, in spite of the fact that it is full of anthropomorphisms.[3] Rather, we perceive nothing else than the mystery-structure in the Person of the living God, namely in the Old Testament's name of God as it is explained as "I am that I am" (Exod. 3:14). Here the Bible says that the essence of God—that *what* He is —cannot be stated; it remains fully impenetrable. But it says that we must always and everywhere reckon with his presence. According to the New Testament, God "dwells in unapproachable light" (I Tim. 6:16); and in his revelation, in the incarnation of the *logos*, he does not cease to be mystery, he does not make himself into a seizable and comprehendible object. Even the fact that the living God of the biblical proclamation speaks, that he addresses human being and calls it to responsibility by no means contradicts his inexpressible mystery, before which silent adoration is finally the only adequate attitude. "Mysticism" and "word" are not so easily to be placed in contrast with one another. Here we should remember the dialectic of speaking and being silent, about which Martin Heidegger has said so much that is important. Speaking—language itself —is not an isolated self-sufficient entity. Rather, it grows out of silence and opens into silence, and even *as* language it still remains penetrated by silence.

The theological decision about which we are speaking has to do with the *niveau* both of our understanding of God and of our understanding of human being. Without this decision, without this concentration on the notion of mystery, religion becomes sectarian, and anthropology becomes superficial. Thus we have turned here our attention toward a theme that includes both interest in anthropology and in religion, in so far as it affects each of these fields equally.

The decision around which our reflection circles has yet a third implication. It has to do with the dialogue between the religions that has to be so open that it requires no common doctrinal presuppositions and expects no doctrinal results. Rather, this dialogue leads simply to a mutual respect in which the experience of one religion enlightens the other and allows itself to be enlightened by the other. For whether the absolute mystery is thought and experienced, for instance, as the Trinitarian God or as Sunyata, Nothingness, God and Sunyata cannot actually be compared, contrasted or harmonized on the doctrinal level. They are, however, the two focal points of a discussion that may prove to be so fruitful that it never ends. In a discussion of this kind "mystery" is not something like a common superimposed concept that the discussion partners agree upon in advance or hope finally to arrive at. It is rather the expression of the self-understanding that the dialogue as such implies as it proceeds in openness. It arises during the dialogue itself. For the dialogue is not simply the product of the necessity of getting along peacefully with one another in a world that has grown small. The motivation to the dialogue we have characterized rather includes the expectation of being enlightened through the perspective of the other and indeed of being strengthened in one's own experience of faith and in one's own confession. And therefore the dialogue presupposes—not doctrinally but implicitly and existentially— that the dialogue partner too, in his very specific religious experience, is nevertheless touched by one and the same mystery. Thus this notion of mystery which refers us to the superrational (not the antirational!) and to the inexpressible (not the speechless!), is in itself a guarantee that it cannot be misused as a new superstructure that would violate the openness of dialogue.

We have said that the participants in a dialogue between different religions can, in the midst of all their differences, be moved by the same inexplicable mystery. This statement is not a harmonizing theory about a common denominator, nor about a minimum of identity of conviction and feeling. Rather, the statement only describes the dialogical condition in which such a totally open yet totally engaged encounter first becomes possible—the encounter we described at the beginning of this paper as characteristic for this age.

Let me close with another statement: To say "God has encountered us and we give testimony to the encounter", is the word of those who are sure of their task and true to their conviction. But to say "God has encountered us alone and only we can witness to the encounter" is the word of those who feel first of all the need of securing and assuring themselves. How we deal with the problem described in this paper, the problem of dialogue, depends finally on whether or not we are truly ready to allow room for the mystery, the omnipresence and sovereignty of God.

FOOTNOTES

1 Cf. Karl Rahner, "Über den Begriff des Geheimnisses in der katholischen Theologie", *Schriften zur Theologie IV* (1962).

2 *Ibid.*

3 The real intention of the Bible is not anthropomorphism but personalism in its talk about God. There must be drawn a clear distinction between personalism and anthropomorphism! Personalism—for which I pleaded in my books *God* and *Der persönliche Gott* (1969)—aims at the nearness of God and the mutuality or reciprocity between God and the human (cf. Martin Buber!), which is implied in such nearness. Whereas anthropomorphism means an objectifying of God's eternal Mystery into an imaginable being alongside the inner-worldly beings.

The Hindu Conception of God

T.R.V. Murti

I am grateful to the organizers of New ERA for inviting me to participate in this Conference on God. I deem it a great honour. This gives me an opportunity to expound, however briefly, the particularly Hindu and Buddhist conceptions of God.

I

A survey of the world of cultural groups, especially of the so-called primitive tribes and backward peoples, would invariably show that none of them at any time in their history was without practices and modes of behaviour implying knowledge of the presence of a Spirit or spirits, of some Transcendent Being whom we call God or gods. The Transcendent Being was also understood as different from man and the empirical world, and in some unmistakable way superior to, governing and controlling, man and things. The evidence of historians and anthropologists is so unanimous and incontestable in this regard that I need not labour the point. A history of the ancient cultures like those of Egypt, Assyria, Babylon, the Greeks and Romans, the Hindus and Germanic tribes would show that they worshipped many gods and goddesses. These gods were adored, abhorred, and certainly propitiated in various ways by appropriate rites and rituals, ceremonies and sacrifices.

That many of these gods have dropped out is not surprising: the adherents of these cults and religious communities themselves went out of existence or their fashions changed. The 'Death of God', although much trumpeted in the West at the present moment, is no new phenomenon. It has been happening right through the ages. Denial or death of a personal God need not necessarily mean the denial of Transcendence, although in the West it perilously amounted to materialism. Buddhism, Jainism, the Sāṃkhya and the Mīmāṃsā and even some adherents of the Advaita Vedānta certainly denied a personal God as a creator and arbiter of the Universe. They did not, however, deny spiritual transcendence. These are great religions, and most of them are current today. Ignorance and exclusiveness of the West are responsible for identifying denial of a personal God as materialism or atheism.

There are thus not two alternatives. Actually, there are three: Personal God, Impersonal Transcendence, and Materialism. Only the last could be called atheism in the strictest sense. Atheism may take either of two forms, crass materialism or humanism. The impersonal spirit or Godhead is known by various names as Brahman, Dharmakāya, Tathatā, Tao. Plato and Aristotle were aware of this as the Good and Pure Act. Plotinus speaks of the One as beyond the World Soul. John Scotus Erigena and Eckhart conceive Godhead as the highest reality. The philosophies of Fichte, Schelling, Hegel and Schopenhauer among others did accept an Absolute Spirit.

All religions accepting God and Godhead also accepted the survival of man or the finite spirit. For, what would be the meaning and value of God if there is no finite being who is in some intimate manner related to God? There are, however, some differences in the conceptions of the finite spirit and its survival. In the semitic religions there is not only an absolute difference between God and man; man is created and has one life only; after his physical death he is in a kind of suspended animation till called on the Judgement Day before the tribunal of God to be assigned to Heaven or everlasting Hell. In contrast, the eastern religions conceive the finite spirit as more intimately related to God, and in some forms, as in the Advaita Vedānta, even identical with God. Physical death does not mean the end of man's career in the world. In fact, this life is one link in the series of births and deaths before and after. The law of Karma operates and determines the kinds and varieties of different births and the status of the individual.

It is from this unending series of births, deaths and re-births that we want to escape. It is taken as suffering, and one wants to achieve freedom or mukti. In the finite state every being is subject to birth, decay, old age and death in various ways. The Buddha describes suffering graphically: "Birth is ill; decay is ill; sickness is ill; death is ill; to be conjoined to things which we dislike, to be separated from things which we like—that is also sorrow".[1] These conceptions and ideologies can be neither strictly proved nor disproved.

Suffering, unlike enjoyment which lulls us into a sense of false security, engenders reflection. Man becomes aware of himself when he becomes aware of his deep involvement. To be conscious of suffering is to be conscious of an alternative to the present state in which we happen to find ourselves. Without the contrast between what is and what might have been, between the actual state and the possible, there could be no sense of grievance; hence no suffering. If everything that happens to us were thought to be completely inevitable and inexorable, there could be no grievance. We feel that things could be helped; they could have been otherwise; we could have done better. Thus in all suffering man is conscious, however implicitly, of the present situation and his ability to help it. Suffering is evidence that our nature is different from the environmental world.

If there were no suffering or if suffering could be removed totally and finally by known objective and scientific means, through technology and application of social laws, there could be no occasion for turning to God, for religion in general. It may be held that, if we could conquer Nature and exploit her resources, we might satisfy all our wants and that as soon as they arise in us. The modern man in the atomic age with his immense faith in technology is prone to think that the solution lies this way. Wants, though, may still outstrip our ability to satisfy them; a leap-frog race may result. The root problem is left untouched. Technology cannot provide the wisdom and the goodwill necessary to make a wholesome use of our power. Control over Nature without control over oneself (self-restraint) can lead only to rivalry, domination, conflict and suicidal warfare. The human problem is basically spiritual; it lies in self-control and self-education.

The root cause of suffering is the egoistic and the megalomaniac attitude—the selfishness of man. The aim of all religion has been to get rid of this egoism altogether, as in the absolutistic systems, or to disarm it sufficiently by conceiving all beings as progenies of the same Father, as in the theistic religions. Mankind has therefore always depended on the unseen, perfect and eternal being called God to bring about change in the worldly order.

II

Does such a God or Godhead exist? Theologians and philosophers in the East and the West have tried to prove God's existence and His nature by appeal to scriptures and by arguments, although they are not completely agreed. The cosmological, teleological and ontological proofs in various forms have been adduced. The *Nyāya Kusumāñjali* of Udayanācārya formulates, in addition, some other interesting arguments:

> The Omniscient Eternal Being (God) is proved by these reasons: Effect, Structuring, Sustenance, usage of words (Language-convention), through Revelation (pratyayataḥ), the existence of Scripture and the usage of Numbers (Sankhyā).[2]

Many others, like the Buddhists, the Jainas and before them the Mīmāṁsakas, have tried quite vehemently to refute God's existence. Kant in his Rational Theology (in the Transcendental Dialectic of his *Critique of Pure Reason*) could also be considered in this connection.

The cosmological proof takes the world as contingent, as effect, and considers God as the first cause or the agent to bring it into existence. The contingency of the world may however be denied; it can be contended that it has always existed without beginning or end as the Mīmāṁsakas, Buddhists and Jainas aver. Diversity in the world and the things that affect us may be due to the operation of the law of Karma (Karmajaṁ loka-vaicitryam) without requiring a personal God. Even if the world were contingent, God need not be the cause. Nature in its potentiality, like the Prakṛti of the Sāṁkhya, may plausibly be taken as its cause; Prakṛti is autonomous. The teleology of the world may be innate in Nature. The moral governance of the world may be traced to the natural good sense and justice implicit in all men. The law of Karma which is a moral law operates in the world and is quite impersonal and invariable. Language may not be a convention made either by man or by God, or by God first and then communicated to mankind. Convention itself presupposes language, which is derived from convention. To make convention, words have to be used and understood by persons participating in the convention. This reasoning is clearly circular. Invoking God does not help here. How could God make known his intention, his conventions between particular words and their specific meanings, to persons who did not use language already? There would be a communication gap. If men were already using language, God's convention does not obviously initiate language, as claimed.

Thus, as there are alternative and plausible modes of explaining the world, its design and moral governance and the presence of language, the so-called conventional proofs do not necessarily prove the existence of God.

The ontological proof, first formulated by St. Anselm and also adduced by Descartes, Spinoza, Leibniz and Hegel and sought to be restated by Charles Hartshorne with great ingenuity and sophistication, fails to carry conviction. The ontological proof tries to prove God by defining the concept of God as including existence, thus begging the question. No idea of a perfect being or coherence of ideas carries with it existence. Idea and being belong to two different orders. A Hegel may assume the identity of thought (or the gamut of ideas) with reality; this, however, remains a pure assumption.

Nor can scripture or revelation vouchsafe the nature and existence of God. There is no unanimity in the different revelatory deliverances of the scriptures of different religions. They are conflicting and even contradict each other on vital issues. To settle the dispute among different revelations one has to appeal to reason. At best, revelation can inform us of the possibility of God's presence; it cannot guarantee His existence. In fact, all these proofs may give an idea of God and suggest his possible existence. As these are not the only modes of explaining the world and its governance, none of them carries with it any existence or reality of God.

At this stage, I should like to make my position clear with regard to the respective roles of Reason and Revelation. Revelation or insight into the nature of the transcendent is conveyed to us through Myths. It is only Mythology couched in symbolic and metaphorical language that could intimate and introduce us to things far removed from the empirical world. Revelation is the inspired intuitions of seers (Rishis) and prophets. Sensuous perception and discursive thought are incapable of revealing God and transcendental truths. These primary utterances of any tradition are through myth. The Vedic Mythology is probably the oldest and richest of all such ventures. Even myths cannot convey to us knowledge of things of which we were completely ignorant, the utterly unknown. If God or Brahman were completely unknown, no enquiry would be possible; if fully known, no enquiry would be necessary. We can make a leap from a position which we have already occupied. Creativity and new intuitions of the transcendent pertain to revelation through myths. The knowledge given by Revelation is taken as Śruti or Śravaṇa (Hearing or Harkening)—the very first step.

The Vedic or other scriptures are not merely to be preserved and repeated by rote, but have to be understood, clarified and interpreted according to the principles of reason. Food taken must be chewed, masticated and swallowed, and thus subjected to the process of assimilation. In fact, without reasoning we cannot understand the true import of scripture. There is the fear that we could become literalists and fundamentalists without reasoning.

In interpreting scriptural revelation by the human intellect, we do open revelation to the hazards of subjectivity and difference (diversity). This risk must be accepted. The Veda and the Vedānta (Upanishads) have been interpreted and explained in several different and opposed standpoints by a number of Āchāryas (Teachers). We have not surely exhausted all the possible ways of interpretation. This second step is called *Manana*, thinking or cogitation. Its purpose is to remove impropriety (asambhāvanā) and opposed understanding (viparītabhāvanā). Reason and Revelation are not to be conceived of as incompatible with each other. Intuitions are given only through revelation; reasoning only arranges, classifies, explains and understands the given intuitions.

The second step, although it helps in appreciating and appropriating the given intuitions of the transcendent, does introduce a measure of separateness and remoteness. The quest in religion is spiritual realization, and not the thinking criticism of things. We have, therefore, to cultivate a process which removes the separation and remoteness. This is the third step called Deep Meditation (Nididhyāsana). Here we know God or our Deepest Self not externally through representation, but by being it entirely (Brahma veda brahmaiva bhavati). We become identical with the real. These three stages are the time-honoured ones accepted by all religious denominations in India. This three-tier formula has its origin in the *Bṛhadāraṇyaka Upaniṣad* passage:

> The Self (Ātman) is to be directly perceived (draṣṭavyaḥ), through Hearing (of Scripture) (Śrotavyaḥ), by Thinking (Mantavyaḥ), and in Deep Meditation (Nididhyāsitavyaḥ) Br. Up. IV, v.6. (ātmā vā are draṣṭavyaḥ śrotavayaḥ, mantavyaḥ, nididhyāsitavyaḥ).

We cannot also adduce the performance of miracles—the so-called violation of the normal laws of nature—as proving God's existence. Of all the world religions it is Christianity which depends upon miracles to some extent to prove the truth of its religious contentions. Some 'Godmen' of present-day India also claim to perform miracles and miraculous cures and confer favours on devotees. Most of these miracles are simply leger-de-main. The miracles like telepathy and clairvoyance are nothing but psychic phenomena. Some born psychics have them. They could also be acquired by constant practice of concentration of mind (the inner sense-organ) and other rules. Patañjali in his *Yoga-Sūtras* gives a systematic exposition for the concentration of mind. He devotes a separate chapter to describe the Vibhūtis or siddhis, psychic attainments like making one's body very light or heavy, minutization, grossification, disappearance, captivation and control of others, flying in the air, telepathy, clairvoyance and scores of others.

The Buddha deals with the Siddhis, psychic attainments. In fact, most of the saints belonging to various religions also possessed many of these powers. Both Buddha and Patañjali[3] are, however, emphatic in deprecating the exhibition of these attainments, taking them as hindrances, (antarāya) which contribute to pride and vanity of the ego. The acquisition of siddhis and their exhibition do not contribute to spiritual insight into the nature of the transcendent.

Many persons, especially prophets and saints in the different traditions, have claimed to have seen God and even conversed with Him. A recent instance is that of Ramakrishna Paramahamsa who claimed to have had constant and intimate experiences of Kālī, the Mother Goddess. We need not deny or doubt the veracity of such intimate experiences of saints in the various traditions down the ages. The explanation is different. Firstly, these intimate experiences are not and could not be shared by other persons; they are not objective or public. It can be said that the saints and the mystics were only communing with their unconscious or with the deeper level of the Self. The very fact that the descriptions and expressions of these experiences given by the different saints are couched in different forms and in different spoken languages is indicative of their subjective character. Moreover, God being universal, formless, uniformly and evenly present everywhere and at all times cannot appear in individual forms and talk to persons in different languages. The intimate experiences of saints can therefore be taken only as versions or the different modes in which each religious tradition functions. The God who appears at any particular time, in any specific place, or in any particular mode, cannot be the universal God.

III

A God who is completely Other and external to man is unknown and unknowable. The most fatal objection against this conception of God is that it lacks existence and immediacy. So if we are to look for God, we are to look for him in the composition or the structure of man, in the Self (Ātman). The existence of the self has been doubted and denied. Hume, for instance, states that there are only mental states of knowing, feeling and willing and not anything over and above. He says: "For my part, when I enter most intimately into what I call *myself*, I always stumble on some particular perception or other, of heat or cold, light or shade, love or hatred, pain or pleasure. I never can catch *myself* at any time without a perception, and never can observe anything but the perception. When my perceptions are removed for any time as by sound sleep; so long am I insensible of *myself*, and may truly be said not to exist."[4]

Hume's search for the self is misdirected. He seeks to find it as an object, as one among other things cluttered in front of him. Even if one were to fix upon something as the self, it would be dead and inert like any object. Is not the doubter himself the self? *Cogito ergo sum*. Or as Śaṅkara says the self cannot be denied; the denier of self is himself the real self. (ya eva nirākartā tasyaiva ātmatvāt; Ātmanaḥ pratyākhyātum aśakyatvāt). Descartes commits the great mistake of identifying the 'I' or the self with the mental states which are perceived and are therefore objects. We experience the states of waking, dreaming and deep sleep. The self cannot be identified with any of these states or mental modifications, for if it were identified with any of these, it could not be *aware of these states as such*. That which is continuous and pervasive amid constant change and flux is different from these changes. The principle is that that which is unchanging and continuous amid change and difference is different from the changeful states, as the thread in a garland is different from the individual flowers hanging on the thread. (yeṣu vyāvartamāneṣu yad anuvartate, tat tebhyo bhinnam, yathā kusumebhyaḥ sūtram).

The self knows and illumines all external objects and mental states, but itself is not *known* as object by any knowledge or mental state. This knowledge which cognizes the so-called self would lead to a *regress ad infinitum*: a series of knowledges and cognitive states chasing one another. If we were not aware of the self at any stage there would be utter blankness and darkness; we could not make any statement whatever, even the statement that there is utter blankness. Hence the real self is not known as object and yet we are immediately aware of it. It is the ultimate and invariable light which lights up and illumines the entire universe (svayaṁ prakāśa: avedyatve sati aparokṣa-vyavahārayogyatvam). The self-luminous and self-existent Self (Ātman) is God *par excellence*. This ultimate truth is conveyed through the Great Sentences (mahā vākyas) of the Upaniṣads: That thou art (Tat tvam asi), I am Brahman (Ahaṁ brahmāsmi), the Self is Brahma (Ayam Ātmā brahma), and Knowledge or Consciousness is Brahman (Prajñām brahma).

IV

Why do we not ordinarily look for God as the deepest or the ultimate Self? The Holy is overwhelming and floods everything; we primarily look *outward* to the object. This is the natural attitude. We get inwardized or reflective only when there is a breakdown of our ordinarily normal functioning. As the *Kaṭho-paniṣad* points out:

> The Self-existent (svayambhū) pierced the opening of the sense organs outward. Therefore one looks *outward*, not within oneself (antarātman). The wise man, while seeking immortality, beheld the Self, turning within, face to face.[5]

All religions conceive God as an *Other* confronting the finite self. Religion is a stupendous symbolism. It externalizes our deepest self *as an Other* existing outside of us. The paradox of all symbolism is that it has to be taken literally if it is to work. This attitude emphasizes the non-contamination with the finite self, its purity and all powerfulness and universality. In doing so it compromises the immediacy and intimate (intrinsic) existence which are associated with the Self. It facilitates, however, the attitude of worship, surrender and appropriation.

A similar anomaly obtains with regard to what we take as the Self. We naturally identify the self with the body, the sense-organ, with the mental states, with the I-sense (egoism). A closer reflection would show, as already pointed out, that the real self is Pure Subject and not object, not something known as Other. That which is an object is constantly changing, varied, unstable, without the identical element to impart unity and oneness.

We will find many layers, stages and phases of the self, and although the self may be wrongly identified with the states and changeful aspects it is really different from them. Otherwise, we shall have to take the changeful states themselves as the self or deny the existence of the self altogether.

It may be thought that in deep sleep there is utter blankness, unwitnessed and unreported. Then how do we become conscious of the state of deep sleep at all? Do we not say on getting up, 'I was sleeping soundly, not knowing anything then'. Of course, this is known retrospectively as a kind of remembrance on waking up, but it certainly refers to the experience of the previous state. If there were no consciousness, a self aware of the state of deep sleep, how could we refer to the state of deep sleep at all, even as utter blankness? The other alternative would be that the self dies when we go to sleep, and there is a totally new self created the moment we get up. The new self created every time is just like the previous self with the added feature of remembering the so-called dead unconscious state of deep sleep. This hypothesis is far from convincing, nor does it explain the situation.

V

These attempts at knowing the self have failed because we try to have a sense perception of the self or a discursive knowledge of it. Over against this, we have a non-sensuous intuition (Intellectual Intuition) of the self. In intuition the essence and existence coincide. We know the self not by having a representation of it but *by being it*. To know is to identify oneself with the thing known. This mode of knowing is basic and fundamental. Our sensuous intuitions and conceptual thought are possible because of this mode of knowledge.

In the West the dichotomy has been sensuous intuition or reason. The empiricists try to derive everything from sense experience; there is nothing in the intellect which is not derived from sense. Opposed to this, the rationalists decry the role of sense-experience and derive everything from reason. The most consistent rationalist we find is Hegel. Kant, however, speaks of two ultimate sources of knowledge: "Our knowledge springs from two fundamental sources of the mind, the first is the capacity of receiving representations (receptivity for impressions), the second is the power of knowing an object through these representations (spontaneity in the production of concepts). Through the first an object is *given* to us, through the second the object is *thought* in relation to that given representation. Intuition and concepts constitute, therefore, the elements of all our knowledge."[6]

The problem of reconciling or harmonizing sensuous intuitions with forms of thought is left unresolved in Kant. His successors tried to tilt the balance one way or the other. Kant also speaks of God knowing things through intellectual intuition. But he doubts and even denies that human beings can have intellectual intuition.

> We have not indeed been able to prove that sensible intuition is the only possible intuition but only that it is so for us. But neither have we been able to prove that another kind of intuition is possible. Consequently, although our thought can abstract from all sensibility, it is still an open question whether the notion of a noumenon be not a mere form of a concept, and whether, when this separation has been made, any object whatsoever is left.[7]

How could Kant be aware that God's knowing is intellectual intuition, if he were not aware of it in himself? Even scripture can only speak to us of things of which we are implicitly aware. It cannot reveal to us something completely and totally unknown. Ultimately our knowledge of God or any other entity must have some reference to basic human experience.

We therefore have a non-sensuous intuition of the self. In fact it is a misnomer to speak of intuition *of* the self. The intuition is the self, and self is the intuition. There is no difference between existence and essence or between substance and attribute. The self is *caitanya-svarūpa*, consciousness itself. All other modes of knowledge and experiences are variations or versions of this basic intuition which invariably and always lies at the back of these modes.

VI

Why are we not aware of the deeper nature of self as the self-luminous Brahman-consciousness, as absolute? We are covered by ignorance. As the *Chāndogya Upaniṣad* (VIII, iii, 2.) says:

> As a treasure of gold hidden is not perceived by persons unacquainted with the knowledge of the hidden spot, likewise all these beings going every day (in deep sleep), are not conscious of the Brahman-world; because they are covered *by the veil of falsity* (anṛtena pratyūḍhāḥ).

This is the principle of māyā or avidyā to which the finite self is subject and because of which the Self appears as the ego, as numerous finite selves vying with one another. The justification for accepting a quasi-real entity called māyā is because of the actuality of evil (finitude, vice and suffering); yet evil could be transcended and negated completely. That is, all our endeavour towards attainment of truth, perfection, and goodness presupposes the presence of evil. If however evil were permanent and absolutely real, we could never get rid of it.

The principle of māyā could be compared to the doctrine of original sin. This mythology is too little understood. There was never a time when man was free, sinless and not self-alienated. For, being free we cannot get into the state of primordial ignorance or bondage by some such trivial act as eating the fruit of the forbidden tree. The evil one or Satan is our own attitude of selfishness, egoism. God is the real basis of universality, unselfishness, goodness and perfection. Satan though actual is not ultimately real, not a real anti-God. The ontological status of Satan is not made clear in Christianity. He is not a real ultimate entity but has only an epistemic status. This is exactly what the doctrine of māyā stands for.

VII

The non-sensuous intuition of the Self is God or rather Godhead. In fact, the intuition is God and God is the intuition. There is no distinction between consciousness and content. There is not consciousness *of*; even intentionality is not intrinsic to consciousness.

Godhead transcends all relations and distinctions. The basic distinction, accepted by the theist and the monotheist, of God on the one hand and the finite self on the other—the I and Thou relationship—itself presupposes a basic unity, the ground on which the distinctions stand according to Advaita Vedānta. The principle involved is that wherever there are distinctions and differences they are based upon an identity on which they stand (abheda-pūrvako hi bhedaḥ). Rāmānuja, the great Indian theist and advocate of difference, therefore, refuses to accept a differenceless, attributeless reality (nirviśeṣa Vastu), or any knowledge which is entirely intuition (nirvikalpa pratyakṣa). For the theist, The Holy (personal God) is fundamental. Although the Advaita is not opposed to God (Īśvara), the Ultimate reality is Godhead or Brahman which is the unity of God and finite creatures. The ultimate aim or value of man is to realize his Freedom—his unity and utter identity with the Godhead. This is the state which transcends all I-ness or egoism. Spiritual attainment in the last analysis is the getting rid of the ego in its various forms.

VIII

Godhead is completely real and accomplished (pariniṣthita vastu). There is nothing to become or to be completed by any developmental process in Him. The Indian view is in full accord with the Aristotelian and the Christian concept of God as Pure Act or Pure Being. It is opposed to conceptions of deity proposed by some of the contemporary philosophers, like Alexander or Hartshorne, who envisage God as an ever-increasing and developing reality. This God which is yet to be, to become what he should be, can never be finalized at any time and cannot serve as the focus of our worship or adoration. A slight distinction may, however, be made between Brahman who is really the Timeless, and God, who is eternal. The eternal is the unchanging reality, over against the changeful and disappearing world. The term "eternal" could therefore be used only in confrontation with the changeful.

The relation between the transcendent—God or Godhead—and the finite world is tenuous, one-sided. The finite world depends on and cannot be anything without God. But God is not compelled or necessitated to create the world. The finite world must be taken as appearance or free phenomenalization of God. The relation between the transcendent real and the world is one of appearance.

As there is a free relationship between God and the finite world, it follows that the realization of God is not by any one monopolistic path. There could be, and there have been, many such paths. The different religions have investigated the paths of realization. They may be incommensurable. Even in each religion there are specific differences under a generic unity.

The different religious modes are the expressions of the spiritual temperament or of the taste of each basic tradition. For instance, one may emphasize the truly intellectual or cognitive approach (jñāna-mārga). The ideal here is to realize God or Godhead as Truth by negating or disassociating it from false appearances, as do the Advaita-Vedānta and many schools of Buddhism. Emphasis may be placed on the predominantly emotional attachment to God, conceiving him as Love; that attitude is one of surrender and obedience. Christianity and Islam and most of the non-advaitic schools of Vedānta like those of Rāmānuja, Madhva, Vallabha, Caitanya, Śaivism, Vaiṣṇavism and many others may be cited as examples of this attitude. Even in the emotional Bhakti approach there may be and there have been different modes: God may be conceived of as father, as mother, as master, as friend, as spouse or as beloved. Love is not *agape*, but *eros* as well. These are not logical alternatives, but they are actual living religions with a long continuous tradition accepted by millions of followers.

One may emphasize (as the ideal) the active role or the doing of good deeds in a dedicated spirit. This would mean emphasizing God as the Ultimate Will and activity. The Bhagavad-Gītā, which teaches the performance of niṣkāma-karma, unselfish dedicated actions, is an example of this emphasis. The main Buddhistic approach and that of Kāshmir Śaivism should also be taken as exemplifying the Will or the Act as basic.

It should, however, be noted that in each of these approaches, the cognitive, the emotional, and the active, there is the co-operation of all the other factors, at least on the lower levels; they are not exclusive of one another. The spearhead, or the drive behind each approach, may emphasize one of these aspects. They may be incommensurable in the ultimate stage. Whether the Absolutes are many and incommensurable or ultimately non-different is a vast and fascinating topic. It is not proposed to pursue this consideration further. It may, however, be noted that in another way spirituality may be either exaltation, glorification, by an intimate inalienable relationship with the Holy Personal God, or utter identity with the Real or Impersonal God. For Rāmānuja and other theists, the relationship with a Personal God is the highest value and ultimate state for man. Śaṅkara points out that where there is a duality between man and personal God there is some deeper and more fundamental unity on which they both stand. This is also God or Brahman, the ultimate Reality or Absolute.

From the above consideration we may conclude that universal Consciousness is God or Godhead; in the last analysis it is the ultimate and only reality. The finite self and other finite beings are limitations or appearances of the universal. The real self is identical with universal consciousness, or with God. The empirical self or ego is a partial embodiment or limitation of that Ultimate Self.

In the theistic religions there is God on the one hand and finite beings on the other, both real, although the reality, superiority and transcendence of God are emphasized. Not only does there arise the perplexing question of two orders or grades of reality, but also about the being of God, His omniscience and power belong to a different order altogether. Theologians are aware that the terms "Being", "Existence", "Knowledge", "Power", etc., although used for finite beings are not used *uni voce*. The fact that man is made in the image of God and was created by a fiat of God, and that God is conceived as the soul of the soul or inner essence of man also indicate the sole reality of God. The ego or the finite self is not thus another reality standing out, opposing God, but is an appearance, a limitation or version of God. Man, and this applies also to all finite beings, is ambivalent: basically God but with an admixture of evil or finitude in varying degrees. The egoism or selfishness makes for estrangement and self-alienation. These have to be eliminated or at least rendered harmless by surrender to God as in the theistic religions.

IX

The ego appears in myriads of forms. We have the individual ego, class, caste, national, cultural and religious egos. Some are acquired, many—like the cultural, social, linguistic and the religious—are inherited. The individual ego or the 'I' *par-excellence* is intrinsic and invariably present. The theistic religions take it as ultimate. Advaita-Vedānta considers this egoism itself as accidental though beginningless, but not endless.

The ego motivates, directs and is the source of all drives and actions. It is really undesirable as it tends towards selfishness, narrowness and pettiness. In the spiritual there is the identity between the means and the end: we should be chaste or truthful not because of some ulterior ends to gain; they are to be taken as ends in themselves. We should love God not because we have to gain anything by that love; loving God itself is the ultimate end (sādhyā bhakti, not sādhana). The worldly or ordinary man uses God as a means to gain favours or relief from painful situations. He is also actuated by fear or dread. This is a lower order of religion and is present in all religious traditions. Again in the spiritual there is complete identity between the good of one and the good of all: the good is an undivided whole. Altruism is based on the conviction that doing good to others is really being good to oneself. In this sense egoism or selfishness is to be eschewed in all forms and to the utmost extent. The attainment of universal selfhood is God or the divine.

God's transcendence and utter freedom from empirical determinations induce the different spiritual approaches. As indicated already, these different approaches are ultimately dependent upon spiritual tastes and the temperament of individuals and traditional groups. Not only are there differences in the basic standpoint of world religions, but there are also various specific differences within each basic religion. The approach to the transcendent is a free venture into a relatively unknown field. Hinduism and Buddhism encourage innumerable spiritual experiments to reach the absolute spirit. There are spiritual accommodation, tolerance and enrichment. The monotheistic religions, however, are dogmatic and monopolistic in their attitudes. Major differences are treated as heresies and they are frowned upon; these religions are generally intolerant. The plea of Symmachus deserves to be heeded: "The heart of this great mystery deserves to be investigated by more than one path".[8] Tolerance of other religions and other doctrinal differences should be based on this conviction of the deep mystery and its approachability by various paths. This openness makes possible the co-existence of equal and different religious communities. Tolerance based upon our practical inability to convert other religionists or on good manners is distinctly superficial. It breaks down sooner rather than later.

Our analysis has been to show that God or Godhead is the ultimate basis of all finite beings. It is the only reality. Finite beings are appearances or accidental divisions or particularizations of that Universal Being. Man, and this applies *mutatis mutandis* to all other creatures as well, is ambivalent in nature: on the basis of Universal Being there is the apparent superimposition of various particular differences which constitutes their egoism or selfishness. Egoism or I-ness is not only the individual egoism but takes on various modes: as class, caste, linguistic affiliations, racial and national denomination and religious fanaticism. To realize God or our deeper spirituality we have to transcend these restrictions and divisions which cramp our outlook and make for pettiness. I draw attention to one or two of these egoisms: caste and religious denomination. Hinduism advocates caste and practices it. It should, however, be noted that this hierarchical attitude is only empirical and procedural. In the ultimate analysis there is only Brahman which is utterly devoid of all differences of any kind whatever (apeta-brahma-kṣatrādi-bhedam asaṁsāri ātmatattvam). It is pure consciousness, being and bliss. The practice and abuse of caste deserve to be condemned in the severest terms. Caste is also practiced internationally by white races against others. Apartheid and racial legislations are instances. This is real caste, based on colour (varṇa).

There is also the practice of caste by followers of one religion against other, alien religions. The monotheistic religions are specially guilty in this regard. They take the followers of other religions as *untermensch* and as not deserving equality with themselves. Such theories and practices are ultimately the denial of man as God or divine. They really deny God. Because each traditional religion has some blind spots and is not truly universal, Tillich advocates that each religion should ultimately transcend its limitations. The current world-religions are parochial and provincial. They appeal to certain types of temperament and taste. Conversion to a particular religion is a sort of imposition and imperialism in the religious sphere. It does not solve any problem; it creates deep spiritual fissures, a kind of religious schizophrenia. It drives the original culture of the converted deep into the unconscious. Besides, each practiced religion is an idolatory, as it worships, while seemingly avoiding physical and tangible idols, the mental, verbal and doctrinal images. These images or idols are so subtle and invariable that they are seldom noticed. Any particular version or expression of God in any form is a perversion, although eminently useful in many ways. The Advaita Vedānta and the Mādhyamika are truly iconoclastic; they reject all such versions and limitations as false impositions (dṛśyatvāt, paricchinnatvāt mithyā). Everything is Śūnya, devoid of the supposed characteristic, and even the Śūnyatā by which we get rid of all things and "isms" is itself śūnya ultimately.

Our main contentions have been that God is none other than the Self; an external and utterly other God is unknown and unknowable. Such an "Other" would lack existence and immediacy. The Self cannot be denied; it is the Self-Luminous Consciousness, not known as object but immediately evident to itself. The Self should not be identified with the individual 'I' or the Ego or any of its ramifications; it is the Universal Consciousness or Pure Being. All religion is a stupendous symbolism, externalizing the Self as a Holy Other, to emphasize its utter purity and universality. All religions speak of God, each in its own way. Each way must be transcended ultimately; because taken literally each is a particular version or expression. Each becomes a caste in the religious sphere and leads to pettiness, blindness and fanaticism. As God is none other than the Deeper Self in the last analysis, it can act only implicitly and unobtrusively. If it were really an Other, it could coerce and bring about a revolution in the mentality of people radically and at once. Rather, its influence is pervasive and persuasive. It is incessantly active and exerts its wholesome influence through the higher impulses of man and other beings. We have to repose confidence in its ultimate victory over evil. As the *Mundaka-ponisad* says, "Truth alone conquers, not Falsity (Satyam eva jayate nānṛtam)".

FOOTNOTES

1 Samyutta Nikāya, Nidāna Vagga XV (Assu Sutta).

2 Kāryāyojanadhṛtyādeḥ padāt pratyayataḥ śruteḥ; Vākyāt samkhyāviśeṣāc ca sādhyo viśvavid avyayaḥ. Nyāya Kusumāñjali. V.i.

3 *Yoga Sūtra* III-37, Te samādhā vŭpasargā vyutthāne siddhayaḥ.

4 David Hume, *A Treatise of Human Nature*, ed. L.A. Selby-Bigge (Oxford: Clarendon, 1888), Book I, Section VI, p. 256.

5 Parāñci khāni vyatṛṇat svayambhūs tasmāt paraṇ paśyati nāntarātman; kaścid dhīraḥ pratyagātmānam aikṣad āvṛttacakṣur amṛtatvamicchan. Kaṭha. Up. IV.i.

6 Immanuel Kant, *Critique of Pure Reason*, trans. Norman Kemp Smith (London: Macmillan, 1929), p. 92, see also p. 65.

7 *Ibid.*, pp. 270-71.

8 As quoted by Arnold J. Toynbee, in *An Historian's Approach to Religion* (London: Oxford Univ. Press, 1956).

The Holiness of God
in Eastern Orthodoxy

Petro B.T. Bilaniuk

The concept of the holiness of God has attracted attention in Western Christianity to a limited degree during the last hundred years; however, concomitant with the theological research on this topic, there was a definite increase of secularization, desacralization and loss of the sense of holiness.[1]

The title, as it stands, is careful not to stress the holiness of God in Eastern Orthodox *theology*. For as we shall see, on the holiness of God, Orthodox theology is underdeveloped.[2] There are few paragraphs or short chapters dedicated to this extremely important and central mystery of the triadic faith. However, this does not mean that there is no general awareness in the Eastern Orthodox spiritual, liturgical, mystical and monastic life of this mystery. In fact, all the Eastern Churches, regardless of their confessional or denominational affiliation (Orthodox, Catholic, Nestorian or Monophysite) have many things in common. One of them is an intense awareness of the Triadic God as a Holy Mystery, or the Very Holiness Itself. God makes his holiness accessible to his creatures in different degrees of intensity. First, to the sacred humanity of Jesus, then to the Mother of God, the saints and all animate and inanimate creatures, or better, the whole visible and invisible cosmos. Therefore, the Christian East is intensely aware of the eschatological fulfillment as the definitive revelation and participation in God as absolute, infinite, all-fulfilling Holiness.

The Holiness of God in the Old Testament.[3]

The Hebrew equivalent for the English word "holy" is *qādôš*, from which is derived the noun *qōdĕš*, "holiness". These words are both of the root *qdš*. The meaning of the word is "to separate, divide" (Note Lev. 20:26). Hence "holiness" in the Old Testament means "separatedness" from the profane, from that which is not holy (I Sam. 21:5; Ezek. 22:26). In the Old Testament, the Greek equivalent to *qādôš* is *hagios* (and infrequently *hieros*). The New Testament uses *hagios* exclusively. Therefore, both the Greek and Hebrew etymologies of the term "holy" point to a reality which is "separated". Besides, it suggests that what is "clean" or "pure" is also related to "holy" in a ritual and juridical sense: that is, a potentially holy state free from defilement by the profane and sinful. The highest sense of holiness which is proper to God is the absolute ontological or substantial holiness, consisting in his eternal uncreated and infinite transcendence and majesty, his total "otherness" of which his glory is an external manifestation. Derived from this concept of holiness is holiness in the moral sense (i.e., absence of sinfulness, with absolute incapacity for sin): that is, absolute moral righteousness. Besides, there is a cultic holiness, which is the quality of an object withdrawn from the profane sphere and consecrated to God alone, therefore clean, sacred, holy.

Old Testament authors often use the term "holy" of God Himself as well as of holy things and persons. Religions of neighboring nations attached the term "holy" predominantly to cultic objects and usages, but seldom to the Godhead. In the Old Testament, the personal God is "Holy" because he is inapproachable in the absolute transcendence of his being; nevertheless, he reveals himself in his divine Lordship as the Creator and Ruler of all things (I Sam. 6:20; Hos. 11:9). The holiness of God has no analogy in the created realm and therefore cannot be deduced from anything known or experienced by man. The most striking example of this is to be seen in Isa. 6:1-3 (cf. Ps. 99) which contains the famous trisagion. The three-fold exclamation of "holy, holy, holy" as a description of the divine being—according to Hebrew grammar—expresses an extraordinary superlative of unheard-of intensity. Therefore in this passage, holiness points to the exaltedness and omnipotence, as well as the awe-inspiring and glorious existence of God. This holiness, however, is radiated into the created realm; in a limited fashion, creatures can participate in it. Thus the holiness of God reveals a personal God, who by his penetrating and immanent will, influences all creatures—human beings, things, places, times and events. In order to describe this dynamic holiness of God, the Bible uses the expression "He glorified himself" (Exod. 14:4; Lev. 10:3; Num. 20:13). Furthermore, his holiness is exclusive, for he demands all honour for himself, and does not permit other gods

(Exod. 20:5; Deut. 17:2-7; Isa. 42:8). In the eschaton, in the last days, the holiness of God will penetrate all things (Num. 14:21); then it will signify the definitive fulfillment.

God elects people and things from the profane world and accepts them into his holiness (Exod. 19:5ff). Therefore Israel is holy (Deut. 7:6, 14:2, 28:9). The election of Israel is sealed by a permanent covenant (Isa. 51:4; Jer. 31:33; Amos 3:2; Ps. 33:12). Furthermore, all dwelling places of God and his manifestations are called holy, e.g., the heavens (Ps. 20:7), the burning bush (Exod. 3:5), Jerusalem (Isa. 52:1), Sion (Isa. 27:13).

The cult is the event and the place of the meeting of God and man. The place of the cult and its many objects are called holy. The elect are holy persons (Exod. 19:14, 24:1ff; Josh. 7:13), the levites, the priests and the high priests (Num. 8:5-22; Exod. 27:1-35; Exod. ch 28, esp. v. 36). Besides, the tent (Exod. 28:43), the temple (I Kgs. 9:3), the holy of holies (Lev. 16:2), the altar (Exod. 29:37), the cultic utensils and the arc of the covenant (II Chr. 35:3), the vestments (Exod. 29:29), the offerings and sacrifices (Exod. 28:38), and the feast days (Gen. 2:3; Exod. 35:2) are holy. By contrast this explains the catalogues of impure animals (Lev. 11; Deut. 14:4-26), the prescriptions for cultic purity and the Holiness Code (Lev. 17-26).

In the later developed writings of the Old Testament, cultic purity and holiness had a didactic function, expressing God's holiness, also demanding moral perfection and holiness in Israel. The divine moral exaltedness is the foundation and measure of human holiness (Lev. 11:44, 19:2, 20:26—P source). In the history of salvation, God appears as redeemer of Israel in spite of its sinfulness (Isa. 41:14, 43:4f). Israel has an obligation to strive after moral holiness, avoiding purely external ritualism (Isa. 1:10-17; Jer. 7; Hos. 6:6; Mich. 6:6-8). Thus the prophets stressed the moral aspect of holiness and purity (cf. Amos 2:7; Isa. 6:5-7, 10:17; Hos. 11:8f).

The Holiness of God in the New Testament.[4]

The New Testament writers show a further development of the

tradition which had begun in the later Old Testament writings. I Pet. 1:15-16 takes up the theme of the Holiness Code (Lev. 19:2, 20:6):

> ...as he who called you is holy, be holy yourselves in all conduct; since it is written "You shall be holy, for I am holy."

This theme of reflection of the holiness of God was taken as a model for analogous expressions:

> Be ye perfect even as your Heavenly Father is perfect (Matt. 5:48). Be ye merciful even as your Father is merciful (Luke 6:36).

I John 3:3 speaks of being pure as God is pure; I John 3:7 speaks of being righteous as God is righteous. This thought pattern is continued in the Apostolic Fathers: I Clem. 33:1, on being adorned with good works as God is adorned with good works (cf. also Polycarp *Phil.* 12:3). Thus in the New Testament and Apostolic Fathers, by analogous expressions, the basic idea is made more explicit and thus stressed: being holy as God is holy.

St. Paul exhorts the Christians to "holiness" (II Cor. 7:1, I Thess. 3:13), but he especially sees holiness in Jesus Christ who was "designated Son of God in power according to the Spirit of holiness" (Rom. 1:4). Jesus is designated the "Holy One Of God," in the evangelists (Mark. 1:24, Luke 4:34, John 6:6—allusion to such texts as Isa. 43:14-15). Thus in the New Testament, the holiness of Jesus Christ is pre-eminent. In its light, the Christians "are called to be holy" (Rom. 1:7).

The Holiness of God in the Fathers of the Church and Subsequent Thought.

Pseudo-Dionysius the Areopagite (*De div. nom.* xii)[5] mentions the divine attribute of "Holy of Holies" and understands it as the "Very Holiness" of God, about which he says, "Now, Holiness is that which we conceive as a freedom from all defilement and a complete and utterly untainted purity."[6] Dionysius stresses that God is the overflowing Cause of all that exists in beauty and orderliness, and at the same time is the utterly Holy Transcendent One. "Out of God, the All-Transcendent Cause"—he writes:

> hath, in one single act, come forth collectively and been distribut-ed throughout the world all the unmixed Perfection of all untaint-ed Purity; all that Law and Order of the world, which expels all disharmony, inequality and disproportion, and breaks forth into a smiling aspect of ordered Consistency and Rightness, bringing into their proper place all things which are held worthy to partici-pate in It; all the perfect Possession of all fair qualities; and all that good Providence which contemplates and maintains in being the objects of Its own activity, bounteously bestowing Itself for the Deification of those creatures which are converted unto It.
>
> And since the Creator of all things is brim-full with them all in one transcendent excess thereof, He is called "Holy of Holies" ...by virtue of His overflowing Causality and excess of Tran-scendence.[7]

The remaining Fathers of the Church do not deal separately with the holiness of God, but always refer to it in connection with their comments on God's divine majesty,[8] goodness,[9] purity, free-dom from sin and lust,[10] etc. The Fathers understood divine good-ness primarily as a moral quality. After them, the mediaeval theo-logians commented on the holiness of God in the context of the attributes of the divine Will, in spite of the fact that holiness and moral rectitude or goodness are not synonymous.

Since God is the exemplary and efficient cause of all that exists outside of Himself, his holiness is the exemplar and principle of all other holiness. The doctrine of the holiness of God has always been the peaceful possession of the Church, and has stood as an unchal-lenged and divinely revealed truth of the Christian faith. Conse-quently, it never has been necessary to raise it to the dignity of an extraordinary and solemn pronouncement. Therefore, the teaching authority of the Church has proclaimed the truth about the holiness of God only indirectly in the enumeration of the divine attributes, in the course of discussion of the divine nature, and in the context of the Holy Trinity,[11] Majesty,[12] Infinity in all perfection, Exaltedness above everything,[13] etc. Also, God's holiness has been stressed in the context of the goodness of His creatures and in the context of divine Providence,[14] of the goal of the world,[15] and of predestination.[16]

The Holiness of God in Modern Theological Thought.

It is to the credit of modern theology, under the influence of modern philosophy of religion, that it has singled out *the holiness of God* as an independent category and value. Especially important was the work of Rudolf Otto, *Das Heilige*.[17] Consequently the content of the biblical message concerning holiness has been re-examined. It has become clear that holiness does not consist primarily in a moral quality, but that the Godhead Himself in His absolute dignity, in His infinite majesty, inapproachability, transcendence and exaltation exhibits infinite holiness. It is precisely this holiness which stresses the radical distance between God and the creature. Holiness is not just any of the divine attributes, but the radical quality which reveals God as God, and is the description of the personal God of biblical revelation. Thus holiness has been recognized as the most fundamental description of the divine being, the fullness of divine existence in its uniqueness and glory.

Needless to say, the holiness of God is the deepest mystery with respect to the being and inner life, light and love of the Triadic God. It is the highest thing that we could possibly utter about God. It is greater in dignity than the many attributes of God, and this designation should better be classed among the names of God: He is the Holy One of Israel (Isa. 43:14).[18] The holiness of God, from the point of view of the contemplating creature, consists of many different moments even if in reality the holiness of God is identical with his infinite essence and with the three divine hypostases. First of all, the holiness of God consists in the infinitely perfect and immutable love by which the three divine hypostases love each other and love the divine goodness for its own sake. Thus God's holiness is a substantial holiness. Consequently, we can identify God as Holiness Itself (Isa. 6:3; Rev. 4:8).

In the substantial holiness of God, we can distinguish God's ontological holiness, that is, the infinite divine goodness; and his moral holiness, that is, God's love for his infinite divine goodness.

Consequently, we can deduce that holiness exists in God formally and absolutely because it belongs to God by reason of His essence and nature which are the foundation and the root of the divine activity *ad extra*. Divine holiness is infinite and unchangeable, just as the divine essence itself. Since divine holiness is an absolute perfection flowing from the substantial nature of God, it is infinitely perfect in itself, neither seeking nor receiving perfection from anything extrinsic to God. Thus, it can be described as an absolute divine perfection which is God's love of Himself and of His creatures.

Another important moment implied in the concept of the divine holiness is the absolute divine purity. God's love for the supreme and infinite good is utterly pure because its norm is the divine essence, and no good which is extrinsic to Divine Being can rival the goodness of God's essence. God necessarily and ontologically is holy, for he necessarily loves the greatest Good, or Himself. His holiness cannot be diminished, for He cannot turn to a good other than his own essence. Divine holiness is absolutely unchangeable, for it is infinite and eternal and therefore implies an infinite firmness. Negatively speaking, God's holiness implies an infinite separation from all evil, which makes it inviolable and without sin.

The Holiness of God in the Liturgy.

The term "holiness" in reference to God is very strongly accentuated in the Christian Liturgies of both the East and the West. Needless to say, such hymns as the *Te Deum* and the *Sanctus* of the Latin Liturgy and the *Trisagion* of Holy Week are the best examples in the West. However, the most beautiful and explicit description of the holiness of God and its effects on the Church and creatures is to be found in the Divine Liturgy according to St. John Chrysostom.[19] There are two major references to the holiness of God as his most exalted attribute: the first is the famous *Trisagion* and the accompanying prayers. While the choir sings the appointed *Troparia* the priest reads the Trisagion Prayer:

O holy God: who dost rest in the saints; who art hymned by the

Seraphim with the thrice-holy cry, and glorified by the Cherubim, and worshipped by every heavenly power; who out of nothing hast brought all things into being; who hast created man after Thine own image and likeness, and hast adorned him with Thine every gift; who givest to him who asks wisdom and understanding; who dost not despise the sinner, but instead hast appointed repentance unto salvation; who hast vouchsafed to us, Thy humble and unworthy servants, even in this hour to stand before the glory of Thy holy altar, and to offer worship and praise which are due unto Thee. Thyself, O Master, accept even from the mouths of us sinners the thrice-holy hymn, and visit us in Thy goodness. Forgive us every transgression, both voluntary and involuntary. Sanctify our souls and bodies, and enable us to serve Thee in holiness all the days of our life. Through the intercessions of the holy Theotokos and of all the saints who from the beginning of the world have been well-pleasing to Thee.[20]

The significance of this prayer is enormous, for it starts with the ontological statement about God's holiness, and exhibits an incredibly thought-through progression in its explication of the theological contents. The exalted ontological holiness of God is the exclusive mode of existence of His being; this means that He is infinitely exalted and infinitely different from the creature and its experience. Furthermore, in His free pantocratic activity He creates nature and brings the history of salvation to realization. The wholly-otherness of God reveals itself as inviolable, unapproachable, and an awe-inspiring Majesty; and at the same time, as an Attracting-Drawing, Beatifying, Blessing Power—as Judgement and Grace, as Justice and Love, as *mysterium tremendum* and *fascinans*.

Therefore the Divine Holiness reveals itself in the eyes of the creature as the most explicit case of *coincidentia oppositorum*. This is so because, in the human being such feelings and experiences as fright and love, awe and enthusiasm, actually can coincide. The holiness of God holds the human being back, and at the same time draws him forward. These ambivalent experiences unite and become more intense in the act of prayer and adoration. This text also presents God as Creator; it presents the principal elements of Eastern Christian anthropology, the nature of the Church as the doxological community, and the goodness and holiness of God as the source of salvation and sanctification; and it presents the fact that the holiness of the creator is a participatory holiness in the holiness of God. The elaborate ritual accompanying the *Trisagion* continues with the following polylogue:

DEACON: Bless, Master, the time of the thrice-holy.

PRIEST: For holy art Thou, O our God, and unto Thee we ascribe glory: to the Father, and to the Son, and to the Holy Spirit, now and ever and unto ages of ages.
TRISAGION

CHOIR: Amen.
Holy God! Holy Mighty! Holy Immortal! Have mercy on us (3 times) Glory to the Father, and to the Son, and to the Holy Spirit, now and ever and unto ages of ages. Amen. Holy Immortal! Have mercy on us. Holy God! Holy Mighty! Holy Immortal! Have mercy on us.
(The celebrants bow three times before the Altar. The deacon says:)

DEACON: Command, Master. (As they go to the High Place, the priest says:)

PRIEST: Blessed is he that comes in the name of the Lord.[21]

One would think that the *Trisagion* represents a certain climax in the liturgical drama, but closer scrutiny reveals that it is an imperial acclamation before the procession of the priest and the deacon to the High Place behind the altar, which is reserved for the bishop alone who represents God the Father on earth. This is clear from the liturgical action which takes place behind the altar:

DEACON: Bless, Master, the High Place.

PRIEST: Blessed art Thou on the throne of the glory of Thy Kingdom, who sittest upon the Cherubim; always, now and ever and unto ages of ages.
(He then stands on the right hand side of the High Place, the center being reserved for the Bishop.)[22]

Thus we can say that the *Trisagion*, with all the prayers accompanying it, forms a real ritual celebrating the highest attribute of God, i.e., His holiness, in all its ontological, existential, and moral dimensions.

    The second major celebration of the holiness of God can be

found in the very heart of the Divine Liturgy of St. John Chrysostom—in the *Anaphora*. The first introductory prayer, which the priest recites quietly, does not mention explicitly the holiness of God, but it enumerates all those divine attributes which point to God's holiness and to His transcendent and exalted majesty:

> It is meet and right to hymn Thee, to bless Thee, to praise Thee, to give thanks to Thee, and to worship Thee in every place of Thy dominion: for Thou art God ineffable, inconceivable, invisible, incomprehensible, ever-existing and eternally the same; Thou and Thine only-begotten Son and Thy Holy Spirit. Thou it was who brought us from non-existence into being, and when we had fallen away didst raise us up again, and didst not cease to do all things until Thou hadst endowed us with Thy Kingdom which is to come. For all these things we give thanks to Thee, and to Thine only-begotten Son, and to Thy Holy Spirit; for all things of which we know and of which we know not, whether manifest or unseen; and we thank Thee for this Liturgy which Thou hast deigned to accept at our hands, though there stand by Thee thousands of archangels and hosts of angels, the Cherubim and the Seraphim, six-winged, many-eyed, who soar aloft borne on their pinions.[23]

The priest then concludes this quiet introductory prayer aloud, exclaiming:

> Singing the triumphant hymn, shouting, proclaiming and saying: (As the priest chants the above the deacon touches the paten with each of the points of the star [making the sign of the cross], then kisses it and lays it aside; he goes to the right side of the altar.)
> CHOIR: Holy! Holy! Holy! Lord of Sabaoth! Heaven and earth are full of Thy glory! Hosanna in the highest! Blessed is He that comes in the name of the Lord! Hosanna in the highest![24]

Thus the "Holy, Holy, Holy" forms a high dramatic plateau towards which the preceding prayer was leading. The text is based on the vision of the prophet Isaiah (6:1-3) who experienced the infinite distance between himself and God, as well as God's infinite majesty. Besides, the text suggests that the threefold (and therefore infinite) holiness of God is the ontological property of His very being and

His glory. But even the "Holy, Holy, Holy" serves as an introduction to a prayer, which the priest recites quietly, and which can be called the prayer of divine holiness *par excellence*:

> With these blessed powers, O Master who lovest mankind, we also cry aloud and say: Holy art Thou and all-holy, Thou and Thine only-begotten Son and Thy Holy Spirit! Holy art Thou and all-holy, and magnificent is Thy glory! Who hast so *loved* Thy world as to give Thine only-begotten Son, that whoever believes in Him should not perish but have *everlasting life*; who when He had come and had fulfilled all the dispensation for us, in the night in which He was given up—or rather, gave Himself up for the life of the world—took bread in His holy, pure, and blameless hands; and when He had given thanks and blessed it, and hallowed it, and broken it, He gave it to His holy disciples and apostles, saying: Take! Eat! This is My Body which is broken for you, for the remission of sins.
>
> CHOIR: Amen. (As the priest says the above words, the deacon points to the paten with his stole.)
> PRIEST: And likewise, after supper, He took the cup, saying: Drink of it, all of you! This is My Blood of the New Testament which is shed for you and for many, for the remission of sins![25]

This magnificent prayer is the highest point and very heart of the Divine Liturgy, for it contains the words of the Eucharistic consecration. But these consecratory words are made meaningful only in the context of the proclamation of the ontological and existential holiness of God's being: "Holy art Thou and all-holy (*panhagios*), Thou and Thine only-begotten Son and Thy Holy Spirit! Holy art Thou and all-holy, and magnificent is Thy glory!" Besides, the glory of the holiness of God is manifested as love, everlasting life, sanctification, and the sacrifice of the only-begotten Son of God for the remission of sins and sanctification of the whole world.

There are many other prayers in Eastern and especially Byzantine Liturgies which express and illustrate the holiness of God. For our purposes the above texts sufficiently clarify the point under discussion. Let us now turn our attention to the Third Person of the Most Holy Trinity, whose proper name is "Holy", that is, the Holy Spirit.

The Byzantine Liturgy glorifies the Holy Spirit as Sanctifier on Monday of Pentecost:

> The Holy Spirit always was and always shall be, for He is with the Father and the Son, One of the Trinity. He is both Life and Life-giving; He is Light, and by nature, the Giver of Light; He is All-holy and the Source of holiness. Through Him, we know the Father and glorify the Son, understanding that the Holy Trinity is a single Power, Three of equal rank and equally to be worshipped.
>
> The Holy Spirit is Light and Life, a living fountain of all spiritual reality; He is the Essence of Wisdom, the Spirit of Knowledge; He is Goodness and Understanding, the Leader of Righteousness; He cleanses us from sin; He is divine and makes us so; He is Fire proceeding from Fire; his word is action, the distribution of gifts. Through Him God witnesses, prophets and apostles were crowned. Oh, the marvel of this truth! Oh, the marvel of this sight! Tongues of fire bringing about the distribution of gifts.[26]

This beautiful hymn is a very good *status quaestionis* concerning the mystery of the holiness of God and the participatory holiness of the creature.

It is precisely the Third Person of the Most Holy Triad, the Holy Spirit, who is the witness to the fact that holiness is the exclusive description of God's being. Thus the Holy Spirit is the hypostatized Holiness of the Father and the Son. It is the Holy Spirit in whom is rooted the absolute monarchy of God and the divine command to worship Him.

On the part of the creature, the holiness of God implies an absolute postulate of subjection and worship which is animated by the Holy Spirit. It is God the Father, through the Son and in the Holy Spirit, who by his power introduces order into creation and who sanctifies it.[27]

However, by appropriation, it is the Holy Spirit who is the Sanctifier, that is, a dispenser of the uncreated divine energies and of participation in the inner life, light and love of the Most Holy Trinity.[28] The most fundamental work of the Sanctifier—the Holy Spirit—is the cleansing of the sinful rational creatures from their sins by application of the redemptive merits of Christ. This cleansing displays both ontological and psychological effects. It is the

Holy Spirit who comes to the rational creatures to open their minds and hearts and to transform them into people who listen to the word of God through which they realize their sinful condition, and reverting from it, are converted to Christ and through him to God the Father with prayerful contrition (Acts 2:40, 9:31, 11:22ff, 13:15, 14:14; Rom. 8:23-30, 12:8; I Cor. 14:3; II Cor. 8:4; Heb. 12:5; I Tim. 4:13). It is this gracious activity of the Holy Spirit which comes to the rational creatures as a call or as a warning or as a strengthening of the will and sometimes of the body too, or as a consolation or as an illumination of the mind. Furthermore, it is the Holy Spirit who sanctifies the human being and makes him capable of saying the faithful and prayerful "Yes" to Jesus the Lord (I Cor. 12:13; I John 4:2-3; Eph. 1:17-18). He is the Spirit of divine adoption, for he gives an internal witness to the human spirit that he or she is a child of God (Rom. 8:16; I John 3:19-24). It is also the Holy Spirit who prays in the human being when he is silent before God (Rom. 8:26ff; John 2:20-27, 16:13).[29]

Thus we can say that the whole economy of the Holy Spirit is holy. He is the Spirit of the Divine Beauty who expresses Himself in Eastern Christian art and who is the reflection of the Divine glory. The Holy Spirit sanctifies the Church and transforms her into a doxological community—in the Spirit of Love. The Mother of God is the Bride of God the Father; and she is the Pneumatophora, or the carrier and distributor of the Holy Spirit. Thus she becomes the Triadophora, or the carrier of the Most Holy Trinity and His sanctity. The Holy Spirit inspires and leads the Ecumenical Councils which are the expression of the *sobornost* (i.e., conciliarity) of the Church. Any honest human being, but especially a believing and practicing Christian, is a pneumatophor, a carrier of the Holy Spirit and of His gifts and Charisms. The Holy Spirit also exercises His mission as the Sanctifier of the individual, of the Church, and of the cosmos. He does this through the Sacraments, especially through Chrismation (or Confirmation) which is the pneumatic Sacrament *par excellence* having as its formula the following words: "The seal of the Gift of the Holy Spirit". The Holy Spirit transfigures, divinizes, and glorifies the people of God. This continues until the definitive eschatological fulfillment which is the definitive Pentecost.

This brings us to the role of the Holy Spirit in that moment of the economy of salvation which is called glorification.[30] Needless to say, glorification can be understood objectively—theologically as the glory of the Triadic God Himself which is His Holiness manifested *ad extra* both in nature and in the divine economy of salvation. Glorification can also be understood subjectively—economically, inasmuch as the creatures glorifying the Triadic God are themselves also being sanctified and glorified by the divine activity of the Holy Spirit who makes it possible for the creatures to participate in the holiness and glory of God. These two aspects are clearly echoed in the innumerable hymns of the Byzantine Liturgy, for instance:

> Let us glorify the one Nature in three Persons, the one indivisible glory, the undivided Trinity in one Godhead that is praised without ceasing in heaven and on earth; in piety let us worship the Father, with the Son and the Spirit.[31]

> It is alien to evil-doers to glorify the Trinity that has no beginning, Father, Son, and Holy Spirit, the uncreated and sovereign Power that founded the whole world by an act of His might.[32]

Very closely connected with the reality of the divine glory are the image and mysticism of light, for instance:

> The Father is Light, His Son is Light, and the Spirit, the Comforter is Light for, shining forth as from one sun, the Trinity divinely illuminates and preserves our souls.[33]

Again the *exapostilarion* of Mattins of the Transfiguration of Our Lord reads:

> Today on Tabor in the manifestation of Thy Light, O Lord, Thou unaltered Light from the Light of the unbegotten Father, we have seen the Father as Light and the Spirit as Light, guiding with light the whole creation.[34]

However, divine glory and light are different aspects of the holiness of God, a fact which can be gathered from I Pet. 2:9. "You ... are a chosen race ... a holy nation, a purchased people; that you may proclaim the perfections of Him who has called you out of darkness into His marvellous light".[35]

The Hebrew *kābôd* and the Greek δοξα, both meaning "glory", occupy one of the most prominent places in the Bible.[36] Divine glory is visible in spectacular thunderstorms (Ps. 97:3-6), or in fire (Exod. 19:16-18) or in a cloud (Exod. 24:15-17), or in the column of cloud or fire in the Tent of Meeting (Exod. 33:9; Lev. 9:22-24), or as a cloud enveloping the Ark of the Covenant (IV Kgs. 19:15; III Kgs. 8:10-11). From the image of cloud and fire slowly emerged the idea of the divine illumination.[37] To Ezekiel "the vision of the likeness of the glory of the Lord" is expressed by a glorified man riding a heavenly chariot in fiery tumult, drawn by four chimeric creatures (Ezek. 1:26-28). A further step toward personalizing the glory of God was taken by Isaiah in chapters 56 and 65, for the spiritual *kābôd* begins to blend with the ideas of God's power and lordly majesty (Isa. 60:1-3).

In post-exilic biblical literature, the divine glory became the symbol of God's universal triumph over heaven and earth (Ps. 57:12, 96:3). In Daniel 7:13-14, the "son of man" is a glorified pantocratic and eternal being.

In the New Testament the presentation of glory is Christocentric (Matt. 28:3; Mark 14:61-62; Luke 1:35, 2:9). John sees Jesus' glory as visible only to those who believe, especially after "signs" and miracles: "He manifested his glory and his disciples believed in him" (John 2:11; cf. also John 17:5, 11:70). According to St. Paul the apostolic life is a reception of light in order to reflect the "glory of God, shining in the face of Christ Jesus" (II Cor. 4:6). However, the most important text which harmonizes the Christological and pneumatological aspects of glory is II Cor. 3:18: "and we all, with unveiled face, beholding the glory of the Lord, are being changed into his likeness from one degree of glory to another; for this comes from the Lord who is the Spirit".

This text points out several important aspects: the spiritualized human being, in the full revelation of his personality, can behold and participate in the glory of God in different degrees of intensity. This seeing and participation is transfiguratory in its effects and draws the creature into the spiritual existence of God through acceptance of an ever clearer image of Christ and in the ever-growing dynamism of the Holy Spirit.

The intrinsic glory of God is His holiness, goodness, beauty and all the other attributes. The extrinsic glory of God is the true goal of creation, for it is a reflection and manifestation, through creatures, of the intrinsic and substantial glory that is God Himself. Therefore God necessarily ordered all things to His extrinsic glory. Consequently the intrinsic perfection of any creature is in reality the extrinsic glory of God.

There can be no theological objection to calling the Holy Spirit the Spirit of the glory of the Father and the Son. Also, there can be no objection to calling Him the glorifier of human beings and of the whole extra-divine reality. On the contrary, the above quoted text, II Cor. 3:18, and all the other texts presenting Him as the Sanctifier, Transfigurer, and Divinizer point to His being the Glorifier as well. Furthermore, we could say that the Holy Spirit is the Spiritualizer of the whole of created reality, for it is He, the Holy Spirit, who, as the dynamic power of God, creates, loves, attracts, vivifies, enlightens, strengthens, illumines, spiritualizes, purifies, sanctifies, reunites, transfigures, divinizes and glorifies the creatures of God the Father through the Son: or simply, the One who leads them to God through His Pentecostal condescension and their synergetic cooperation.

In summary, let us draw together the main threads of our discussion. We dwelt upon the holiness of God, that unique and primal attribute of God which reveals God as God; then we could proceed to understand the importance of saying that it is precisely the Holy Spirit who is the witness to the fact that holiness is the exclusive description of God's being. Thus the Holy Spirit is the hypostatized Holiness of the Father and of the Son; and it is the Holy Spirit consequently who makes creation holy, who orders and sanctifies it. This sanctification is very easily observed in the charism of prayer.

This brings us full circle in our discussion as we come to a few thoughts on the *glory* of God; for the glory of God is the reverberation of His holiness. His holiness belongs to his essence; his glory is manifested in nature and in the economy of salvation. The glory of creatures is their participation in the glory of God; the Holy Spirit, in his role as Sanctifier, makes this possible. The glory of mankind is at its fullest in conscious glorification of God: "Let us glorify the

One nature in three Persons ... let us worship the Father, with the Son and the Spirit."

FOOTNOTES

1 On holiness as an attribute of God see: Karl Vladimir Truhlar, "Heiligkeit", *SM* vol. 2, col. 627-34; J. Lachowski, "Holiness in the Bible", *NCE* vol.7, pp. 51-52; J.D. Fearson, "Holiness", *NCE* vol. 7, p. 51; H. Gross and J. Grotz, "Heiligkeit", *HtG* I, 653-62; H. Graf Reventlow, *Das Heiligkeitsgesetz form-geschichtlich untersucht* (Neukirchen-Moers, 1961); G. Thils, *Christliche Heilig-keit* (Munich, 1961); Michael Schmaus, *Katholische Dogmatik* vol. I (Munich: Max Hueber, 1960), pp. 562-67; B. Thum and A. Lang, "Heilig, das Heilige", *LThK* 2nd ed., vol. 5, col. 84-89; W. Koester and L. Szeffczyk, "Heiligkeit Gottes" *LThK* 2nd ed., vol. 5, col. 133-36; E. Pax, "Heilig", *Bibeltheologisches Wörterbuch*, ed. Johannes B. Bauer (Graz, 1959; rev. 1962) I, 398-403; G. Lanczkowski, "Heilig", *RGG* 2nd ed. 3, 146-55 (bibl.); O. Schilling, *Das Heilige und das Gute im Alten Testament* (Leipzig, 1956); J. Hessen, *Die Werte des Heiligen* 2nd ed. (Regensburg, 1951); B. Häring, *Das Heilige und das Gute* (Munich, 1950); F.K. Feigel, *Das Heilige*, 2nd ed. (Tübingen, 1948); H. Ringgren, *The Prophetical Conception of Holiness* (Uppsala, 1948); Matthias Joseph Scheeben, *Handbuch der Katholischen Dogmatik*, Zweites Buch, *Got-teslehre oder die Theologie im engeren Sinne* (Freiburg: Herder, 1948) 249-64; P. van Imschoot, "La sainteté de Dieu dans l'ancien testament", *La vie spirituelle* 309 (1946), pp. 30-34; O Procksch, "hagios, etc.", *ThW* I, 87-116; J. Hänel, *Die Religion der Heiligkeit* (Gütersloh, 1931); M. Schumpp, "Das Heilige in der Bibel", *Theologie und Glaube* 22 (1930), pp. 331-43; J. Dillersberger, *Das Heilige im Neuen Testament* (Kufstein, 1926); E. Williger, *Hagios. Untersuch-ungen zur Terminologie des Heiligen in den hellenischen und hellenistischen Religionen* (Giessen, 1922); J. Stufler, *Die Heiligkeit Gottes und der ewige Tod* (Innsbruck, 1903).

2 Frank Gavin, *Some Aspects of Contemporary Greek Orthodox Thought* (n.p.: Morrehouse, 1923; reprint: N.Y.: American Review of Eastern Orthodoxy, 1962) which has been an influential manual among English readers has only one paragraph, pp. 101-2, on the holiness of God:

> As one aspect of Holiness means separation from the world and from every earthly thing and imperfection (thus in the Old Testament) so the ethical aspect includes this same note of separation, inasmuch as things earthly are contaminated and unclean. Hence Holiness may be defined as "that property according to which the Divine Will is perfectly identified with the Good which it seeks; in relation to man, this object is moral cleanness, and the carrying out of the ethical law implanted in man's conscience." This good with which the Divine Will is equivalent may not be understood as something outside the Divine Nature, as if the Will of God were to be conformed to some higher Good external to It, for this would take away the Absolute Character of His Will, but this Good is "the expression of the internal identity of the Divine Nature with it." The scholastic question as to "whether good is good, hence God wills it," or "because He does will it, it is good," creates an unnecessary distinction. God can only by His

nature will what is good, and what He wills, as proceeding from His Nature must be only what He is, that is, good.

The confusion and lack of clarity point to the fact that Gavin has been influenced by pessimistic Western thought, especially Calvinism. Hardly better is: Panagiotis N. Tremitias, *Dogmatique de l'Eglise Orthodoxe Catholique* vol. 1 (Athens: Editions de Chevetogne, 1959). Cf. also Platon (Metropolitan), *Orthodox Doctrine of the Apostolic Eastern Church* (Manchester, 1857), p. 41; Peter Hauptmann, *Die Katechismen der russisch-orthodoxen Kirche* (Göttingen: Vandenhoeck & Ruprecht, 1971) *passim*; Emilianos Timiadis, *Lebendige Orthodoxie* (Nürnberg und Eichstätt: Johann Michael Sailer, 1966), pp. 13-31. We submit to the reader: Petro B. T. Bilaniuk, *Studies in Eastern Christianity* (Munich-Toronto: Ukrainian Free University, 1977); and Petro B.T. Bilaniuk, *Theology and Economy of the Holy Spirit: An Eastern Approach*, (Bangalore, India: Dharmaram Publications, 1980).

3 R.J. Faley, "Holiness, Law of", *NCE* vol. 7, p. 53; H. Gross, "Heiligkeit", *HtG* vol. I, pp. 653-58; Klaus Hemmerle, "Heilige, das", *Sacramentum Mundi* vol. 2, cols. 575-82; W. Koester, "Heiligkeit Gottes", *LThK²* vol. 5, cols. 133-34; B. Kraft, "Heilige, das Heilige iii", *LThK²* vol. 5, cols. 89-91; J. Lachowski, "Holiness in the Bible", *NCE* vol. 7, pp. 51-52; X. Leon-Dufour, *et al.*, *Vocabulaire des theologie biblique* (Paris, 1962), pp. 981-87; A. Michel, "Sainteté", *DTC* 14.1: 841-854; M.F. Morry, "Holiness of God", *NCE* vol. 7, p. 54; Karl Vladimir Truhlar, "Heiligkeit", *Sacramentum Mundi* vol. 2, cols. 627-34.

4 See previous note; also Isabel Ann Massey, "Interpreting the Sermon on the Mount in the Light of Jewish Tradition as evidenced in the Palestinian —Targums of the Pentateuch: Selected Themes", Diss. University of St. Michael's College 1980, pp. 63-66.

5 C.E. Rolt, trans., *Dionysius the Areopagite: The Divine Names and the Mystical Theology* (London: SPCK, 1977).

6 *Ibid.*, p. 181.

7 *Ibid.*, p. 182.

8 Lactantius, *De ira Dei* 3.

9 Augustine, *Civ. Dei* xi. 24; *Enchiridion* 3; *Enarr. in Ps.* 134,3.

10 Gregory of Nyssa, *De beatitudinibus orat.* 6; Augustine, *Ep.* 186,6,20.

11 *DS* 275, 343, 482.

12 *DS* 343, 461.

13 *DS* 1782.

14 *DS* 428, 706, 1783ff.

15 *DS* 1783, 1805

16 *DS* 200, 316, 322, 627.

17 The first edition was published in Breslau, 1917; English version: *The Idea of the Holy* (London: Oxford Univ. Press, 1958); cf. Th. Siegfried, *Grundfragen der Theologie bei Rudolf Otto* (Gotha, 1931); R.F. Davidson, *Das Heilige. Kritische Abhandlung über Rudolf Otto's gleichnamiges Buch*, 2nd ed. (Tübingen, 1948).

18 The classification among the *names* of God attaches a greater dignity to the idea than classification among the *attributes*—per discussion with Dr. Isabel Ann Massey. See the early theological development on the topic as summarized in A. Marmorstein. *The Old Rabbinic Doctrine of God: 1. The Names and Attributes of God* (1927; reprint in *The Doctrine of Merits in Old Rabbinical Literature and The Old Rabbinic Doctrine of God*, N.Y. KTAV, 1968), esp. pp. 97 and 208-17.

19 *The Divine Liturgy according to St. John Chrysostom with Appendices* (N.Y.: Russian Orthodox Greek Catholic Church of America, 1967); abbr. hereafter *DL*. Cf. also Casimir Kurcharek, *The Byzantine-Slav Liturgy of St. John Chrysostom* (Allendale, N.J.: Alleluia Press, 1971); D. Plazidus de Meester, ed. Η ΘΕΙΑ ΛΕΙΤΟΥΡΓΙΑ ΤΟΥ ΕΝ ΑΓΙΟΙΣ ΠΑΤΡΟΣ ΗΜΩΝ ΙΩΑΝΝΟΥ ΤΟΥ ΧΡΥΣΟΣΤΟΜΟΥ: *Die Göttliche Liturgie unseres Hl. Vaters Johannes Chrysostomus* (Munich: Salesianischen Offizen, 1938). Most Reverend Joseph Raya and Baron Jose de Vinck, *Byzantine Daily Worship* (Allendale, N.J.: Alleluia Press, 1969). Hans Joachim Schulz, *Die Byzantinische Liturgie* (Trier: Paulinus, 1980).

20 *DL*, 38-39.

21 *DL*, 39.

22 *Ibid.*

23 *DL*, 62-63.

24 *DL*, 63.

25 *DL*, 64.

26 *BDW*, pp. 898-99.

27 Cf. Hans Urs von Balthasar, *Spiritus Creator* (Einsiedeln: Johannes Verlag, 1967); Regin Prenter, *Spiritus Creator*, trans. John M. Jensen (Philadelphia: Muhlenberg Press, 1953); H.P. Van Dusen, *Spirit, Son and Father: Christian Faith in the Light of the Holy Spirit* (New York: Scribner's, 1958).

28 Cf. Luis Maria Martinez, *The Sanctifier*, trans. Sr. M. Aquinas (Paterson, N.J.: St. Anthony Guild Press, 1957).

29 Cf. Willibald Pfester, *Das Leben im Geist nach Paulus: Der Geist als Anfang und Vollendung des christlichen Lebens* (Freiburg, Sw.: Univ. Verlag, 1963).

30 On the glory of God and glorification of the extradivine reality see: T.A. Smail, *Reflected Glory: The Spirit in Christ and Christians* (London: Hodder and Stoughton, 1975); Humbert Bouëssé, "Ehre Gottes", *SM* vol. 1, col. 998-1001; D.J. Ehr, "Glory of God (End of Creation)", *NCE* vol. 6, pp. 514-15; J.T. Burtchaell, "Glory (in the Bible)", *NCE* vol. 6, pp. 513-14; E. Pax, "Herr-

lichkeit", *HtG* I, 680-85; Hans Urs von Balthasar, *Herrlichkeit. Eine theologische Aesthetik* vols. I-III/2 (Einsiedeln: Johannes Verlag, 1961-1967); R. Schnackenburg, "Doxa", *LThK*, 2nd ed., vol. 3, col. 532-24; W. Eichrodt, *Theologie des Alten Testaments* (Berlin, 1957), vol. I, pp. 9-12; Z. Alszeghy and M. Flick, "Gloria Dei", *Gregorianum* 36 (1955), pp. 361-90; L.H. Brockington, "The Septuagintal Background of the New Testament Use of Doxa", *Studies in the Gospels*, ed. D. E. Nineham (Oxford, 1955) pp. 1-8; C. Mohrmann, "Note sur 'doxa': Sprachgeschichte und Wortbedeutung", *Festschrift Albert Debrunner* (Bern, 1954), pp. 321-328; G. von Rad, *Studies in Deuteronomy* (London, 1953), pp. 37-44; M. Steinheimer, *Die Δοξα τοῦ Θεοῦ in der römischen Liturgie* (Munich, 1951); I. Efros, "Holiness and Glory in the Bible: An Approach to the History of Jewish Thought", *The Jewish Quarterly Review* 41 (1950/51), pp. 363-77; A.M. Ramsey, *The Glory of God and the Transfiguration of Christ* (London, 1949); B. Zielinski, "De doxa Christi transfigurati", *Verbum Domini* 26 (1948), pp. 291-302; B. Stein, *Der Begriff Kabod Jahve und seine Bedeutung für die alttestamentliche Gotteserkenntnis* (Emsdetten, 1939); H. Kittel, *Die Herrlichkeit Gottes* (Giessen, 1934); J. Schneider, *Doxa. Eine bedeutungsgeschichtliche Studie* (Gütersloh, 1932); I. Abrahams, *The Glory of God* (London, 1925); G.P. Wetter, *Phos* (Leipzig, 1915); *idem*, "Verherrlichung im Johannesevangelium", *Beiträge zur Religionswissenschaft* 2 (1915), pp. 32-113; A. von Gall, *Die Herrlichkeit Gottes* (Giessen, 1900).

31 Mattins of the Entry of the Most Holy Theotokos into the Temple, *FM*, p. 193.

32 Mattins of the Birth of Our Most Holy Lady, *FM*, p. 124.

33 Mattins of the Entry of the Most Holy Theotokos into the Temple, *FM*, p. 178.

34 *FM*, p. 495. It is significant that the hymn is being sung three times. The glorifying effect on the apostles flowing from the glorious Transfiguration of the Lord Jesus Christ is described in the following hymn: "Today as He has promised, Christ, shining on Mount Tabor, dimly disclosed to His disciples the image and reflection of the divine brightness; and filled with godlike and lightbearing splendour, they cried out for joy: "Let us sing unto our God for He has been glorified",' *FM*, p. 482.

35 Paul Evdokimov, "La notion biblique de la lumiere dans la tradition orientale", *Bible et vie chrétienne* (1953), pp. 31-39; *idem*, "Le mystere de la lumiere dans la Bible", *Bible et vie chrétienne* (1953), pp. 40-52.

36 Cf. *GEL*, 202-3; *ThW* 2, 236-58.

37 The notion of glory is very closely connected with the mysticism of light and illumination. See on this: B.L. Mullahy, "Light, Liturgical use of", *NCE* vol. 8, pp. 747-50; J. Ratzinger, "Licht", *HtG* II: 44-54 (bibl.); Jaroslav Pelikan, *The Light of the Word* (New York, 1962).

ABBREVIATIONS

BDW   *Byzantine Daily Worship.* Trans. and ed. Most Rev. Joseph Raya and Baron José de Vinck. Allendale, N.J. and Combermere, Ont.: Alleluia Press, 1969.

DL   *The Divine Liturgy according to St. John Chrysostom with Appendices.* N.Y.: Russian Orthodox Greek Catholic Church of America, 1967.

DS   *Henricus Denzinger—Adolfus Schönmetzer. Enchiridion symbolorum definitionum et declarationum de rebus fidei et morum.* Edition XXXII. Barcinonae: Herder, 1963.

FM   *The Festal Menaion.* Trans. from the original Greek by Mother Mary and Archimandrite Kallistos Ware, with an introduction by Archpriest Georges Florovsky. London: Faber and Faber, 1969.

HtG   *Handbuch theologischer Grundbegriffe.* Ed. Heinrich Fries. 2 vols. Munich: Kösel, 1962-63.

LThK *Lexikon für Theologie und Kirche.* 2nd. Freiburg: Herder, 1957ff.

NCE *New Catholic Encyclopedia.* 17 vols. New York: McGraw-Hill, 1967.

RGG *Religion in Geschichte und Gegenwart.* 6 Vols. 3rd ed. Ed. Kurt Gallig. Tübingen, 1957-65.

SM   *Sacramentum Mundi. Theologisches Lexikon für die Praxis.* Karl Rahner *et al.* eds. 4 vols. Freiburg: Herder, 1967-69.

ThW   *Theologisches Wörterbuch zum Neuen Testament.* G. Kittel-G. Friedrich. Stuttgart, 1933ff.

God at The Head
of Religion:
A Search Through
Buddhism

Jotiya Dhirasekera

Now is not the time for the great religions of the world to be disputing, down here on earth, about the identity of the kingdom of heaven above. Conceptually there are unanimity and agreement that these two, life on earth and the kingdom of heaven, must be spanned. It is widely felt and universally recognized that the human situation as we witness it is not an ideal situation for man to be in. However, the techniques of gauging this, and the results of such reckoning, widely vary through the history of civilizations.

Man's Inheritance and Expectations

Insecurity on account of disease and death appears to have disturbed man, almost from the beginnings of life on earth, when much less was known about the human body, its health and pathology. For example, prayers for freedom from disease, decay and death were addressed by early Vedic Aryans in India to greater non-terrestrial powers in whom they had begun to believe and with whom they had cultivated relationships of varying intensity. Several passages in Vedic literature, including the Ṛgveda and the Atharvaveda (Rv. VI, 74.4; VII, 88.7; Av, II. 10. 1; IV, 16.6) refer to god Varuna as responsible for inflicting men with the then much dreaded disease dropsy as a punishment for sin. This role of gods comes from the desire of men that the gods should safeguard the moral order among men. Together with Mitra, Varuna is said to be a dispeller, hater and punisher of falsehood. They afflict with disease those who neglect their worship:

> The folk, O Miture-Varuna, who hate you, who sinfully hating pour you no libations,
> Lay in their hearts, themselves, a wasting sickness, whereas the righteous gaineth all by worship. (Rv. I,122.9.)[1]

Beneath this mantle of moral guardianship, one sees the morbid tones of vindictiveness, revealing unwittingly the creation of the gods in the image of man. Indra and Varuna, as guardians of human progeny in such situations, feature prominently in the Vedic religion of India. A greater degree of domesticity and intimacy is seen in a prayer addressed to the Guardian of the Homestead (Vastospati), Rv. VII, 54, to keep away disease and decay:

> O Guardian of the Homestead: bring no disease, and give us happy entrance.
> May we never-youthful in thy friendship: be pleased in us as in his sons a father....
> Protect our happiness in rest and labour. Preserve us evermore, ye Gods, with blessings.

Likewise, prayers are offered to Varuna requesting that the life of the worshipper be spared and safeguarded:

> Let me not yet, King Varuna, enter into the house of clay:
> Have mercy, spare me, Mighty Lord. (Rv. VII, 89.1)

Extra Paternal Protection

These failings like decay and disease, as well as declining material fortunes, and the fury of a hostile world in storms, floods and earthquakes, together with the wrath of enemies, made man turn towards a power beyond himself. Looking upon the world as a larger home, he wanted a second father to safeguard his place therein and provide for his physical needs and mental security. Thus he began to learn to pray for better fortunes here and for a better life beyond this. It is primarily towards the achievement of both these ends that man turned towards the superhuman and the divine and submitted himself to a way of life which could thereafter be termed religious. What was believed to be beyond human ken and human power was inevitably placed in the realm of the superhuman. On the other hand, it did not require a penetrative intellect of a very high order to become convinced of the recurrently discovered inadequacy and inefficiency of human life. These failings, at the human level, although partially relieved from time to time, continued to be lamentably irremediable.

The Buddhist Vision

The Buddhists too start by unhesitatingly declaring the human situation as being far from satisfactory. There is no uncertainty whatsoever in the teachings of Gotama, the Buddha, that the highest bliss of man and his highest attainment lie in his transcendence of the mundane. Thus the term *lokuttara* has come to be used in Buddhist texts to refer to everything transcendentally supreme. As a religion, Buddhism recognizes the limitations and frailties of human life. Decay, disease and death derive from the purely physical basis of life; greed, hatred, enmity and jealousy with consequent states of frustration and bitterness, emanate from within man and are not inflicted from without. In themselves they constitute no evil which exists in the world, outside and independent of man. They are on account of man. Buddhism's cardinal theme of *dukkha* (Skt. dukkha) or unsatisfactoriness of life, emerges from these observations. The unfailing law of constant change or *anicca* (Skt. anitya) together with the consequent truism of the absence of an abiding and enduring substance which is generally rendered as soullessness or *anatta* (Skt. anatman) form the cornerstones of the philosophy of early Buddhism whose main burden has been the suffering of man. Thus its religious message invariably deals with the cessation or termination (*nirodha*) of this suffering. It is to be noted that thus from the point of view of salvation, the emphasis has come to be laid at this end. Gotama, or more accurately speaking Siddartha, in his early years as Bodhisattva or the Buddha to be, was rightly vexed with the problem of the origin of this unsatisfactoriness associated with life. The question has often been asked, as repeatedly recorded in the Buddhist texts, whether the responsibility for this lies with an outside agency, a power beyond man (param katam sukhadukkham S. II, 19, 22). This appears to have been the general run of religious inquiry, as we have already shown above with reference to ancient India, and perhaps has been elsewhere too. It was a searching probe into this, namely the why and the wherefore of the presence of unsatisfactoriness in human life, which brought out the second of the Four Noble Truths of Buddhism, i.e., the Truth relating to the origin of *dukkha* or *Samudayasacca*. The very reckoning with the existence of the unsatisfactoriness of the life of man, as referred to above, constitutes the first or the primary truth of *dukkha* (*Dukkhasccaya*).

The Point of Departure

It is here at this point, on the analysis and explanation of the unsatisfactory nature of life, that Buddhism appears to part ways with the other widely prevalent religious systems of the world. The Buddha's analysis of the problem of the unhappiness of man proceeds on the basis of an analysis of the causal genesis of unhappiness. Thus his view proceeds from what is known and observable in the world of man rather than seeking an agent or mediator outside the world of man. According to him, whoever was enough within the world of man to have an impact on him, had in turn to be impacted by it. Taking up the contemporary theological assumption of his day in India that the Great Brahma is supreme in the Thousand World System (*Sahassilokatdhatu*) and presides over it, the Buddha argued that the Great Brahma must then also be subject to the laws that govern this World System, namely, that he must himself be subject to change. (*Yavata bhikkhave sahassilokadhatu Mahabrahma tattha aggam akkayati Mahabrahmuno pi bhikkhave atth'eva annathattam atthi viparinako.* Anaguttara Nikaya V., pp. 59-60.) Far from conceding the manipulation of the affairs of the world of man by a power or person from outside, he sought to locate the source of changes in the world of man, both physical and psychological, within the very conditions which shape human existence. Thus while the Buddhists share with most of the major religions of the world the aspiration to transcend the mundane, they have clearly maintained the Buddhism of Gotama, the Buddha of the sixth century B.C. In its early Indian form, as well as in the form preserved in the Theravada tradition, this anthropocentric bias has been upheld.

These basic points of Buddhist thinking do certainly make

Buddhism appear to be different from most of the other religions. But this lack of uniformity is in itself no cause for lament. It does not leave Buddhism in a vacuum. It only implies a different approach to and analysis of the problem. But some have criticized Buddhism on this point. The following comment made by one such critical analyst may be noted in passing:

> The development of mankind in our present time urges the Buddhists also to reconsider their way and to take history seriously. They can no longer exclude the social dimension from their system. World peace, without which even personal liberation remains impossible, can be established only if mankind forms a unity, a community in which every individual is considered formed only if the love of God frees man from this egoism and inspires them with self-giving love.

The Burden of Buddhism

The Buddha was essentially a religious leader, one whose major concern was to help man to relieve himself of his suffering. By starting more from the core than from the periphery, he selects his specific areas of activity and confines himself to those alone. In fact, he refuses to be dragged into arguments and discussions which do not relate to this problem of the salvation of man. For example, he resisted ontological problems which relate to cosmology. In one of the widely known discourses of the Majjhima nikaya, the Cula-malunkya sutta, the Buddha makes this position of his very clear.

> That the world is eternal has not been explained by me, Malun-kyaputta: that the world is not eternal.... And why, Malun-kyaputta, has this not been explained by me? It is because it is not connected with the goal, is not fundamental to the Brahma-faring,[2] and does not conclude to turning away from, nor dispassion, stopping, calming, super-knowledge, awakening nor to nib-bana.... (MLS. II, p. 101.)

His main mission is the clarification of the unsatisfactoriness of the life of man (*dukkhan ca aham pannapemi*) and an enunciation of a way for its eradication (dukkhassa ca nirodham M. I, 140). This is reiterated in the Malunkya sutta as follows: "And what has been explained by me, Malunkyaputta? 'This is anguish'[3] has been explained by me.... This is the course leading to the stopping of anguish has been explained by me" (MLS. II, p. 101). It is with perfect awareness of his field of activity that the Buddha says that he visualises the world to be within the fathom-sized body of man (A. II. 48). If that is properly corrected, then all other matters correct themselves consequently. Hence the Buddha's promulgation of the Causal Genesis of Paticcasamuppada is primarily in relation to the presence, origination and elimination of the unsatisfactory life processes of man. His main line of inquiry was 'what being there does this naturally unsatisfactory human life come to be perpetuated' (*kismin sati idam hoti*). It is a question, an inquiry and an analysis relating to a specific problem. It is the answer to these questions and the ways recommended for their solution which gave rise to a total and comprehensive religious system which has come to be designated today as Buddhism.

Unity and Dignity of Man

Having thus analysed the plight of man in the world in terms of his samsaric inheritance[4] at birth, his own correct or incorrect action through thought, word and deed and the extent to which he finds himself in the grip of his environment, the Buddha saw no justification for laying the responsibility for the suffering of man in the hands of a Supreme Being, who at the same time is credited with the responsibility of creation. Not only does the Buddha through his theory of Causal Genesis eliminate the role of an external agency and the process of creation, but he also highlights the contradiction between the benevolence of creation and the painful presence of suffering in the world.

Thus in place of fear and dread which come in the wake of a concept of sin and transgression and in place of submission which follows from authoritarianism, Buddhism starts with the culture of man and the elevation of his dignity. A first step in this direction is the insistence on the virtue of *maitri*, of the practice of loving-kindness. It is basically the state of friendliness, of being a friend of mitra that links man to a society. It is no doubt extended to all grades of life, human and animal and further extends through time and space, leaving no room for caste, creed or ethnic differences. It is in fact interesting to observe that the future Buddha on whom the salvation of the present world is said to be hinged is named Maitreya. This insists as it were that the salvation of man rests on the mutual love of and respect for one another.

Far from harping on petty ideological differences within creeds, man must learn to respect man in his own right and in spite of differences and disagreements. Nothing short of such a down-to-earth and meaningful value can stop the carnage that is being embarked upon, day after day, on the basis of race, colour and creed. And friendliness or *maitri* is increasingly more needed within groups than between groups.

Society and Moral Order

The Buddhists are thus required to look upon humanity with a sense of unity, working towards the goal of eliminating one another's stress and turmoil which result from the misguided and miscalculated behaviour of each one. It is not their mission to propagate a creed, in response to a divine will, and to win over the rest of mankind to their side. The virtues they uphold both for self-redemption and for the welfare of mankind have a universal applicability. They are directly and intimately connected with human nature. Through a process of self-education Buddhists are expected, for this purpose, to regulate their lives by refraining from certain types of behaviour which are personally and psychologically corroding and socially and externally disruptive and damaging. The deterrent in these cases is a healthy and constructive value-awareness, rather than a fear which represses and inhibits. In the field of Buddhist morality, two basic considerations which regulate social behaviour are:

1. an awareness of what degrades human life (*hiri*)

2. an awareness of what damages its furtherance (*ottappa*)

These are described as regulative factors which put the world on the right track (*lokapālaka dhamma*).

The value of these restraints which are sponsored by Buddhism in its religious ethics lies in their cohesive power of integrating society into a harmonious whole on a basis of mutual respect which is directly reciprocal on the human plane, deriving its validity at a grass-root level. As far as the Buddhists are concerned, more than any other virtue, *maitri* or loving-kindness, reaches farthest in this direction. It is an unfailing stimulus to ego-reduction. According to Buddhism, egoism in the form of the assertion of 'I' and 'mine' (i.e., *ahamkāra mamimkāra mānānusayā*) stands very much in the way of salvation. The mutual character of the virtue of *maitri* also develops benevolent affection leading to a spirit of giving and sharing (*dāna, dānasamvibhāga* and *cāga* of the Buddhist texts) which is a much needed virtue in the world of today and tomorrow, where imbalances of resources as well as of production will continue to prevail indefinitely, exposing man to risks or poverty and starvation. Practised with adequate seriousness at an individual level, it must necessarily penetrate into the psychology of nations at a group level. Buddhists who are prompted by *maitri* to contribute towards the very basis of sustenance and consequently of peace and comfort of their fellow beings, could not generate thoughts of destruction through wars or quarrels with rival groups nor within their own.

The no-God stand

My brief introduction to the basic tenets of Buddhism which give Buddhism its distinctness with regard to the rejection of a Creator God who presides over the world he has created and contrives for the redemption of the worldlings whose lot has come to be suffering both in mind and body, was mainly intended to emphasize the non-traditionalist character of the religion of the Buddha in its historical beginnings. One of the basic recognitions in early Buddhism about the nature of the world, as already outlined, is its view of unsatisfactoriness with regard to the experience of man living in it. The physical inheritance of man at birth, according to Buddhism, brings in its wake and by virtue of it, a host of unpleasant and unwelcome situations like disease and decay, not to speak of death at a time when it is least expected, in the physical sphere, as well as a complicated network of psychological aberrations like greed, hatred, jealousy, pride. This view of the sources of suffering stands in opposition to a view of a Supreme Being who either has control over unwelcome and unpleasant situations or could provide succour in relation to them (*attāno loko anabhissaro*, M. II, p. 68).

In this context it must be adequately stressed that no serious student of Buddhism could afford to miss the significance of the two Pali words *tāna* and *abhissara* which are embedded in the above quotation. The word *tāna* means protection, shelter, refuge and in its negative, *attāna*, what is asserted is the absence of such a source of comfort or security for suffering worldlings, external to themselves. Bring into this context the Buddha's oft-repeated injunction: "Be ye your own refuge. Provide for yourself your own security. Seek it not from another. Seek it and find it in the Dharma." (*Attadīpā bhikkhave viharatha attasaranā anaññasaranā dhammadīpā dhammasaranā anaññasaranā*, D. II, p. 100.) *Abhissara*, on the other hand, even more than the Sanskrit word *isvara* which means over-lord, Supreme Being or God, with the prefix *abhi* added to it, means a deity presiding over and controlling the destiny of the world. The concept of its negative in *anabhissara* fits in harmoniously with the Buddhist theory of Causal Genesis as far as the life of man is concerned. On this Causal Genesis alone depends, positively, life through the word "process" or *samsāra* and negatively or reversely, the salvation of man in *nirvāna*.

As for the authenticity of the quotation which we have discussed so far and which is given in the text as one of four postulates of doctrine or *dhammuddesa*, it is not only quoted in a learned discussion by a Buddhist disciple, the venerable Ratthapala, as a fundamental point of doctrine, but it is also authenticated by the king of Kurus, who himself asserts that it is a statement made by the Buddha: "*Acchariyam bho Ratthapāla abbutham bho Ratthapala yāva subhāsitañ ca idam tena bhagavatā jānatā pasatā arahatā sammāsambuddhena attāno loko anabhissaroti. Attāno hi bho Ratthapāla loko anabhissaro*" (M. II. p. 70).

By now it should be sufficiently clear that the Buddhist explanation of the phenomenon of life in the world and its assessment necessarily shows a deflection from the general run of religious thinking the world has witnessed so far. To assume a position of importance or authority to go so far as to say that it should or should not be so shows very little sense and much less logic. Such a purist stance can by no means lead to universally acceptable and wholesome results. What is first and most desirable in the study of a religion, at least in the social context of today, is profundity in theology; and the grandeur of its metaphysics is necessarily moved to take a second place. As to the evaluation of the contribution of a religion to the culture of mankind, different criteria are being adopted, depending on considerations like world position: east or west, north or south, etc.

The Buddhist Impact

In terms of the lessons the world is learning today, or perhaps refusing to learn, it should not be difficult to discover common norms of human value which would be universally applicable. We should have more than a desire to consolidate a set of beliefs. We should have the desire to maximize the good that religions can bring upon mankind collectively. In such a scheme religiousness or spirituality should loom larger than theology. Anything to the contrary should prove to be like the use of atomic weapons to conquer the world, or putting it less nakedly, to secure peace. To look upon differences or the absence of one's major themes in the creed of another as a defect or deficiency shows a lamentable lack of magnanimity. Others attempt to obliterate differences and to impress one stamp on everybody. One would be led to believe that such moves are prompted either by wishful thinking or blissful ignorance or a spirit of repressive aggression. The world today, at least in the realm of religion, would do well to learn to agree to disagree.

In order to explore the possibilities of an inter-religious dialogue, not for its own sake, but to save man from the brink of disaster on which he is presently perched, let us examine the tone in which students of religion speak of the faith of each other. Making a general appraisal of Buddhism in the history of the world, the author of *The God of Buddha* says:

> ...So, we, too, if we are sincere seekers of the way of the Buddha, must return to that early India which was the cradle not

only of the physical and mental personality of the Buddha, but also for the tremendous spiritual message of His doctrine—a doctrine eventually destined to go beyond the confines of its homeland and ultimately become the basis of a human civilization for the major part of Asia and praxis of life for all sentient beings in their quest for immortality.[5]

To this historical evaluation of the role of Buddhism for the furtherance of human civilization and world culture, very little needs to be added except in point of detail. With regard to Buddhism's impact on western Asia, almost as far as the Caspian Sea, which it reached even before the dawn of the Christian era, what remains as archaeological evidence, for various historical reasons, is scanty. The colossal Buddha statues of Bamiyan together with the sculptural remains of Fondukistan in Afghanistan eloquently testify to this. Over and above these, one notes the historical records of al-Biruni who wrote about a thousand years ago, detailing the prevalence of Buddhism, even prior to the arrival of Zoroaster, in those regions. Moreover, Buddhism contributed to civilization in general, and art and culture in particular, of eastern Asia. China, Korea and Japan are adequate proof of our claim, not to speak of what still lies buried under the sands of Central Asia. So it was with Asoka in the Indian sub-continent and in other countries of south and southeast Asia like Sri Lanka, Burma and Indonesia.

Having explained Buddhism's very peculiar position with regard to God at the head of religion, I also made an attempt to show that, in spite of it, Buddhism has had enough inner strength to revitalize man to embark on a journey of spiritual ascent. It is an ascent based on and gathering its momentum from a carefully reorganized social order. It was also shown, through reference to history, that for more than twenty-five centuries Buddhism has contributed to the well-being of man, at a modest and moderate pace, though, contributing more to stablizing peace than to escalating material prosperity. While it reckoned with the possible corrosion that could come in the wake of the latter, it never upheld poverty as a virtue itself. Charity, on the other hand, with which the good life of the Buddhist invariably begins, was born both of a love of fellow beings and a desire to keep the irksome ego within restricted boundaries.

Buddhism's no-God position has been very much misunderstood. Some fail to see any evidence in Buddhism which either directly supports this notion or even implies it. Others are categorical in stating that no religion of any worth could possibly take up such a position. This latter group takes up two lines of action. One forcibly reads into the Buddhist texts implications pointing to God, the Absolute, the Eternal and the Ultimate. Language-wise, in rendering Pali or Sanskrit terms, these views are untenable. Idea-wise they are inconsistent and contradictory and do not fit in, even clumsily, to the general thesis.

Leaning on the word *kalyāṇa* which means benevolent, wholesome or charming, in the inoffensive compound *kalyāṇamitta* (i.e., a benevolent or charming friend) a certain writer tries to render it as the Lovely, giving the compound the meaning *a friend, associate and intimate of the Lovely*. Thereafter, he equates this *Lovely* with the *Absolute*. In consequence of this seemingly Don Quixotic adventure, the said writer loses himself in a verbal tangle with almost amusing results.

> Now, while Brahma-faring culminates in Nirvana and is synonymous with Nirvana, it cannot be equated with *the Lovely* because of the following distinction: Brahma-faring can lead to friendship, association and intimacy with *the Lovely*, but friendship, or association or intimacy, is not the same as identity with *the Lovely*. The Buddha, too, who on occasions has claimed identity with Dharma and also that He had attained the highest Nirvana, makes no claim of identity with *the Lovely*, but states that, because of His friendship with *the Lovely*, beings are able to have Nirvana. Hence this Lovely is higher than the Buddha, since friendship, association and intimacy with It are vital for Buddha's task of salvation. Moreover, since the Buddha too had to seek salvation, one could logically assume that the Lovely was also instrumental for the Buddha's own enlightenment.[6]

Some others would, in the interest of mankind, call upon the Buddhists to revise their major thesis. They are certain of the absence in Buddhism of the concept of God without which, they are equally certain, there can be no salvation for mankind either here or hereafter. Let me repeat here for further examination such a verdict, which comes from a non-Buddhist source, to which I have already referred.

> The development of mankind in our present time urges Buddhists also to reconsider their way and to take history seriously. They can no longer exclude the social dimension from their system. World peace, without which even personal liberation remains impossible, can be established only if mankind forms a unity, a community in which every individual is considered as a being of infinite value and equal rights. Such a community can be formed only if the love of God frees men from their egoism and inspires them with self-giving love.[7]

This criticism is obviously missing the point. Starting with the problems of man at a grassroots level—problems as seen, known and discerned by man himself—Buddhism takes account of history, and therefore of the need even to regulate its course. It is for the others to get to know how much the Buddhists, in their system, deal with social considerations, and how much they strive to make the unity of mankind a reality. Buddhism prescribes the elements for a just and benevolent rule, and for social and economic stability, while exposing at the same time the foibles and cunning of leaders of men at all levels. But it drives no wedge that divides, not even at the level of man and animal. This attitude of the Buddhists is born of a primary adoration of life, which forms, in fact, the first precept in their ethical system. The consequence is that Buddhism works negatively for the protection of life against destruction and positively for the development of unbounded love throughout the entire universe. It needs hardly to be stressed at this stage that the very goal of Buddhism is the overthrow of egoism and the perfection of loving-kindness. The first step towards that goal is symbolized by the very name of the future Buddha, the Buddha-to-be, whom the Buddha Gotama has already named as Maitreya or the Compassionate One.

Since I have now indicated briefly two ways in which non-Buddhists have reacted in response to Buddhism, particularly with regard to its non-acceptance of the idea of God, let me conclude with a question. As we approach the end of the century today, would you accept either of these positions or would you explore the possibility of a new approach in the light of what has been said so far about the core of Buddhism, its scope and concern for mankind?

FOOTNOTES

1 See Macdonnell, *Vedic Mythology*, pp. 26ff.

2 This refers to the Buddhist religious life, specially of the mendicant, known as brahmacariya. It has nothing to do with Brahman or Brahma of pre-Buddhist Indian religions.

3 Here, the translator uses the word anguish to refer to *dukkha* which we explain as 'unsatisfactoriness of life'.

4 For example, the psycho-physical condition, manifest or latent, in which a human being finds himself, at birth or later in life, on account of his own conscious, volitional activity or *karma*.

5 Jamshed Fozdar, *The God of Buddha* (New York: Asia Publ. House, 1973), p. v.

6 *Ibid.*, p. 144.

7 Theobold Diederich in *Religious Dialogue and Human Development—The Asian Scene* (Sri Lanka Foundation Institute Pocket Book 2), p. 44.

God and Creation in Unification Theology

Unification Theology

Chung Hwan Kwak

How can we know God? As the unique and eternal first cause of everything, God cannot be confined within the space-time of this world. As the standard of perfection and the source of all ideals, God is absolute and unchanging. How can we, who live in a spatiotemporal and changeable world, know God, who is unique, eternal, absolute, and unchanging?[1]

We can know God because we are created in His image (Gen. 1:26). Although studying an image can never yield complete knowledge of its original source, a deep understanding of our own human nature should reveal something about God's nature. However, if we examine our own nature in an attempt to know God, we are immediately confronted with the problem of evil and sin. We have evil tendencies which often thwart the good that we would do. If we had only our own sinful nature as a guide, we would have to conclude that the Creator of the universe is self-contradictory and self-destructive; but God has provided us with an example of a person with no evil tendencies, who not only embodies human nature undistorted by sin, but who also reveals something to us about God's nature. That person is Jesus Christ.

Jesus taught us to call God "Father," and to love all human beings as our brothers and sisters. He taught us that our own true happiness is to be found only in the Kingdom of God; and out of his love for God and his love for us, he singlemindedly dedicated himself to establishing God's ideal. Even when that dedication led to his death at the hands of those whom he had come to help, Jesus forgave his persecutors. His self-sacrificial love, manifested in an unwavering effort to lead us to true happiness, reflects the most essential aspect of God—what Unification theology[2] calls "heart."

Heart is the impulse that seeks joy through loving someone or something. It is not the same as emotion, since it would obviously be a mistake to say that the most essential aspect of Jesus and God is emotion (just as it would be a mistake to say that the most essential aspect is intellect or will). Heart manifests itself in love, which is not merely a sentimental emotion or a romantic longing—but a purposeful activity which serves, benefits, and invigorates someone or something. As such, love involves intellect and will as well as emotion; so heart is deeper than intellect, emotion, and will, and is the starting point and motivation for all three.

Jesus did not love abstractly, in a vacuum. He loved real human beings. Joy arises only when the lover has a beloved to love. Although the lover exists independently of the beloved, joy is dependent on the relationship between them. Since the purpose of heart is to give love, heart includes the impulse to find or create a suitable recipient for love. Thus, the creation follows from God's desire to seek joy through sharing His love. However, because of the nature of love, the lover cannot fully experience joy unless the beloved is also joyful; so God's primary desire must be for His creation to be joyful. By understanding God's heart in this way, we may conclude that God's motivation for creating the universe is joy—joy for creation and joy for God.

If God is our "Father," then He must have created us to be His "children." According to Unification theology, this follows from God's motivation for creating the universe. Just as the joy experienced by someone who loves another human being is potentially greater than the joy experienced by someone who loves an animal or inanimate object, so also the joy experienced by God is potentially greatest when the object of His love most nearly resembles Him. Thus God's children, like all other things in His creation, have aspects of "internal character" (mind) and "external form" (body), which are distinguishable but inseparable; and these reflect God's "internal character" (intellect, emotion, and will, with their roots in heart) and God's "external form" (the divine energy which sustains the creation and provides for its harmonious operation). Likewise, God's children exhibit aspects of "positivity" (initiative or assertiveness) and "negativity" (receptivity or responsiveness), reflecting the fact that God both initiates and responds in His relationships with us. Furthermore, in addition to a physical mind and body, each of God's children has a spiritual immortality, human beings are more like God than are other creatures. However, the characteristic possessed by all human beings which most nearly resembles God, and which most distinctly sets them apart from the rest of the creation, is *creativity*.

As God's sons and daughters, we are similar to Him primarily because we are co-creators. In a minor sense, we are co-creators because we are capable of participating actively in the process of perfecting ourselves as sons and daughters of God. Thus, Jesus taught us that we must become perfect as our Heavenly Father is perfect (Matt. 5:48). To be a co-creator in this sense means to be responsible for directing our behavior in such a way that we do not misuse the love we receive from God. Love is fundamentally important as the basis of all true relationships; and as such, it must be properly ordered, so that the "vertical" relationship with God takes priority over "horizontal" relationships with other created beings. This is the significance of Jesus' "Great Commandment" to love God with all our heart and soul and mind and strength, and to love our neighbor as ourselves (Mark 12:30-31). According to Unification theology, the love that flows between a person and God, if not misused, would gradually establish an unbreakable unity of heart between them. A person in such a relationship with God would "inherit" God's internal character, and especially God's heart. Consequently, that person would share God's purpose and God's feelings, and would become capable of manifesting perfect divine love. Furthermore, although free (like God), that person would never do evil, because an evil act would cause that person the same grief that it would cause God. It is because Jesus established such a unity of heart with God that we can look to him in order to know God.

However, co-creatorship also implies the freedom to choose a purpose different from God's purpose. Unless human beings were free *not* to establish a perfect unity of heart with God, their co-creatorship would be a sham. But if perfect unity of heart with God is unbreakable, then there must be a period of time, before that unity is established, during which human beings may "sin," or act in ways that cause God grief instead of joy. Unification theology calls this period of time the "growth period." Between the original formation of a human individual in birth and infancy, and the time when a person reaches spiritual maturity or "perfection," the individual in the growth period has the responsibility to "create" himself or herself as a child of God. As the necessary condition for co-creatorship, this growth period follows from God's original desire to seek joy through loving someone who resembles Him as much as possible. Therefore, God could not create us perfect instantaneously, but had to provide a process through which we could exercise our co-creatorship.

Furthermore, although animals, plants, and inanimate objects (unlike human beings) do not have any portion of responsibility for their growth, the growth process itself is reflected throughout the whole of creation. Thus, the physical universe developed through many stages over a very long period of time before living things were created; living things evolved progressively from relatively simple beginnings to their present complexity and diversity; and each individual organism grows through several stages on its way to maturity. However, all of these processes were specifically instituted by God to prepare the way for His children. None of them are random or undirected, since the ultimate goal was fixed in advance; so Unification theology is imcompatible with theories which rely primarily on random mutations and natural selection to explain evolution. For that matter, Unification theology is incompatible with any theory which takes the material world as its starting point to explain life and spirit. Life does not arise spontaneously from inanimate matter, but represents a fundamental transformation of "internal character," effected by God. Similarly, the immortal human spirit is not a mere epiphenomenon of matter, but (like matter and life) has its origin in God.

Therefore, human nature cannot be explained materialistically, but only by relation to God. According to Unification theology, all relationships can be analyzed in terms of a "four position foundation," wherein an origin divides into two complementary aspects which constitute a unity by relating harmoniously to each other on the basis of their common origin. For example, human perfection can be understood as a four position foundation with God as the "origin," mind and body as the "division," and perfected individuality as the "union." In relation to God, the mind establishes a unity of heart; while in relation to the body, the mind initiates actions which are consistent with God's purpose. The body is made of elements which (to a limited extent) reflect God's characteristics, and it responds to the mind's direction. The perfected individual would thereby reflect God's nature, and could be said to be created in God's image.

In order for our first human ancestors to achieve individual perfection, they had to exercise a portion of responsibility. The biblical story of the fall casts this responsibility in symbolic terms, as the duty not to eat the fruit of the tree of knowledge of good and evil (Gen. 2:17). But our first ancestors neglected their responsibility. Consequently, they not only failed to inherit God's heart, but also acquired a deformed "fallen nature" riddled with contradictory tendencies. As the original parents of the entire human family, our first ancestors thereby transmitted fallen nature to all their descendents, making it necessary for God to institute a process of restoration before human beings could again become capable of fulfilling their responsibility to grow to perfection as His children.

Since the most essential aspect of God is heart, God's original desire had been for human beings to reflect His nature in such a way as to produce the greatest joy. But instead of being a joyful culmination of the long process of creation, human beings broke God's heart. In Unification theology, God is not seen as a wrathful judge who sentences people to death and eternal damnation, but as a loving parent made sorrowful by the failure of His children. Therefore, the most important consequence of the fall is God's grief.

God could not overcome His grief by unilaterally and arbitrarily restoring people to their pre-fallen condition, since such an act would have negated their freedom and responsibility and made it impossible for them ever to reflect God's nature. Unless human responsibility is preserved in the process of restoration, God's ideal can never be realized. Thus, throughout Old Testament history God called upon people to obey His commandments and fulfill His will; and despite repeated failures, the people of Israel finally succeeded in overcoming, at least symbolically or conditionally, the failure of our first ancestors. Jesus came on the foundation of their success, to a nation waiting for the Messiah.

Jesus was born sinless as the "second Adam." He fulfilled his responsibility and inherited God's Heart. However, as the true son of God, his purpose went far beyond his own perfection, and he desired that everyone become a child of God. Since Jesus was united with God, by uniting with him as their mediator people could unite with God and thereby be cleansed of their fallen nature. Through this process, God could restore in fallen people the capacity to fulfill their responsibility as co-creators. Of course, Jesus could not force people to unite with him against their will; so he attracted them by sharing God's love with them, and he taught them to "believe in him whom He has sent" (John 6:29). Nevertheless, while Jesus was alive nobody followed him wholeheartedly, and when the persecution became serious even his closest disciples deserted him. Although Jesus had come to bring joy through unity with God, he was misunderstood, rejected, and crucified. The crucifixion added to the grief which God felt because of the fall, and God's grief has persisted up to the present day.

The present state of the world is hardly such as to make God joyful. The very fact that human beings are still so far from reflecting God's nature is evidence that the process of restoration has not been completed. Yet Jesus was definitely the Messiah who came to establish the Kingdom of God. What went wrong? We can begin to answer this question by examining in more detail God's original ideal—what Unification theology calls the "Three Great Blessings." God told our first ancestors to (1) be fruitful; (2) multiply and fill the earth; and (3) subdue the earth and have dominion over every living thing (Gen. 1:28). The First Blessing refers to individual perfection, or unity of heart with God. Jesus achieved the First Blessing. However, through the faithlessness of other people rather than through any failure on his part, Jesus was prevented from achieving the Second Blessing.

From the very beginning, God's image was female as well as male (Gen. 1:27). The Second Blessing indicates that God intended the original man and woman to be the "True Parents" of the human family, transmitting God's heart and love to all their descendents. However, our first ancestors failed to achieve the First Blessing, and became "false parents" instead. The Messiah comes to rectify this failure by restoring True Parenthood to the human family, which must be "reborn" to become the true family of God. The femininity as well as masculinity of God's image, the importance of True Parents, and the need for fallen people to be reborn into the true family of God all suggest that the messianic office is to be exercised not by a single individual, but by a husband and wife. However, Jesus was crucified before be could establish a true family on earth. Only after death did Jesus receive a "bride": in the Christian tradition, the "bride" of Jesus is the "Mother" Church, filled with the Holy Spirit, which together with Jesus gives spiritual rebirth to faithful believers.

Whereas the First Blessing calls upon people to become God-centered individuals, and the Second Blessing calls upon them to establish God-centered families, the Third Blessing calls upon them to develop a God-centered relationship with the rest of the creation. Unification theology interprets "subdue" and "dominion" in such a way as to emphasize God-centered stewardship. With physical bodies that reflect God's nature, perfected individuals would serve as mediators between God and His creation, bringing joy to both. Practically speaking, by achieving the Third Blessing human beings would acquire the knowledge and technology to minimize problems such as disease and hunger, and to provide the best possible physical environment for the Kingdom of God.

Because of the fall, our first ancestors failed to achieve any of the Three Great Blessings. Because of the crucifixion, Jesus was prevented from achieving more than the First. But until all human beings are able to achieve all three, God's joy will not be complete, because God's heart will always seek perfect joy for every individual, and perfect joy consists in achieving our full potential as co-creators and children of God. God, our invisible Heavenly Parent, is the eternal origin of true love. Despite the fall and despite the crucifixion, God will not be satisfied until the human family can inherit His heart and reflect His nature. This must begin with True Parents at the family level and expand from there to societies, nations, and the world. The True Parents must share God's love with everyone, establishing the brotherhood and sisterhood of all humankind, the Kingdom of God. Then God, humankind, and all creation will be united, centered on God's heart. God's grief will be wiped away, and God's joy and our joy will be complete at last.

FOOTNOTES

1 The English version of this paper was prepared with the assistance of Jonathan Wells.

2 More detailed expositions of Unification theology may be found in the following books:

Divine Principle (New York: Holy Spirit Association for the Unification of World Christianity, 1973).

Outline of the Principle: Level Four (New York: Holy Spirit Association for the Unification of World Christianity, 1980).

An Asian (Philippine) and Christian Concept of God (A Philosophical and Theological Perspective)

Vitaliano R. Gorospe, S.J.

The Asian Faces of God

In Asia, the cradle of the world's great religions, God has many faces. There are as many concepts of God in Asia as there are diverse religions and cultures. What is distinctive and peculiar to Asia is its multi-faceted religiosity; that is, cosmic and animistic religions have been integrated with one or another of the great Asian religions like Hinduism, Buddhism, and Islam. The only concept of God of Western origin which has somehow been inculturated in Asia is that of Christianity.

The purpose of this paper is to bring one Asian concept of God which is a symbiosis of East and West into the contemporary discussion on God. This paper is an attempt to present (from a philosophical and theological perspective) the Filipino and Christian concept of God which is found in Philippine "popular religiosity" or the "religion of the people."[1] One value of an international ecumenical conference which brings both East and West into dialogue is what John S. Dunne calls a double process of "passing over," a shifting of standpoint, a passing from one culture to another, from one way of life to another, from one religion to another, and a "coming back," a returning with new insight to one's own culture, one's way of life, one's own religion."[2]

Inculturation

In any discussion of God today, one cannot escape the challenge of inculturation of the concept of God "from within" today's culture, whether Eastern or Western or a worldwide cross-cultural phenomenon called modernity.[3] Hence, this paper is divided into three main parts. First, from a philosophical viewpoint, we shall point out elements of a philosophy of religion which underlie the Filipino and Christian concept of God. Secondly, we shall indicate what the Filipino and Christian way to God has in common with Western traditional and contemporary approaches to God. We shall focus on the "Filipino dimension" of universal human and religious experience. Thirdly, from a theological perspective, we shall show the mutual reciprocity between Philippine culture and the Christian faith in the evolution of a contemporary concept of God which is both Asian and Christian.

Traditional approaches to God address themselves to two fundamental questions: "Does God exist?" and "Who is God?". Perhaps contemporary approaches to God have shifted to the question of the final meaning of reality, of man, and of the future. In any case, this paper hopes to make a two-fold contribution to the ecumenical discussion. First, Filipino popular Christianity underscores the truth that the question of God today cannot be resolved by reason alone. This is not to say that the truth of Filipino popular Christianity is not philosophically and theologically verifiable.[4] Whatever is authentically human in Filipino popular religiosity is shared by other religious faiths. Secondly, Filipino popular Christianity serves as a paradigm of the inculturation process whereby Christianity is to be incarnated from within indigenous cultures to the mutual enrichment of both. Filipino popular Christianity is a unique blending of East and West.

The Filipino Faith in God

Although Christianity is a minority religion in Asia (2.3%), the majority religion in the Philippines is *Catholicism*. Among all the countries in the world, the Philippines, with a total population of 47,000,000, ranks sixth place in the number of Catholics (39,931,000). In proportion to the total population of the Philippines, Catholics are 84.97%; Moslems (4.32%), Protestants (3.06%), indigenous religious sects like *Aglipayans* (3.5%) and *Iglesia ni Kristo* (1.6%), and Buddhists (.09%). Today *animism* (belief in the spirit-world, both good and evil) which is the religion of close to four million (about 10%) mountain tribal Filipinos already shows Christian influences.

This study is limited to *Filipino popular Christianity* or *"popular Catholicism"* and is based on an emerging Filipino philosophy and theology, the findings of the social sciences, a re-discovery of Philippine myths, symbols, and folklore, and new insights from Philippine literature.[5] For the authentic interpretation of these resources the benchmark is contemporary Filipino experience.

"Popular Catholicism" reflects the faith and the "religion of the people" (i.e., the less educated majority) and refers to the beliefs and practices of indigenous origin, regardless of orthodoxy, either tolerated or disapproved by "official Catholicism."[6] Popular Catholicism, urban or rural, is characterized by trust in God, church attendance, and a year round mixture of Filipino culture and the Christian religion. An international comparative study shows that among child-rearing values of the Filipino family, trust in God ranks highest.[7] Trust in God is also a dominant theme in Philippine literature. But, as we shall see later, the meaning of trust in God is ambivalent: it could mean a Christian trust in Divine Providence or a sort of fatalism in religious guise.

Filipino popular Christianity emphasizes practical solutions to problems of daily life and is concerned with birth, marriage, health, death and immediate temporal concerns. That is why Filipino popular Christianity is characterized by a *thaumaturgical thrust*—e.g., faith healing, "possession trances" (*langkap*) or ecstatic preaching, vows and penitential rites like flagellation, ritual dancing and popular devotions to gain favors, and *animistic* beliefs and practices—e.g. predicting the future, dream interpretation, spirit-communication, corporeal rites, good luck amulets, rituals for the dead, exorcism. The widespread growth of faith-healing through the medium of preachers in a state of trance has flowered into a new religious movement called the New Mysticism to which we shall return later.

Elements of a Philosophy of Religion

Two World Views: East and West
In order to situate the Filipino world view of God, the individual, and this life, a word about the contrast between two world views is necessary. Both Eastern (Hinduism and Buddhism) and Western philosophy (Plato, Hegel, Husserl, Louis Lavelle) have in common the concept of God as the Absolute and the method of intuition through self-reflection.[8] To arrive at God as a Totality which includes everything requires an extra-rational method of reflection —intuition or a vision of the whole. In both Oriental and Occidental philosophy, God is reached through reflection on man's most pro-

found self; the way of immanence leads to the discovery of transcendence. To think of God as an indivisible whole—"the All in all"—leads logically to a pantheistic way of thinking in all primitive and natural religions. However, to say that the Absolute is All in all is not to be taken in the literal or perceptual sense. Both Oriental and Occidental thought conceive the Absolute as One but the Absolute can present itself in myriad forms. Whereas the Eastern concept of God is impersonal, the Western concept (at least the Christian) is personal.

The major difference between Oriental and Occidental philosophy is in their treatment of individual selfhood and of human life. The East does not glorify the individual because the ego is of no importance. In Hinduism and Theravada Buddhism, individuals are not real but illusory; Buddhism de-emphasizes the individual as a source of sorrow and misery. The West glorifies the individual self as the source of personhood, personal freedom and responsibility. The East looks on human life as suffering and misery and therefore undesirable; the individual must be liberated from life in this world. "Nirvana" in Hinduism means the annihilation of the individual self and absorption into the Great Self; in Buddhism, the fading out of suffering. The West looks on this life as pleasurable and desirable and therefore human life must be prolonged as far as possible.

The Filipino World View of God, the Individual, and This Life
If the Filipino world view of God, the individual, and this life resembles the Western rather than the Eastern world view, this is mainly due to the influence of Christianity from the West. The pantheistic way of thinking about God as a Totality that includes everything is foreign to Filipino thought and the Filipino approach to God is intuitive rather than rational. In Filipino popular religiosity God is transcendent, personal, and One. Even Filipino animism acknowledges only one supreme god who is distinct and superior to other minor deities. *Bathala* is the traditional title given to the supreme god. *Diwata* and *anito* are names given both to lower divinities or spirits (non-humans) and to *kaluluwa* (souls of the dead), departed ancestors. There is also a hierarchy among evil and benign, friendly spirits. In pre-Christian Philippine creation myths, the creator god is personal and given human attributes. In Filipino

official Christianity, God is One and is revealed as Three Persons, and the Filipino Christian adult who reflects profoundly on himself becomes aware that he is God's son. But in the religion of the people, the focus is on Jesus Christ, the Virgin Mary, and the saints.

In Filipino thought today, the individual is very important. A traditional Filipino value is self-esteem (*amor propio*) and the Filipino looks at himself as a self (*kalooban*), conscious of his dignity and freedom as an individual.[9] If Filipino tradition has emphasized the importance of the tribe, family, the group (*sakop*) over the individual (versus rugged individualism in the West) and the next life rather than this life, Christianity has purified and enriched Filipino tradition by emphasizing both the dignity of the individual as God's image, the value of the human community and the importance of this life and its continuity with the next. The Filipino common man (*tao*) does not espouse flight from this world (*fuga mundi*) and its concerns. On the contrary, Filipino popular Christianity is mainly concerned with practical solutions to the problems of daily life. Belief in the doctrine of "harmony of opposites" enables the Filipino to look on sorrow and suffering as part of the rhythm of nature. Filipino religious festivals and rituals, the town *fiesta* are symbolic of the Filipino as a religious man of joy who celebrates life and believes in the importance of this world.

The Filipino Concept of God
The existence of God is a fact for ordinary Filipino Christians. If man can know by his reason about the existence of God from nature, then the Filipino rural adult lives by nature and sees in the signs of nature their Unseen Owner. Among rural Christians, omens or signs of the divine are seen in nature—in the rainbow, sun, moon, stars, streams, trees, birds and flowers. This belief is by no means superstitious but manifests man's natural approach to the invisible God through visible creation (Rom. 1:19-20).

Unlike the Eastern pantheistic and impersonal concept of God, the Filipino concept is always in personalistic terms. *Bathala* and its translation— *Ginuo/Panginoon/Apo*—means "Lord." He is almighty (*makapangyarihan*), eternal (*laon/gugurang*) and in Filipino animism God is remote and inaccessible except through intermediaries (minor deities). On the one hand, any polytheistic meaning of God in

Filipino animistic religions is purified and transformed by the Christian faith. On the other hand, the Filipino concepts of Creator (*Maykapal, Ang Lumikha, Makapangyarihan*) already provide the human basis for the Christian meaning of Almighty Creator in Genesis. In the Christian faith, God is revealed as Father, Son, and Holy Spirit. By transsignification, *Ginuo/Panginoon/Apo Diyos* becomes the equivalent of the Old Testament "Yahweh" and the New Testament "Kyrios" or Lord God. Since Jesus Christ is the fullest revelation of God, He is truly *Panginoon, Apo Diyos*. Although God is Trinitarian in "official Catholicism," in popular religiosity the concept of God is often unitarian. The most popular Filipino Christian concept of God is Merciful Father (*Amang Maawain*) which, although culturally conditioned, because of the innate Filipino national character of mercy (*awa*), takes on the added meaning of *Abba* or Daddy (Gal. 4:6).

The Filipino Concept of Creator (Maykapal)
Since in the Oriental cyclic view of history there is no beginning nor end, there is no need of a Creator to explain the origin of the world. But the concept of God as Creator which is essential to the Christian religion is already found in pre-Christian Philippine myths and folklore. Of interest are two versions of several Filipino creation myths about the origins of the human race and of the first man and woman; the former giving superiority to the brown race over the black and white races and the latter giving equality to the first man (*Malakas* or Strong) and first woman (*Maganda* or Beautiful) inasmuch as both sprang simultaneously from the same bamboo stalk. Philippine creation myths are significant for two reasons. First, they are pre-Christian and therefore, although colored by the Filipino character and culture, are part of the worldwide stream of mythology and folklore and mirror the history of the human spirit in its struggle against the forces of evil, ignorance, and irrationality since the fall of man. Secondly, they bring home the truth that technocratic society "has deprived the human mind of the myth and the rite, two things by which human beings enact their deep yearnings and keep themselves sane in mind and body."[10]

The Sacred and Profane in Filipino Life

Religion is nothing but the experience of reality in a special way and reality is not composed of two domains: a profane and a religious.[11] The sacred (holy) and the profane (human) are inseparable in Eastern thought and life. Similarly in Filipino life there is a spontaneous and harmonious blending of the holy and the secular. Among tribal Filipinos, religion is a way of life which is not separated from daily economic and social life. Among rural Christians, prayers or offerings to God are made in times of planting, harvesting, fishing and hunting, in the life-phases of birth, marriage, and death because these once-in-a-lifetime events are somehow sacred times. The Filipino philosophy of religion is incarnational; that is, God's active presence is incarnated in certain persons, places, things which are therefore considered sacred.

Like the Asian man, the Filipino wants to be in harmony with God, spirits (both good and evil), nature, family, fellowmen, and with himself. This "harmonizing tendency" inclines the Filipino to blend the sacred and profane in his daily life. Examples of this harmonious blending of Filipino culture and Christian faith abound. In a rural hut, a suburban home, or in a public bus, one finds a picture of a sexy movie star alongside that of Christ, the Virgin Mary, or a prayer card. Stickers in jeepneys (most common public transportation) combine sex and religious humor, e.g., "Sexy, free" (no fare) and "God knows Hudas not pay" (play on "who does" —Hudas—not pay). All Souls Day is a mixture of candles, blessings, prayers as well as holiday picnic. A jeepney driver passing in front of a church, or a Filipino boxer entering the ring, blesses himself with the sign of the cross. The harmonious blending of the sacred and profane, of Filipino culture and Christian faith, is most evident in Philippine religious festivals and rituals: e.g. a religious procession and beauty pageant (*Santacruzan*), a fluvial procession in honor of the Virgin Mary (*Penafrancia*), a carabao festival in which water buffaloes are made to genuflect in honor of the Virgin Mary (*Birhen sa Turumba*), ritual dancing for fertility to obtain the intercession of St. Clare.

While it is necessary to distinguish the sacred and the profane to avoid over-sacralization, at the same time one must not separate the sacred and profane so as to do away with the sacred altogether.

103

Although the process of secularization, on the one hand, can lead to authentic religion by purifying magical religion from fatalism, superstition, and other irrational and dehumanizing elements, on the other hand, it can also lead to secularism and contemporary atheism. Despite secularization, Filipino popular Christianity has remained immune from today's culture of unbelief in God and illumines the truth that the sacred and profane are distinct but complementary moments in human experience. The sacred is known *in* and *through* the profane. The sacred and profane ought to be inseparable and the sacred should influence the profane in human life.

The Filipino Concept of God as Mahal-Banal

The majority of simple, poor, ordinary Filipino Christians often refer to God as *Mahal-Banal*. The Filipino term—*mahal*— stands for both *value* and *love* and best expresses the concept of God as Supreme Value and God as Love. It also expresses the Christian obligation of love of God and neighbor. The Filipino term—*banal*— means *holy* and points to God as All Holy and the source of all love and holiness. Thus the Filipino concept of God as All Love and All Holy (*Mahal-Banal*) is the "Filipino dimension" not only of the harmonious blending of the sacred and profane but also the experience in the people's religion of Rudolf Otto's *The Idea of the Holy*. According to Otto, in the presence of the "Holy," God is experienced as *mysterium numinosum, tremendum, et fascinosum*.[12] Nowhere is the Filipino experience of the "Holy" (*Banal*) more evident than in the thaumaturgical thrust and animistic practices of Filipino popular Christianity. In contrast to the Scientific, Secularist, and Marxist visions of man, the Filipino philosophy of religion is permeated with a profound sense of the "holy," a sense of awe-inspiring mystery (*kila-bot*), numinous (*pambihira*), and a sense of admirable wonder (*kahanga-hanga, mahiwaga*) in the presence of God.

The Primacy of the Spirit

In the past a common interpretation by Western social scientists of Filipino animism was ignorance or superstition. For instance, on the island of Mindanao in southern Philippines, a *balete* tree refused to be felled to make room for the Japanese *Kawasaki* steel mill which was being built, because the tree was believed (by the local folk) to have been inhabited by spirits. The tree that refused to be felled is a symbolic protest, unspoken but real, in the psyche of the local inhabitants against the devastation of the environment which once was permeated with humanity, understanding, compassion and love. For tearing up the area in order to give way to the vast and giant industrial complex, tore people's lives; it is spirits that are invaded; in short, it is the primacy of the spirit over matter that was being felled.[13] Today, animism in Asia stands out as a symbolic protest of the Third World against the exploitation not only of nature but of the vast majority of Asian poor by the First World in the name of scientific and technological development. The animistic beliefs and practices of Filipino popular Christianity are a strong reaffirmation in a modern technocratic culture that has lost all sense of transcendence and of the sacrality of man and nature, of the primacy of things of the spirit—the need for faith, prayer, and spirituality in man's search for and union with God.

Filipino Approaches to God

To appreciate the Filipino approaches to God, a few preliminary remarks are helpful. First, Filipino approaches to God are based on *intuition* rather than logic, on faith rather than reason. But the Filipino intuition of faith, both human and divine, can be shown to be based on philosophical and theological grounds. In the religion of the people, what is important is not what is *thought* or *said* about God but how the people's faith is *lived*. Secondly, in the corpus of Filipiniana writings, there are no systematic philosophical "proofs" of God's existence similar to Western traditional and contemporary approaches to God.[14] Instead one finds the "Filipino dimension," colored by the Filipino character and culture, of the universal religious experience of mankind. Herein lies the point of contact between East and West, North and South, in an ecumenical, inter-cultural, and interfaith conference. Thirdly, in Filipino popular Christianity, whatever resembles the religious thought of the West is mainly due to the influence of Christianity.

The Question of God from a Filipino Perspective

Despite secularization, secularism, and contemporary atheism, the question of God remains but it must be framed in a new cultural perspective. What is the Filipino perspective today? Filipino popular Christianity does not approach God as a cosmological but as an anthropological, religious, and existential question.[15] God as Almighty Creator, All Love-All Holy, as Merciful Father is more relevant and meaningful to the ordinary Filipino Christian than Absolute Being, Prime Mover, First and Final Cause, not only because Filipino thought and language are concrete but because man's concepts of God evolve with the historical and cultural context. Asia and the Philippines share with the rest of the Third World the context of massive poverty and widespread structural injustice. It is within this context that Asian man, the Filipino common man, asks the question of God. The poor of the Third World are asking whether justice, human liberation and development are signs of the true God, of God's active presence today. The question of God in a Philippine context acquires a new meaning and takes on a socio-economic and political dimension. Who is the Filipino today? What are the future and destiny of the Filipino people? In a country where seventy per cent of the people are poor, deprived, oppressed because of injustice, what is God doing in all this? Where is God to be found today? The majority of the Filipino poor are beginning to find God in grass-roots "communities" where the Christian *faith* is palpably lived and Christian *justice* is being promoted. Other Filipino Christians find God in the lives of the "New Mystics" who are paragons of simple but deep faith, prayer, and spirituality and whose healing ministry is exercised mostly among the poor.

Three Images of God in Filipino Popular Religiosity

The traditional metaphysical and cosmological "proofs" for God's existence and the contemporary philosophical and anthropological approaches to God are totally alien to Filipino popular Christianity. However, Philippine literature which reflects the religion of the people shows three different images of God in the person of Jesus Christ arising out of a different historical situation. In the Spanish period, Christ is portrayed as the Model of Man (*Uliran ng Tao*); in the American period, Christ is the Reason of the World (*Katwiran ng Mundo*) and consequently the Foundation of the Moral Order; and after World War II, Christ is presented as the Messiah of Society (*Mesiyas ng Lipunan*).[16]

The most popular Filipino book read by ordinary Filipino Christians is the local version of the Passion of Christ in the Gospels called the *Pasyon*. With regard to the first image in the *Pasyon*, Christ becomes the Filipino model of obedience to God, parents, Church, and the Spanish monarchy. With regard to the second image of Christ as the Reason of the World, in the name of Reason (*Katwiran*), the Realistic tradition (theme of country) gave a socialist view of society, whereas the Romantic tradition (theme of love) taught love as the basis of the moral order, the way to human happiness. With regard to the third image of Christ as Messiah of Society, the *Pasyon* was first used by the Spaniards as an instrument of Filipinization and colonization but later was used by the Filipinos as an instrument of the Philippine revolution against Spain. Thus, in Philippine literature, the Filipino faith in God evolved from passive obedience and resignation amidst hardship and adversity to active self-reliance in the struggle for political freedom and independence.

The Filipino Moral Approach to God

In these three images of God which are the conclusions of the intuitive faith of the Filipino people in their history, one who thinks in Western philosophical categories will look in vain for logical arguments towards a moral and personalistic approach to God as the future of man. These three contemporary approaches to God are implicit and unthematized in Philippine literature. In the religious consciousness of the people, it is taken for granted that God is the model of Filipino moral behavior, the Reason of the World and the Foundation of the moral order, and the future of the Filipino people. Newman's moral approach to God is reflected in the Filipino popular approach that takes conscience as the "voice of God." In the struggle for freedom, Filipino nationalist leaders took for their moral guide right reason (*katuwiran*). *Katuwiran* comes from the Filipino "*tuwid*," meaning "straight" or "right." In Spanish the word *derecho* means "straight" but it is also the term for "law" (the law of right reason). In Thomas Aquinas, the Latin *recta ratio* or right reason (the natural moral law) is the objective norm of morality. True, the Filipino concept of right reason is a gradual development from Western influences such as found in European Rationalism; still God in Filipino popular religiosity is the ultimate basis of right reason. Hence, God is the Reason of the World and the Foundation of the Moral order. Moreover, it has been shown that Filipino tribal customary law (*adat*) reflects the primary precepts of the natural moral law before the advent of Islam or Christianity.[17] The Thomistic natural law theory that the law of right reason is nothing but a participation of the "eternal law" strikes a strong resonance in the Filipino moral approach to God.

The Filipino Personalistic Approach to God

Much has been written on Filipino personalism by social scientists and psychologists. Since Philippine culture is person-oriented and the Filipino way of thinking and behaving is highly personalistic, it is most natural and logical for the Filipino to think and speak of God as Personal. Like the Asian tendency to be in harmony with everyone and everything, the Filipino traditional value of "getting along with others" (*pakikisama*) or "smooth interpersonal relations" provides experiential grounds for a personalistic approach to God.

In the Filipino nationalist tradition, the ideal of nationalism (*pagkabayani*) is to be united by national consensus (*pagkakaisa*), by means of neighborly sharing of goods and services (*pakikisama*), in order to build a community in which every person is self-possessed and responsible (*pagsasarili*), and it is ultimately based on the universal value of human brotherhood (*pakikipag-kapwas-tao*). Implicit in the five Filipino nationalist values is the belief in a Personal God who is the necessary ground, condition, and goal of universal human brotherhood and community (*pakikipagkapwa-tao*), a deeply rooted Filipino tradition and value which underlies the Filipino aspiration for unity (*pagka-kaisa*) brought about by communal sharing (*pakikisama*).[18]

The Filipino is deeply aware of his human dignity (*pagkatao* which is equivalent to the Chinese *jen* or humanity) and of his worth as a person (self-esteem or *armor propio*) and is very sensitive to personal affront and the violation of his person. Hence, like the Asian "politeness" or "etiquette," respect (*paggalang*) for persons ranks very high as a Filipino value. Of all the anthropological "proofs" for God's existence, Gabriel Marcel's personalistic approach to the "Absolute Thou" comes closest to the experience of the Filipino. Marcel's concept of "being-with-others" as the ground of the God-man relationship finds a much richer and deeper expression in the Filipino concept of *kapwa* (neighborliness) which in the Filipino experience and language has at least eight levels of nuanced meanings. *Kapwa* best expresses "shared identity" or the unity of the "self" and "others."[19] The Filipino classic, *Urgana at Feliza*, a treatise on the traditional Filipino family and on etiquette and proper behavior, describes the harmonious relationships between husband and wife, parents and children in terms of Marcel's "I-thou" interpersonal relationships. The traditional Filipino family is God-centered and stresses person-oriented values which are rooted in "love of neighbor" (*paki-kipagkapwa-tao*) and ultimately on "love of God" (*pagibig ng Diyos*).

Whereas the Eastern concept of God is impersonal, nothing could be more personal and concrete than the Filipino images of God in the person of Jesus Christ found in popular devotions such as *Santo Niño* (Infant Jesus), *Hesus Nazareno* (suffering Christ), *Santo Entierro* (dead Christ), *Sagrado Corazon* (Sacred Heart), and *Kristo Rey* (Christ the King). These popular devotions have been influenced by Spanish Christianity and have been culturally and historically conditioned by the suffering and death of the Filipino people under the Spanish colonial era. The point is that they express the centuries-old faith of the people in a Personal God who suffered and died out of loving concern, in a Risen Savior who promises them final victory.

The significance of the Filipino personalistic approach to God to the contemporary ecumenical discussion on God is twofold: first, Filipino personalism represents the personalist philosophy which is strikingly manifested in Philippine culture, language, customs, and habits; and, secondly, a personalist philosophy and theology of God would seem to be the natural area in which the Filipino might be expected to make a genuine and distinct contribution.

The Filipino Approach to God as the Hope and Future of Man
The colonial history of the Filipino people and their continuing

struggle in the midst of poverty and injustice for liberation and total human development has given them a philosophy of history and a philosophy of hope whose final fulfillment is God as the future of man. This Filipino-Christian view opposes merely humanistic and nihilistic views of man. The Filipino popular view is that each human life has a history with a beginning and a goal. Unlike the Eastern cyclic view of history, the Filipino concept of history is spiral but always directed towards the future and a Power that is personal. The Filipino Christian does not look back to a repetition of the past but looks forward to a new and definitive future in God. Within the Christian faith, a strictly cyclic view of history cannot be reconciled with the linear Christian history of salvation.

"God—He is the Hope of the world" (*Ang Diyos siyang pag-asa ng mundo*) from a very popular song sums up well the Filipino approach to God as the hope and future of man. The recurring theme in Filipino short stories and novels is the undying hope of the Filipino poor and oppressed in Christ, the Messiah of society. Throughout their history even in their darkest hours, the Filipino masses have never lost hope in the future or in God. During the Philippine revolution against Spain, the Filipino symbol of oppression and injustice was darkness (*dilim*), the darkness of prison and despair; a turning to light (*liwanag*) was the symbol of hope, freedom, salvation, and Paradise. The hope of the Filipino people, their liberation from the darkness and prison of oppression, their turning to light, drew its inspiration from the example of Christ in the *Pasyon*. Even to this day, even among the most abject poor, one rarely sees the face of despair. What is the explanation of this deep and lasting hope that is innate in the Filipino national character? It cannot be mere human optimism. At bottom, it can only be Christian hope. As immortalized in the words of a contemporary Filipino poet, the ultimate basis of Filipino Christian hope is Jesus Christ —He and none other is the Hope and Future of mankind.

The Filipino Mystic Approach to God

A religious-mystical movement (which may be called the New Mysticism and its practitioners, the new mystics), a post-World War II phenomenon, is going on all over the Philippines, mainly in the poorer sections of the country.[20] Characteristic of the mystic is the

110

trance state (*langkap*) whereby, without willing it, s/he is "possessed" by the Holy Spirit, the Virgin Mary, or some saint. While in this state of trance, the mystic delivers a religious message about the sinfulness of man, the need for repentance, and the threat of foreboding calamities. At this point, the devotees present their problems and ask for advice or for healing. Cures are *de facto* plentiful. Today, these core Mystic groups have somehow become institutionalized: some have fused with the Charismatic movement; others speak of their religious "mission" here and abroad.

A psychological explanation behind the trances, possessions, reading of hearts, speaking in tongues, foretelling of the future, and other wonders which the mystics perform has been given by psychologists: they explain these phenomena as possession by an internal image or psychological exorcism of the "possessed" person. But the theological question is whether it is truly God speaking to the Church and to the world through the mediumship of the mystic. There are many instances of prophetism and discernment of spirits in the Bible to show that God can speak through a person's unconscious just as He can speak through a person's conscious mind. But it is necessary to discern between true and false prophets who claim to speak in God's name. The Bible itself offers four criteria: empirical, behavioral, canonical, and theological.[21]

The official Church may ignore, tolerate, or disapprove these new mystics, but the challenge of the New Mysticism remains. The lives of many of the new mystics are paragons of simple faith and the complete surrender of the self into the hands of God. They lead poor lives and their teaching and healing ministry is mostly among their fellow poor. Perhaps the flowering of the New Mysticism in the Philippine Church may teach the Filipino clergy and religious their true vocation to mystic prayer and union with God or at least act as a complement to a more rational inner approach to God.[22] Maybe through the indigenization movement the official Church will accept and absorb a spirituality of the people that is genuinely Filipino.

The Filipino Approach to God's Presence in the World and in Man
In the modern world where God seems to be absent, contemporary questions like evolution and God's creation of the cosmos, God's

eternal plan and man's freedom, fatalism and Divine Providence, the existence of evil and God's existence, pose many difficulties that question God's active presence in the world and in man. What is the popular Filipino Christian approach to these modern difficulties? The Filipino traditional and popular view on these difficult questions contains many ambivalences but it is precisely in this area of ambivalence that the Christian faith has played a major role in purifying and transforming Filipino beliefs and practices.

The common Filipino view acknowledges God as Creator and His active presence without in any way denying scientific evolution and process philosophy.[23] In a poem entitled, *"Ebolusyon,"* a Filipino writer warns against the dangers to the Christian faith of learned knowledge and science. The author is by no means against true science but is attacking scientism and secularism. It is most natural for the Filipino rural adult to see God's presence in nature. Belief in God's presence everywhere is very strong in Filipino popular Christianity. In a Christian culture like the Philippines, the presence of so many Christian symbols in the Filipino home and in public places and vehicles is a forceful reminder of God's omnipresence in the consciousness of the people. One of the traditional themes in Philippine literature is the contrast made between God's presence in the rural village and His absence in the city. Although this lyricized dichotomy is a misconception of God's presence, nevertheless, this romanticized concept associates God's presence with good and His absence with evil.

The Filipino Approach to Divine Providence
Earlier it was mentioned that the Filipino faith in God could mean a genuine trust in Divine Providence or a sort of fatalism in religious guise. In Filipino popular Christianity many practices and beliefs show a tension or ambivalence between fatalism and contingency. On the one hand, some Filipino proverbs express a fatalistic attitude: e.g., "Man's life is like a wheel; today it is up, tomorrow it is down." On the other hand, other proverbs express man's freedom: e.g., "Even if your fate is good, you will never attain it unless you pursue it." It is commonplace in Filipino culture to attribute everything to good or bad luck (*suwerte* or *malas*) or fate (*tadhana* or destiny *kapalaran* or fortune) which likewise has an ambivalent

meaning, either negative (fatalistic) or positive (includes human effort, risk-taking, trust or hope).

The most noted traditional Filipino value—*"bahala na"*—defies literal translation because this attitude and expression carry many meanings. It could mean "Come what may" or "God will provide." The negative meaning of *bahala na* is a kind of fatalistic resignation which really represents an escape from involvement or a shirking from personal decision and responsibility. Thus thinking that whatever will be will be, one blindly trusts fate and passively accepts one's situation or condition with patience, long-suffering, and endurance. The attitude of apathy, of not caring and doing nothing, is better expressed by the phrase *"pagwawalang bahala."* *Bahala na* could also refer to *"Bathala,"* some vague notion of God reduced to fate or destiny. The positive meaning of *bahala na* is rooted in the notion of "responsibility," either personal or collective: e.g., "I or we will be responsible" (*ako* or *tayong bahala*). It is this root meaning of "responsibility" that has been transformed by the Christian faith into genuine trust or hope in God which includes human effort and cooperation. This is the meaning of the Filipino proverb: "If man will do his part, God will take care of His part" (*Tao ang gumagawa, Diyos ang Namamahala*). God helps those who help themselves.

A scholarly study entitled *"And God Said, 'Bahala Na,'"* develops the theme of God's Providence in a lowland Filipino context.[24] The author shows how by the process of theological-cultural interchange patterned after the Incarnation, the Filipino value of *bahala na* as modified by another Filipino value—*malasakit* or concern —has evolved into the Christian notion of God's Providence or concern for the world and man. God's concern (*malasakit*) manifests itself in three ways: (1) in God's risks for man and his well-being; (2) in God's will for man to realize his full potential as a "situated freedom"; and (3) in God's trust in man. A good example of indigenization is the creative transformation of *bahala na* through *malasakit*, that is, from a traditional Filipino to a Christian understanding of the risks of God for man out of concern for him.

In the religious thought of Dr. Jose Rizal, the Philippines' greatest national hero, the convergence point of his thinking about God and religion is Divine Providence.[25] There are three elements of

Rizal's trust in Divine Providence. First, the Filipinos ought to place their trust in God even and especially in time of injustice and persecutions. Secondly, such trust in God implied trust in one's own self and one's own God-given resources. Rizal wrote to Blumentritt: "The majority of the Filipinos have already lost all hope in Spain. Now we await our fate *from God and ourselves*, never more from any government." Thirdly, an inseparable corollary to trust in God was Rizal's uncompromising resolution that the means to be employed must be morally right, noble, and just. Why must the Filipinos appeal to God? Simply because the Filipino people were God's people and God was leading them in their historic task of laying the foundations of the nation. The Filipinos must now look beyond alien institutions to the God who guides the destinies of men and nations; under God, they must work out their own redemption; they must now take their future where God has placed it—into their own hands. For Rizal, trust in God was not a fatalistic resignation to the course of history, but the pursuit of one's *tadhana* (destiny), the acceptance of an awesome task, namely, the founding of the Filipino nation. Briefly, for the Filipino national hero, *"Bahala ang May Kapal"* meant "God will provide! Our fate has come. Let us trust in our own strength."

The Filipino View of God and Evil

In Filipino popular Christianity, the existence of evil is not a major obstacle to belief in God. Besides fatalism, there are at least four elements which underlie or influence the Filipino philosophy of evil: (1) animism, (2) the harmony of opposites, (3) the doctrine of retribution, and (4) the Christian popular view of suffering.

First, the Filipino animistic view gives a dualistic explanation of the problem of evil: whatever is good is due to the good or friendly spirits; whatever is bad must be attributed to evil spirits. The practical concern of Filipino folklore medicine is to cure sickness and ward off misfortune. Evil spirits must be placated by offerings, prayers, rituals or exorcised by various Filipino faith healers and mystics. Secondly, the Filipino common man explains evil in terms of the "harmony of opposites" so evident in the rhythms of life and nature. Health is a balance between hot and cold. Good and evil are part and parcel of the harmony of nature, e.g., day and night, low and high tide, dry and rainy season, good and bad harvest, as well as the harmony of life, e.g., birth and death, joy and sorrow, health and sickness, good and bad luck. This non-dualistic ("both-and") view of good and evil is influenced by the Asian "harmonizing tendency" which reconciles contradictories, e.g. *yin* and *yang*, bent and straight, empty and full.

Thirdly, a very common Filipino explanation of evil is in terms of the doctrine of retribution. Any evil that befalls a person is believed to be a payment for a debt of wrong doing and there is always a strict balance between the wrong done and its punishment. The doctrine of poetic justice is summed up by the Filipino proverb: "If you owe life, you must pay with your own life." The Filipino belief in the curse (*gaba*) is akin to the Indian doctrine of *karma* (you reap what you sow). Inasmuch as this doctrine of retribution could be connected with the Filipino concept of fate and freedom, the cause of evil could be ambiguous.

Fourthly, although one finds in Filipino popular Christianity a residue and interplay of the fatalistic, animistic, harmonious, and retributive explanations of evil, the Christian meaning and attitude towards suffering predominate. Poor, simple, ordinary Filipino Christians are so used to a life of poverty, hardship, and suffering, it is not difficult for them to identify themselves with the suffering Christ. Only the God who suffers and dies can save. That is why the most popular devotions of the Filipino poor and oppressed are those of *Hesus Nazareno* (suffering Christ), *Santo Entierro* (Holy Sepulchre representing the dead Christ), and *Sagrado Corazon* (the wounded heart of Christ). In the solemn reading (*pabasa*) of the Passion of Christ (*Pasyon*) during Lent, the people see a picture of their everyday life of hardship and suffering. In Philippine history there have been individuals and religious groups who came to see in the colonial situation of oppression and injustice a permanent *Pasyon* condition of Philippine society. Religious leaders exhorted the Filipino masses to control the inner (*loob*) at the cost of suffering (*dusa*) in order to share (*damay*) in the suffering of Christ and thus reach the light (*liwanag*), freedom (*kalayaan*), and Paradise.[26] Today, some Filipino revolutionaries see once again in the suffering, crucifixion, and death of the Filipino people, especially the poor and powerless, the victims of injustice, the passion and death of Jesus Christ.

The Filipino Way of Speaking about God

Perhaps one contribution Linguistic Philosophy has made to the contemporary discussion on God is the renewal of religious language. Linguistic heterogeneity in Asia and in the Philippines is an added advantage for a philosophy and theology of God because each language is a *distinctly new way* of experiencing God. Religion begins with language. For language is the "experience" of reality and religion is its "expression."[27] In Filipino popular Christianity the way of thinking and speaking about God is through myth and folklore, proverbs and aphorisms, parables and allegories, song and dance, rites and rituals. To convey religious and moral truths, the Filipino uses poetic idiom of which the most popular expression are proverbs. "To God belongs mercy, to man belongs the work," (*Nasa Diyos ang awa, nasa tao ang Gawa*) teaches the religious truth that God helps those who help themselves. Terms referring to God in the Filipino languages are concrete, symbolic, poetic, metaphorical, and personalistic. A favorite popular title of God is *Maykapal* (Creator), and concrete metaphorical images of God abound in Philippine poetry, short stories, novels, comics, and popular love songs. In one short story that takes place in a rural area, a little boy, seeing the rosy sky at dawn, exclaims, "Look, God also cooks his breakfast."

The problem and meaning of God-talk which is the main preoccupation of Western Linguistic philosophy is alien and far removed from the faith experience of the majority of Filipino Christians. Despite the Filipino's love for flowery and poetic speech, faith in God in Filipino popular religion is expressed not so much in words as in action. The religion of the people finds its best expression in popular devotions, in processions, in song and dance, in religious celebration and festivity. Filipino Christians do not "learn" about their Christian faith; the people "believe" and "live" the faith. In a Philippine context the renewal of religious language means the inculturation of the Christian faith within the cultural experience and in the language of the people.

Mutual Reciprocity between Filipino Culture and Christian Faith

Principle of Mutual Reciprocity

In the past it was mistakenly thought that in order to embrace the Christian faith which has become synonymous with Western culture, one had to renounce one's own culture. Similarly, faith in God need not be realized only by means of Western experience and categories. It was thought that Filipino culture had nothing to give to the Christian faith. Today, in the words of the 1977 Roman Synod of Bishops, "a true 'incarnation' of the faith through catechesis supposes not only a process of 'giving' but also a 'receiving.'"[28] Speaking on behalf of Asian cultures, Cardinal Sin of Manila stated that "the mission of the Church does not simply consist in giving what she has but also in receiving what she does not have."[29] Let us try to see, from a theological perspective, how the indigenization of the Christian faith within Filipino culture consists in a two-way process of "giving" and "receiving."

Christian Culture

In the first place, the Christian faith "gives" by interpreting, purifying, transforming and enriching Filipino experience and Filipino values. Filipino popular Christianity makes *better Filipinos* because it fosters Filipino values like family solidarity and community solidarity and makes *better Christians* because the Christian message is indigenized or Filipinized. With regard to the role of Christianity in Philippine education in the last four hundred years, the Christian faith has tried (1) to preserve, and even to improve, to enhance, to build upon the native culture; (2) to impregnate it with the spirit of the Gospel; and (3) to purge it of those elements which are un-Christian and inhuman.[30]

It is not difficult to show how Filipino experiences and questions about the ultimate meaning of life—about the possibility of hope and trust, about problems of evil, sin, guilt, friendship, unity, harmony with nature, sexual identity, the after life, and final lasting peace—are interpreted and transformed by the great mysteries of the Trinity, the Cross and Resurrection, salvation and grace, the Eucharist, the Church, baptism, Mary, heaven and the return of

Jesus Christ.[31] The Christian gospel "judges" every culture.[32] It is the Christian faith that purifies Filipino popular religiosity from distortions of religion, superstition, magic, fatalism, false syncretism, and any dehumanizing factors. Here are a few examples. Although the Filipino tribal and customary law (*adat*) is one source of natural law justice, it took un-Christian forms in the past, such as headhunting. It is the Christian faith that has done away with this practice and today it is the Christian Church that is vigorously defending the cultural way of life of the tribal Filipinos. It has already been pointed out that *bahala na* modified by the Filipino value of concern (*malasakit*) has creatively transformed the traditional fatalistic attitude of *bahala na*, a false sense of resignation or an escape from decision and responsibility as well as the vague notion of *Bathala* or God now reduced to fate or destiny, into the Christian trust in Divine Providence as the risks of God out of loving concern for man. The Christian doctrine of sin and Paschal Mystery (suffering, death, and resurrection of Jesus Christ) purify the Filipino concept of evil, sin, and guilt from explanations based on dualism, harmony of opposites, curse (*gaba*), or the doctrine of retribution (*karma*).

In the area of morals, a very strong Filipino cultural value is shame (*hiya*) which acts as a social sanction for non-conformist behavior. Nevertheless *hiya* tends to remain somehow external and superficial: that is, Filipinos tend to say to themselves, "Don't be caught," or else suffer shame. This cultural value could well be purified and interiorized into a principle of Christian spirituality by relating it to the internal presence of the Holy Spirit. "What will other people say" usually determines Filipino moral behavior; it is "conscience from the outside." It is the Christian faith that contributes to the formation of "conscience from the inside" or a mature religious conscience which can be clearly distinguished from the voice of society or the authority figure (superego). In short, in the words of Vatican II, The Christian gospel "never ceases to purify and elevate the morality of peoples."[33]

The significance of contemporary atheism is the denial or rejection of false images and wrong concepts of God or of religious language that has become irrelevant or meaningless for modern man. The great majority of Filipino Christians believe God in their hearts but may worship false gods in their minds. They are trying sincerely to lead a good moral and Christian life, but they may be incorrect in their thinking about God. It is precisely in regard to the traditional Filipino concept of God that the Christian faith has played a significant role in correcting the vague, mistaken, or inadequate ideas of the people's religion. It is the Christian gospel that continues to challenge the practical if not theoretical atheism that guides the behavior of the materialistic Filipino elite. It is the Christian faith that gives the people the true identity of God, and educates them towards maturity in their faith.

The norm for judging the orthodoxy of the Filipino faith in God as expressed and practiced in Filipino popular devotions to Christ is conformity to the Christian gospel. If these popular devotions which focus on the baby Jesus, the suffering and dead Christ, the wounded Heart of Christ, have been criticized on theological grounds, it is not because they are false but rather incomplete images of Christ. They continue to foster an unawareness of the central event in the life of Christ, namely, His Resurrection which alone gives ultimate meaning and value to these popular devotions. But how to propose and not impose a new devotion to the Risen Christ which is theologically adequate without destroying the faith-expression of the people?

Suffice it to say that Christian faith and worship follow a people in the various stages of its history and must take people "where they are at," giving them a pedagogy that accompanies them toward all the dimensions of the Christian life. No people can live meaningfully all the dimensions of the Christian life simultaneously. Each period of history will have its own emphases, its own focus. If the Filipino people are in great poverty and suffering, Christian faith and devotion must first lead them to an existential acceptance of a situation they can do very little about as individuals. This is not passive resignation but Christian realism to acknowledge facts and to face them within the dimension of faith. In the past, the faith expression of Filipino Christians has been shaped by realities largely beyond their control. But with regard to the present and the future, there is, of course, need to re-orient the people's devotion and link their faith to what is possible and desirable. But even here, a realistic appreciation of the simple but genuine faith of the humble and the poor is in place. In developing a theology of the people, theologians must study the meaning of the Christian faith within the "wisdom of the humble and poor."[34] To do this demands real immersion in the popular culture, a real sympathy with an "insider's heart."

Filipino Culture

In the second place, Filipino culture not only "receives" but also "gives" to the enrichment of Christian faith and culture. It has already been shown how the elements of the Filipino philosophy of religion give the human basis in Filipino experience of the Christian concept of God. After all, grace builds on nature, the holy on the human. The concept of God as Creator is already found in Philippine creation myths, as if pre-Christian Filipino experience was already proportioned and ready to hear the Christian revelation. These pre-Christian creation myths even try to improve on the Genesis account by focusing on the superiority of the brown race and the equality of man and woman.

In the past Filipinos were led to believe that the animistic religion of tribal Filipinos and the animistic rituals of popular religiosity contribute nothing to Christian faith. Cardinal Sin, with regard to Catholicism in Asia, said that "a certain kind of animism can still be used for deeper spirituality."[35] Animism is a "signal of transcendence," points to the presence of the "Holy" and preserves man's sense of God as *mysterium numinosum, tremendum, fascinosum.* Filipino animism is a persistent reaffirmation of the primacy of the spirit. What is sorely lacking in the Marxist, scientific, secular visions of man is the sense of mystery of man and nature. Man is always "more" than matter; he is also spirit. Filipino animism treats things as persons. A seventy-eight-year-old Filipino farmer, after a long dry spell when at long last the rains fell, exclaimed in joy: *"tuwang tuwa ang mga halaman"* (how happy the plants are!). Some Filipinos pray to the spirits before chopping down trees, unlike unscrupulous loggers who exploit Philippine forests for profit from abroad. The 1972 disastrous floods were believed to be the spirit of nature punishing the people for their irreverence to nature. Superstitious? Only to the Marxist, secular, technological man who has lost all sense of the sacrality of nature. Today the wages of the desecration of nature is environmental pollution. The conflict between tribal Filipinos and government or business development projects is a forceful reminder that people are more important than objects, that we must respect the bond between man and nature, that we must not destroy indigenous cultures and the integrity of a people in the name of modern technological development.

What does the Filipino harmonious blending of the holy and the human teach us? Perhaps the separation of the sacred and the profane, of religion and morality from human life, explains secularism and contemporary atheism. Today, sad to say, a practical secularism in the form of Western consumerism guides the behavior of many so-called Filipino Christians among the educated, rich influentials of Philippine society. That is the price one pays for separating the holy and the human. The denial of God and the exclusion of religion and morality from marriage and family life have wrought untold havoc to the family in the modern world. At the 1980 Roman Synod of Bishops "On the Role of the Family in the Modern World," the Filipino bishops made a unique contribution by presenting the Filipino family as the paradigm of the Christian family. The Filipino family is different from other Western models in the appreciation of values because it is Oriental, and from other Asian countries, because it is Christian. The typical Filipino family is God-centered and child-centered. The extended family is involved in the moral and religious education of the child at home. Old and sick parents continue to live and are cared for in the homes of their children. The Filipino family stands out as a strong bulwark against the evils of divorce, abortion, pornography, drug abuse, against a Western funded population control movement which undermines cultural and Christian values and which promotes a contraceptive culture that leads to a sterilization and abortion mentality. In the West, the family is in a serious crisis. It is in this area of marriage and family life that Filipino culture can make a genuine and distinct contribution to the Christian faith.

How rich Christian worship and devotion have become because of Filipino culture. It was the native creative imagination and artistry of the village folks that transformed the four gospels of the Passion of Jesus Christ into something truly and distinctively Filipino. Today the Christian gospel of the Passion is used in four ways, Filipino style: (1) *pabasa* (solemn reading of the *Pasyon*), with the Filipino addition of *pagkain* and *inuman* (food and drink for the devotees); (2) *kalbaryuhan* (outdoor re-enactment of the Way of the Cross and Calvary); (3) *sinakulo* (dramatic Passion play from the Cenacle to Easter, all throughout Lent); (4) *tapatan* (leveling) or *pananawagan* (calling), both in the form of *bugtungan* (riddle-rivaling or contest). Today the indigenization movement has creatively transformed the Christian liturgy into Filipino art, music, hymns, and folk dance that is the envy of the liturgical renewal in the West.

Finally, on the basis of the Christian faith, are the animistic and corporeal rituals of Filipino popular religion to be accepted, rejected, or modified? Two things are presupposed: first, differences between the Christian faith and elements in Filipino culture may be irreducible, complementary, or successive stages in the process of development;[36] secondly, in the case of irreducible or contradictory elements, the Christian gospel never ceases to purify popular religion from its inhuman and less than human or un-Christian forms, such as magic, sorcery and witchcraft, personality cult, demonic spiritism, and sectarianism. Given these presuppositions, how can the animistic and corporeal rituals of Filipino popular Christianity contribute to the enrichment of Christian faith and culture?[37]

In general, popular religion manifests a thirst for God which only the simple and poor can know; shows generosity and even heroic sacrifice in the matter of belief; makes us profoundly aware of the fatherhood, providence, loving and constant presence of God; fosters patience, the sense of the cross in daily life, detachment, openness to others, devotion.[38] Popular religiosity gives a sense of spiritual values, fosters ascetical discipline, promotes a deep and innate religious sense, values filial piety and attachment to the family, believes in the primacy of the spirit, and shows a hunger for the supernatural.[39]

In particular, what can *animistic* rituals like faith-healing, possession trances, knowledge of hidden things through medium of *tawas* (candle drops), give to the Christian faith? Faith healing reminds us of the need of "faith that moves mountains" and of prayer, not only the need of the individual person but also of a believing, praying and healing community that is hungry to experience community and engagement. Christ the Healer, and salvation as the healing of the whole person and community, can be trans-signified in Filipino folk medicine and indigenous faith healing rituals.[40] Christians are made aware that the sickness of the spirit, emotions, and of the body caused by sin, disease, psychic stress, and the demonic can be healed by the sacraments of reconciliation, anointing of the sick (Jas. 5:14-15), and exorcism.[41]

Possession trances and ecstatic preaching of the New Mystics may recall biblical prophetism in St. Paul. The biblical prophet speaks to men in the name of God for their upbuilding (edification), their encouragement, their consolation (I Cor. 14:3). God's word can be incarnated in any indigenous ritual that authentically fulfills the function of biblical prophetism in responding to the needs of particular Christian communities. However, it is an error to affirm that God is physically present in the ecstatic mystic. But the feeling or simple apprehension of God's presence dramatized in the state of trance is authentic. These stylized rituals subconsciously dramatize certain objectives, aspirations, needs, anxieties, desires, and values collectively felt by the community. *Vox populi* or the sense of the faithful, can be an authentic expression of *vox Dei*. Furthermore, the New Mysticism points to the pastoral possibility of gospel preaching through the medium of ecstatic preachers. Certainly it calls for homiletic renewal and the need of "Holy Spirit inspired" homilies.

How about *corporeal* rituals? *Tawas* (candle drops), *anito* (idol), *anting-anting* (amulet) can be idolatrous or superstitious in exaggerating the sentimental value of the material symbols of God's presence, as when a medallion is used to show one's macho image or an amulet is believed to be bullet-proof. But these corporeal rituals can be cultural styles of expressing spiritual realities through material symbols. In those who are authentically conscious of God's presence and goodness, they foster obedience to God's commandments. These corporeal rituals can be incorporated into new *sacramentals* as the need becomes apparent.[42] *Tawas* has a Scriptural basis in the Pauline charism of "reading hearts" (I Cor. 14:24-25) and "knowledge of hidden things" (I Cor. 2:7f; I Cor. 4:5). The statues, images and medals are not worshipped, but they symbolize God's presence. If idolatrous, these statues, images, medals, and amulets are not as serious as the idolatry of the educated elite whose super-idols are wealth, pleasure, power, prestige, and movie superstars.

Ritual dancing, for fertility, evokes faith and religious devotion to Christ and the saints. It is a concrete example of how Filipino folk liturgy can be incorporated into the Christian liturgy. Penitential flagellations have been regarded in the past as signs of perversion, exhibitionism, sadomasochism, fanaticism, or anti-clericalism and are now being exploited by the tourism industry. But these penitential rites can be sacramentalized by bringing in the Sacraments of Reconciliation and the Eucharist and by harmonizing the reading of the Passion with these flagellation penances. They can become "signals of transcendence" for ascetical renewal and self-denying love. The conflict between indigenous grass-roots tastes and the alien and corrupt taste of the elite class unmasks the craving of the hippie generation for instant mystical experience through "sensory deprivation" or "sensory overload." There are no shortcuts to mysticism. The value of the flagellation rite can be defended by relating it to a primary principle of Christian asceticism, the need for self-discipline.

To sum up, in focusing and stressing the positive aspects and virtues of animistic and corporeal rituals, one may get the over-all impression that there is absolutely nothing wrong with these rituals and practices. What has been said positively about Filipino popular religion should in no way be taken to mean that we are denying or minimizing the aberrations, exaggerations, and excesses in practice nor closing our eyes to the dangers to which popular religiosity is always open. One should be slow in making generalizations; it is better to judge Filipino animistic and corporeal rituals on a case by case basis according to objective biblical criteria mentioned earlier.

Conclusion

From a philosophical and theological study of Filipino popular Christianity based on (1) elements of a Filipino philosophy of religion, (2) Filipino approaches to God which universal religious experience also shares, and (3) the mutual reciprocity of Christian faith and Filipino culture, we have discovered an explanatory and explorative concept of God that is uniquely Asian and Christian. What significant implications and conclusions can be drawn from the study of popular religiosity for the contemporary discussion on God?

First, from an ecumenical perspective, the Eastern mystic and spiritual approaches to God are a much needed complement to the over rationalistic approaches of the West. It is impossible to discuss God outside a religious and spiritual context. In the future, it is hoped, Eastern thought will play a much larger role than Western thought which in the past has always played a dominant role. Secondly, more and more it is becoming clear that the philosophical way to God by itself alone is a dead end. No matter how consistent, comprehensive, convincing philosophical approaches to God may be, they never arrive at the true identity of God. Reason alone can never bring true faith in God. Thirdly, from the perspective of the Third World, any discussion of God today has to face the challenge of inculturation, indigenization, or contextualization of the concept of God "from within" each culture. Each culture and each language is a new and distinct way of experiencing God. In Asia and in the rest of the Third World, the question of God cannot be framed meaningfully except in the context of massive poverty and widespread injustice. The poor of the Third World are desperately asking where God is to be found in all this. Unless the contemporary discussion addresses itself to this question, all God-talk is in vain. Finally, any philosophizing and theologizing about God can no longer afford to ignore, much less despise, popular religiosity or the "religion of the people." A renewal of the contemporary approaches to God means "rooting" reflective and systematic thought in the wisdom and faith experience of the people and in their own language. Filipino popular Christianity has shown that popular religiosity has much to contribute to the Christian faith.

FOOTNOTES

1 For a sociological description of "popular religiosity," see "Let the People Be: Popular Religion and the Religion of the People," *Pro Mundi Vita Bulletin* 61 (July 1976): 1-31.

2 John S. Dunne, *The Way of All the Earth* (New York: Macmillan, 1972) is widely read because of the author's refreshingly human and ecumenical approach to theology.

3 Marcello de Carvalho Azevedo, S.J., "Inculturation and the Challenges of Modernity," International and Interdisciplinary Seminar on Inculturation, Jerusalem, 16-26 June 1981, p. 3 (Mimeographed).

4 David A. Pailin, "The Function of the Philosophy of Religion; Is the Christian Faith True?" *The Expository Times* 84 (August 1973): 324-29, uses the general criteria of coherence, fruitfulness, comprehensiveness, and convincingness to show the reasonable grounds for a mature, responsible religious faith.

5 Among the principal sources are Leonardo N. Mercado, S.V.D., *Elements of Filipino Philosophy* (Tacloban City: Divine Word Univ. Publ., 1974); *Elements of Filipino Theology* (*Ibid.*, 1975); ed., *Filipino Religious Psychology* (*Ibid.*, 1977); *Filipino Thought on Man and Society* (*Ibid.*, 1980); the author's *The Filipino Search for Meaning* (Manila: Jesuit Educational Assn., 1974); *The Filipino Search for God* (*Ibid.*, 1978); ed., *Filipino Theology Today* (Quezon City: Ateneo de Manila Univ. Press, 1979); Ramon C. Reyes, "Sources of Filipino Thought," *Philippine Studies* 21 (Fourth Quarter 1973): 429-37; Francisco R. Demetrio, S.J., *Myths and Symbols Philippines* (Manila: National Book Store, 1978); *Christianity in Context* (Quezon City: New Day Publishers, 1981); Rodrigo D. Tano, *Theology in the Philippine Setting* (*Ibid.*, 1981). Reyes, *art. cit.*, points out two basic stages of Filipino thought: vital thought by way of myth, ritual, song and language, folklore, traditional sayings and aphorisms, and customary legal, political, and religious codes, and reflexive or systematic thought, e.g., philosophy, theology and the social sciences.

6 Frank Lynch, S.J., "Folk Catholicism in the Philippines," in *Society, Culture, and the Filipino,* ed. Mary R. Hollnsteiner *et al.* (Quezon City: Ateneo de Manila Univ. Press, 1975), pp. 227-38.

7 Emma Porio, Frank Lynch, and Mary R. Hollnsteiner, *The Filipino Family, Community, and Nation,* IPC Papers no. 12 (Quezon City: Ateneo de Manila Univ. Press, 1978), pp. 41-44.

8 Emerita S. Quito, *Oriental Roots of Occidental Philosophy* (Manila: De la Salle Univ., 1975).

9 Mercado, *Elements of Filipino Philosophy*, p. 71.

10 Aloysius Pieris, S.J. "Towards an Asian Theology of Liberation: Some Religio-Cultural Guidelines," in *Asia's Struggle for Full Humanity,* ed. Virginia Fabella (New York: Orbis Books, 1980), p. 86.

11 H. Mertens, "Religion as an Experience of Reality," *Tijdschrift voor Theologie* 14 (1974): 129-30, shows that religion gives a sense of depth, a sense of the future, a sense of totality so that the man of religious faith experiences reality as grace.

12 Rudolf Otto, *The Idea of the Holy* (New York: Oxford Univ. Press, 1958).

13 Demetrio, *Myths and Symbols Philippines*, pp. 262, 279.

14 For example, see W. Norris Clarke, S.J., *The Philosophical Approach to God: A Neo-Thomist Perspective* (Winston-Salem, North Carolina: Wake Forest University, 1979).

15 For an explanation of the question of God as an anthropological, religious, and existential question, see Gorospe, *The Filipino Search for God*, pp. 35-36.

16 Jose Maria Francisco, S.J., "Panitikan at Kristianismong Filipino: Ang Nagbabagong Larawan ni Kristo," *Philippine Studies* 25 (1977): 186-214.

17 Vitaliano R. Gorospe, S.J., "Sources of Filipino Moral Consciousness," *Philippine Studies* 25 (1977): 278-301.

18 Horacio de la Costa, S.J., "The Filipino National Tradition," in *Challenges for the Filipino*, ed. Raul J. Bonoan, S.J. (Quezon City: Ateneo de Manila Univ. Press, 1971), *passim*.

19 Virgilio G. Enriquez, "*Kapwa*: A Core Concept in Filipino Social Psychology," paper presented at the twentieth annual conference of the Japanese Society of Social Psychology, International Christian University, Tokyo, Japan, 3-5 September 1979, gives eight levels of the meaning of *kapwa*: (1) transactions/civility with (*pakikitungo*), (2) inter-action with (*pakikisalumuha*), (3) joining/participating with (*pakikilahok*), (4) in conformity with/in accord with (*pakikibagay*), (5) being-along-with (*pakikisama*), (6) being in rapport/understanding/acceptance with (*pakikipagpalagayan/pakikipagpalagayang-loob*), (7) getting involved (*pakikisangkot*), (8) being-one-with (*pakikiisa*).

20 Jaime Bulatao, S.J., "The New Mysticism in the Philippine Church," *Witness* 1 (First Quarter 1981): 14-25.

21 Bulatao, *ibid.*, pp. 23-24, explains the fourfold criteria as follows: empirical —the verification of predictions; behavioral—a good and fruitful life; canonical —obedience to Church authority; theological—profession of Jesus Christ as Son of God.

22 Clarke, *The Philosophical Approach to God*, pp. 11-32, develops the Neo-Thomist transcendental approach to God from the dynamism of the human spirit.

23 Clarke, *ibid.*, pp. 66-109, discusses the Christian doctrine of creation and Whiteheadian process philosophy.

24 Jose M. de Mesa, *And God Said, "Bahala Na!"* (Quezon City: Publishers' Printing Press, 1979.

25 Raul J. Bonoan, S.J., "Rizal on Divine Providence and Nationhood," *Philippine*

Studies 25 (1977): 145-162.

26 Reynaldo Clemena Ileto, *Pasyon and Revolution* (Quezon City: Ateneo de Manila Univ. Press, 1979).

27 Pieris, *art. cit.*, p. 77.

28 Pedro S. de Achutegui and Joseph L. Roche, S.J., *Word, Memory, Witness: The 1977 Bishops' Synod on Catechesis*, Loyola Papers no. 11 (Quezon City: Cardinal Bea Institute, 1978), p. 46.

29 *Ibid.*, p. 129.

30 Miguel A. Bernad, S.J., "Our Ages of Discontinuity," *Proceedings of the Conference/Dialogue on the Role of Christianity in Philippine Education*, ed. Armando F. de Jesus (Manila: ACEAM-ECERI, Univ. of Santo Tomas, 1979), p. 8.

31 Andrew M. Greeley, *The Great Mysteries* (New York: Seabury, 1976).

32 H. Richard Niebuhr, *Christ and Culture* (New York: Harper, 1956).

33 *Gaudium et Spes*, no. 58 in *The Documents of Vatican II*, ed. Walter M. Abbott and Joseph Gallagher (New York: America Press, 1966), p. 264.

34 Juan Carlos Scannone, "Popular Culture: Pastoral and Theological Considerations," *Lumen Vitae* 32 (1977):158-74.

35 Jaime Cardinal L. Sin, "The Future of Catholicism in Asia," *Boletin Ecclesiastico de Filipinas* 52 (October-November 1978): 572-84.

36 Bernard Lonergan, S.J., *Method in Theology* (London: Darton, Longman and Todd, 1975), pp. 128-29.

37 For this section of the paper, see Vincent Marasigan, S.J. "Rituals in Manila's Catacombs," *Philippine Studies* 27 (1979):74-81; "Tagalog Ecstatics," *Philippine Priests' Forum* 10 (March 1978):23-32; "Grassroots Ascetical Renewal," *Ibid.*, 7 (March 1975):92-95.

38 Paul VI, *Evangelii Nuntiandi: On Evangelization in the Modern World* (Pasay City: Daughters of St. Paul, 1976), no. 48.

39 1978 Federation of Asian Bishops' Conferences, no. 7.

40 The communication of the Christian gospel or meaning in the process of being incarnated in the symbolic rituals indigenous to the culture is called *"transsignification"* or "creative assimilation and translation" (*idem*).

41 Francis McNutt, O.P., *The Power to Heal* (Notre Dame, Ind.: Ave Maria Press, 1977).

42 *Sacrosanctum Concilium: Constitution on the Sacred Liturgy* in *The Documents of Vatican II*, no. 79.

Total Well-Being:

Salvation and God in the

Experience of an

African People

Christian R. Gaba

The task of this paper is to examine an African people's experience of salvation.[1] Africa shall be understood as black Africa; an African people shall be ethnically defined and salvation shall be made to refer to the indigenous,[2] autochthonous, conception of it rather than to the Christian or the Islamic conceptions which mainly share the religious milieu in varying proportions with the host indigenous religion in any African society today. The prime material for investigation shall be the people's formal expression of man's religiousness as it is visible in worship. Two main reasons direct this choice of worship. First, worship is the ritual in what Ninian Smart refers to as the numinous religious experience, which engages the most frequent attention of *homo religiosus*. It is therefore, a main source for our knowledge of religious ideas. And second, the ritual utterances[3] that form part of worship constitute a main source of a people's own account of their religious experience. This source is indispensable to the investigation of religion *qua* religion. If one considers also the fact that African peoples whose values are prescribed by their indigenous religious traditions are, at present, generally unlettered, then worship and ritual utterances, becomes a primary source in the study of the religious experience not only of African peoples but also of non-scriptural peoples in general. This is one reason why this paper argues that scholarly accounts of non-literary cultures and non-scriptural religions must include works that aspire to be the *ipsissima verba* of believers themselves. Therefore, prominence must be given to ritual utterances that arise not from artificially arranged sacred times but from what W. Cantwell Smith calls "actual moments of involvement in transcendence".

The main questions that this study will explore are: What is the nature and meaning of salvation in the experience of an African people when we use the principles and standards of the people themselves? How does this experience serve as an index not only of this people's world view and their conception of man's religiousness but also of the nature of the current discussion involving God in this particular milieu? Finally, to what extent does this mode of "God-talk" contribute to a new environment for ecumenical conversation? To what extent does it participate in ecumenical dialogues that will ultimately result in the realization of a family of religions within a transformed entire human society, conceived as a huge family?[4]

The specific African people studied here is the Anlo people of West Africa. Presently, the Anlo people are part of Ghana politically but ethnically they are a section of the Ewe people. *Dagbe* is the traditional Anlo word that is translated into the English word salvation. The word "*Dagbe*" is particularized for ritual usage and seldom occurs in non-ritual circles. Outside the ritual sphere of life the ritual connotation is still present for it always expresses a prayerful wish for the promotion of human well-being. In my study, *Scriptures of an African People,*[5] *abundant life* rather than salvation is employed as the English translation of *Dagbe*. This is largely because abundant life rather than salvation is a more appropriate English rendering of this religious concept in indigenous Anlo experience. If one can conceive the Anlo understanding of salvation as the Hebrew *Shalom*, understood as total well-being in body, mind and soul in relation to personal and societal issues, as Bolaji Idowu observes of African indigenous religious experience in general, then one possesses the right understanding of this Anlo concept. It is in conformity with usage in English theological and religious circles as the word to categorize the religious man's concept examined here that *salvation* rather than *abundant life* is employed in this study to translate the Anlo *Dagbe*.

To gain an insight into the Anlo indigenous conception of salvation one must grasp the concept of *Dagbe*. It, however, must be stated that etymology cannot be of assistance here in view of the fact that *Dagbe*, unlike some other Anlo concepts, is not analyzable etymologically.[6]

Ritual utterances during worship picture *Dagbe* as deriving from more than one source. This is revealed by the following passages:

Take them (the offerings) to the abode of *Mawu*,
the Creator, and bring us abundant life (LX1, 15, 17).

O Grandfather *Nyigbla* give to all your male and
female servants abundant life (LXXX111, 18-19).
Asitenu, owner of abundant life (LXV1, 1-2).
Please give us abundant life (XXXV1, 14).
Please take it to *Mawu* (God)
And bring back to us abundant life (XX1, 34-35).

The first three passages occur in the context of rituals performed in the shrines of the deities[7] and the last two form part of an
ancestral ritual. The first and the last passages make *Mawu*, God, the
source of *Dagbe* and the deities and the ancestors are pictured as
messengers who run errands between God and man, whenever the
latter is in need of *Dagbe*. However, in the second and the third
passages the deities are the source of *Dagbe* and in the fourth
passage *Dagbe* comes from the ancestors. In my earlier study, I have
two whole chapters of Anlo sacred utterances which are examples of
general intercessory prayer that open Anlo indigenous worship in
the shrines and are, therefore, poignant petitions for the realization
of *Dagbe*. These are chapters XXIII and XLIX, which are exclusively
addressed to the deities and the ancestors respectively. Nowhere in
them is the name of God mentioned. Ritual utterances thus make
both God and the lower spirit powers that manifest themselves in
the deities and the ancestors dispensers, in their own right, of *Dagbe*
in the world of men. This view seriously questions the Anlo concept
of God as "the Ground of all being" (LXXIII, 19), i.e., the origin of
all things, and the "Creator" (LXI, 15) even of the lower worshipful
spirits. However, the Anlo people themselves do not seem to be in
any serious predicament here.

It is quite true that Anlo sacred utterances make all worshipful
manifestations of the holy[8] sources of *Dagbe*. It must, however, be
pointed out that sacred utterances that occur in the context of
organized or formal ritual can only form part of ritual directly
involving the deities or the ancestors and never God because they,
and not God, are always the objects of organized ritual. Then the
concentration of the worshippers' full and undivided attention on
particular spirit powers as the direct objects of formal worship when
God is not invoked, leads to a permissible exaggeration of the
functions of these spirit beings in order to excite them into quick
and decisive action. It is, however, worth noting that whenever the

name of God is mentioned in the context of organized worship, even though he is not the direct object of attention, the direct objects who are either the deities or the ancestors, then at once assume inferior roles as God's representatives in the world of men. This is clearly substantiated by all the sacred utterances the writer has documented and in which the name of God is invoked. For example, the sacred utterances in question reveal that these lower spirit powers are specifically requested to take to God all the sacrifices which apparently are intended for them since they are offered in their shrines. So in God's presence the lower spirit beings are explicitly limited to their representative roles in the world of men suggesting that they qualify for cultic attention simply because they are the vicegerents of God who is the ultimate source of all worship. The Anlo people may thus explicitly address the lower spirit beings at times as "owner of abundant life" (LXVI, 2). Nevertheless they are aware that God is the real source of *Dagbe* and that it is from him that the lower spirit beings receive it for onward transmission to men. One only needs to watch the Anlo man at his wits' end. Whenever he appeals for *Dagbe* to his object of worship in such a situation, it is on God and never the other two categories of worshipful spirit beings that he calls. Above all, it should be re-membered that the sacred utterances of the Anlo people do not as yet constitute reasoned and clear theological statements but *ex tempore* expressions of their religiousness. Therefore the Anlo con-cept of *Dagbe* reveals that in the experience of this African people God is the source of man's salvation and that the dispensing of salvation in the world of men on behalf of God by his vicegerents, who are the other worshipful spirit beings, does not in any way threaten his position as the "Ground of all being", i.e., the "Source-Being" (LXIII, 19), in Anlo life and thought.

Anlo traditional thought also holds that God offers *Dagbe* to all men regardless of their moral standing. The general communal meal that forms part of Anlo indigenous festivals comes to mind here. It is taken by all people who may be present during the sharing of it. It could even be taken out of the sacred place to those who are not able to present themselves for worship. Participation in this meal does not require any serious self-examination to ascertain if one has been faithful to the moral demands of the Anlo society. In fact one does not need such a self-examination at all. Chapters LIX and LX of the writer's study of Anlo sacred utterances provide examples of ritual utterances that accompany the sharing of the meal in question. It is interesting to note that nowhere is there the slightest reference to imprecations on one's enemies. This is not coincidental but central since all men are the children of God. Hence, they automatically qualify, in spite of their moral condition which may be unacceptable by Anlo standards, for the realization of *Dagbe* which worship, as it is visible in the sharing of this communal meal, confers. Another element in the Anlo traditional experience of salvation that a study of *Dagbe* reveals is that every human being by his humanity alone has salvation within his reach.

However, to qualify for the realization of *Dagbe* does not imply an actual realization of it. Even though it is true that every human being, as God's child, has an automatic right to the realization of *Dagbe* which comes from God, this realization, however, is potential. The individual is expected to take a personal and a conscious step to bring *Dagbe* within his reach. The second festival communal meal provides a ritual illustration for this personal decision. This meal may be beer brewed specially by the ritual specialist himself or a blood meal prepared with pieces of the sacrificial animal cooked with its own blood. This meal is shared only by those who are convinced they satisfy the demands of all that is of good report in the thinking of the Anlo people. Anyone who participates in it, knowing full well that his moral standard does not measure up to that expected of an Anlo man, does so at his own risk for his personal well-being will be seriously impaired. The prelude to a typical Anlo prayer is intended to remind worshippers of the cardinal requirement for effective participation in worship and, for that matter, the realization of *Dagbe*. This prelude divides society into two on moral grounds reminding worshippers of the lot of each group, namely that the morally unacceptable forfeit their right to the realization of *Dagbe* and that the morally acceptable are those that have a firm grip on *Dagbe*. Worshippers are accepted to publicly declare their moral standing, which must be good, by formally identifying themselves with the morally good before joining in worship. Therefore in the Anlo indigenous experience of salvation, as this is exposed by their concept of *Dagbe*, salvation may be meant

135

for all people that on earth do dwell. But the actual realization of it is conditional on a personal decision. Simply, a personal response to one's object of worship then is a *sine qua non* to man's salvation in the estimation of the Anlo people. This points to the endowment of man by the Creator with a free will in Anlo thought and life with its attendant responsibility for one's action.[9]

Another important dimension of the Anlo conception of salvation is that once salvation is realized, the corresponding human condition must be free of all life-negating phenomena and be full of life-affirming ones. One recalls here the sacred utterances that the priest uses to welcome worshippers to the place of worship and to dismiss the congregation at the end of worship.

> You shall not worship trouble; You shall not worship poverty; You shall not worship sickness; You shall not worship death; It is only Grandfather that you shall always worship. May he provide a firm support before you; And also behind you. Should the heat of misfortune surround you, May it all be turned into abundant life for you (LXXVI).
>
> *Priest:* Gathered as we are here today, Grandfather, it is life that we desire. Here is the life that we need.
>
> *Congregation: Akufia!*[10] *Akufia! Akufia!* (LXIII 27, 32-34)

A third passage of note here is the ritual utterance that features in the immolation rite in the drama of sacrifice.

> All the members of the *Vifeme* clan say: If trouble seizes them; May trouble leave them alone; If poverty seizes them; May poverty leave them alone: If sickness seizes them; May sickness leave them alone; But if abundant life should ever seize them, May abundant life seize them and cling very firmly to them for ever (X, 6-16).

The immolation, it must be remarked, is the culminating point of worship, signifying complete human self dedication and surrender to the divine will in return for which man must enjoy divine protection which manifests itself in the realization of *Dagbe* in all its forms and in all spheres of human activity. It is appropriate here to note in some detail the life-affirming phenomena that characterize the realized state of salvation in the Anlo indigenous milieu. This is seen in the following sacred utterance:

> Bless those who have no children with plenty of children and grant increase to those who already have them. Grant good health to the farmer that . . . the harvest (may) far outweigh his labour. When the fisherman goes out in his canoe allow (him) to catch only edible (fish) and very plentifully. Help out traders too that they may also succeed in all they do . . . . Let no one die prematurely. It is for good health that we pray . . . . Good health to all; Long life and prosperity to all (LXXVII).

One can say that human experiences like poverty, trouble, sickness and death "indeed all manner of misfortunes" (LXVIII, 5) suggest the absence of *Dagbe* from the human condition and that a life that enjoys good health and immeasurable success in all endeavours and eventually ends in ripe old age (XXXVI, 55) is typical of the human condition in which *Dagbe* is realized. In other words, salvation in the Anlo traditional experience implies deliverance —deliverance from all life-negating phenomena for an unrestrained enjoyment of material property that is filled with all life-affirming phenomena.

However, the Anlo people also believe in the existence of spirit powers which are essentially evil and these operate through human agents known as sorcerers and witches. In the Anlo milieu, man's experiences involving evil spirits are as real as those involving the good ones. In fact they constitute perhaps the principal element that renders life a meaningless riddle in this African society. There is also the concept of destiny. According to this view, the day-to-day experiences of man are part of his life-plan prearranged for him by God[11] before his birth. And life-negating phenomena also form part of the Anlo man's experiences and, therefore, of his destiny. Thus the presence of the ills of life in the human condition does not necessarily signify an unwillingness to consciously pursue *Dagbe*. The indigenous Anlo experience of salvation may suggest a deliverance from all life-negating phenomena, yet an unrestrained enjoyment of material prosperity is not a necessary index to the well-being that characterizes the human condition in which salvation is realized.

The Anlo concept of destiny seems to suggest that God is the cause of man's misfortunes since it is God alone who prepares the individual's destiny. But the concept of *dzitsinya* in Anlo thought qualifies this view. *Dzitsinya* means conscience in English. It is regarded as emanating from God and entering the individual at birth as the life-soul. In functional differentiation, *dzitsinya*, as conscience, acts as God's voice in man, in fact as the God in man, forewarning him before he plunges himself into any situation that may make or mar his well-being. Any experience of man that is favourable or unfavourable to him is regarded as a direct result of the individual's reaction to his conscience, that is, the God in him. So that misfortunes may form part of man's God-given destiny. Yet according to the Anlo conception of conscience, the ills that man suffers may be his own responsibility. Therefore, man rather than God is made responsible for the life-negating phenomena that signify the absence of *Dagbe* from the human condition. Simply stated, in the Anlo experience of salvation, God is the origin of all things in the world but man is blamed for his inability to attain salvation.

Even though evil in the form of suffering is not incompatible with the realization of *Dagbe* and therefore of salvation in the life of the sufferer, yet moral evil definitely is. The individual who opts for a life that brings misery and woe to himself and his fellow men is godless, in fact irreligious, simply because God who is the source of *Dagbe* is a moral being, always on the side of fair-play. This leads to the consideration of imprecations that form quite a significant part of Anlo prayers. The following passages are of relevance:

> If any wicked people should plot that what we are about to do should fail, may this gin turn into blood in his stomach. May *Avadatsi* expose him by all means. Abundant life to all of us. May the wicked people perish in twos and threes (XXVII, 28-33).

> He does not wish anyone evil. But should anyone wish him evil, may the evil come on that person himself. May the person fail utterly in any venture (XX, 13-15, 21).

> If anyone wishes death to this lineage, may he also suffer death. The wicked people are like fire which must be extinguished before the good people enjoy a perfect peace. Abundant life to all of us (XXVI, 30-34).

Those who may scheme that (your) children and grandchildren should not continue to live, may they become the victims of their own machination and perish in large numbers. Abundant life to all of us (XLV, 30-35).

Those who are studying in the educational institutions, grant that they drink deep in the well of knowledge. But should any wicked people plan evil against these children who are your male and female servants, please you know you alone are our refuge. And he who takes refuge behind an ox never gets trapped down by a rope. It is only to your call that we answer. And whenever we go out it is in your name alone (LIV, 28-35).

According to these passages, moral evil leads to the unattainment of *Dagbe* and, therefore, of salvation. All those who perpetrate moral evil must not enjoy material prosperity but suffer, even to the point of complete removal from society through early death. However, the fifth passage in this section clearly shows that references to wicked people in ritual do not always have an imprecative motive. It may be a way of positively asking for divine protection but leaving it entirely to the divine to employ a means that he considers proper for the protection of the morally good. In any case, another important element in the Anlo experience of salvation is that suffering does not necessarily imply the non-attainment of salvation but suffering is a necessary part of a wilful forfeiture of salvation.

A problem presents itself to the inquirer here. Quite often one finds those who cannot, after serious self-examination, pin-point any moral evil in their lives which could render salvation unattainable. Nonetheless, they take steps that generally imply that they have done some wrong which they may have forgotten and which is responsible for their loss of salvation. For example, one may refer to a sufferer who may willingly submit to the performance of a ritual that implies an atonement for wrongs that he has done. This obviously questions the view that suffering is not a necessary part of a personal loss of salvation. But it also serves to emphasize the finite and the dependent nature of man on the divine. It also shows that the Anlo man does not take any chances, mobilizing all the means at his disposal, to make salvation a reality in his life. Above all, it should not be forgotten that ritual which is intended to achieve the goal of atonement is practically the same as that which aims at the removal of life-negating phenomena for which man himself may not be responsible. Herein arises the problem that is being considered here.

What then constitutes sin? What leads to the performance of the ritual signifying atonement in Anlo life and thought? Suffice it to observe that sin is not so much a state as acts which are life-negating for the actor and his fellow men. In the Anlo indigenous experience, man is considered as coming pure, that is, sinless, into the world, and he makes himself sinful by his own acts and personal choices.[12] Some of these acts may, in their immediate reference, be directed against other men but they too, like those that are in direct contravention of stipulated injunctions by one's objects of worship, have a divine dimension. Sin then consists, in Anlo thought and life, of any kind of human behaviour that leads to the experiencing of life-negating phenomena in the human condition. This implies the withholding of the protective presence of one's objects of worship, effecting a separation between the worshipper and the worshipped and suggesting that the acts of behaviour in question are against the worshipped. Hence, we find it irrelevant to classify sins as ritual or moral, since the former are considered at best of less importance than the latter and at worst as no sin at all. This study also finds unacceptable the employment of the word "taboo" as a designation for a religious category. Social proscriptions and prescriptions as well among the Anlo may have to do with diet yet not be founded on any conceivable health grounds, or with the well-being of man as in the taking of life directly through murder or indirectly through sorcery and witchcraft. Yet all are of equal importance since the consequence in each case is practically the same: the impairment of human well-being emanating from the divine. To commit sinful acts means flouting the divine will. So the designation of sins, as ritual or moral is not meaningful in considering the life and thought of the Anlo people. All the wrong choices of man in this society are ultimately the flouting of the divine will, a simple disobedience with an inherent pride. If, then, the Anlo experience of salvation involves the absence of life-negating phenomena considered as evidence of sinful acts, then petition for deliverance from these ills is an implicit petition for deliverance from sinful acts as well. It is a plea to be divinely aided to make the right personal choices which testify to the subjection of the human will to the divine. This is vital to the realization of salvation.

The Anlo conception of salvation does not assign the sinful to a perpetual loss of salvation. There is provision made for the realization of salvation once more by those who have lost this opportunity. The prelude to Anlo traditional prayers is again instructive. This prayer divides society into two groups on a moral basis and then reminds worshippers of the fate of the morally bad, the sinful, and the morally good, the faithful. Worshippers must declare that they are among the faithful so as to qualify for worship. In other words, all the sinful people are always reminded during worship that they have to and can give up their sinful ways in order to realize *Dagbe*, salvation, occasioned by and visible in an effective participation in worship, for which they have, on their own accord, presented themselves. But the clearest illustration of the point being made here is provided by the general communal meal already discussed. That all people can participate in this meal, regardless of their moral standing, shows that the sinful are not assigned to permanent condemnation in the Anlo scheme of salvation. The door for readmission into the company of the faithful is always very widely open to all those who, by their own action, have forfeited the right of sharing in man's salvation. This readmission is effected through sacrifice.

The sacrifice in question here is the *nuxe* type. *Nuxe* is made up of two Anlo words: *nu*, a noun, means a thing; *xe*, a verb, means to pay or prevent. *Nuxe*[13] means either to prevent a thing from happening or to pay a price for something. By means of *nuxe* sacrifice, then, the Anlo people seek to pay the requisite price for their sins so as to remove the ills of life that have resulted therefrom, or to prevent the evil results of their sins from manifesting themselves in human affairs. Sacrifice then has the intention of realizing salvation.

The sacrificer formally announces his purpose for coming into the divine presence to show that he has come to a personal realization of his numinous unworthiness and that he is willing to be made worthy again. The following passage is an illustration of what the sacrificer says as he presents himself for *nuxe* sacrifice.

Every year brings me the same round of misfortunes. (I) consulted the diviners and I was advised to perform some rites. As I present myself before you (i.e., the object of worship) all the misfortunes that are after me, grant that they all leave me alone (LXIV).

The sacrificial victim is used to wipe the body of the sacrificer. This is done by the sacrificer himself or the officiating priest or by both of them, the latter after the former. Ritual recitals which accompany this act may take these forms:

I wipe away death, sickness, poverty, trouble, indeed all manner of misfortunes from (my) person. May the days of my life here be long and full of prosperity and peace. May my earthly life reach its natural evening safely (LXVIII).

I wipe away all death, all sickness, all poverty, all troubles, all evil from your person. All the misfortunes that are after you I wipe them away all completely from your person (LXIX, 13-19).

In this rite the individual identifies himself with the sacrificial victim in order that the latter may take the place of the former. The victim also takes away the sacrificer's sins and their evil consequences as he transfers them to the victim by wiping his body with it. The rite of self-identification of the sacrificer with the sacrificial victim also reveals that in Anlo indigenous experience sacrifice is ultimately the offering of oneself to the divine.

The priest then cuts off pieces of the string used to tie the victim as he addresses the sacrificer thus:

All strings that bind you to death, sickness, poverty, trouble indeed all misfortunes, all these I now cut off from your person (LXIX, 1-6).

This is a ritual of absolution. Its aim is to bring into the personal experience of the sacrificer the fact that his numinous unworthiness, visible in sinful acts that prevents him from the realization of salvation, has been removed and that he is once more qualified for an actual realization of salvation.

The sacrificial rite culminates in the immolation. Here a poignant petition is presented by the officiating priest on behalf of the sacrificer to his object of worship:

> *Naki's* fervent prayer (is) if sickness, trouble, poverty, death, any manner of evil seize her, may they leave her alone. But if abundant life should ever seize her, O grant that abundant life may seize *Naki* and cling very firmly to *Naki's* person for ever (LXX).

As the words "very firmly for ever" are pronounced, the sacrificial victim is immolated and given to the object of worship. If it is an animal, the entire blood is given to the divine except where part of it is to be used in preparing the special meal to serve the purpose of a sacrament of holy communion which is not lawful for the sinful to share. In *nuxe* sacrifice where an animal victim is always used, the head is offered to the object of worship with these words:

> As long as one offers the head of an animal, one's head can no longer be claimed. Today I have offered the head of a chicken in exchange for her head. Henceforth her head is fully her own (LXXV).

This recital very explicitly states that the sacrificial victim has completely taken the place of the sacrificer and that even though self-removal from the divine presence through sin leads to the death of the wrongdoer, yet a timely realization of one's shortcomings and the expression of the desire to make the requisite amends lead rather to the death of a substitute that is acceptable to the divine and this ultimately results in the salvation of the repentant wrongdoer.

Parts of the sacrificial victim are presented not only to the object of worship but also to all other spirit powers both good and bad—to the bad so that they withdraw their presence from the affairs of the sacrificer; to the good spirits to reinstate their protective presence. The rest of the sacrificial animal is then shared in a meal with fellow worshippers. This signifies a reunion with the deity on the one hand and with the community of the faithful on the other. In other words, worship, as it is visible in sacrifice, is the dramatization of the realization of salvation in the experience of the Anlo people.

Though the analysis of sacrifice reveals an intense use of ritual, yet ritual is not considered as mechanically effecting man's salvation. The meticulous performance of the requisite ritual assures man of only the potential realization of salvation in Anloland. Its actual realization demands that the sinful must not only publicly confess his sins but also solemnly promise to pursue henceforth that which is of good report in the thinking of the Anlo people.[14] And when the man in search of salvation is required to observe that which is of good report constantly in his life before his salvation is assured, then, morality is given a central place in the Anlo indigenous religious experience; it is made a prerequisite for the realization of man's salvation. It makes the one who ultimately grants salvation and his representatives in the world of men moral beings as well. It is not, therefore, unknown in the Anlo indigenous experience that it is only the pure in heart that shall realize salvation. And when one couples this moral requirement with strict ritual demands, it can be submitted that salvation is achieved very largely by works.[15]

It has also been noted that salvation is deliverance and this deliverance is from all life-negating phenomena which must be completely replaced with life-affirming ones apparently in the here and now. Peace (*fafa* in Anlo) which very commonly occurs, second only to *Dagbe* in Anlo ritual utterances can, on this score, be equated with life-affirming phenomena visible in material prosperity. Even though there exists a belief in innocent suffering in Anlo thought yet the existence of this belief does not seriously question the view that, on the whole, the Anlo experience of salvation suggests an inseparable link with immeasurable prosperity in this world. However, it must be quickly objected that this is not materialism because matter does not have any say in human existence in Anlo thought. The material prosperity that characterizes the human condition in which salvation is realized obviously does not differ from that which obtains in the human condition in which salvation is not attained. But the Anlo people will regard the material prosperity characteristic of the unrealized state of salvation at best as not *total* well-being and at worst as not well-being at all. And the crux of the matter is that salvation is total well-being that shows itself in material prosperity and not vice versa; namely, that immeasurable material prosperity is evidence of total well-being and therefore signifies the realization of salvation. This view provides the reason for the Anlo man's lack of appreciation for the human condition, however materially prosperous, that has no divine dimension. This conception of salvation is the Anlo version of the religious man's conceptualization of the totality of existence in the presence where no life-negating forces dwell.

This view of salvation as total well-being is reflected in all spheres of human existence. Human existence, in the language of Mircea Eliade, may comprise both sacred and profane dimensions, as the Anlo people are aware. But in their thinking, there must be a total dissolution of the sacred and the profane, with the pattern for life prescribed by the sacred before total well-being, salvation can be realized. Hence all human activities be they political, social, economic, recreational, which others may compartmentalize and designate secular in contradistinction from the sacred, are regarded as given situations[16] for the expression of this holistic world view which is dominated by the sacred. In short, the view of salvation which links salvation with material prosperity, is the Anlo way of objectifying a universal concept of religious man: salvation is the totality of involvement of the totality of being in Being.

Salvation is also restoration in the Anlo traditional experience. First, two passages from Anlo ritual utterances may be noted.

> Exactly as our forbears have done it, on my knees as I am, may I also do everything strictly according to the ancient custom of our forebears (VII, 45-48).

> The prayer which our forebears used to offer from very ancient times, the whole lineage has given me this calabash (of water) that I may offer the very prayers (XXVIII, 8-11).

The two passages affirm that the dramatization of salvation in worship must be performed exactly as it was done "in very ancient times" and "strictly according to the custom of our forebears", in Eliade's terms as it was done *in illo tempore*. One can say that when the salvation which worship dramatizes is actualized, it will be a reinstatement of that which was and now is not. Secondly man is, in Anlo thought, considered born sinless into the world and it is when he consciously starts making wrong personal choices that he gets into the state of numinous unworthiness with its attendant loss of salvation. If one adds to this the practice whereby children are employed as mediums in divination by water—and mirror gazing, because they have not yet made themselves numinously unworthy —then an additional reason is supplied for the conception of salvation as restoration since salvation, as making numinously worthy again, implies the retrieving of that which has been lost. There is also a myth which makes all man's expressions of his religiousness a quest to restore himself in a divine presence lost in the distant past.

In the light of these examples, one can consider the Anlo indigenous experience of salvation as restoration. That is, when salvation is realized the condition of life will be just as it was in the distant past before the dawn of the human condition that is characterized by salvation-negating phenomena. This makes the realization of salvation in finite existence partial or it is not achieved at all. Total well-being, complete salvation, must be completely free of life-negating phenomena in Anlo thought. In fact, the people's constant quest for salvation, visible in their preoccupation with the religious life, is itself proof that salvation has not yet been completely attained. This gives salvation a future dimension. But it is a future which, paradoxically, is rooted in the past since realized total well-being will not be a "new" life but an "old, lost one" now restored.

Are the Anlo people participants in the contemporary discussion involving God? If discussion is conceived as a conscious effort to reason out an issue that has become unclear so as to state it logically and coherently, then one can say that the Anlo people are not participants in the contemporary discussion on God in their milieu. But if discussion is considered essentially in terms of its end product, namely, using words to express one's position on an issue and not the *mode* of arriving at this expressed thought, and granting that discussion, understood in this way may lack logic and coherence, then it can be said that the Anlo people are in their own way involved in a discussion about God—God in the sense of the entire sacred dimension of life. This discussion is contemporary because it is an activity that characterizes the people's current life. One is thinking here again mainly of the people's *ipsissima verba* as they appear in their worship which is a day-to-day affair. And when one couples this material with their proverbs which originated in the distant past and constitute an attempt to conceptualize their experience of life, and which are still freely used, then one is implying that the contemporary discussion on God is not essentially different from what it used to be. These people are not literate, neither are they professional thinkers. Moreover, modern ways of achieving well-being in secular and religious dimensions are not considered a serious threat to the survival of their way of realizing salvation. I am thinking here of the Euro-Christian mode of achieving total well-being and not the Islamic, since the latter does not seem to have any real attraction for the Anlo people and since Islamic life is not linked with enviable life-affirming phenomena in the Anlo society, unlike the Euro-Christian mode with its scientific, technological and educational (more direct) advantages. The Anlo people regard these as testifying to the enviableness of this mode of achieving total well-being. This admiration expresses itself in the tendency to borrow whenever it becomes necessary. But they incorporate the borrowed[17] elements into their own system to augment and not to *displace* their own mode of achieving total well-being. They cannot imagine giving up their own system of realizing salvation in preference to another because they regard God himself as directly responsible for the coming into being of all ways of realizing salvation.[18]

Thus, the Anlo experience of salvation affirms religious pluralism as a fact of life which must be recognized by all peoples in the world. Every people, as it pursues individually its way of achieving salvation, must make sure that this must also make realizable the well-being of all peoples as separate units and taken together as one unit. The Anlo form of worship bears testimony to this attitude. Anlo "God talk" today, as visible in their worship, gives full attention to the well-being of the individual and the community in a way that should lead to the goal of total well-being in the individual and corporate dimensions of society.

The Anlo discussion involving God, therefore, makes all life dependent on him through his vicegerents the lower worshipful spirit beings. He is "the Creator" (LXI, 15), "the Great Determiner of destiny, the Ground of all being" (LXXIII, 9), "the Almighty, the Great Artificer who makes the hands and the feet" (LXXVII, 9-11). Human existence in need of realizing the well-being characteristic of salvation must be completely dependent on God, i.e., must acknowledge the indispensability of the sacred dimension of life. Therefore, "whenever we go out it is in your name alone, and it is only to your call that we answer" (LIV, 34-35). Any way of life that does not uphold the view of total well-being founded on the sacred, however materially prosperous, will not be characterized, in the Anlo view, by that well-being which salvation reflects. And any way of life that aims at achieving total well-being must recognize pluralism, i.e., the diversity of ways of achieving salvation as a divine institution and must not attempt to uphold only one mode of realizing salvation. The way of life that envisages achieving total well-being must, at the same time, consider *all* human activities —even those commonly regarded as purely secular and, therefore, outside the domain of the divine—as activities in which salvation is present and God is operative. In other words, this way of life must not divorce any sphere of life from religion.

Finally, the Anlo experience of salvation encourages ecumenical conversation and dialogues in that the quest for total well-being must take full cognizance of, and actively involve, all known ways of achieving total well-being. Moreover, the eventual realization of total well-being involves the whole inhabited world. In that world inevitable differences in world views shall exist, differences epitomized by the various ways of realizing salvation. But within a transformed world, one characterized by the overcoming of the divisions between the sacred and the profane, these differences will no longer lead to opposition. In the Anlo view, the sacred is central to all of life; in theistic language, a wholly transformed society is one in which God's rule is present in all spheres of life. This society shall be a huge family because "for us the spouses of others we treat as our own. Likewise, we regard as our own the children of others" (XXXVII, 39-40). In other words, the way in which the Anlo people are pursuing this ultimate goal of all humanity—through their unceasing performance of ritual as a constant enacting of this never-ending desire to realize total well-being within their own milieu—is evidence of their hope for the coming into being, one day, of a transformed human society wherein salvation is realized.

FOOTNOTES

1 This paper is a revision of a chapter by the author in *Christianity in Independent Africa*, ed. E. Fasholé-Luke, R. Gray, A. Hastings and G. Tasie (London, 1978).

2 Indigenous, autochthonous, and traditional are used interchangeably and, except where otherwise stated, refer to the host religious experience of black African peoples, to which the Christian and the Islamic experiences came as guests.

3 Ritual recitals, ritual utterances and sacred utterances are all employed to refer to the documented *ipsissima verba* of the studied people collected during worship.

4 Here I am indicating my intention to try to relate this paper to the aims and purposes of the New Ecumenical Research Association (New ERA).

5 Except where otherwise stated Roman numerals followed by the Arabic refer to quotations from my book, *Scriptures of an African People*.

6 According to a speculative etymological analysis, *Dagbe* derives from two Anlo words: *daa* which means always, forever, eternally, and *gbe* which means day. Put together *Dagbe* means literally to have only the day always, forever, eternally. And if we remember that the night in Anlo thought is symbolic of all life-negating phenomena *and the day of all life-affirming phenomena* then this attempt at etymological analysis of *Dagbe* may be acceptable since *Dagbe* implies the eternal absence of life-negating phenomena from the human condition and the eternal experience of life-affirming ones.

7 "Deities" in this study refer to the worshipful spirit beings which exist side by side with God and the ancestors in the Anlo concept of the sacred.

8 Holy is used in the sense in which it is used in R. Otto's *Idea of the Holy*. "'Demons' and 'gods' alike spring from this root and all are nothing but different modes in which it has been objectified" (Oxford, 1923), pp. 14-15.

9 For further information see the author's "African Traditional View of Freedom and Responsibility", *Orita*, X/I June, 1977.

10 *Akufia* is an untranslatable Anlo word. It is onomatopoetic and, therefore, meaningful only when one sees the action that goes with it. It is accompanied by worshippers throwing both hands alternatively over their shoulders as if scooping water over the whole body during a bath—symbolizing a total immersion of oneself in, and a dramatization of the total well-being that *Dagbe*, as salvation, confers.

11 Hence God is known as *Segbo*, i.e., "the Great Determiner of destiny" (LXXXIII, 9).

12 The question of original sin in the biblical sense is not meaningful in this milieu.

13 *Vosa* is another Anlo word for this type of sacrifice. It is made up of two Anlo

words: *vo*, a noun, means evil; *sa*, a verb, means to tie and pass over or by (a person). *Vosa* then means the tying of evil or rendering evil to pass by a person or a community—evil that manifests itself in form of life-negating phenomena consequential to sins. *Nuxe* is preferred in this study because it is the word that is commonly used in Anlo traditional milieu to describe the type of sacrifice being considered here.

14 Relevant here is the surrender by repentant witches and sorcerers of all that they use in their destructive activities as a demonstration of their change of heart.

15 I think there is an element of grace, understood as divine aid, because prayers as petition, are intended to seek divine assistance to achieve a goal implying that one cannot do it all by oneself. However, it is of minor significance in the sense that ritual performance through sacrifice and informal expression of religion through doing that which is a good report, are regarded as absolutely indispensable for realizing salvation.

16 See the author's "African Traditional Way of Nation Building", *Orita*, IX/I, June 1975.

17 From their indigenous neighbors: e.g., the national deity, *Nyigbla*, believed by some people to have come from the *Shai* people; *Yewe* cult from the *Fon* (Dahomey, now Benin Republic); the cult of *Adudu* from their *Ewe* neighbors in Togo. The cult of *Tigare* was adopted from a Northern Ghana neighboring people through the *Asante*. There is not borrowing as such from Christianity. But the Anlo people take a lively part in Christian worship periodically especially during the Christian festivals of Christmas/New Year and Easter by way of augmenting their own mode of realizing salvation as total well-being—a testimony to their ecumenical spirit and, therefore, of their acknowledgement of religious pluralism within the human condition with an attendant promotion of dialogue since total well-being of each and all is the ultimate goal of this people. The refusal by Christians in Anloland to participate in the indigenous festivals raises grave doubts in the minds of thoughtful Anlo people as to whether Christians are actually pursuing the total well-being characteristic of a God-centered world view.

18 Consider, for example, the case in *Ewe Kristo Hame Nutinya* (Bremen, 1936), pp. 10-11 where an Anlo man listening to a sermon preached by a missionary asked whether Jesus was the same as *Nyigbla*, the Anlo national deity. In the view of the Anlo people both Jesus and *Nyigbla* were God's sons sent by Him to reveal His character and purpose to the Europeans and the Anlo people respectively.

Being and Giving:
Heidegger and the
Concept of God
John Macquarrie

P robably no modern philosopher has exerted such an influence on the theology of the twentieth century as has Martin Heidegger. Bultmann, Tillich and Rahner, to name only three of the most outstanding theologians, are all deeply in Heidegger's debt. One could hardly hope to understand them in any depth without knowing the Heideggerian background to some of their ideas. It is not difficult to point to what theologians have owed to Heidegger, but what is much more difficult is to discover just what Heidegger himself thought of theology and of religion generally. Clearly, for instance, he must have influenced the way in which Christian theologians, including some very important ones, have thought of God. But did Heidegger himself have any concept of God? Is there any place for God in his philosophy?

Of course, we may recall that in his youth Heidegger spent some time in a Jesuit seminary. Many years later, he frankly declared, "Without my theological origin, I would never have attained to the way of thinking".[1] But during most of his career he kept theology at a distance and believed that the tasks of the theologian and the philosopher are quite different. In the sentence which I have just quoted, Heidegger meant by "the way of thinking" philosophy itself, for in his later work he tended to drop the term "philosophy" and speak of "thinking" instead. So there is something of a contradiction between the confession of the indebtedness of his thinking to theology and another remark of his from a slightly later writing, when he says: "Someone who has experienced theology in his own roots, both the theology of the Christian faith and that of philosophy, would today rather remain silent about God when he is speaking in the realm of thinking".[2]

Heidegger's own aloofness from theological questions has led to some questioning of the legitimacy of employing his philosophy in theological work. But surely his own attitude to theology is irrelevant to the application of his ideas. He believed himself that language always says more than the author means to express and that sometimes interpretation will be like an act of violence in so far as it wrests new meanings from what has been said—and, even more, from what has been written. It is the case that not only theologians but psychiatrists and educationists have drawn on the resources of Heidegger's philosophy, though he did not deal explicitly with these topics.

Yet, although Heidegger was reticent on the themes of God, religion and theology, there are many allusions to these themes scattered through his works. Many of the allusions are brief, some are obscure, and they are not all easily harmonized. But there is more than enough to show us that we are dealing with a man deeply interested in theological questions, even if he did not think that the philosopher ought to involve himself directly in them. When Heidegger died in 1976, a former student of his, the philosopher Hans-Georg Gadamer, entitled his memorial lecture "An Invocation to the Vanished God", and declared: "It was Christianity that provoked and kept alive this man's thought; it was the ancient transcendence and not modern secularity that spoke through him".[3] Surely it was no accident that the words "Only a God Can Save Us" were chosen as the title for a piece in the magazine *Der Spiegel*[4] reporting an interview that Heidegger had given in 1966 on condition that it would be published only posthumously.

Near the beginning of *Being and Time*, there is brief but densely packed mention of theology, running as follows: "Theology is seeking a more primordial interpretation of man's being toward God, prescribed by the meaning of faith itself and remaining within it. It is slowly beginning to understand once more Luther's insight, that the 'foundation' on which its system of Dogma rests has not arisen from an investigation in which faith is primary, and that conceptually this foundation not only is inadequate for the problematic of theology, but conceals and distorts it".[5] The remark occurs in a passage in which Heidegger has been discussing what constitutes progress in a science. He holds that it is not the accumulation of information that counts as progress, but the capacity of the science to undergo a revolution in its basic concepts—a view which in some ways anticipated the theories of Thomas Kuhn. He then gives examples of fundamental changes taking place in mathematics, physics, biology, the historical sciences and, finally, theology. When we remember that these words were being written in 1926 and that Heidegger was at that time teaching in the University of Marburg where he had as a colleague the theologian Rudolf Bultmann, then it is not difficult to identify the profound theological changes to which Heidegger is referring. Barth, Gogarten, Tillich, Bultmann and other theologians of what was then still the younger generation were asserting the independence of their subject, recapturing the insights of the Reformers, going back to the New Testament sources and, generally speaking, finding the foundations of faith within faith itself. In particular, they were discarding the old natural theology and the metaphysics that went along with it, in the belief that these were alien importations into theology and damaging to its work.

That this is the correct interpretation of Heidegger's comment on theology can now be confirmed from a lecture on theology which he gave in 1927. Because of his reticence on the subject, this lecture was held back from publication for forty years. The lecture is in fact very revealing, and one of its main aims is to keep philosophy and theology as far apart from one another as possible. Philosophy, we are told, has to do with the question of Being, but theology is a special or positive science, and this means that it deals not with Being but with a special area of beings. "Theology", says Heidegger, "is a positive science, and as such absolutely different from philosophy". A positive science—also called an "ontic" science —deals with a region or specific area of beings or objects. "Ontology, or the science of Being, on the other hand, demands a fundamental shift of view; from whatever is (the beings) to Being". So he declares that "theology, as a positive science, is closer to chemistry and mathematics than to philosophy". Theology's closest neighbour, Heidegger suggests, is history. "Theology, as the science of faith, that is to say, of an intrinsically historical mode of being, is to its very core a historical science".[6]

There are a few other mentions of theology in *Being and Time*, and these vary between hostility and a kind of patronizing friendliness. Thus, while Heidegger in the passage quoted seemed to be giving approval to the efforts of theologians to reconstruct their study anew on a foundation drawn from faith itself, we find him equally concerned that philosophy should purge itself of any surviving theological influences. He speaks of "residues of Christian theology which have not as yet been radically extruded from philosophy".[7] An example of such a residue is mentioned by Heidegger —the belief that there are "eternal truths", and this he rejects because it conflicts with his own understanding of truth as an event, namely, the event of uncovering. On the other hand, we find Heidegger acknowledging that certain ideas that are of importance both for his own philosophy and for the philosophy of other thinkers with whom he has some sympathy, have their origins in Christian theology. For instance, he observes that "transcendence", understood in the sense of the human being's reaching out beyond itself, has its roots in theology.[8] He also declares it to be "no accident" that the phenomenon of anxiety, so important for his own early philosophy, has been studied chiefly in the history of Christian theology.[9]

The ambivalent attitude to theology and the insistence on the complete separation of theology and philosophy continue to be seen in Heidegger's *Introduction to Metaphysics*. That book opens with the famous question of Leibniz: "Why are there beings rather than nothing?" According to Heidegger, this is the basic question for philosophy, and this of course accords with his earlier view that philosophy has to do with the question of Being. But this is not a question for theology, and is not even seen to be a question by the theologian. The Christian theologian thinks he already knows the answer to the question of why there are beings rather than nothing. His answer, according to Heidegger, is: "Everything that is, except God himself, has been created by him. God himself, the increate creator, 'is'".[10] Now, such an answer is said to miss the point of the question, understood at the philosophical level. The question, philosophically understood, is an ontological question, asking about the relation—or perhaps one should say, the difference—between the beings and Being. The Christian doctrine of creation has misunderstood the question as an ontical one, and so traces back everything that is, except God, to something else that is, namely, God. It tries to account for the existence of the beings in terms of another being.

This is what Heidegger calls "onto-theology", always with him a pejorative term that stands for a confused mixture of theology and metaphysics. Its error is to confuse Being with the beings, indeed, to assimilate Being to the beings, for, says Heiegger, "we think of

Being rigorously only when we think of it in its difference with the beings, and of beings in their difference with Being".[11] As he had already maintained in his inaugural lecture at Freiburg, one must think of Being as wholly other to the beings. Indeed, from the point of view of the positive sciences which concern themselves with "what is, and nothing else", Being must be counted as nothing, for it is not anything that is.[12]

But let us come back to the discussion in *Introduction to Metaphysics*. While he is critical of onto-theology as an ontic science which can only confuse the issue if it is allowed to influence philosophical inquiry, Heidegger immediately goes on to offer some defence of theology within its own field as an exposition of faith. "There is", he writes, "a thinking and a questioning elaboration of the world of Christian experience, that is to say, of faith. That is theology. Only epochs which no longer fully believe in the true greatness of the task of theology arrive at the disastrous notion that philosophy can help to provide a refurbished theology if not a substitute for theology that will satisfy the needs and tastes of the time. For the original Christian faith, philosophy is foolishness".[13]

On the one hand, Heidegger seems to be saying, much as Hegel did before him, that theology is inferior to philosophy for it speaks out of faith and cannot answer or even entertain the radical philosophical question of Being. Theology has not achieved conceptual clarity, and, in particular, has remained on the ontic level so that it is more akin to chemistry or history than to philosophy. Yet, on the other hand, Heidegger acknowledges, as we have seen, that from the theological point of view philosophy appears to be mere foolishness. Perhaps that is because philosophy's quest for conceptual clarity cannot adequately express the concrete content of faith. So we find Heidegger saying in another place: "*Causa sui* is the right name for the God of philosophy. But man can neither pray nor sacrifice to this God. Before the *causa sui*, man can neither fall to his knees in awe, nor can he play music and dance before this God. The godless thinking which must abandon the God of philosophy, God as *Causa sui*, is thus perhaps closer to the divine God".[14] Surely in this there is an echo of Pascal's famous contrast between the God of philosophy and the God of Abraham, Isaac and Jacob.[15]

The question must be raised whether Heidegger has not permitted himself to generalize in an impermissible way about the immensely diversified fabric of Christian theology and even so-called "natural theology". Has all theology been of the onto-theological variety? Have Christian thinkers considered God as another being in addition to the beings of the world, as something else that "is" beyond whatever is in the world? Or has the very use of an expression such as *ens causa sui* indicated a reality that cannot belong within the realm of *entia*, for the qualification *causa sui* would seem to indicate that it is "wholly other" to anything that we commonly designate an *ens*? Admittedly, Christian theology may have been confused on the point and much of its language inadequately analysed or used with care and consistency. But Christian theologians have themselves been more or less aware of the inadequacies of their language. Some have been aware of the tension between the God of faith and the hypostatized God of philosophy; some, like Karl Barth, have used for God in relation to created things precisely the expression which Heidegger used to differentiate Being from beings—the "wholly other". Perhaps the mystical tradition has been particularly aware of the difference between God and the beings and the consequent limitations on our language about God. Though our language objectifies God, the reality of God lies beyond the objectification. In his conversation with Heidegger, a Japanese interlocutor says to him: "For us, the Void (*das Leere*) is the highest name for what you like to express by the word 'Being'".[16] Admittedly, this remark is made from the standpoint of Buddhism, but Christian mystics too, including John Eckhart whose thought has many similarities to Heidegger's, could have said much the same. They were aware that God is not to be found in the realm of what is, that is to say, he is nothing that is.

It is not only among explicitly mystical writers but in a much broader stream of Christian theology that there struggles to find expression the difference between God and the objects that are found in the world. Some of these theological writers do express themselves in ways that seem close to the ways in which Heidegger speaks of the difference between Being and the beings. Perhaps Paul Tillich has been most explicit in linking God with Being in something like a Heideggerian sense, but he has not been alone in this, and especially since Nietzsche's proclamation of the death of

God and the decline of the old monarchical concept of God, many theologians have been searching for an understanding of God in terms that could not rightly be called "onto-theological". We must therefore be careful not to allow Heidegger to decide what it is permissible for theologians to say or to decide unilaterally where the boundary between philosophy and theology is to be drawn.

In this connection it may be mentioned that in 1964 there was set up at Drew University under the auspices of the late Carl Michalson a conference for American theologians troubled by the problems of God language and especially by the question whether one can speak of God in language that does not objectify him. Heidegger was invited to attend, and although he did not come, he sent a paper on "The Problem of a Non-Objectifying Speaking and Thinking in Today's Theology".[17] The paper was brief. In general terms, Heidegger acknowledged the objectifying tendency of language and lamented that in modern times everything seems to be represented as an object for control and manipulation. As against that tendency, he declared his belief that what is most proper to language is "a saying of that which reveals itself to human beings in manifold ways". But he stopped short of drawing any implications for theology. He reiterates that theology must confine itself within Christian faith, and it is in that context that theologians will have to decide about their own problems of language. It may be noted, however, that he no longer calls theology an ontic or positive science, and raises the question whether it is proper to regard it as a science at all.

So far our results are somewhat negative. We have seen that although Heidegger often refers in one context or another to God and theology, he wants to stand off from these questions. Perhaps we could press the matter further. Is there anything in Heidegger's philosophy that might properly be called "God", even if he himself avoids God language? One of his many distinguished former students, Karl Löwith, has declared that Heidegger's philosophy "is in its very essence a theology without God".[18] But a theology without God or without some holy Reality even if it is not called "God" is a contradiction. If, in spite of all that he has said, there is a theology in the philosophy of Heidegger, then there must be an idea of God or of a surrogate for God.

Is Being a candidate for the role of God in Heidegger's philosophy? I have mentioned the near identification of God and Being in Tillich's theology, but that is only a recent example of what has been a very long association. Let us consider for a moment the classical theism of St. Thomas Aquinas.[19] It is true that in the five ways of proving that there is a God, Thomas uses descriptions which seems to suggest a being (*ens*), something which is, even if it is in a highly distinctive way. Yet if one considers what must be involved in notions like "first cause", "prime mover", "necessary being" and so on, one sees that these cannot be additional items of the same order as causes, movers, beings, however distinctive. Rather each is the very ground of all the items that are to be reckoned causes, movers or beings. What we have here is not an attempt to explain some entities in terms of another entity, but to indicate the ground of all entities or beings. This is the case, even if the attempt is not successful or if it is confused. Again, when Thomas says that *Qui est* or *He who is* is the most appropriate name of God, this might seem to be a clear proof that he thinks of God as a being or entity. Yet he explicitly says that this name is appropriate because "it does not signify any particular form but rather Being itself (*esse ipsum*)". God is therefore the same as Being itself. Thomas explains that "since the existence of God is his essence and since this is true of nothing else, it is clear that this name is especially appropriate to God, for the meaning of a name is the form of the thing named". But we ought to notice here that whereas Thomas holds that it is true only of God that his existence is his essence, Heidegger claims that this is also the case with human beings.[20]

Let us now examine Heidegger's concept of Being and ask whether or how far it might correspond to what a theologian means by "God". The question of Being was, of course, central to *Being and Time*. That was not a book of philosophical anthropology and not even a book of metaphysics, though it still does not evince Heidegger's later antipathy to metaphysics. His rejection, or better, his overcoming of metaphysics finds clear expression in the introduction to his little book, *Was ist Metaphysik?* This book consists of three parts: his inaugural lecture at Freiburg, which gives its name to the book; a postscript written fourteen years later; and the introduction, entitled "Der Rückgang in den Grund der Metaphysik" which did not appear until twenty years after the lecture. In this introduction, he recalls Descartes' remark, that the whole of philosophy is like a tree, of which the roots are metaphysics, the trunk physics, and the branches which come out of the trunk the other sciences. But Heidegger wants to push the inquiry further back. "We are asking", he says, "what is the ground in which the tree of philosophy has taken hold". The trouble about metaphysics is that it has never got beyond the roots of the tree, and has never inquired about the ground in which the tree is planted. It is at this point that Heidegger distinguishes between philosophy and a more fundamental thinking about Being. He writes: "A thinking which thinks of the truth of Being can no longer be satisfied with meta-physics, though its thinking is not opposed to metaphysics. To continue the metaphor, it does not tear up the roots of philosophy. But it digs and ploughs the ground for philosophy. Metaphysics remains the origin of philosophy, but it does not attain the origin of thinking. Metaphysics is overcome in the thinking of the truth of Being". Metaphysics, Heidegger holds, has been concerned with beings, with what is. It is onto-theology, and takes two forms. It may try to trace back all the beings to some common substance, or it may fix attention on the highest, divine being. In either case, it remains in the realm of beings, and falls short of that more original thinking in which one thinks of the truth of Being. From the point of view of ontical science, this, of course, is nothing. Yet Heidegger claims that here we have to do with a reality more real than any of the things that are, and he speaks of awe and wonder as the apppopriate response. Is Being then Heidegger's equivalent to God?[21]

It is in his *Letter on Humanism* that Heidegger uses the most exalted language about Being and its relation to human beings. He declares that "before he speaks, man must let himself be addressed by Being".[22] Man is the recipient of Being's self-communication. Some characteristics of Being are now made clearer. On the one hand, Heidegger declares explicitly that Being is not God, but in the very next sentence, he makes it clear that by "God" he here under-stands a being in the discredited onto-theological or metaphysical sense. On the other hand, he explicitly dissociates himself from atheism, and in particular from the atheism of Sartre. The latter had quoted a sentence from *Being and Time* which says that only as long as a human understanding of Being is possible, "'is there' Being",[23] and had taken this to mean that man himself is the ultimate and that Being is an idea produced by human subjectivity. But Heidegger now says that this is a misinterpretation of his thought. In German, the expression "'there is' Being" is written "'*es gibt*' *Sein*", and although the words "*es gibt*" are used in everyday German in the weak sense of "there is"—Sartre had in fact translated them as *il y a* —they mean literally "it gives." Heidegger insists that he meant these words to be taken in their literal sense as denoting an act of giving, and in the original text they do indeed appear in inverted commas to indicate that they have a special sense. We may ask then: "What gives?" Heidegger's answer is that Being gives itself and communicates itself to human beings. Thus, in contrast to Sartre's existentialism, which is also an atheistic humanism, Heidegger is able to declare: "Man is not the lord of beings. Man is the shepherd of Being".[24]

The almost accidental introduction of the expression *es gibt* into *Being and Time* turns out to have considerable importance for Heidegger's later thought. We shall see more of it shortly. It has already established the close connection between Being and giving. Being takes on the character of an act of giving.

Before we leave the *Letter on Humanism*, we may note another instance of Heidegger's typical reluctance to speak of God. Although, as we have seen, he dissociates himself from atheism, he tells us that nothing is decided about God. One would have to move beyond the traditional metaphysical question about God's existence or non-existence. We are told in cryptic terms: "Only from the truth of Being can the essence of the holy be thought. Only from the essence of the holy is the essence of divinity to be thought. Only in the light of the essence of divinity can it be thought or said what the word 'God' is to signify".[25]

This seems to leave the question of God open. It is clear that Heidegger is not a theist in the traditional metaphysical sense, but even clearer that he is not an atheist, if that term is taken in its broad sense to mean the godlessness of Being. There is much to be said in favour of John R. Williams' suggestion that "panentheism accords well with the elements in Heidegger's thought that are relevant to religion".[26] This label, "panentheism", is not in itself important, but it does place Heidegger in the succession of mystics like John Eckhart, who spoke of a "Godhood" (*deitas*) that cannot be contained in the traditional concept of God (deus), a Godhood moreover which cannot be hypostatized and set over against the world as a transcendent being. It is interesting to note also that at the present time forms of panentheism are embraced by many Christian theologians, including such diverse figures as John Robinson and Jürgen Moltmann.

Heidegger's relation to the mystical tradition is further evidenced by what he teaches about thinking.[27] He takes over from the mystical tradition the term Gelassenheit, which might be translated "collectedness", "serenity", "imperturbability". This collectedness is attained by meditation, a kind of thinking that is open and receptive. This is the kind of thinking advocated by Heidegger and apparently seen by him as the goal toward which philosophy leads. He considers this meditative thinking to be close to the reflection of the poet. On the other hand, he contrasts it with the active, calculating thinking of the technician and also with the assured faith of the theologian. Whether in making these comparisons Heidegger does justice to philosophers, poets, technicians or theologians, we need not pause to inquire.

The thinking of which Heidegger speaks is also a thinking which waits. This idea of waiting introduces another important aspect of what he has to say about God or the divine. At the very beginning of *Being and Time*, he had declared that time supplies the horizon for any understanding of Being,[28] and Heidegger has always considered Being in dynamic, temporal and historical terms. Being is not timeless; it includes becoming and has a history. (This again, by the way, could be said of God as conceived by panentheists). Heidegger believes that in the West, from the time of the Greek philosophers onward, there has been a forgetting of Being and an increasing preoccupation with the beings, culminating in the technological era. He writes: "In the beginning of Western thinking, Being is thought, but not the 'It gives' as such. The latter withdraws in favour of the gift which It gives".[29] Here we come back to the understanding of Being as a primordial act of giving, but the act is forgotten through preoccupation with what is given. But it seems doubtful whether Heidegger would attach any culpability to the forgetting of Being. He seems rather to suggest that Being sometimes withdraws itself, and it may be the fate of a whole historical epoch to experience the absence of Being. "What is history-like in the history of Being", he says, "is obviously determined by the way in which Being takes place and by this alone . . . this means, the way in which it gives Being".[30]

This notion of the absence and then the possible return of Being is another echo of the mystic's experience of God. It also reflects the poetry of Hölderlin, of whom Heidegger was a great admirer. Hölderlin gave expression to the sense of alienation that was mounting in the nineteenth century, and his language was definitely religious, though perhaps as much pagan as Christian. The gods have departed; they have not ceased to exist, but they are absent. Still, the very perception of the absence of the gods is a tacit acknowledgement of them and of their possible return. But Heidegger does not believe that there is anything we can do to bring about that return. "Whether God lives or remains dead is not determined by the religiousness of man and still less by the theological aspirations of philosophy and science. Whether God is God is determined from and within the constellation of Being".[31] There is surely a touch of fatalism in that sentence. But Heidegger is not a pessimist. Let me allude again to the interview with him that was published posthumously in *Der Spiegel*. As I mentioned earlier, it was entitled "Only a God Can Save Us", a remark made by Heidegger during the interview. He was asked whether he is a pessimist. He replies that he is neither a pessimist nor an optimist. Even the experience of the absence of God is a liberation from complete fallenness into preoccupation with the beings. But we cannot think God into the present; we can only make a preparation either for his appearing or for his continuing absence. So we live, as it were, between the times, but we may hope for a new advent.[32]

Mention of this dynamic and even mildly apocalyptic element in Heidegger's thinking about God and Being directs our attention to still another concept which appears in his later writings—the event (*das Ereignis*). John R. Williams believes that finally it is "the event" rather than Being which most closely corresponds to God in Heidegger's philosophy. What then is "the event"? It seems to be the "It gives" whereby Being communicates itself to man and, in a sense, entrusts itself to man, and this event also appears to be ultimate. We read in one place: "There is nothing else to which one could trace back the event or in terms of which it could be explained. The event is not the result of something else but an act of giving that reaches out and imparts like an 'It gives', something which even Being needs to attain its own character as presence".[33] These sentences would seem to support Williams' contention that "the event is the ultimate concept in Heidegger's philosophy".[34] But I would be reluctant to follow him when he says that the event is "beyond Being". It would be hard to know what could be meant by declaring the event "beyond Being", especially in the context of a discussion of Heidegger, for whom "Being" never means the sum of what is or the sum of the beings, but is declared to be wholly other from the beings, and so, in a sense, already beyond them. I would think myself of the event as an event within Being, or perhaps the event of Being or even the event which constitutes Being and reveals that the essence of Being is giving. If the event is the " It gives" and if this event is the truth of Being, then surely we are close to what the religious believer names as God. Does not Heidegger's thinking on the truth of Being and his finding that truth in an ultmate act of giving bring us close to the Christian assertion that God is love?

Let me come back to Gadamer's memorial lecture. He says, I think rightly, that those who have studied Heidegger will never again read the words "Being", "Spirit", "God", in the way they were understood in traditional metaphysics. But then he asks why someone who found theological questions as fascinating as Heidegger did was not himself a theologian and indeed explicitly avoided direct involvement in theology. "Because", replies Gadamer, "he was a thinker, it was thinking that was at work in him. He felt no empowerment (Ermächtigung) to speak of God. But what would be needed to speak of God, and that it would not do to speak of him as the sciences speak of their objects, that was the question that stirred him and showed him the path of thinking".[35]

FOOTNOTES

1 Martin Heidegger, *Unterwegs zur Sprache* (Pfullingen, 1965), p. 96.

2 Martin Heidegger, *Identity and Difference* (New York, 1969), p. 55.

3 Hans-Georg Gadamer, *Aufsätze* (Freiburg, 1976), p. 204.

4 *Der Spiegel*, No. 23 (1976), pp. 193-219.

5 Martin Heidegger, *Being and Time* (London, 1962), p. 30.

6 *Ibid.*, p. 6.

7 *Ibid.*, p. 272.

8 *Ibid.*, p. 74.

9 *Ibid.*, p. 492, n. iv.

10 Martin Heidegger, *An Introduction to Metaphysics* (New Haven, 1959), p. 7.

11 Heidegger, *Identity and Difference*, p. 62.

12 Martin Heidegger, *Was ist Metaphysik?* (Frankfurt, 1949), pp. 26-7.

13 Heidegger, *An Introduction to Metaphysics*, p. 7.

14 Heidegger, *Identity and Difference*, p. 72.

15 Blaise Pascal, *Pensées* (Paris, 1973), No. 737.

16 Heidegger, *Unterwegs zur Sprache*, p. 109.

17 Martin Heidegger, *The Piety of Thinking* (Bloomington, 1976), pp. 22-31.

18 Karl Löwith, *From Hegel to Nietzsche* (Garden City, 1967), p. 207.

19 St. Thomas Aquinas, *Summa Theologiae*, Ia, 2, 3 and Ia, 13, 11.

20 Heidegger, *Being and Time*, p. 67.

21 Heidegger, *Was ist Metaphysik?*, pp. 7, 9, 19, 47.

22 Martin Heidegger, *Über den Humanismus* (Frankfurt, 1947), p. 10.

23 Heidegger, *Being and Time*, p. 255. See Heidegger, *Über den Humanismus*, p. 24.

24 Heidegger, *Über den Humanismus*, p. 29.

25 *Ibid.*, pp. 36-7.

26 John Reynold Williams, *Martin Heidegger's Philosophy of Religion* (Waterloo, 1977), p. 154.

27 Martin Heidegger, *Discourse on Thinking* (New York, 1966), p. 54.

28 Heidegger, *Being and Time*, p. 19.

29 Martin Heidegger, *On Time and Being* (New York, 1972), p. 8.

30 *Ibid.*

31 Martin Heidegger, *Die Technik und die Kehre* (Pfullingen, 1962), p. 46.

32 *Der Spiegel*, No. 23 (1976), p. 209.

33 Heidegger, *Unterwegs zur Sprache*, p. 258.

34 Williams, *Martin Heidegger's Philosophy of Religion*, p. 126.

35 Gadamer, *Aufsätze*, pp. 204-5.

Is God Personal?

John Hick

A Jew, a Christian or a Muslim is tempted to use the word 'God' as though it had a fixed and unproblematic connotation: the personal creator and lord of the universe. But when we see theistic religion as part of the wider range of forms of religious life it becomes natural to regard 'God' as our theistic term for the Ultimate, the Real, the Divine, the Transcendent. It is then a question whether, rather than an unproblematic fact that, God is personal.

Or rather, the question is not *whether* God is personal—for there can be no doubt that the Ultimate is known as personal within the traditions of theistic experience and thought—but *in what sense* God is personal.

We need to begin by asking what it is to be personal. We have a family of words, 'person', 'personality', 'personhood', 'personal'; and they all, I suggest, arise from observation of the same basic fact. This is the fact that as a baby grows and interacts with other human beings, undergoing his/her own unique stream of experiences, and reacting in his/her own way—partly on the basis of a genetic groundplan and partly in the spontaneous creativity of life through time—he/she develops a psychic structure, which is his/her character, with a psychic 'face' which is his/her personality. Each such living organism of character expressed in a personality can be called a self: roughly, the character is the unconscious self, whilst the personality is the conscious self. For the character is the underlying and relatively slowly changing structure which the personality expresses, and the personality is the conscious surface which lives in interaction with other selves. Thus the psychic 'face' is an interface. For personality is essentially interpersonal. To be a person is to be a person in inter-action with other persons. A human baby is not born a person but becomes one by being drawn into the human community. (Having once become firmly established as a person he/she may of course retain the capacity for personal response through long periods of solitude; but still his/her very existence as a person remains a gift of human society.) Thus a person is not adequately characterized, in Boethius' classic definition, as 'an individual substance of a rational nature'.[1] For on this account there would be no necessity for more than one person to exist; whereas modern psychology and sociology have shown us that, as has been said, 'for there to be one person there must be at least two'. A person, then, is better described as an individual who is capable of inter-personal relationship and who is (or has been) part of a system of such relationships.

If personality is thus interpersonal, can we think of God *an sich* (i.e., God in him/her/itself) as personal?

In modern Christian thought there has been, on the one hand, a strong emphasis on the awareness of the divine in personal I-Thou encounter and, on the other hand, a reluctance to speak of God as *a* Person. And so it has become almost a commonplace of recent Christian theology to say that God is personal but not a person. For a person is thought of as inherently finite, one person among others. And so we find God described as, for example, 'the Eternal Personal',[2] or as 'the personal absolute',[3] or as 'infinitely personal',[4] or again as 'transpersonal, superpersonal'.[5] The point of the distinction between a person and a personal being lies in the assumption that whereas a person is necessarily finite a personal being may be infinite. However, the distinction is entirely stipulative and has no further use than to avoid problems connected with the concept of an infinite person. The notion of a personal being who is not a person is a self-contradiction; and the idea of an infinite personal being is thus the same as the idea of an infinite person. Whether this concept is viable is not easy to determine. However, I do not propose to attempt to determine it here, since the question is superseded when we take seriously the modern insight that personality is essentially inter-personal. This interactive conception of personality is, I think, so well supported by psychological evidence, and has become so widely established, that it can now be used with some confidence as a stepping stone to further explorations.

There would seem to be two possible hypotheses under which ultimate reality could be said to be intrinsically and eternally personal. According to one, the infinite divine reality exists eternally in inter-relationship with finite persons. According to the other, the ultimate is internally a community of persons, such as is affirmed in some versions of the Christian doctrine of Trinity.

The first hypothesis would involve the view, which some theologians have indeed held, that the Ultimate is essentially creator and cannot be conceived as existing without a dependent universe; together with the further belief that the created realm has eternally included personal life. Each of these demands the sacrifice of some other principle or insight whose relative value must be carefully weighed. If the Ultimate is not self-sufficient, being capable of existing only in relation to and thus in interdependence with another reality, then the divine Being will be less than 'that than which no greater can be conceived'. This is a high theological price to pay. The other presupposition—that the created universe has always included finite persons—is also costly. For man has existed for no more than a million years at most, and the affirmation of other forms of personal life, collectively co-eternal with the Creator, would be an *ad hoc* speculation in which many will not feel entitled to indulge.

But cannot this problem be met by invoking the other hypothesis, perhaps in the form of the Christian conception of God as three persons in one? This doctrine has been formulated in a variety of ways, ranging from the virtual tritheism of the 'social' conceptions of the Trinity to the modalistic notion of three distinguishable modes of operation of the one God. The latter, whilst in many ways attractive, does not enable us to speak of inter-personal relationships between the *hypostases* of the Trinity or, thus, to speak of the Godhead as inherently and eternally personal. A society of three, sustaining personal relationships between its members, requires three centres of personal consciousness and will, however harmoniously related. Such virtual tritheism is indeed found not only in popular understandings and artistic representations of the Trinity but also within patristic thought, particularly among the Cappadocian Fathers of the fourth century. Thus Gregory of Nazianzus used the example of Adam, Eve and their son Seth, who were three and yet shared the same human nature, as an analogy for the Father, Son and Spirit, who are three whilst sharing the same divine nature. This kind of Trinitarianism does enable us to think of the Godhead, in its eternal nature independently of the creation, as containing personality; for on this interpretation the Godhead consists of three inter-related personal beings forming together a uniquely intimate divine society. But it cannot be concealed that this is a sophisticated form for tritheism. Such a limited polytheism would not have solved our original problem of how to think of the God of monotheism, or the ultimate known as a deity, as eternally personal.

I conclude, then, that the ultimate is personal, not *an sich* but in interaction with human (and/or other created) persons. For personality is not a substance but a network of relationships, constituted by the ways in which one is seen by, acts upon, and is responded to by others. This relational character of personality is well expressed by the psychological concept of the persona as a role that one has within a certain group. One's personality exists in and is constituted by the range of these overlapping personae. The word 'persona' comes originally from the Roman theatre, where it referred to the mask worn by an actor to indicate the part that he was playing. This mask-connotation is stressed by C.G. Jung in his use of the term. However, I want to put a somewhat different stress upon it. For one's persona in relation to a particular group or individual is not an extrinsic mask one puts on: it *is* oneself within that system of relationships. It constitutes one's self living and interacting in that particular human context. Thus my neighbour's image of me, which is my persona in relation to them, is *me* in so far as I am part of the community which I conjointly form with them. I am present to them through their image of me, which is my persona in relation to them. A persona is accordingly a social reality, living in the consciousness, interactions, memories and traditions of a community

Further, within the different variously overlapping groups of which one is a member, with their variously overlapping centres of interest, one has partially different personae. One may be, to varying extents, 'a different person' in one's family, with colleagues at work, with a group with whom one relaxes after work, with other members of a squash-playing or rambling or stamp-collecting or other leisure group, with fellow activists in a political party, etc., etc. One can thus have several partially different personae within different strands of activity and inter-relationship. And each such persona is built up through the particular sequence of events constituting the life of that group. Thus personality is not only essentially inter-personal but, as a corollary, essentially *historical*—having its concrete character within and as part of a particular stream of events in the creation of which contingency and freedom have played a part. The threads of history of which one is a part may of course exhibit all degrees of distinction and overlap, and one's personae may have varying degrees of fixity and plasticity, and may change more slowly or more rapidly. There is indeed virtually infinite variation in the subtle interactions and systems of inter-relationship and mutual perceptions of different human beings through time.

But let us ask—what is it that *has* this range of personae that constitute a personality? Let us call it the self. This is not another deeper personality but a persisting, but also changing, system of character-dispositions, which has been built up through one's life as a person in interaction with other persons. Thus one's various personae both express one's self and reciprocally contribute to its development. It is the distinctive pattern of character traits that constitutes an unique individual who is *me*. This concept of the self as a persisting dispositional structure is analogous to that of the *linga sharira* in Hindu thought, or of the karmic bundle in Buddhist thought, which in each case is said to be successively reincarnated by forming a series of different empirical personalities. I am, however, putting the notion to a different use in speaking, not of the self's successive incarnations in different bodies, but of its expression in and through overlapping personae in different social contexts.

Pressing further the possibilities of variation between the personae of the same individual, we can imagine someone entering into several quite separate communities with no overlap or communication between them—like Gulliver finding himself first as a giant among the midgets of Lilliput, and then as a relative savage among the superior Houyhnhnms. In such very different contexts he would be related to others through different personae, embodying his different roles within these separate histories.

The varying personae of a human individual within different social contexts provide a partial analogy for the plurality of divine personae which have developed in relation to different human faith-communities. The view that I am suggesting is that the ultimate is always present to human consciousness, with its innate capacity for religious awareness; but that such awareness takes two main forms, theistic and non-theistic; and that the theistic forms consist in the particular divine personae which are reported within different streams of man's religious history. Each of these divine personae has a social reality and power in the life of the worshipping community in relation to which it has been formed; and it constitutes, at a given time, that community's perception of the Ultimate.

A divine persona is thus similar to a human persona in that each is the product of interaction between the knower and the known. A divine persona exists in a community's partial 'perception' of the Ultimate, and thus expresses something of the character of the human worshippers as well as of the divine reality; and is to this extent of the nature of projection. At the same time it mediates the divine presence to a human community, in so far as that community is able at a given time to be conscious of the Ultimate; and it is to this extent of the nature of revelation. On the other hand, a divine persona differs from a human persona in that, in the case of the Ultimate, the object of awareness is utterly disproportionate to the human perceivers. This fact introduces an element which is not present at the level of inter-human awareness.

It should also be stressed that a divine image/persona is not static and unchanging. On the contrary, in the course of a faith-community's religious history its divine image may well undergo development, mediating a fuller or, as the case may be, a less full awareness of the Ultimate. Over long periods, far exceeding the scope of any individual's direct observation but in ways sometimes traceable by the historian, the Gods have changed. For example, it is possible to observe, over the near millennium documented in the Hebrew scriptures, an evolution in the divine persona from the primitive tribal deity who urged his people on to deeds of barbaric savagery ('And you shall destroy all the people that the Lord your God will give over to you, your eye shall not pity them'. Deut. 7:16) to the gracious Lord of heaven and earth who calls his people to be 'a light to lighten the gentiles'. Indeed when a religious tradition is documented over a long period of time it is sometimes possible to write the biography of God as experienced within that tradition.

Let me conclude, however, not with the biography of a god

but with two portraits of gods, one of Indian and the other of Semitic provenance—Krishna and Jahweh.

The specific character of the Lord Krishna, as worshipped in the Vaishnavite tradition of India, is revealed in the mythic story, elaborated in the Mahabharata and interpreted theologically in the Bhagavadgītā, of the incarnation of the supreme God Vishnu; and is expressed in the individual's daily *puja*, in the communal worship, with its priesthood and its music and incense, in the great annual festivals of the Vaishnavite tradition, and in pictorial representations and statues of Krishna and his consort Radha. All this constitutes a rich, complex and satisfying 'form of life' or 'lived myth', which is characteristically Indian, and which has its own massive solidity accumulated by the believing participation of successive generations from time immemorial. And this is the mythic world or 'space' which Krishna inhabits. It would be impossible to indicate who he is except in terms of this particular mythology and in the context of this particular stream of human religious history.

Israel's Jahweh is a quite different divine Person, instantiating the concept of God within a very different context. He is characterised, in narrative terms, as the God of Abraham, Isaac and Jacob, who brought the children of Israel out of bondage in Egypt and established them in the promised land, who made his covenant with them, raised up alien powers to punish them when they turned away from him, and sent his prophets to recall them to true religion, so that they might be a light to enlighten the peoples of the earth. And this lived myth is made real to each new generation by the re-telling of the stories in the synagogue and in the family worship and rituals, and particularly in the great annual festivals—Passover, Yom Kippur, Rosh Hashanah. This tremendous mythic history in which Jews participate constitutes another powerful and spiritually nourishing religious form of life, which has held the children of Israel together through so many centuries and through so much adversity. And once again, it would be impossible to detach Jahweh from his role in this particular stream of religious experience. His nature is revealed in the stories of his actions on the stage of Israelite history, and these stories construct a particular mythic world or 'space' within which Jahweh has his existence.

Thus Krishna and Jahweh, as they are reflected in Hindu and

Jewish faith, are two quite distinct divine personae who appear within quite different cycles of stories. These two cycles are as independent of one another as two traditional fairy tales, each taking place in its own magic space and time. They differ, however, from fairy tales in that the latter are fantasies, akin to dreams, whereas the myths of a religious tradition are stories by which the story-telling community itself lives and in terms of which it understands its life. They thus shape its waking consciousness and affect in varying degrees its entire existence.

Krishna and Jahweh, then, are real divine figures central to different streams of religious life. Each is historical in the sense that he is part of the experience of a people as they have lived out their history through the centuries. Their relationship to the publicly remembered sequence and pattern of past events is different, reflecting respectively the keen Semitic interest and the vague Indian lack of interest in historiography. Jahweh's personal life—that is, his interactions with a group of finite persons—began indeed in the mists of pre-history with his self-revelation to Abraham, but continued through relatively firm tracts of near-eastern history, religiously interpreted and remembered. As such he has a concrete personality, developed in interaction with his chosen people: he is a part of their history and they are a part of his. Krishna, on the other hand, is much more tenuously related to public history. His life on earth cannot be definitely located within secular time. The stories in which he appears have a legendary character. And yet he is a thoroughly historical figure in the sense that he has entered as a concrete personal reality into the life of generation after generation of people within the Vaishnavite religious world. Indeed, so real is he as a person that a Roman Catholic, living in Vrindaban, the legendary scene of Krishna's youth, where he had played with the gopi girls, can report that 'even today the great bhaktas of Vrindaban relate how it is possible to discover Krishna peeping archly from behind a tree, dancing his rose dance with gopis during especially blessed times, or to meet Radha on a lonely path, enquiring after her lover Krishna'.[6]

There are of course many other divine personae, each likewise describable only within the context of a particular strand of religious history: the Allah of Islamic faith, who is known in his self-revelation in the Qur'an through the Prophet Muhammad; the Holy Trinity of Christian faith, known through the distinctively Christian response to Jesus of Nazareth, together with the Church's experience of the Holy Spirit and its inherited Jewish belief in God the Father; Shiva, known and intensely experienced within the Shaivite cults of India...

There remains to add the very important fact that God, the Ultimate, is not only experienced in many traditions as personal, but is also experienced in other traditions as non-personal. The Ultimate is indeed experienced and thought by human beings through one or other of two categorial concepts—the concept of Deity, which presides over the theistic forms of religion, and the concept of the Absolute, which presides over the non-theistic forms of religion. Each of these categorial concepts is concretized in actual religious experience as a range of divine *personae* (Jahweh, Allah, Krishna, Shiva...) or as a range of non-personal 'ultimates' (Brahman, Nirvana, Sunyata...).

Is God, then, personal? No, in the sense that God, the Ultimate, *an sich*, is real beyond all interactive relationship with finite persons. Yes, in the sense that in addition to being authentically experienced in non-personal ways, the Ultimate is also authentically experienced in personal terms by many human persons.

FOOTNOTES

1 Boethius, *Contra Eutychen et Nestorium*, chap. 3.

2 H.H. Farmer, *The World and God* (1935), p. 8.

3 John MacMurray, *Interpreting the Universe* (1956), p. 138.

4 Ian Ramsey, *Theology*, Vol. LXXIV (1971), p. 126.

5 Hans Küng, *On Being a Christian* (1976), p. 303.

6 Klaus Klostermaier, *In the Paradise of Krishna* (1969), p. 15.

The Impersonality of God

John N. Findlay

This paper is intended to be a contribution to Absolute-theory, a discipline of which theology, which treats of the Absolute as some sort of a God, is only one species. Absolute-theory is a discipline which tries to sketch the logic of an Absolute, a unique being necessary in the sense that its existence requires no explanation, and that cannot be thought away, and which is the presupposition of all other existences. The justification of thinking in terms of an Absolute is not, however, to be found in formal logic, whose necessities ignore content, and are arguably not existential: pragmatically it rests on the fact that almost everyone accepts an Absolute of some sort, whether this be material, or spatio-temporal, or sensational, or conscious or whatever, and whether it be placed in an individual or non-individual category, e.g., that of a supreme Eidos or a supreme Value or an ultimate Imperative, or an ineliminable Act or Process, etc. It is sufficient that an Absolute should be what is parasitic upon nothing, and that everything other than itself is in some manner parasitic upon it, and determined by it, though such determination need not take the form of formal logical entailment or any other form of necessitation. An Absolute, if it can be coherently thought of at all, certainly exists, since it covers all possibilities: it can only fail to exist if our thought of it is basically incoherent. The existence of an Absolute is therefore either quite necessary or wholly impossible, though it may not be either for us or epistemically, and the question as to *what* it is may further admit of many alternative answers from *our* point of view, though, from the point of view of the Absolute, no alternatives are conceivable. The logic of absolutes, though superlatively difficult, has, however, been interestingly explored by such great thinkers as Proclus, Aquinas, Shankara, Hegel and Bradley, and so have logics which try to base everything on ultimate, contingent matters of fact, e.g., Wittgenstein's in the *Tractatus*, though whether there is not a subtle contradiction in the latter approaches may well be questioned.

The paper further argues that Absolutes are for us necessarily connected with certain fundamental values, whether these be merely cognitive values of explanation and understanding, or other non-cognitive values which have a closely similar interpersonality. The values, e.g., which guide us in assessments of inductive and other kinds of probability, are closely parallel to those of interpersonal justice. A viable Absolute cannot therefore be wholly value-free. The task of the Absolute-theorist is, however, made very difficult since his discourse will have to modify the sense and use of even the most fundamental connectives and modalities of ordinary discourse: everything said in such discourse may have to be in some measure 'analogical'. The Absolute, e.g., may have to combine the functions of a Property, a Relation, a Value and an individual Subject, as it does, e.g., very ingeniously, in the theology of Aquinas. To what extent, therefore, talk in terms of the personality of the Absolute is to be encouraged or discouraged, is a very complex and difficult question, but such talk will be least doubtfully legitimate if it is freely flanked by discourse in terms of other analogies.

The aim of this paper is to consider how God, conceived as the supreme object of religion, and credited with all the ontological and axiological attributes necessary in such an object, should be related to the concept of a conscious person. Does God include personality among his many attributes? Is he to be conceived of, not perhaps as *a*, but as *the* all-perfect individual person, from whom all imperfect persons derive whatever positive qualities and perfections they may have? Does he as much transcend individual personality as he is thought to transcend anything with a definite position in space or time, anything with a definite shape, size or duration, or anything which moves to some definite consummation, or anything of a sensuous or corporeal nature, or anything of a psychic or spiritual nature that is closely bound up with what is local, temporal, material, sensuous or one-sidedly concrete or abstract?

The gist of this paper will then be that God, conceived as the supreme vehicle of ontological and axiological perfection—I am not considering any other sort of God—must as necessarily transcend personality as he transcends everything else that is limited, local, mutable, or purely one-sided. This does not mean that all these things, including personality and persons, in so far as they have a positive content and worth, may not be counted as excerpts from the inclusiveness of his perfection, excerpts which will, however, misrepresent and distort that perfection if seen in the limited, one-sided form they assume in ordinary existence and experience. Space and Time, to use an analogy which Kant also makes use of in a similar context, can be conceived as containing all definite shapes, sizes and durations within themselves, while not giving them the sharp separateness characteristic of our experience of spatio-temporal things. So God, it may be suggested, contains within himself the possibility of all qualified and related things, some of which are actual and others merely possible, and that he also contains within himself the possibility of all forms of sentience and cogitative reference and conative effort, some of which are actual and others merely possible, but that, *qua* total Godhead, it is wrong to ascribe to him definite, single qualities and relations, or parts outside of other parts in space or time, or movements towards or away from definite regions, or definite conscious states, or personal unities or conscious states, or goal-directed conscious trends, such as are distinguishable within him. Using this analogy, it is arguable that God is, on the one hand, the complete peace in which the one-sidedly, finitely actual subsides into the boundlessly possible that surrounds it, and that is seen as its necessary complement, while the possible is also seen as the possibility *of* all the one-sided, finite actualities that distinguish themselves within it, and which constitute the necessary complement of its mere possibility. God, in this conception, is therefore as much boundless positivity, as also boundless, all-cancelling negativity. To this must, however, be added that God is to be thought of as a boundless active power which *can* determine, at all times and in all ways, which possibilities will be raised to actuality, and which actualities will, in their turn, subside into mere possibilities. He must, in short, not be thought of like the empty space or time which passively accepts contents from other sources, but rather like a space-time which is in some manner self-filling and self-emptying and self-modifying, and which is also, in countless of its parts and aspects, self- or other-sentient, and self- or other-referential, and self- or other-aiming.

God, further, must be taken to be the possibility of harmonious or good forms of being and relation in a more positive sense than he is the possibility of bad or inharmonious forms of being. (My naturalistic identification of goodness with harmony cannot be defended in detail here.) Harmonious forms of being are those in which differences continue one another or bring each other out by contrast, or are in some way single and unified in spite of all their difference, whereas bad forms of being involve inner disruptions and discontinuities, in which unity is in some manner violated or set at naught. God, of course, is the possibility of all forms of disunity and disharmony as of all forms of unity and harmony, and therefore of all forms of evil as much as of all forms of good, but he is in a sense more authentically the possibility of the former than of the latter, since his comprehensive allness comes out more fully when things are brought together in harmony, than when they seek to exclude one another in discord. The goodness of God is, however, impossible without the evil, for the coming together in harmony is most evident and salient when it is a harmonization that overcomes disharmony, but the evil possibilities in God are likewise impossible without the good, since they are only evil because they resist the harmonization, which is more authentically divine. It would be wrong to regard good and evil, though necessary to one another, as of equal status in God: evil, while not merely negative, is in a sense parasitic upon good, which it helps to realize, while good is not parasitic on the evil which it requires. It can be said to use the evil instrumentally, while the evil cannot so use the good. Wicked persons sometimes try to invert this essential pattern of priority, and deepen evil by the greatness of the good they trample on and defile; cruel people are in this respect the most wicked of the wicked. Evil cannot, however, take the place of good, since, if this were possible, disharmony could become a case of harmony. Disharmony may indeed be overridden in a higher harmony, and harmony in a deeper disharmony, but the former direction has an absolute priority over the latter. Divinity can therefore be said to permit disharmony and evil of various sorts, but also always to be positively seeking to *redeem* the evil which is thus permitted, and to reduce it to harmony. Redemptive activity is therefore what most completely characterizes divinity. (The conceptions I have been sketching have been presented full-blown since I cannot hope to explain and justify my theology in the course of a single, brief paper.)

It is not unacceptable to hold that God, as the supreme religious concept must be an intellectually explanatory notion: the idea of something whose existence and basic properties require no explanation, but which could not in any respect be otherwise, and which is also explanatory of everything whose existence and properties might in any way have been otherwise. The notion of an ontologically perfect being, which covers all possibilities and therefore exists of necessity, and whose being and basic properties are in some manner presupposed by the being and properties of all things which could have been otherwise, has been attacked by some as logically incoherent: there cannot be anything which exists of necessity *tout court*, but only if certain prior conditions have been satisfied. If this view is correct, there cannot be a God at all, for nothing that could have been absent or different in essential character could have been a God. I think, however, that practically all thinkers believe in an absolute something or other which cannot be thought away, whether this be material, or spiritual, or spatio-temporal, or conceived as belonging to some abstract category like the One of the Neoplatonists or the pregnant Emptiness of some schools of Buddhism. The omnipossibility or necessity which is here envisaged is not, of course, that of purely formal logic, but involves content, and may be called 'ontological'. That there are necessities and possibilities and other modalities of this sort, and that we have some limited insight into them, is something that I shall not argue for on the present occasion. I shall take it that almost everyone believes in an ineliminable being of some sort, and that theologians and God-worshippers *must* do so.

A God cannot, however, merely be ontologically perfect, but must also be axiologically perfect: he or it must embody all those positive values which represent ends that everyone must desire for everything and everyone, and which are absolute and invariant among things and persons. Here again there are people who think that the conception of such absolute values is incoherent, since all values merely reflect the valuations of concrete persons, and are of necessity infinitely various, and in no sense absolute. I cannot argue with such value-relativists, but, if their view is correct, there cannot be a God, only various imaginary beings decked out with the values of particular adorers. Perhaps one of them is a superhuman spirit who adores himself, and gives himself the honorific title of God, much as Amin or Bokassa gave themselves similar royal titles. If such a spirit exists, we owe him no religious deference, even if he did make us out of nothing, and has the power to elevate us to heaven, or plunge us into hell. Power is nothing without goodness, and a goodness which is absolute: it represents a value, but is nothing without other values of compassion, understanding, sense of beauty, etc., which must complement it, and it may, if complemented by evil, augment, rather than reduce, such evil. Hence God is not God because he made Leviathan, and the other marvels mentioned in the book of Job, but because what he made was good, and because he himself is good, and cannot aim, except instrumentally or interstitially, at anything but what is good. And in default of absolute values which God cannot make or unmake, but at most represent what he as a perfect being necessarily is and seeks to realize, there cannot be a God at all. God therefore represents the unsurpassable extreme of explanatory necessity both in being and value, and if such an ideal is incoherent, then God is impossible, and religion or the worship of God is an absurd and empty self-prostration before nothing or an idol.

I have, in my previous exposition, further connected absolute value with harmony, i.e., with a unity of nature which, while it may tolerate difference and variety, and in fact requires it, none the less always subordinates it, and makes its elements fit in with one another. But this, I think, entails that, whether or not God is personal or a person, the extreme of value realizable in a finite, contingent, being (which cannot be rated as a God) is none the less realizable only in persons, and that persons therefore are nearer to God, more godlike, than anything else which is not divine. Persons involve the possibility of a richer harmony among elements and aspects than anything else can. This possibility follows from the nature of conscious intentionality, the power of a person to direct his thought to the widest possible variety of things and themes, and to fit them all together into a single picture with the maximum of internal coherence and harmony. A conscious person has further the power to coordinate his purposes into unified patterns having the highest variety and internal harmony, and all rational patterns of life involve such a unification. A conscious person has, further, the remarkable power to put himself into the position of other conscious persons, and to see things from their perspective: he is therefore capable of all the higher harmonizations of interest in which the supreme values consist. In contrast to conscious persons, unconscious or poorly conscious beings have only limited powers of harmonization, and obviously all the aspects of such beings, whether qualitative, relational or propositional or what not, have no such powers at all.

The question may next be studied whether God, as the all-embracing case of ontological and axiological perfection, can be deemed himself to be personal or a person. (The use of pronouns such as 'himself' is not meant to prejudge any issue.) It seems clear at once that if God is to be called a person or personal, he is so in a very different sense from ordinary persons. For ordinary persons, however inclusive in their survey and reckoning with other things and persons, are essentially one instance of personality among others, and achieve their highest potential by *trying* to rise above the limitations of their position in time and space and among other persons, without ever being fully able to do so. God, however, includes all that is separately realized in other persons, and contains all that is finite transcended in himself. He cannot be external to anything except in the sense that he brings the infinite complement and corrective to whatever the ordinary person realizes, and this infinite complement and corrective cannot be alien to what it completes and corrects, but must in a sense be the natural extension of what it is trying to achieve. Any other view of God must make him as limited and one-sided as the beings he excludes. He then becomes merely the Great Father or Elder Brother whose insight happens to be infinite whereas ours is only finite, whose power and goodness are infinite whereas ours are finite, and so on. As a mere infinite superior, God cannot then have the absolute authority of the values he exemplifies, since we too in an inadequate manner embody them, and can at best value him *for* the values he embodies, and not for himself. Only if he, in some extraordinary manner, can become identical with the values he embodies, become Very Being Itself, Very Goodness and Beauty Themselves, Very Power Itself and so on, can we reverence him as one with the values which he is said to possess. Religion in its deepest earnestness therefore becomes unavoidably Platonic. Otherwise expressed, in God the distinction between essence and existence, as Aquinas called it, or between the

What and the This, as Bradley termed it, has to be set aside: we must have a unique nature which is also its own, only instance, and we must have an instance which is one with the nature it instantiates, and hence can be present, in varying approximations, in countless other instances. The point I am making agrees also with one made by Kant in terms of autonomy and heteronomy. The values and laws that govern one's action cannot be someone else's laws, however exalted the being who prescribes them: they must necessarily be one's own values and laws, expressions of one's own freedom as a rational being, which rationality means that one seeks, like God, to be a being whose consideration extends to everything and to everyone. This godlike rationality cannot be borrowed from someone else: it must be one's own most absolute property as a being who thinks in terms of unrestricted universals, or in other words a being who thinks and is conscious. God therefore must be present in the hearts and minds and wills of all persons, however misguided and distorted these are, and it is only because he is thus interior, as much as exterior, that he can demand a deference that is unconditional, and that amounts to worship or a bending of the knee. But a being who *is* in some sense the inmost nature of all persons cannot be counted as one person among others, nor can a being who *is* all the values which give virtue and beauty to persons, be a mere example of the virtues and beauties in question.

All this does not mean that it is not appropriate for us to conceive of God in terms of all positive excellences of persons, and also of things, though the eminent sense in which *he* embodies those excellences is not the sense in which *they* embody them. We can certainly think of God as a person, whether of the masculine or feminine gender, but we can equally well think of him as an impersonal, spiritual force which works through persons, e.g. the prophets. The Holy Ghost, though called a person of the Trinity, has never really achieved personality, but appears at best in the form of a dove, flames of fire, tongues, etc. Wilhelm Wundt somewhere wrote of it as a *daimonenartiges Wesen*: it is *from* God rather than God *simpliciter*, and as such it speaks through the prophets, evangelists and others. The same holds of the Word or Logos mentioned in the first chapter of St. John's Gospel: in a deep sense it *is* God, but it also is *with* God, something that radiates from the divine source. And while it was made flesh in Christ, it also lighteth every man that cometh into the world, and hence operates beyond the incarnation, and is suprapersonal rather than personal.

If we now turn to the great eastern religions, we find God conceived of impersonally rather than personally: for Taoism, Deity is like water which pervades everything, and which is glorious in its fluid weakness rather than in resistant hardness. For Hinduism there is indeed a form of divinity which is conceived personally, and which decides to assume many personal guises, but there is also a form in which differences vanish like an illusion, and which is without quality or the opposition of object to subject. This is in fact the highest form of Deity, but not all can achieve the union with it which its nature requires: for them devotion, *bhakti*, to differentiated expressions is the only approach to deity of which they are capable. And while in Buddhism there are countless exalted personal Buddhas and Bodhisattvas with a special mission to help mankind to emancipation, the true deity of Buddhism is the Buddha-eye or Buddha-nature present like a jewel in all men, which can lead them to an ultimate peace in which all the clutter of finite being vanishes. The analogy of empty space is here employed, and in the meditative ascent of the mind to Nirvana it passes through a stage which contemplates the infinity of unoccupied space, then through one which contemplates an infinity of consciousness undiversified by objects, while the goal of the series is Nirvana itself, which is better thought of as a big Void than as anything occupied or diversified. Some of you will feel critical of the oriental reverence for emptiness and nothingness, but it must be remembered that such an emptiness is in a sense rich with the forms that are in it swept away. It must be remembered too that many Christian thinkers have placed a God who is No-thing, i.e., Nothing in particular, at the heart of their theology. Thus Origen conceived the supreme godhead as an abyssal depth, while Erigena interpreted the biblical creation of everything out of *nothing* as a creation by God of everything out of *himself.* The great Alexandrian theology which sprang from Plato and Pythagoras, and to which many Christians belonged, was also one which believed in an ultimate unity in which all particularities would vanish, though all such particularities also derived from it and looked back towards it, and discerned in it a multiplicity which was first actual for them rather than for their source. There were also Christian theologians who tolerated an infinity of different analogies in their conception of God. Thus the pseudo-Areopagite, in his treatise on the Divine Names, says that, while God is from one point of view unspeakable, having neither figure nor quantity, nor bulk, nor position, nor mutability nor anything sensuous, and being also void of conceptual determinations, and so unconnected with Science, Truth, Kingship, Unity, Spirit, Sonship, Fatherhood, etc., he is also positively characterizable in all the ways in which his essence reveals itself. Thus God is at once the greatest of all beings and the most minutely subtle, the most stable and also the most mobile.

Since the Areopagite has thus given one *carte blanche* to conceive God in terms of any positive analogy, I should like myself to put in a claim for the fragrance of certain wild sweet-peas that bloom in the South African veld in spring. Their fragrance seemed to me to articulate nothing but absolute purity, absolute innocence and absolute sweetness, to be in short Deus Odorans rather than anything which merely is *of* God.

It remains to be considered whether, admitting the propriety of a vast number of personal and impersonal, positive and negative analogies, one should not also accord some special virtue to analogies in terms of consciousness or thought or mind or spirit. Is God best thought of by analogy with a perfect mind, which timelessly envisages all possibilities of differentiated and contingent being, and which relates them all to the absolute values which are one with its essence? It is here that I think that the Neoplatonists are valuable mentors. They teach a doctrine of Three Hypostases in Divinity, the first being called the One or Good which is beyond all differentiation, the second the Divine *Nous* or Mind, which embraces all possible forms of being and intellection without any savour of the spatial or temporal or sensuously particular, while the third is the Soul which operates in time and which descends into divided, sensuous particularity, and which is also particularized in countless individual souls as well as in a cosmic soul diffused throughout the universe. It is in the conception of the *Nous* that one sees the Neoplatonic equivalent of personality in God. This *Nous* is not, however, my mind or your mind or any particular super-mind, but is rather a mind present in, and shared in by all souls, and which conceives everything from every point of view. Its distinctive peculiarity is, however, that all objects, and all subordinate minds, are in it present in a peculiar interpenetrating manner, so that each can be said to contain all the others within itself, and to exihibit clear distinction without division. The Divine Mind has therefore none of the separation of parts characteristic of objects in our experience or of particular minds. In it all are all, and each all, and the glory infinite, as Plotinus says in a famous passage. Its unity resembles that of a well-blended drink in which countless savours can be distinguished, but not divided, or the noise of the talk at a drinking party in which there is a similar blend of multitudinous voices. All this does not prevent the whole blend of savours or voices from having its own distinctive, unitary character, and in some such fashion must the Divine Mind contain all minds and all objects of mind, without thereby becoming a mere amalgam and confusion of separates.

The notion of interpenetrating unity we are considering is not, moreover unintelligible to us: everywhere in experience we meet with things tending in its direction. If we have heard musical phrases or a melodic whole, the phrases, and the whole, linger on as a mood in the soul in which all the elements remain distinct but are undividedly unified. A similar concentration occurs when we achieve understanding of some single proposition, or complex of propositions, as when we clearly see that a certain number is prime, or divisible by another number. In such an insight, complex detail is present, but it is present as a whole, and no part is isolated and seen apart from the others. The same thing occurs in many momentous decisions which change the course of our lives, and it certainly occurs when we suddenly achieve deep understanding and emotional unity with some other person. If we imagine all this extended into an infinitely embracing unity, we achieve a vague impression of the spritual life at the divine centre which sums up all we know and infinitely more beside. The infinite is readily brought into such an embrace, since infinity is only inaccessible when it has to be arrived at by a *piecemeal* summation of parts, one after another in time. When the piecemeal element, and the element of temporal supersession, vanish, an infinite whole must be as simple to grasp as a finite one: it simply contains, non-successively and without any division, parts exemplifying any and every finite number. The kind of life that is thus achieveable can, however, only be by a remote analogy personal. For it is not opposed to other persons or objects, and it does not advance or develop in time. If one likes to call it personal, one may do so, but one is using the word in a new sense, which one can never hope to illustrate, though one has some inkling of what it may involve, and can progress *towards* it along the routes we have indicated. It lies at the point of convergence of all these routes, and we can travel, in its direction; all thought in fact always does so, but we cannot, in this life at least, arrive at the term of the journey. We are therefore free to describe it in a large number of personal and impersonal figures. We can converse with the Divine Centre in personal prayer, if that is the analogy that suits us, but we can equally see it as radiating forth into ourselves, and into everything else, without giving it the responsive form of a person. What I am saying is of course in harmony with the many eastern forms of Yoga, and it is not out of harmony with such experiences as those of St. Teresa and St. John of the Cross, for whom a container of water simply loses itself in a larger body of water, or a flame becomes part of a larger flame. Many of the phrases in the Eucharistic addresses at the end of St. John's Gospel—I in you, and you in me, and all in the Father—tell the same tale. That which terminates in persons, and yet comes from beyond them, and is responsible for their union, comes out in all of them.

I wish to end this paper by considering the charismatic persons who feel themselves to be in some way more absolutely one with the supreme religious object than others are, or who are thought by others to be so. Such consecration of particular persons has taken place in many religions and above all in Christianity where Jesus says, for example, that he and the Father are one, that anyone who has seen him has seen the Father, and where he identifies himself with the Ancient of Days in the superbly ungrammatical utterance: 'Before Abraham was, I am'. While I do not believe that all such statements were made before unsympathetic audiences to the extent that the Gospels suggest they were, there can be little doubt that Jesus experienced in himself an identification in which the Father came down into union with him, or he was raised up into union with the Father, and that, in virtue of this union, he could also enable others to achieve a similar identification, and become sons of God. Buddha similarly experienced an elevation into an absolute vision which was possible for all men, and which had been achieved by countless Buddhas in the past. There have, of course, been charismatic Messiahs of varying stature who have made similar claims, or who have been accorded such a stature by others. The founder of the Church or Society which has organized this meeting is credited with such claims, and he has shown his respect for us by not requiring the slightest acceptance of these claims by those who have come to this meeting. The question is, however, how far, and in what sense, we can admit the possibility of such Messianic identifications or transfigurations, so that a finite human person becomes one with the absolute, necessary source of all being and value. My answer is that we may admit it, since it is true in some measure of all of us, however much we may distort and corrupt it: each of us has a life-line to the absolute centre of being and value, and cannot by any act disrupt it. There is in fact no room anywhere for anything but the absolute source and the radiations which stream from it, and what is defective and evil is only possible because it represents the necessary contrast to the source's positive attributes. In the nature of the Absolute we have, not only what it of necessity includes, but also what it of necessity excludes, and to which it thereby gives a parasitic content which is, however, open to appropriation by many of the limited instances of its excellences to which it freely gives being. A charismatic individual is, however, one in whom the shadows and distortions of the instance are for a great part set aside, so that the absolute source can reveal itself more undistortedly and perspicuously. It can shine with some part of light which, as John says, lighteth every man that cometh into the world. I do not, however, myself believe that this transmitted or reflected light can ever be undiminished, and hence even the greatest exemplars have limitations and distortions of vision due to the traditions and the times in which they grow up, or due also to factors of personal temperament which nothing can eliminate. I do not wish to give examples of such limitations and distortions, since to recognize their presence is also to see around them and beyond them, to the ideal or ideals in terms of which we recognize them as inadequate. A Messianic ideal must further, in my view, specify itself into a variety of forms, some more philosophical, some more practical, some more aesthetic, some more devotional. In the Father's house there will therefore not only be many mansions, but many presences presiding over them, some human, some perhaps superhuman, and we may have an angelic or polytheistic hierarchy terminating in what transcends all forms of speech or praise. I think therefore that Messiahs are necessarily many, and of varying charisma. I am not myself prepared to pass judgement on any genuine Messiah or to grade him favourably or unfavourably in relation to others, any more than I would do so in relation to my dearest friends. For the great assembly of genuine Messiahs, or Saints or Bodhisattvas or whatever, are the blessed company that keep our world from foundering, and whom we must rely on as a body. What I supremely reverence is not, however, this blessed company, but the charismatic light which shines through them all and transfigures them, and which I cannot myself identify with a person or with anything personal.

God, Moral Perfection, and Possible Worlds

Philip L. Quinn

According to the theistic religions, human persons are called upon to worship God. Theists typically hold that reverence and adoration are the appropriate human responses to him. This view presupposes that God deserves or merits worship. If a being were not worthy of worship, then surely worship directed toward that being would be wildly inappropriate. But what features must a being have to be a fitting and proper object of worship? It seems clear that only a morally perfect being could be worthy of the unqualified devotion typical of theistic worship. Moral goodness falling short of perfection might earn a being admiration but never adoration. This is why it is essential to theistic orthodoxy that God be thought of as perfectly good.

Theists also hold that God created the heavens and the earth. God is, therefore, responsible for at least some of the good and evil in the cosmos of contingent things. Theists cannot avoid grappling with the problem of evil. How could a perfectly good being create a cosmos containing as much evil as we find in the world? Possible answers to this question, ranging from a free-will defense to a soul-making theodicy, are common currency among philosophers and theologians. But it is less widely recognized that theists must also confront a problem of good. Evil apart, the created cosmos seems to contain less good than it might have contained. How could a perfectly good being create a cosmos containing less good than the very best he could have created? And if a being worthy of worship would create the best cosmos he could, is a theist committed to holding that this is the best of all possible worlds? We all know that Voltaire ridiculed the Leibnizian doctrine that this is indeed the best of all possible worlds. But is the doctrine really ridiculous, fit only for satire? And, ridiculous or not, is it a doctrine orthodox theists are stuck with, like it or not, in virtue of holding that the creator deserves their worship? In this paper, I propose to discuss these and related questions.

I

In an ingenious paper called "Must God Create the Best?" Robert M. Adams tries to refute the doctrine according to which God, if he creates at all, must create the best of all logically possible worlds.[1] Adams supposes that those who would defend such a view would do so because they accept something like the following principle:

> (1) If a perfectly good moral agent created any world at all, it would have to be the very best world that he could create.[2]

Adams claims that a theist, or at least a typical Judeo-Christian theist, need not accept this principle. He holds that it is plausible to suppose that God could create a world such that (i) none of the individual creatures in it would exist in the best of all possible worlds; (ii) none of the creatures in it has a life which is so miserable on the whole that it would be better for that creature if it had never existed; and (iii) every individual creature in it is at least as happy on the whole as it would have been in any other possible world in which it exists.[3] If God were to create such a world, Adams says, he would not thereby wrong any of the creatures in it, nor would he thereby treat any of them with less than perfect kindness, nor would he thereby exhibit any flaw or defect of moral character. Hence, according to Adams, God's creating such a world would not preclude his being a perfectly good moral agent. But because such a world could not be the best of all possible worlds, or even one of the best if there are several tied for first place, Adams concludes that there simply is no requirement, logical or moral, that God create the best of all possible worlds.

It seems to me clear enough that a being who created a cosmos satisfying the three conditions Adams states would be a good moral agent. What needs further exploration, I think, is the question of whether such a being would be morally perfect in the sense necessary for being worthy of worship. But before beginning such an exploration, I need to give some attention to a fundamental conceptual issue.

According to Alvin Plantinga, a possible world is a state of affairs of a certain sort, and states of affairs are not the kinds of things that can be either created or destroyed.[4] On this view, even God could not, literally speaking, create a possible world. What he can do is bring it about that certain states of affairs obtain or are actual, and so we ought to speak of God actualizing rather than creating a possible world. Of course, we may suppose that God can create ordinary contingent individuals such as tables and chairs or even extraordinary individuals such as angels and demons. But such creatures are not a possible world; they are its inhabitants or denizens. In actualizing a possible world, God, we may suppose, creates its contingent denizens. Some possible worlds, however, have only necessary beings such as numbers and properties as their denizens, and if God were to actualize such a world, he would refrain from creating any contingent individual. Thus strict accuracy forbids us to speak of God creating possible worlds, because this way of talking suggests a power to alter modal status which most theists do not attribute even to God.

Is it plausible to suppose that God could actualize a possible world satisfying conditions (i)-(iii)? It certainly appears to be. Because each of those conditions implicitly involves universal quantification over creatures, a world without creatures would vacuously satisfy them. Surely Judeo-Christian theists would not deny that God could have chosen to actualize a possible world without creatures, for to do so would be to imply that God as a matter of logical necessity had to create something or other. Moreover, if each creature is a denizen of only one possible world, as modern counterpart theorists believe and as Leibniz seems to have held, then any possible world that is less than maximally good in which no creature has a life so miserable that it would have been better for it if it had never existed will satisfy these conditions. A problem arises, however, if we do not accept counterpart theory and consider possible worlds containing creatures. For all I know, every possible world which contains creatures at all contains at least one which could be happier than it is in that world. Or perhaps there is no possible world in which any creature is as happy at it could be; maybe for every possible world w and each creature capable of being happy that exists in w, there is some possible world w' such that w' is diverse from w and that creature also exists in w' and is happier in w' than it is in w. This is not to suggest than any creature could be unboundedly happy, so to speak; it could happen if creatures approached, asymptotically as it were, without ever reaching their upper limits of happiness as possible worlds varied. So it might be, for all I know, that condition (iii) cannot be satisfied except vacuously; but, then again, perhaps condition (iii) can be nonvacuously satisfied. The trouble is that I do not know enough about possible worlds and their creaturely denizens to be able to tell for sure whether what Adams assumes is really plausible. In this situation, the reasonable thing to do seems to be to allow, for the sake of argument, that there are possible worlds with creatures that satisfy (i)-(iii) but to reserve judgment on just how plausible this assumption really is.

But even if this concession is made, some problems remain. A possible world with creatures that satisfies conditions (i)-(iii) is such that every creature in it is as happy as that creature could be, but perhaps another possible world containing the very same creatures is morally better though less replete with felicity. Why should we rule out of court the possibility that a possible world which fails to satisfy condition (iii) but includes compensating exercises of moral virtue in the face of adversity on the part of some of its creatures is a morally better world than another which contains the very same creatures and satisfies condition (iii) but lacks such exercises of virtue? If this is possible, should we not admit that a perfectly good moral agent would prefer a possible world with more moral goodness and less happiness to a possible world with more happiness and less moral goodness? Adams makes use of intuitive notions of the goodness of possible worlds and of the moral goodness of agents without exploring in much detail the philosophical questions such notions give rise to. What are we to understand by the relational predicate '—— is a better world than...' applied to pairs of possible worlds? How are we to interpret the expression '—— is a better moral agent than...' applied to pairs of persons or personlike entities? And what connections are there between the moral goodness of a creator and the goodness of the individuals he creates? Does morality ask for no more from a perfectly good creator than that he wrong none of his creatures, treat none of them with less than perfect kindness and manifest no defect of moral character? I next turn to an exploration of some of these issues.

II

When we assume that possible worlds can be compared with respect to their goodness, we suppose that there are features of possible worlds on which such comparisons are based. But which features are these? Should we say that the goodness of a possible world is a monotonically increasing function of the total amount of moral goodness contained in it? On this view, one possible world would be better than another just in case the first contained more moral goodness than the second. Or should we claim that the goodness of a possible world is a function of some of its apparently nonmoral features? For example, one possible world might be judged better than another just in case the first ranked higher on a scale combining considerations of simplicity and variety, appropriately weighted, than did the second.[5] Of course, it is by no means evident that possible worlds which are very simple and chock full of variety are also particularly morally edifying. Perhaps simplicity and variety constitute an appropriate basis for comparative judgments of aesthetic goodness and yet are utterly irrelevant to moral goodness.

So we need to make some assumptions about which varieties of goodness a morally perfect creator would be concerned about in comparing possible worlds with an eye to actualizing one. I shall assume that the sort of goodness which would be important from the point of view of a perfectly good moral agent envisaging actualizing a possible world is moral goodness, and so I shall suppose that there is a relation expressed by the phrase '—— is a morally better world than...' which does relate pairs of possible worlds. But I shall not give an account of what moral goodness is. In particular, I shall not assume that a possible world in which every creature is as happy as it could be but no pity for suffering is ever felt is morally better than one in which some suffering evokes pity but some creature could be happier than it is. Nor shall I assume that a possible world of the second kind is morally better than one of the first kind. Similarly, I shall remain neutral about whether justice contributes more, or less, than creaturely happiness to the moral goodness of a possible world. All I shall suppose is that, however the moral goodness of possible worlds is determined, some are morally better than others.

What formal properties should we attribute to the relation expressed by the phrase '—— is a morally better world than...'? Doubtless there would be widespread agreement that such a relation must be asymmetric and transitive. From this it follows that it must also be irreflexive and, hence, that it induces a strict partial ordering on the set of all possible worlds.[6] This much seems obvious, but beyond this point things quickly become murky. Is it the case that for any possible worlds w and w', if w is distinct from w', then either w is a morally better world than w' or w' is a morally better world than w? Not obviously so, for perhaps there are two distinct possible worlds exactly equal in moral goodness. Is it even the case that every pair of possible worlds is commensurable with respect to moral goodness? Again the answer is not obvious; maybe there are distinct possible worlds w and w' such that w is not a morally better world than w', w' is not a morally better world than w, and yet neither are w and w' equal in moral goodness. And even if any two possible worlds are morally commensurable, must we suppose that one possible world is the best of all? Once more it is not clear what the answer is. Perhaps for each possible world there is another which is morally better, or, if there is a possible world than which no other is morally better, maybe there are many such possible worlds of maximal moral goodness. Since I can see no way to provide uncontroversial answers to questions such as these, I propose to leave them open in this discussion. Thus I intend to see how far I can get in exploring the topic of this paper with nothing stronger than the assumption that the set of possible worlds is strictly partially ordered.

A simple observation will serve to motivate a definition linking possible worlds with the power needed to actualize them. It may, for all I know, be the case that even an omnipotent being is not able to actualize just any world which is logically possible.[7] Suppose, for instance, there were an inhabitant of some but not all possible worlds such that in every possible world where it exists it is uncreated. Such a thing would be contingent but essentially uncreated. Let us also assume that actualizing a possible world involves at least creating all its denizens which do not exist necessarily. Any possible world which has among its inhabitants a contingent but essentially uncreated being would then be unactualizable. But maybe the best of all possible worlds, if there is a unique one, is for this reason, or for some other, unactualizable. Or perhaps every possible world better than some particular world is unactualizable. In order not to beg any questions about such matters, I suggest that the notion of an actualizable world be defined as follows:

(2) w is an actualizable world = df w is such that it is possible that there is an x such that x is omnipotent and x actualizes it.

Less formally, an actualizable world is one which an omnipotent being could actualize. It may or may not be the case that every logically possible world is also actualizable. I take no stand on this issue.

I shall not assume that there is a best actualizable world or that, if there is one, it is unique. But even without such strong assumptions several definitions of kinds of moral goodness that pertain to actualizable worlds can be formulated. First, there is a notion analogous to the idea of being a best possible world; it is the concept of an actualizable world whose moral goodness cannot be surpassed. This notion is defined as follows:

(3) w is an actualizable world of unsurpassable moral goodness = df w is an actualizable world, and, for all w', if w' is an actualizable world, then w' is not a morally better world than w.

An actualizable world of unsurpassable moral goodness is an actualizable world such that no actualizable world is morally better than it is. Obviously this definition does not entail that there are any such worlds, and it is consistent with there being several if there are any. For all that I have said, two actualizable worlds of unsurpassable moral goodness might either be equally morally good or be incommensurable with respect to moral goodness. A Leibnizian of the strict persuasion would, I suppose, be as unhappy with the suggestion that there are many actualizable worlds of unsurpassable moral goodness as with the suggestion that there are none. In either case it would seem that God could have no Sufficient Reason for actualizing exactly one possible world, and this, after all, is the most he can do. However, if there are several such worlds, God can at least appeal to the principle of Insufficient Reason and decide which among them to actualize by some divine analogue of the process of rolling fair dice. Or nonmoral considerations might serve in such a case to break ties for first place.

Next we need to frame some definitions having to do with possible worlds of the sort Adams holds God could actualize without moral fault. I begin by defining those possible worlds, if any, whose denizens are happy in the appropriate ways. They are to be thought of as possible worlds whose creaturely inhabitants enjoy a felicity as complete as is possible for them. The definition of such completely felicitous actualizable worlds goes as follows:

(4) w is a completely felicitous actualizable world = df w is an actualizable world, and w is such that (i) none of the creatures in w has a life in w so miserable on the whole that it would be better for that creature if it did not exist in w, and (ii) every creature in w is at least as happy on the whole in w as it is in any w' distinct from w in which it exists.

As I mentioned above, for all I know, there are no completely felicitous actualizable worlds other than those vacuously so in virtue of containing no creatures. Moreover, if there are some, some or all of them may, as far as I can tell, also be actualizable worlds of unsurpassable moral goodness. The definitions do not preclude this. Whether or not one thinks this is the case will depend at least in part, I imagine, on one's views of the relations of felicity and moral goodness, and so I would expect opinions on this matter to differ as moral theories vary. Thus, in order to follow Adams in focusing attention on possible worlds less good than the best actualizable, we need to define the notion of a morally surpassable but completely felicitous actualizable world. This concept is defined as follows:

(5) w is a morally surpassable completely felicitous actualizable world = df w is a completely felicitous actualizable world, and there is a w' such that w' is an actualizable world and w' is a morally better world than w.

For all I have said so far, it may be that no actualizable world is morally better than any completely felicitous actualizable world. So perhaps no possible worlds satisfy this definition. But maybe some actualizable worlds which are not completely felicitous are morally better than some which are. After all, there may be features other than felicity which contribute to the moral goodness of possible worlds, and some such features may be weightier than felicity by itself.

A final idea that I will have occasion to use in subsequent arguments is the notion of a possible world which is, among completely felicitous actualizable worlds, morally unsurpassable. It is defined as follows:

(6) w is a morally unsurpassable completely felicitous actualizable world = df w is a completely felicitous actualizable world, and, for all w', if w' is a completely felicitous actualizable world, then w' is not a morally better world than w.

It is evident that this definition does not entail that there are any morally unsurpassable completely felicitous actualizable worlds, and it does not preclude there being several if there are any. Moreover, our definitions entail nothing about whether some morally unsurpassable completely felicitous actualizable worlds, if there are any, are also actualizable worlds of unsurpassable moral goodness.

The point of this somewhat cumbersome battery of definitions is to allow us to pose some rather precise questions about what a perfectly good and omnipotent moral agent would do if he were to actualize a possible world. Would such a being actualize a world of unsurpassable moral goodness even if no such world were completely felicitous? Might such a being actualize a morally surpassable yet completely felicitous world? Must such a being at least actualize a morally unsurpassable completely felicitous world?

Adams seems to hold, in effect, that such a being might actualize a completely felicitous world that is morally surpassable. Is this correct? Before we can return any confident answer to this question, we must reflect a bit on what is involved in being a perfectly good moral agent.

III

Our discussion of the perfections of moral agents may begin with an observation about English grammar. There are many English expressions whose general form is 'a perfectly A N,' where substituends for 'A' are adjectival phrases which admit of the comparative and substituends for 'N' are noun phrases which function as count nouns. Examples are such things as 'a perfectly flat surface,' 'a perfectly splendid dinner,' 'a perfectly frictionless plane' and 'a perfectly respectable place to live.' Among expressions of this sort, there is one difference of logical functioning that has some importance in the present context. In some cases at least, a perfectly A N would be such that it is not possible that there be an N more A than it is. For example, a perfectly flat surface would be such that it is not possible that there be a surface flatter than it is. It is clear that this is one of the features of perfectly flat surfaces, perfectly frictionless planes and perfectly rigid rods which makes them such useful idealizations in physics. In other cases, however, a perfectly A N would be such that it is possible that there be an N more A than it is. Thus, a perfectly respectable place to live may nonetheless be such that it is possible that there be a place to live more respectable than it is. For example, though Rye is a perfectly respectable place to live, Scarsdale is a more respectable place to live than Rye is.

When theists apply the phrase 'a perfectly good moral agent' to God, it may not be obvious whether they intend their usage to be assimilated to cases of the first sort or to cases of the second sort. In order to circumvent any ambiguities, I shall define different locutions to express two interpretations which might be placed on that phrase. The weaker locution is defined as follows:

(7) x is a thoroughly good moral agent = df x is a moral agent, x performs some actions, x does nothing morally wrong, and x exhibits no defects of moral character.

A thoroughly good moral agent is, so to speak, morally good through and through. However, a thoroughly good moral agent may be such that it is possible that there be a moral agent better than he is, for of two moral agents both of whom exhibit sterling characters and neither of whom does anything wrong, one may effectuate more widespread beneficence, perhaps of a supererogatory kind, than another. I believe my definition of a thoroughly good moral agent reflects all those features of moral agents to which Adams makes explicit reference in his statement of what God might properly do in creating, since I take kindness to be a moral character trait. There is, however, another degree of moral excellence. The stronger locution which expresses it may be defined as follows:

(8) x is a superlatively good moral agent = df x is a thoroughly good moral agent, and x is such that there is no possible world in which there is some y such that y is a better moral agent in that world than he is in the actual world.

There could be no moral agent better than a superlatively good moral agent actually is. Of course, comparing the goodness of moral agents is probably no easier than comparing the goodness of possible worlds. Many questions arise. What features of moral agents are to be considered in making such comparisons? What sort of ordering does this relation induce on sets of moral agents? Moral theories can be expected to disagree about the answers to such questions. However, it does seem clear enough that many theists are committed to holding that God is a superlatively good moral agent and, indeed, the only superlatively good moral agent. Such theists would not, I think, be satisfied to maintain that God is merely a thoroughly good moral agent, though he is at least that, or even essentially a thoroughly good moral agent; they would insist that God has to be a superlatively good moral agent, and perhaps essentially so, if he is to be worthy of the kind of worship they believe they owe him. The question such people need to ponder seems to me to be this: What sort of possible world would an omnipotent and superlatively good moral agent actualize if he actualized any world at all? Or, at any rate, since this is a question I find puzzling, I shall next consider some answers to it.

IV

As a preliminary to our discussion of superlatively good moral agents, let us consider briefly what a thoroughly good moral agent would do in creating. A principle with some plausibility is the following:

> (9) If an omnipotent and thoroughly good moral agent were to actualize a possible world, he would actualize some completely felicitous actualizable world.

This principle strikes me as acceptable provided we assume, at least for the sake of argument, that the value properly most cherished by such an agent is the happiness of his creatures. An argument in support of the acceptability of this principle goes as follows. Suppose an omnipotent and thoroughly good moral agent actualizes a world. Since he is omnipotent, it can be any actualizable world. Because he is thoroughly good, he will do no wrong and exhibit no flaw of character in actualizing a world. Assuming that depriving a creature of happiness it might have enjoyed is the only way a creator might wrong that creature or exhibit a moral flaw in creating it, a thoroughly good moral agent might actualize any completely felicitous actualizable world. So if there are some such worlds with creatures in them, he will actualize one of them. I think this is the important positive insight Adams has got hold of, even though I remain somewhat skeptical about the exclusive emphasis on happiness in his treatment. However, it should be noted that it is consistent with (9) that the world actualized by an omnipotent and thoroughly good moral agent be neither a morally unsurpassable completely felicitous actualizable world nor an actualizable world of unsurpassable moral goodness. This is interesting but perhaps not very surprising. After all, it would seem that a thoroughly good moral agent could omit certain moral perfections from his creation without diminishing the happiness of any of its creatures. The difficulty is that (9), though it is at least arguably correct, is not really an answer to the question posed by a theist who wishes to know what sort of world a superlatively good moral agent would actualize if he actualized any world at all. So we should next consider some principles that do address that question.

The first such principle may be stated in the following way:

(10) If an omnipotent and superlatively good moral agent were to actualize a possible world, he would actualize some completely felicitous actualizable world.

It seems to me that this principle is at best misleading. There are some relations among possible worlds which may hold, consistent with everything I have assumed so far, such that if they did hold there would be certain completely felicitous actualizable worlds that an omnipotent and superlatively good moral agent would not actualize. Let me explain why. Suppose an omnipotent and superlatively good moral agent actualizes a world, and assume the world he actualizes is a completely felicitous actualizable world but is also a morally surpassable completely felicitous actualizable world. On these assumptions, it is possible that something actualizes a morally better world than the one which, by hypothesis, he actualizes, since it is morally surpassable. But then it surely seems possible that there is a better moral agent than he actually is, namely, one who actualizes a morally better world than he, by hypothesis, has actualized. This, however, contradicts the assumption that he is a superlatively good moral agent. Hence, if there are completely felicitous actualizable worlds that are also morally surpassable, and a world without creatures would indicate that there are, then an omnipotent and superlatively good moral agent would actualize none of them. He would actualize instead some morally better world.

This line of reasoning suggests that we examine next a somewhat stronger principle. It may be formulated as follows:

(11) If an omnipotent and superlatively good moral agent were to actualize a possible world, he would actualize some morally unsurpassable completely felicitous actualizable world.

But even this principle seems not to capture the doctrine we are searching for. It is consistent with everything I have assumed so far to suppose that there are actualizable worlds morally better than any morally unsurpassable completely felicitous actualizable world. This would be the case, for example, if there is some actualizable world in which happiness is proportioned to virtue and some suffer on account of their sins which is morally better than any completely felicitous actualizable world. But perhaps there are some such worlds; certainly many theists have thought there are. If there are, and if an omnipotent being were nevertheless to actualize a morally unsurpassable completely felicitous actualizable world, then there would be actualizable worlds morally better than the one that he, by hypothesis, had actualized. But then it surely seems to be possible that there is a better moral agent than he, by hypothesis, actually is. Thus he would not be a superlatively good moral agent. So if there are actualizable worlds morally better than any morally unsurpassable completely felicitous actualizable world, as there may well be, then an omnipotent and superlatively good moral agent would actualize one of them and not some morally unsurpassable completely felicitous actualizable world.

These considerations suggest that the correct principle about actualization by a superlatively good moral agent is the following:

(12) If an omnipotent and superlatively good moral agent were to actualize a possible world, he would actualize some actualizable world of unsurpassable moral goodness.

The reasons that support this principle are easy to state. Suppose an omnipotent and superlatively good moral agent actualizes a world. Assume for the sake of argument that the one he actualizes is not an actualizable world of unsurpassable moral goodness. Then either it is not an actualizable world at all, which contradicts the supposition that an omnipotent being actualizes it, or there is another possible world which is both actualizable and morally better than it is. But, in this case, it surely seems to be possible that there is a better moral agent than he who, by hypothesis, actualized a world of surpassable moral goodness, namely, one who actualizes a morally better actualizable world. And this contradicts the supposition that our creator is a superlatively good moral agent. So an omnipotent and superlatively good moral agent would actualize an actualizable world of unsurpassable moral goodness. As was noted above, it is consistent with our definitions that such a world also be a morally unsurpassable completely felicitous actualizable world. What these arguments show, therefore, is only that, if an omnipotent and superlatively good moral agent had to choose between less than complete felicity and surpassable moral goodness when actualizing a possible world, he would choose less than complete felicity.

It is obvious that (12) is a good deal like (1). Since (1) expresses a view Adams rejects, an argument in favor of (12) can reasonably be interpreted as an argument against a position of the general sort Adams defends. I intend the arguments I have given to be successful arguments of this kind. But are my arguments sound? An attentive reader will have observed that in several of them I infer from the premise that there are morally better actualizable worlds than the one which, by hypothesis, has been actualized the conclusion that it is at least possible that there is a better moral agent than its hypothetical actualizer is. Are such inferences in any way dubious? Their validity, it would appear, can be guaranteed by assuming as an additional premise the following principle:

(13) Necessarily, for all w, w' and x, if w is an actualizable world and w' is an actualizable world and w is a morally better world than w', then if x is an omnipotent moral agent and x actualizes w', then x is such that there is some possible world in which there is a y such that y is a better moral agent in that world than he is in w'.

As far as I can tell, (13) expresses a fairly obvious truth. An omnipotent moral agent can actualize any actualizable world. If he actualizes one than which there is a morally better, he does not do the best he can, morally speaking, and so it is possible that there is an agent morally better than he is, namely, an omnipotent moral agent who actualizes one of those morally better worlds.

Another nice feature (13) has is that it does not fall prey to certain counter-examples Adams cites in order to refute a principle he suggests as something which implies (1). The principle in question goes as follows:

(14) It is wrong to bring into existence, knowingly, a being less excellent than one could have brought into existence.[8]

Examples involving animal breeding, e.g., breeding goldfish rather than golden retrievers, and human procreation, e.g., having normal children instead of chemically altered supergeniuses, seem to refute (14) if we allow that what people do in such cases is genuinely to bring something into existence. But clearly such examples do not serve also to refute (13). For one thing, since its scope is restricted to the actualization of possible worlds, no example which concerns bringing something into existence could be so much as relevant to refuting it. For another, (13) does not assert that it would be wrong to actualize a world than which there is a morally better one could actualize; instead it asserts that a being who acted in this way would not do the best that could be done, which in turn implies that such a being would not be a superlatively good moral agent.

From all of this, I conclude that I have gone a long way towards meeting the challenge to the Leibnizian philosophical tradition raised by Adams. For I have formulated a principle, namely (12), which is akin to his principle (1), and I have argued in support of it from a premise, namely (13), which is not refuted by his counter-examples to (14) or by any other examples known to me. In addition, I have tried to indicate why theists are indeed committed to defending some position of this general sort in virtue of their view that God deserves or merits worship of the extreme kinds they typically believe it appropriate to direct toward him.[9]

FOOTNOTES

1 Robert M. Adams, "Must God Create the Best?", *The Philosophical Review* 81 (1972), pp. 317-31.

2 *Ibid.*, p. 317.

3 *Ibid.*, p. 320.

4 Alvin Plantinga, *The Nature of Necessity* (Oxford: Clarendon, 1974), pp. 44-45.

5 Leibniz seems to have held a view of this sort. See Section V of *Discourse on Metaphysics* and Paragraph 58 of *Monadology.*

6 The technical terms from the theory of relations are defined in many set theory texts. See, for instance, Patrick Suppes, *Axiomatic Set Theory* (New York: Van Nostrand, 1960), pp. 68-72.

7 The supposition that an omnipotent being could actualize any logically possible world has been baptized "Leibniz' Lapse" by Alvin Plantinga. See Plantinga, *op. cit.*, pp. 180-84. His examples involve the complexities of free actions.

8 Adams, *op. cit.*, p. 329.

9 I read earlier versions of this material at the University of Illinois at Chicago Circle and at the University of Rhode Island. I thank my audiences on those occasions for helpful discussion.

Creativity, God

and Creation

Theodore Vitali

I. 'Creativity' and Unity

The most serious problem classical theists discover in process philosophy is process philosophy's commitment to a dialectical concept of creativity in which the one and the many are so mutually implied that neither is totally derived from the other. Essentially, the problem faced by classical theists is the age-old problem of the one and the many. In the case of process philosophy, they clearly recognize that process philosophers have reversed the emphasis of western philosophy on unity and have opted instead for a more radical form of pluralism. If we look briefly at Whitehead's Category of the Ultimate we will be able to discover quite easily not only the dialectical character of creativity, but the problems envisioned by classical theists as well.

Let us take for example the Category of the Ultimate:

> 'Creativity' is the universal of universals characterizing ultimate matter of fact. It is that ultimate principle by which the many, which are the universe disjunctively, become the one actual occasion, which is the universe conjunctively. It lies in the nature of things that the many enter complex unity (*PR*31).

If we simply isolate the terms "many" and "one", we can see their dialectical character. "One" refers to the universe conjunctively. The term "one" therefore refers to a complex synthesis of many elements creatively conjoined to form a new unity. On the other hand, the term "many" refers to the many entities constituted by subjective acts of creation, the many "ones" which derive from the synthetic unificatory process of concrescence. Yet, the many are not simply inert ones. They are the objects of prehension and thus the data for future syntheses. They exist to be part of the concrescence of future occasions. The many require the one as their *raison d'etre*, their purpose as objective unities, objective beings. Consequently, unity and multiplicity are mutually implied. Unity without multiplicities would be vacuous, totally abstract, absolutely indeterminate. Multiplicity without unity (future unification) would be impotent, utterly chaotic, absolutely dissimilar. For there to be creativity—at least creativity understood as "the advance from disjunction to conjunction, creating a novel entity other than the entities given in disjunction" (*PR* 32)—both unity and multiplicity must be so dialectically implied that neither one can be totally derived from or reducible to the other. Creativity, in other words, requires the most radical form of pluralism.

Traditional theists have been quick to realize the implications of such a radical form of pluralism. They have been quick to realize that the radical shift from a philosophy of being and unity to a philosophy of becoming and underived plurality entails the following: a) that the intelligibility of the universe can only be partial because of the lack of an ultimate source, an ultimate unity, b) that the affinity implied in creativity between God and the World is terribly obscure if the World is somehow other than God but not derived from God as a primal source, c) that the metaphysical foundations for creativity itself are at best highly suspect because of the absence of an ultimate reason for the fact of creativity and for the normativeness of creativity said to be present in every actual occasion.

At this time, we will examine more closely these concerns. We will develop them out of recent writings on the subject by Norris Clarke and Robert Neville.[1] They provide as clear and as precise a criticism as one could desire. They also offer solutions to the problems. We will take them in turn.

A. Intelligibility and the Problem of Radical Pluralism

When Clarke confronts the problem of the underived status of actual occasions in Whitehead's Category of the Ultimate, he asks, "What then is the ultimate source of explanation of the unity of the universe, or why its two correlative poles, God and the multiplicity of the world, are attuned to each other so as to make up a single system, since neither one ultimately derives all its being from the other?"[2] To paraphrase the question being asked: Given the absence of a doctrine of *creatio ex nihilo* entailing the derivative status of finite entities, how does one explain both the reality of and the intelligibility implied in multiple occasions if these occasions are underived from some primordial unifying source? Following the thought of St. Thomas Aquinas in *De Potentia*, 5, 3, the question can be further refined by focusing on the relationship between unity and diversity, sameness and difference. If intelligibility requires the contrast between sameness and difference and that difference is intelligible only as a diminution of sameness, how can difference be in and of itself the cause of sameness? Put in terms of unity and multiplicity, how can multiplicity (which directly entails diversity) be a source of unity (entailing sameness) if multiplicity can only be generative of diversity?

In Clarke's view, multiplicities cannot account for unity and sameness, and thus the dialectical character of the Category of the Ultimate means in the final analysis that the world is radically unintelligible. Clarke's complaint is constant: "an infinitely fragmented force of creativity cannot be an authentic ultimate, precisely because it is actually a many, and only abstractly one."[3] Intelligibility requires some primordial unity of source in which the many and the diverse derive their being and intelligibility from their status as contingent beings whose existence and intelligibility are due to the "participative" or "derivative" character of their being—are due to their dependence upon God as creator.

The problem with affinity follows from the non-derivative status of actual occasions. The dialectic between one and many presupposes a profound affinity between the World and God. God may not be the creator of the World *ex nihilo*, but He is the source of the World's finality. God provides the subjective aim for each actual occasion, and thus He energizes creativity insofar as He provides the real possibilities constitutive of the determinable (but not determinate) future for each occasion. God keeps creativity from descending into mere repetitiveness and ontological boredom. But on the other hand, God would be in Whitehead's words "actually deficient and unconscious," without the world. There is, therefore, a profound affinity between God and the World as exhibited in creativity. But the problem Clarke sees is, Why is there this or any affinity at all? If God were the creator of the world, the affinity would be due to God's creativity and the World's dependence upon God. But in Whitehead's view, God and World are mutually implied and thus one cannot be said to be the source of the other.

Clarke suggests that Whiteheadians may appeal to creativity itself as the source of affinity, that "inscrutable, faceless, amorphous force of creativity which is just *there*, everywhere in the universe, as a primal fact with no further explanation possible—a kind of generalized necessity of nature..."[4] But if this "inscrutable force" is intrinsically constituted by the dialectic of one and many, it follows that creativity itself is an instance of an "ultimate many, with no unifying source."[5] It too suffers from the problem of being a many attempting to explain a unity. As the first part of this discussion indicated, following St. Thomas, such an appeal won't work.

Robert Neville refines the problem of affinity raised by Clarke by an analysis of the normative character of the principle of creativity. As we observed above, the ontological character of the affinity exhibited between the World and God, the many and the one, depends upon the ontological character of the principle of creativity. In a very real sense, the Category of the Ultimate is ultimate for process philosophy; the rationality of the entire process ontology will extend to the limit of the rationality contained in the principle of creativity. As far as the principle of creativity goes, so goes the rationality of the system. Neville knows this and attacks creativity's normative character accordingly.

Neville moves against the normative character of creativity by examining the relationship of the Category of the Ultimate to the Ontological Principle. Neville's basic concern is to show that a) the Ontological Principle is only a cosmological principle, and thus non-normative, and b) the Category of the Ultimate, while intended to provide the normative foundation for the Ontological Principle, is itself either merely descriptive of matter of fact, and thus non-normative, or ontologically inadequate to meet the demands of the Ontological Principle, and thus, in fact, non-normative.

Neville contends that the Ontological Principle (that every condition to which the process of becoming conforms in any particular instance has its reasons *either* in the character of some actual entity in the actual world of that concrescence *or* in the character of the subject which is in process of concrescence [PR 36]), while accounting for the fact of contingent unity in the process of self-actualization, is by nature only a cosmological and not an ontological principle. It describes how unity is achieved in actual occasions; it does not tell why such unificatory processes *must* occur. The Ontological Principle, therefore, being merely descriptive of fact is, as a result, non-normative. The Category of the Ultimate, however, was intended by Whitehead to provide the reason why such processes must occur. But according to Neville, it too begs the questions. Neville writes:

> The kind of *unity* associated with the category of the ultimate is correspondingly ontological. Whereas cosmological unity is a matter of objective unification of actual entities in the satisfaction of another actual entity, ontological unity is the primordial togetherness of actualities necessary for prehension and articulated by the creativity binding many into one. The category of the ultimate describes the condition for the existence of any actual entity. There could be no harmonious satisfaction, expressive of the ontological principle, were there not the basic relation of ones and manys through creativity.[6]

What constitutes the normativeness of this relationship? If we take creativity as a descriptive generalization, as Whitehead intended it, or if we take creativity as a normative principle "to the effect that pluralities must be unified," then can creativity alone account for the necessity that the many must become one, or, in other words, "why there exist any events of creative unification" at all?[7]

In the first instance, a merely descriptive category tells us what in fact takes place, but does not tell us why. In the second instance, creativity as a normative principle involves a serious internal problem. Creativity apart from concrete events is in and of itself indeterminate, thereby having no character of its own. But, if radically indeterminate apart from concrete instantiations in actual occasions, how can creativity be normative for these specific occasions? How can the indeterminate be the determinate (normative) ground for finite creativity? Neville puts it neatly:

> But then if creativity apart from specific occasions is completely indeterminate, it cannot be normative in any sense that would necessitate creativity in specific occasions.[8]

If creativity is in and of itself non-normative because radically indeterminate, then creativity cannot be an ontological principle in the strict sense, a principle which necessitates (founds the ultimate reason for) the dialectic of one and many. Rather, it would be simply a generalized description of empirical fact; this could hardly be an adequate grounding for an ontology of creation.

In order to have an adequate ontological grounding for creativity, it is requisite that reasons be given which are the foundation for the dialectic of one and many in creativity without at the same time presupposing the dialectic. Any appeal to "creative" decisions as the ontological basis for creativity fails because such decisions are instances of creativity and thus presuppose the dialectic intended to be supported and defined. Neville writes:

> According to the ontological principle there ought to be somewhere a creative decision responsible for any unification. But the decisions of all actual entities, precisely because they are creative, cannot constitute the ontological unity as the condition for creativity. There would be no creative actual entities if there were no unity of one and many through creativity.... Therefore, *given the ontological principle*, with no possibility of an ontological decision, the ontological unity of many and one in creativity is impossible![9]

For process cosmology to be ontologically grounded, a normative principle must be discovered which is capable of providing the reasons for finite creativity (the unity of the dialectic of one and many) without itself being an instance of it. In other words, if process cosmology is to be grounded in a valid and coherent ontology, it must be grounded in an ontology which transcends the categories of process. Process cosmology must be grounded in an ontology of being and creation.

B. *Creatio ex Nihilo and Finite Creativity*

Clarke believes that he discovers in an oft-neglected concept of "transient energy" (apparently used much earlier by Whitehead) a way of solving the ontological problems surrounding the irreducible pluralism intrinsic to creativity; as a result of this solution Clarke perceives a way of solving the problem of the non-normative character of creativity which directly affects the ontological character of affinity between God and World. Clarke argues that if at the satisfaction of an actual occasion creative energy is transmitted over to or erupts into a new occasion (his phrase is "evokes a new occasion"), then a causal explanation is available for explaining why there are new occasions at all, rather than a total cessation of activity. New occasions do not simply appear out of nowhere, thus violating the principle *ex nihilo nihil fit*, or for that matter, Whitehead's own ontological principle, but rather new occasions appear because the creative energy contained in an actual occasion, upon its satisfaction, transmits over into a new occasion.

Because this font of energy is finite, it cannot of itself account for its own being. Clarke argues, therefore, that the font of energy exists because it has been created by God *ex nihilo*.[10] In Clarke's theory, God creates the primordial font of energy which then becomes the explanatory cause or principle of the emergence of new occasions. One can easily recognize then that multiple actualities have at least a fundamental unity in their causal dependence upon the energy of creativity. They are all instances of creative energy. This energy in turn is not without explanation or reason. It, too, being finite, has its reasons in a primal cause, God the creator. Multiplicity in such a view is thus reduced to unity by way of material and efficient causalities.

This theory also helps us solve the problem of intelligibility and affinity discussed earlier. A theory of *creatio ex nihilo* unifies all disparate realities through a form of closure, that is, through a form of ontological dependence. From event to God, the line of causality is always from the complex to the unified insofar as each stage of dependence or causal reduction entails the move from multiplicity to unity. Each event is an instance of creativity (creativity being the primordial energy) insofar as each event not only is evoked from this primordial energy but also articulates and determines this energy as well. Nevertheless, each event, though formally determining creativity, is materially one insofar as each event is creativity in this or that way. Furthermore, creativity itself, though radically indeterminate *in se*, is other than but dependent upon God. Even *qua* indeterminate energy, creativity is not totally other than God, totally independent. Creativity's being is dependent upon God as creator and conserver. Therefore, the energy of creativity is one with God as any effect is one with its cause.

The affinity between God and the World, so crucial for the intelligibility of finite creativity, is equally established in the *creatio ex nihilo* doctrine. The affinity exhibited here is the relationship of ontological dependence of the World upon God its creator and conserver. The affinity, in other words, is the relationship of ontological dependence. The intelligibility of creativity, dependent as it is upon the God-World dialectic, is ultimately grounded in creativity's primordial dependence upon God the Creator. In the Creator-created relationship there lies the ultimate ground for the being and intelligibility of the affinity exhibited between the World and God in creativity.

Neville's solution is more radical than Clarke's and more in keeping with the dialectical character of process philosophy. As we saw above, Neville contends that for creativity to be inherently intelligible it must be grounded in an act which is not itself an instance of creativity. It must be a primordial act in and by which the dialectical relationship of one and many, crucial to creativity, is established. Neville locates this act in the eternal act of creation.

One and many come to be in dialectical contrast by the act of creation. Neville writes:

> This kind of creativity does not presuppose an ontological unity because it is not a reduction of a multiplicity to unity through a novel entity, nor a production of a multiplicity out of a unity. It is the creation of both unity and multiplicity *ex nihilo*, the creation of determinateness as such.[11]

Neville dubs this form of creativity *ontological creativity* in contrast to the cosmological creativity evidenced in the empirical happenings in the world. The ontological unity required by and for the intelligibility of finite or cosmological unity is founded on ontological creativity. One, many and creativity are normatively together in a primal unity through the act of creation in which one, many and creativity are created *ex nihilo*.[12]

The problem in this explanation is that since "ontological creativity is productive of all determinate plurality, including its own character, it cannot proceed according to any pre-established principles. In this sense, then, there is no explanation of why this world is created that has process in it rather than one without process."[13] Yet, one is not dealing with a total irrationality since there is available the explanation of how such a world is possible, i.e., that such a world of process is created *ex nihilo* by God who in creating the world makes Himself creator in the act of creating a world other than Himself.

To summarize Neville's position, God is the necessary and thus normative ground for the ontological principle. In the act of creation God constitutes (creates) Himself both as One and as Creator and thus One in contrast to Many. Neville seems to share Paul Weiss' view that reality requires that entities be determinate and that determinateness requires in turn a state of being in contrast with another. For God to be determinate, therefore, He must be constituted in a state of contrast with that which is other than Himself, the World. In the eternal act of creation God constitutes Himself determinate because in His eternal act of producing another *ex nihilo*, He also produces *ex nihilo* the dialectical contrast of author-product, one-many. He creates Himself as Creator by creating *ex nihilo* that which is other than Himself, the World.

One must recall, however, that Neville is not advancing a thesis here in which God must be viewed as necessitated to create *this* or *that* particular world. He is free to create any world He pleases, though by the logic of determinateness, there must be something other than Himself. In terms of *this* or *that* specific world, there is no reason evidenced *why* God created as He did. Empirically, what we discover is that *in fact* God created a world exhibiting process or substance characteristics. What can be necessarily known, however, is that given an empirically contingent world, the requirements of intelligibility entail that this world be created *ex nihilo*, that cosmological unity necessarily requires ontological unity. A principle of sufficient reason is thus given without sacrificing divine freedom.[14]

C. *Creatio ex Nihilo and Divine Relativity*

From the perspective of process philosophers, a theory of ultimate causal unity runs the risk of jeopardizing the key insight of process philosophy, namely, that all events are creative unifications of past data forging a novel, determinate actuality out of what was merely a future potentiality. This key insight rests upon the prior insight that the future is the continuum of potentiality and not the locus of actuality. Therefore, any ontology brought to shore up process cosmology, must enhance the ontological status of the continuum of possibility.

In my judgment, Clarke and Neville are quite concerned with developing a consistent ontology of the future which is compatible with process philosophy. Both have developed theories of divine relativity to allow for the radical indeterminacy of the future. Clarke's position, however, appears to me to be more important to our discussion because it contains a radical revision of the Thomistic doctrine of divine absoluteness and thus forms a crucial bridge between process and Thomistic philosophies. Therefore, I will examine Clarke's revised notion of divine absoluteness at this time.

To fuse together a theory of divine transcendence (the kind of transcendence necessary for a theory of *creatio ex nihilo*) and process cosmology, Clarke revises the classical concept of infinity along personalist lines. He does this to a) shore up (what he considers) the "undeveloped" theory of the Primordial Nature thus facilitating its role in an ontology of creation and b) develop a Thomistically acceptable notion of divine relativity needed to secure a genuine theory of creativity. If Clarke's attempts at revision should prove fruitful, he will have developed a workable concept of divine relativity coupled with an adequate ontology of derivation (participation) and thus an ontology suitable for grounding a genuine process cosmology.

Clarke's revision of the classical doctrine of infinity (and thus his revision of the classical doctrine of divine absoluteness) begins along traditional lines but then radicalizes itself through a personalist interpretation of perfection. God is said to be infinite *in se*. God is infinite in the inner qualitative intensity of His being.[15] God's infinity is the unlimited, unqualified excellence of his primordial being, His pure actuality. To avoid a static or "block" view of divine infinite perfection, Clarke interprets perfection along personalist lines. The divine infinite perfection, the divine excellence, is to be understood as the unlimited capacity for *personal* relationships, i.e., personal love and concern.[16] This personalist interpretation of infinite perfection allows Clarke to move from the concept of divine infinity to the concept of divine relativity because the barrier has been removed from fusing infinite perfection (transcendence) and real relationships (immanence).

Clarke writes that:

> our metaphysics of God must certainly allow us to say that in some real and genuine way God is affected positively by what we do, that He receives love from us and experiences joy *precisely because* of our responses; in a word, that His consciousness is contingently and qualitatively *different* because of what we do.[17]

From this text we can see that Clarke has expanded the Thomistic concept of God to include *real internal relationships* with creatures insofar as the divine consciousness is positively affected by "what we do." However, he warns us that he does not intend to imply that God is passive to creatures as an effect is passive to its cause.[18] Rather, being *infinitely* perfect, God is in no *need* of creation and therefore cannot be affected positively or negatively by what transpires in the world. The infinite intensity of His being precludes the possibility of "increase or decrease in the Infinite Plenitude of God's intrinsic inner being and perfection..."[19]

If this is true, how do we reconcile the two statements that God's consciousness is "contingently and qualitatively different because of what we do" and that the infinite intensity of His being precludes the possibility of "increase or decrease in the Infinite Plenitude..."?

Clarke's response is that creatures make a difference to God insofar as they possess specific determinations and thus "specify" or determine the modalities of God's experience of His infinite power. Clarke writes:

> It is that God is constantly working in and through us with His supportive and collaborative power, supporting both the being and action of every creature. But He allows this power to be determinately channeled by the respective natures, especially the free-will decisions of creatures. Thus God knows what we are *doing by how we allow His power, in itself indeterminate to flow through us; by how we determinately channel this flow of power,* according to our own free initiatives. Thus *He knows* not by being

acted *on, but through his own action in us*. He knows what we are doing by doing with us whatever we are doing, except that it is we who supply the determinations to specify in-itself-transcendent (and thus indeterminate) fullness of His power (italics added).[20]

From this text we can see that God's infinity, though utterly rich in inner intensity, is in and of itself indeterminate. The determination experienced in the divine infinity derives from the determination creaturely activities exercise upon the divine power insofar as these finite activities channel the flow of divine collaborative causality. Nevertheless, it must also be kept in mind that God's infinite richness is eternal. This means that though in itself indeterminate, God does not move from indeterminacy to determinacy through time. God's act of creation is eternal and thus the richness of His relationships to His creatures is equally eternal. There is no increase or decrease in God because God's creative act is eternal, totally outside of time and change. Therefore in God's eternal creative act all actions are present as determinate modalities of God's "supportive and collaborative power." God is related to His creatures *actively* through His power; the creatures supply only the determinations of this power; that is, they supply only the determinations of *how* this power is concretized. Clarke clarifies what he means in this text:

> I still insist..., that all such "novelty" and "enrichment" in God (new joy and so forth), authentically new as they are, can only be new *determinate* modalities of expression of the already infinite intensity of the actual interior joy in God, and hence can never rise higher in qualitative intensity of perfection than the already infinite Source of which all finite modalities are only limited participations.[21]

In the light of these three texts we can piece together the move Clarke has made. He has conceded to process philosophers the all important point that God must be conceived as really related to the world. On the other hand, Clarke understands this relativity in terms of the divine infinity. God is relative to the world insofar as His infinite and indeterminate power is channeled and determined by creatures. Since God's act is eternal, the various determinations of the divine expression which creatures contribute are also eternal. God, therefore, does not increase or decrease in His infinite intensity of being.

In this theory Clarke appears to have it both ways. He is able to retain a classical concept of God as creator of the world *ex nihilo*, and at the same time he is able to advance a theory of divine relativity which supports a theory of genuine creativity and simultaneously avoids conflicting with the doctrine of divine infinite perfection, pure act.

Returning to the original problem of *creatio ex nihilo* and the indeterminacy of the future, Clarke appears to have found a way to reconcile aboriginal unity and genuine creativity. The theory of divine relativity holds the key to this reconciliation. The fact that the divine power is intrinsically indeterminate and thus capable of being channeled by creaturely activity allows for a strong distinction between potentiality and actuality in temporal processes. If God's power were totally determinate, then all activity would be eternalized in the divine activity. No true sense of emergence would be possible. If the divine power is indeterminate, as Clarke suggests, then the future could be understood as the indeterminate divine power in regard to possible determinations. Time would be real because the future would truly be the realm of the determinable, not merely the determinate "hidden from creaturely view." In terms of eternity, however, God would not be before or after these determinations but co-terminous with them. Thus, while time would be real in that the indeterminate would become determinate for creatures, for God in Himself no increase or decrease would be suffered since He is already and eternally His own fullness of being and perfection.

In this view, one would have a theory of ontological unity (unity of source) fused with a theory of creativity in which creativity is seen to be a derivative effect of the primordial unity. Clarke therefore seems to have both an explanation for the fact of creativity (*creatio ex-nihilo*) and an explanation for the affinity exhibited between the World and God (theory of participation). The question we must now ask is, Does the theory work?

D. The Logic of Eternity and Divine Relativity

It is my contention that Clarke's theory does not work because the doctrine of eternity, so crucial to his ontology of unity, precludes necessarily the possibility that finite values can have causal impact on the divine being and thus precludes the possibility for a real notion of divine relativity.

Clarke, of course, is extremely sensitive to such a counterclaim. His revision of the traditional concept of infinity along personalist lines was intended to offset such a claim and enhance a theory of creativity. The pivotal notion in this discussion, however, turns out to be, not infinity, but eternity. In Clarke's theory, God creates the world (and thus constitutes Himself in relation to the world) in the non-durational moment of eternity. God's specific relationship to the events of the world flows from His intention that the world in coming-to-be exercises real, though limited causality. Thus, in creating the world, God also intended that there exist in the world secondary causes which in their being and causality "channel and determine" God's supportive and collaborative power.

Nevertheless, the question still comes to mind, despite the theory of secondary causes, whether a doctrine of eternity can be fruitfully wedded to a doctrine of genuine relativity without sacrificing the meaning of relativity. I don't believe it can. If we take "to determine" to mean the act of making a difference, the act of affecting another in some real way, then the two terms, "eternity" and "relativity", if taken to refer to *actual* states in God, become mutually exclusive. Clarke tells us that whatever meaning "channeling" and "determining" may have, these terms do not and cannot mean that God is different because of these creaturely exercises of power, as an effect is different because of its causes. Clarke is aware that the logic of eternity precludes any potentiality in the divine inner being and thus *a priori* precludes the possibility of God truly changing because of creaturely activity. If "eternity" and "relativity" are taken in strong senses, they must be exclusive of each other. Therefore, the meaning of relativity must be amended. Clarke makes this move when he clarifies the exact role that secondary causes play in "determining and channeling" the divine power. Clarke is certainly aware that his theory is paradoxical if one considers creaturely causality as an active or positive influence on the divine power. Such a position would have to argue that God is directly affected by secondary causes and thus must be subject to change. This, of course, would diminish any real meaning to pure actuality and eternity.

But what if one considers finite causality as "channeling and determining" the divine power through the *negative* role of *limiting*? In other words, what if creatures "channel and determine" God's power insofar as they *limit* the flow of that power? This seems to be the route Clarke wants to take. The unlimited, indeterminate power of God is limited in its exercise, not by its intrinsic quality or power, since this is absolute, but by the limited agencies through which it exercises itself as creator and collaborator of all finite being and activity. The divine power is thus "determined," not by what is *positive* (in being) but by what is *negative*. This is the only way God can be really related to the world without somehow being related as an effect to a cause. God's relationship to creatures is thus real because He is related to what is truly real, His power-as-limited by the secondary causal agencies. God, in other words, is really related to the world as that which limits His power. To use Plato's apt phrase, God is related to the world insofar as the world is "existent non-being." Now Clarke and process philosophers agree on this much at least: creativity is real. They also agree that creativity means qualitative increase in value. But increase in value requires in turn real relatedness on the part of any subject, God included, to that value. If this were not true, then this value would lack ontological status, would lack being, because it would lack the power to affect another. If we were to argue that such novel values have power to affect other finite subjects, but not God, then we would be faced with the problem of arguing that finite being, though valuable and affective in time, would be invaluable and impotent as far as the ultimate reality is concerned, God's own being in eternity. Time would diminish in value before eternity. To offset such a claim, it is necessary that even for God creative novelties must make positive differences to His inner life and being precisely insofar as they are new qualifications of reality, new unities. God must be affected by what each new unity *is* in itself, by the very *being* of its unity.

Clarke's theory of creation, even with his important revisions in the doctrines of infinity and divine absoluteness, fails to meet this requirement. In this theory, divine relativity (because it is wedded to his doctrine of God as pure and eternal act) can only refer to God's direct and positive relationship to Himself, His own being and power, even though the latter is understood to be active under the condition of creaturely limitations.

But as we have argued, creativity requires real relationships based upon real power (Whitehead's Principle of Relativity). A genuine ontology of creativity requires that God's relationship to novel entities be taken in the strongest possible sense. Clarke's theory takes God s relativity in the weakest possible sense. It is for this reason that Clarke's attempt fails. The ontology of being, culminating in the doctrine of pure and eternal act, precludes *a priori* the possibility of genuine creativity in which novel occasions leading to novel unities add qualitatively to the wealth of reality. For God, no such increase is possible. For Him, these occasions make no internal difference and thus have no value, have no being (Plato).

II. Creativity and Dialectical Unity

Does our conclusion that a doctrine of creation is inimical to an ontology of creativity lead to the further conclusion that no form of unity is possible for and in process philosophy? Does our conclusion mean that no theory of participation or derivation is possible for process philosophy and that, as Clarke complains, process philosophy is radically pluralistic and thus seriously jeopardized by all that such radical pluralism entails? My answer to these questions is simply "no". Some form of unity is possible and necessary for process ontology. Furthermore, a theory of derivation can be and, in fact, already has been developed from process principles, a theory which depends upon a process theory of unity and thus a theory which is compatible with the whole architectonic of process philosophy.

At this time, I would like to develop this theory of unity and derivation. I will be dependent upon Lewis S. Ford's recently developed theory of God as the future of all actual occasions. After presenting Ford's views, I will incorporate my own views on the unity of dialectic as grounded in God's necessary existence. Hopefully, I will be able to propose a theory of dialectical unity in which

God's necessary existence is the ultimate reason for the unity of the creative process, what Neville called the normativeness of creativity, and what Clarke called the Affinity between God and World.

A. God as the Future of All Actual Occasions

Lewis Ford has become convinced over the past few years that the complaints of some Thomistic philosophers, especially Norris Clarke, are valid and must be addressed. He has accepted Clarke's criticism (flowing from Aquinas' claim that only unity can account for sameness, not multiplicity [De Potentia, 5,3] that some form of participation is necessary if multiplicity and difference are to be intelligible. Ford is also sensitive to Clarke's claim that without such a theory, Whitehead's own theory of creativity may well be in violation of his ontological principle.[22] Ford is also aware that whatever form of unity is developed, it must be a form of unity in which multiplicity is derived from a causality other than efficient causality. Efficient causality is understood in diametrically opposite ways by Process and Thomistic philosophers. For the Thomists, efficient causality is active in producing passive results. In Whiteheadian philosophy, "each occasion is the present active reception of objective causal factors. Instead of being produced by its causes, each occasion produces itself out of its causes." Receptivity is active, not passive.[23] To argue that creativity is produced by efficient causes would amount to arguing that creativity, which is the source of prehensive activity, is itself the result of the activity of which it is the source.[24]

Ford is quite aware that since efficient causality cannot be the principle of unity, whatever form of unity that remains must be in the future of each occasion, since it cannot be in the present or past. The causality exercised by God must be final, not efficient causality. Ford's revision of Whitehead's concept of God comes in at this point. Ford seeks to envision God as the principle of unity within a coherent theory of creativity. In one of the few published accounts of this theory, Ford writes:

How can God, as future, exert any power? No satisfactory answer is forthcoming, I submit, as long as causation is understood in terms of the cause producing its effect. But if causation is in terms of the event actively producing itself out of passive, objective causes, these causal factors could include future possibilities functioning as lures just as well as past facts functioning as conditioning determinants. God is then the power of the future operative in our present as the source of those possibilities that address us for good or for ill, in terms of which we must decide and act.[25]

What this seems to be suggesting is that it is wiser to conceive God and his activity as futural, rather than as past or present. God is, in one of Ford's expressions, the "activity of the future." As the activity of the future, God provides the future required for the prehensive activity of each occasion, the continuum of possibility without which prehension would lack its mental/conceptual and creative pole.

God's activity insofar as it is future consists in the production of "infinite possibility." God contemplates the entire wealth of conceptual forms and, out of this contemplation, unifies "his experience of past actualities into real possibilities..."

There are two foci to this process of possibilization within God. On the one hand, there is the use of timeless forms to unify all his diverse spatio-temporal experiences of the world into one final experience, quite inaccessible to us; on the other hand, there is the diversification of possibility into those which are immediately relevant to us, in terms of which we achieve concrete determinations. Yet throughout, God remains the unity of the whole; it is finally the creatures which pluralize the domain of possibilities into many actualities.[26]

In another place, the most recent elaboration on this theme by Ford, he tells us that God acts as future insofar as he creates the "conditions of the present." As each occasion concresces, becomes, God prehends it from every future standpoint, thereby unifying all these physical prehensions in "every way that they can be unified." Nevertheless, God does not effect "the final determinate unity of that particular multiplicity." Such determinateness, as the earlier papers acknowledged, belongs to the "arbitrary, finite decision of particular actualities, deciding *this* rather than *that*. Only the finite can ultimately produce the determinate."[27]

To summarize, God as future means that God's unificatory activity, God's own concrescence, forms the continuum of possibility which in turn constitutes the future of each actual occasion. More strongly put, God's unificatory activity *is* the future of each occasion because he is the unity of possibility, the lure of feeling, which draws the many into ever greater unity, ever greater complexity, through the attractiveness of the possible good. The divine unificatory activity is thus the source of finite creativity because it is the future or conceptual pole of each actual occasion.

In the same recent article, Ford elaborates:

> In this transference [of divine creativity to finite creativity] God is not objectified for the present creature, as something to be prehended. Instead he grants the power of prehending, for it is from God that the occasion receives its prehending of the past and its future, i.e., the specific ways in which that given past may be unified, and the creative activity of unification. The occasion is a brief present space in which past and future are reconciled.[28]

Despite the fact that finite creativity is derived from infinite creativity, finite subjectivity from infinite subjectivity, it does not follow that finite subjectivity lacks ontological autonomy from the divine subjectivity. In order for finite subjectivity to lose its autonomy, it would be necessary that God would have to be the full determinant cause of what takes place, the final determinate unity. Ford is clear, as the texts above show, that the divine subjectivity accounts for only possibility, what might be, not for what becomes or determinately is. The actual occasion determines its own actuality as it "pluralizes the domain of possibilities into many actualities." God is thus neither the determinate actualities themselves nor their total cause. He is simply the unity of possibility which provides the aim, the finality, that lures the occasion into creative self-completion. It is the subjectivity of the actual occasion which accounts for the determinate unity achieved, even though the occasion's subjectivity is derived from God. An important distinction is thus maintained between the occasion's actuality (unity) and God's actualizing process. This distinction between actuality and possibility provides, finally, the ontological safeguard for the autonomy of the creature.

In my judgment, Ford's theory partially meets the primary objections raised by Clarke and Neville. Ford has developed a theory of unity which is consistent with process principles, yet one which is capable of at least partially providing an adequate ontological foundation for a theory of participation (derivation), and for the normativeness exhibited in and by finite creativity. But, it must be noted, because God in His unificatory activity is not the absolute creator of the world *ex nihilo*, but rather is in fact dependent upon the world for his own self-actualization, a more radical form of unity is required than simply the unificatory process of divine concrescence. A form of dialectical unity is needed, one which is grounded in the necessity of divine existence. We will address this issue at this time.

B. *Dialectical Unity and God's Necessary Existence*

From our discussion so far, it is evident that if one is to develop a theory of unity, one must do so within the principles of process philosophy. To do otherwise, as Clarke and Neville have attempted to do, is to run the risk of losing what one has set out to save, a genuine theory of creativity. Therefore, a theory of unity has to be developed which embraces the dialectical character of creativity and at the same time contains a principle of necessity. It is this principle of necessity which will ground the normative character of creativity and the affinity between God and the World. It is this principle which will provide the ontological unity requisite for an intelligent and coherent theory of creativity.

Ford's thesis that creativity (finite) is ultimately derived from God's unificatory activity implies, as stated above, the continual and necessary existence of a world containing finite centers of creative activity, the world extending infinitely into the past and into the future. The divine concrescence therefore requires the multiplicities of the world as its material principle. Furthermore, the divine concrescence requires that this multiplicity be emergent, not static ("the many become one and increase by one") because if it were not emergent, God's experience of the world would become static, monotonous and, by definition, non-creative. As I hope to argue, though, this is *a priori* impossible. God's existence, being necessary, necessitates as well His creativity. The divine creativity requires by its own dialectical nature the existence of other centers of creativity. Therefore, the divine necessity requires the existence of other creativities by the logic of its own necessity. It is because of the divine necessity that finite creativity, derived from God's activity, is *a priori* necessary and thus ontologically normative.

Charles Hartshorne may well have given us the most important ingredient in our discussions in his analysis and defense of the Ontological Argument.[29] Without attempting to go into a complete treatment of Hartshorne's defense of the Ontological Argument, I feel it will be adequate for our discussion to simply state that Hartshorne has given us this much at least, a convincing proof that God's existence cannot be conceived as merely possible; it must be conceived as either necessary or impossible. God's definition, that than which nothing greater can be conceived, precludes *a priori* mere possibility as a modal qualifier for the divine existence. Only "necessity" or "impossibility" can be proper modal qualifications. If God's existence is not necessary, it is *a priori* impossible.[30]

Hartshorne is also clear in telling us that while the divine existence must be understood as necessary, the divine states must be understood as contingent. God's necessity, in other words, entails only that God have actual states and that God be maximally related to all the events of the world. But, the divine necessity does not specify how and in what way God will be directly related to the world. The world itself specifies this through its own concreteness. The divine necessity simply entails that God must exist as maximally relative to all that is and transpires.[31]

But as we stated above, God's self-actualization, God's unificatory activity, requires that there be a world of self-actualizing events. Though the divine necessity does not specify what these events must be in their concreteness, it does specify that there must be creative events in the universe. God's own necessity therefore entails the existence of other centers of creative activity, though these centers account for their own unity and being, their own determinateness.

If we translate this into Ford's language, we can see the connection between the divine unificatory activity and the divine necessity. God's necessity *in concreto* is the impossibility of there being a moment in which God's unificatory activity could cease. God's existential necessity, therefore, is the reason why God's unificatory activity is not only constitutive of the future of all actual occasions, but the *a priori* reason why occasions exist at all. Finite creativity must occur because the divine unificatory process can *never* cease. The dialectical character of the divine unificatory process, grounded as it is in the divine existential necessity, means in the end that its dialectical counterpart, finite creativity, must exist and exhibit the ontological characteristics described in the Category of the Ultimate.

God as the future of all actual occasions is thus God in a specific aspect of the whole dialectical process. The ultimate unity grounding this dialectic is the necessity of the divine existence. In this necessity, God's unificatory process is the normative ground for all finite creativity.

Clarke and Neville objected that a surd existed at the heart of Whiteheadian ontology because the Category of the Ultimate, which was intended to ground the ontological principle, was itself without a reason found in an actuality. It thus violated, in their view, the very principle it was intended to uphold. From what we have seen, however, Lewis Ford's revision of Whitehead's concept of God (coupled with Hartshorne's doctrine of divine necessity) meets these objections. Creativity is not simply there, an amorphous force totally underived, a multiplicity underived from a primal unity. Rather, creativity is the metaphysical structure of God's own existence. This structure, being both *a priori* necessary and dialectical in structure, not only provides the unity requisite for derivation but also provides the reason for the necessity of finite creativity. The Category of the Ultimate is normative, therefore, because the dialectical relationship of one and many contained therein is grounded in and required by the normative character of divine existence.

Though this argument leads to the conclusion that the ultimate unity in the universe is dialectical unity, it does not lead to the conclusion that God is nothing more than one ingredient among many in the composition of the universe. God's transcendence is upheld in this theory because God's existence alone is necessary. All other existences in the universe are contingent and limited. Furthermore, all finite existences, finite creativities, derive their creativity from God as their futures. Thus, while the unity of the universe is dialectical, its ultimate ground is the divine necessity. God's own necessity is the final reason for creativity, the final reason for the normativeness exhibited between one and many, that the "many must become one and increase by one."

Summary and Conclusion

Norris Clarke and Robert Neville saw the need for a form of unity in process philosophy if it were to become internally coherent. Both attempted to locate this form of unity in God the Creator, who created the world *ex-nihilo*. Their attempts, as I have argued throughout this paper, failed because the ontology of being which they espoused led in the end to the negation of time and creativity.

It seems to me that any attempt made to revise Whiteheadian ontology along classical lines is doomed to failure. The ontology of being, because it must lead to an ontology of pure act, must in turn lead to a doctrine of creation which is wedded to a doctrine of eternity. The logic of eternity, in my judgment and as I have tried to argue, precludes the possibility of genuine creativity because it devalues the ontological status of time and novelty. In the end, creativity makes no "real" difference to a being totally complete, a being Who is pure actuality. Only an ontology of becoming, an ontology in which time and creativity are central, an ontology in which the potentiality for new appreciations of value is the hallmark of activity, can consistently meet the demands of Whiteheadian, or for that matter, any process philosophy. In my judgment, Ford's revised theory of God, if coupled with Hartshorne's metaphysics of necessity meets these demands. In my judgment, in Ford's theory (as so qualified) one has the metaphysical foundations for process cosmology, the ultimate ground for the normative character of creativity, the ultimate ground for the unity of the world, the affinity between World and God.

Before bringing this paper to a close, I feel it is important to at least mention some of the problem areas Christian philosophers and theologians must face if they are going to take seriously the implications of process theism. Norris Clarke has already pointed to at least one of them. Process theism demands, as our discussion has shown, the rejection of a *creatio ex nihilo* account as traditionally defined. Clarke has told us, and is correct, that this will place process theism in direct conflict with the main tradition of Christian thought. For the Catholic, the problem is even more severe. This position will force a head-on collision with defined Catholic doctrine dating back to the last decades of the Second Century.[32]

The doctrines of omnipotence, omniscience and divine sovereignty will also be in jeopardy, at least as traditionally formulated. In line with these difficulties, the Christian doctrines of grace, predestination, divine providence, will also be in for some serious difficulties.

Finally, the central doctrine of the Incarnation will be in trouble if one chooses to follow process ontology. The reason for the difficulty here is the process notion of person. In Christian theology, the Blessed Trinity is one being with three Persons. In process philosophy one cannot distinguish between person and actuality. Process theism runs the risk of tri-theism rather than Trinitarianism. Obviously, the theology of the Incarnation suffers under such a system.

I mention these things because for the Christian philosopher these issues are extremely important if he is to philosophize in and as part of the great Christian tradition. I mention these things, too, because I deeply believe that aside from and beyond the problems of internal consistency and rational coherence, the future of process philosophy will depend upon its ability to function within the great Tradition. If process philosophers and theologians are unable to retain and enhance the formal elements in the Christian Creeds, it is my opinion that process philosophy will slip off onto the wayside of Western thought. To put it in a word, I believe process philosophy, if it fails to become an ingredient within the Christian tradition, will become a mere footnote in the history of the West. At this point in time, I am very unsure how things will turn out. Fortunately, the discussions have just begun. Fortunately, too, there is an atmosphere of honest discussion and debate, not political rancor, permeating the scene. I feel confident that if these discussions continue in this vein, Christian philosophy will be blessed by all that transpires.

FOOTNOTES

1 Norris Clarke, *The Philosophical Approach to God* (Winston-Salem, N.C.: Wake Forest Univ. Press, 1979). Robert Neville, *Creativity and God* (New York: Seabury, 1980).

2 Clarke, p. 72.

3 *Ibid.*, p. 73.

4 *Ibid.*, p. 72.

5 *Ibid.*

6 Neville, pp. 39-40.

7 *Ibid.*, p. 41.

8 *Ibid.*

9 *Ibid.*, p. 43.

10 Clarke, pp. 76-77.

11 Neville, pp. 44-45.

12 *Ibid.*, p. 45.

13 *Ibid.*

14 *Ibid.*

15 Clarke, p. 87.

16 *Ibid.*, p. 98.

17 *Ibid.*, p. 92.

18 *Ibid.*, p. 93.

19 *Ibid.*, p. 92.

20 *Ibid.*, pp. 96-97.

21 *Ibid.*, p. 98.

22 Lewis S. Ford, "The Search for the Source of Creativity," *Logos* 1/80, pp. 47-48.

23 *Ibid.*, p. 48.

24 *Ibid.*

25 Ford, "God as the Subjectivity of the Future," *Encounter* 41/3 (Summer 1980), p. 289.

26 *Ibid.*, p. 291.

27 Lewis S. Ford has kindly allowed me to see in manuscript form his paper on "The Divine Activity of the Future." This article will be forthcoming in *Process*

243

Studies. Here the page references are to the article in manuscript form, p. 6.

28 *Ibid.*, p. 7.

29 Charles Hartshorne, *The Logic of Perfection* (LaSalle, Ill.: Open Court, 1962), *Anselm's Discovery* (LaSalle, Ill.: Open Court, 1965), *Creative Synthesis and Philosophic Method* (LaSalle, Ill.: Open Court, 1971).

30 Hartshorne, *The Logic of Perfection*, p. 57, *Anselm's Discovery*, p. 3, *Creative Synthesis and Philosophic Method*, pp. 100-101.

31 Cf. Theodore Vitali, "The Ontological Argument: Model for Neoclassical Metaphysics," *Modern Schoolman*, Vol. LVII, no. 2 (January 1980), pp. 130ff.

32 Clarke, pp. 70-72.

God: A Contemporary
Indian Discussion

Kapil Tiwari

One of the striking features of the last few decades has been a reawakening of interest in God and spirituality. Contemporary Indian religious thinkers are as preoccupied with the issue as are thinkers in the contemporary West. Their analysis and description of the problem have developed along different lines. Too often, an overgeneralization is made regarding the issue. Many scholars insist that contemporary Indian thinkers persist in speaking about the above concepts in more or less Christian terms. In my opinion the concepts, at base, are alien to Christianity as usually interpreted. It is true that Truth or Reality and the concept of spirituality based on the realization of Truth are universally the same, but it is also true that it manifests itself differently to the mediums and cultures into which it is embedded. Distinctive cultures involve distinctive outlooks and perspectives, and each of the world's religions may be understood in this way. I try in this article to shed some light on how thinkers like Swami Vivekananda, Rabindranath Tagore and Mahatma Gandhi have grappled with the issue and to what extent they can be helpful in further understanding of the concept in the contemporary discussion. I make no claim that this essay will solve many enigmas of the contemporary discussion on God; perhaps it may impel further re-evaluations of the Eastern sphere of spirituality as represented by the above thinkers. It should be noted that these thinkers are not academic philosophers but spiritual leaders, mystics and poets. Often this makes it difficult to understand precisely the general trends of their thought. It is not the intention of the paper to polarize many issues which these thinkers speak to. Rather an attempt is made to collect their insights into basic themes in the hope that issues involved will become clearer. For this reason, much descriptive detail is omitted. It is only hoped that little of what is basic is left out. Lastly, my intention, in the face of their inner realization of the Truth, is to let it stand, thus avoiding unnecessary defilement by rational argumentation particularly when the thinkers intend silence. In this respect, much of what I say is at best 'noisy'. Regretfully such 'noise' seems necessary when one has to talk about anything.

As a beginning I want to suggest that the Indian approach to God and spirituality differs from the way in which thinkers in the West approach these topics. These differences reflect certain basic assumptions of the Indian mind which are either absent or less dominant in Western religion and culture. For example, God is not the starting point of Indian religions. 'Spirituality' is the central thrust of Indian religious life. Spirituality is altogether a different concept in different philosophies and religions of India. Whatever may be the differences between various systems, they are all concerned with a 'meditative' approach to spirituality.[1] The meditative approach is uniquely Indian, and it is the same for contemporary Indian thinkers as it is for the Vedic and Upanishadic sages. In this respect, the contemporary Indian approach is more traditional and less modern, more interpretive and less creative, more authoritative and less rational. The broad assumption of this method is very simple; it leads toward inwardness which is the realm of innocence, peace and tranquillity. The secret of spirituality consists in becoming aware of the true nature of Truth in contradistinction to mere outwardness or externality which is perceived as a causal link that does not affect the tranquil structure of Truth.

The Truth in itself is inexpressible; it is an eternal mode of existence and can be experienced by all who are enlightened to find it. The realization takes place here and now and must transform the nature of man to such an extent that it is his new birth. The contemporary Indian thinkers do not look at Truth only in terms of God; it matters little for them whether one calls this Truth, God or deity, personal or impersonal, qualified or unqualified, masculine, feminine or neuter. Whatever He, She or It may be, one must find the Truth in oneself. This approach is based on the implied traditional belief that Truth is a many-dimensional Reality and can be viewed from many perspectives, each of which is valid for the seeker who is equipped with the right framework of mind. The problem of the two Absolutes—the religious and the philosophical (*Deus* and *esse*) and the relationship between the two—has not vexed contemporary Indian thought; the different answers given to these questions are many and the contemporary Indian thinkers are not interested in such questions at all. The western religious consciousness in the debates over these questions has resulted in an ever-increasing loss of religious consciousness and in this respect the thinkers under discussion exhibit a tendency of thought which is different from that in the West. The first principle which we have called the Truth has been accepted in the simple statement 'the Truth is'. The way it has been interpreted is slightly different according to the various thinkers, but they have not made a great issue of it. The acceptance of the Truth has led some thinkers to connect it with God, but the character of this connection is not philosophically coherent and in my opinion it is deliberately vague. It is not as much an issue as we find it to be in philosophy of religion in the West.

Arnold Toynbee tells us of criticizing his mother for omitting a foreground detail in the landscape she was drawing. She replied that in sketching the first principle is deciding what to leave out. This is also the first principle to be learned in speaking of Truth, the contemporary Indian thinkers would insist.[2] Since all these thinkers are greatly influenced by Vedanta, the first principle, that is Brahman, has been accepted as 'It is'. Our minds cannot grasp the nature of the Truth as it is not a product of intellectualism; it is not a rational concept or a phenomenon out of several phenomena. The problem is not that our minds are not sharp enough; the issue lies deeper. To put it simply, the Truth which is ground of everything is transcendent to thought, and it cannot be grasped in terms of the empirical. The logical faculty of thought breaks up the immediacy of Truth into differences of subject and object and relation between the two and distorts the nature of Truth as a necessary precondition of all existence. As a necessary condition of all existence, it is called *advitiyam* (without a second) and *amrtam* (immortal). Every knowledge serves to reveal, though partially, the immediacy of Truth but by no means can represent it. The whole complex of knowledge is based on the delusive structure of *Vrtti-jñān* (reason) which because of its inherent procedure understands the unconditioned as conditioned and equates the empirical with the ontological. All these contemporary thinkers reject the confusion between the two and in doing so, they do not reject or displace anything except a misconception about the Truth.[3] In this sense, all of them are absolutists. Any attempt to establish Truth, for all of them in one way or the other, implies God. Philosophy and religion mingle. If Truth is a philosophical inquiry and God a religious inquiry and Truth pre-supposes God, the connection is automatically established. It does not make any difference whether one calls this position absolutistic or theistic. Theism, according to these current thinkers, though it might appear pluralistic, is actually governed by the spirit of abso-lutism owing to its total and complete emphasis on God. The implication of this standpoint is two-fold: first, it reaffirms the positive idea of life against nihilism or scepticism and, second, it purifies religious experience from the dogmatism which has domi-nated western philosophy and theology.

Many critical thinkers might raise objections to the above position. The philosophical Absolute, according to them, is differ-ent from the Absolute of theism, but a case may be presented to indicate that the two are really not different. The bracketing of the Truth with God gives the Reality the status of being both omnipo-tent and omniscient. The omnipotence of the Reality would not be possible if there were not an underlying unity behind phenomena, and its omniscience cannot be intelligible if it is not spiritual and the illuminator of everything. The Upanishads have clearly affirmed that the Reality is both omnipotent and omniscient (*Yasya bhāṣā Sarvamidam vibhāti*). The approach of the contemporary Indian thinkers is to show how the meditative technique can unite philoso-phy with the religious quest for Reality. Mahatma Gandhi, for example, makes this reconciliation possible in his doctrine of *Satyā-graha* (Insistence on Truth). The word Truth has a philosophical base whereas insistence stands for commitment with all its religious implications. Mahatma Gandhi has put 'love' into his philosophy by making Truth accessible by love. Truth for him is not only God but also Love. He offers no argument to convince us of Truth as God and Love through reason, as faith transcends reason. Swami Vivekananda in a similar way reconciles the Truth with Reality (*Sat*), Consciousness (*Chit*) and love (*ānanda*). Rabindranath Tagore does not make any distinction between philosophy and religion. Philosophy is the 'vision of the Real' and the aim of religion is to unite man with the Real through Love. In love alone the sense of difference is obliterated, and Reality manifests itself in total unity. The meaning of this is that in whomsoever we love we find our own soul in the highest sense because in them we have grown longer, in them we have touched the great truth which comprehends the whole universe. Neither in the case of God nor in that of love, do the questions 'how', 'why', 'what for' exist.

The above interpretation looks strikingly similar to the essence of Christianity, but here again there is another fundamental difference. All these thinkers attach enormous significance to the complete suppression of the passions, to the cultivation of total *Vairāgya* (sacrifice and detachment). Owing to this spirit that runs through them all, the aim of spirituality for Indian thinkers may be characterized as transcending morality or conscience as they are commonly understood in Western thought. In other words, the goal of Indian spirituality lies as much beyond morality as it does beyond rational categories of thought. On account of this it is clear that contemporary Indian thinkers talk of spirituality in terms of tranquillity which does not have the slightest element of guilt or anguish. It is necessary that ethics with its rational base be understood only in the phenomenal sense and be barred completely from the sphere of spirituality. That is why all these thinkers have put the realm of spirituality above the doctrine of *Karma-Saṁsāra* (the cycle of birth and rebirth) which is a feature of phenomenal consciousness. The secret of love and wisdom consists in becoming aware of the true nature of *Karma-Saṁsāra* itself which is *nāma-rūpa* (name and form), and being causal and rational in nature has nothing to do with the Reality as it is. The concern of the seeker is to rise above passion and egocentric desires. Detachment (*vairāgya*) accomplishes this task, for without detachment there can be no realization of the tranquil sphere of spirituality. This particular philosophy has been expressed in the doctrine of desireless action (*niṣkāma karma*), systematically spelt out in the *Bhagavad-Gītā*:

> The *Yukta* (united one) attains to tranquillity, by relinquishing the fruits of action; but the *ayukta* (ununited one) is impelled by desire, and by being attached to fruits (of action) is bound. Action is said to be the means of the sage who wishes to attain to yoga (union); when he has achieved yoga serenity is said to be the means.

It is interesting to note that even Rabindranath Tagore, who was greatly influenced by Christianity and by poetic sentimentality, distinguishes love from attachment and brings into love the element of sacrifice of all personal considerations. Since the concept of 'individuality' is more or less absent in Indian spirituality as it is a mere 'mask' or name and form, the doctrine of love assumes a status which is neither rational nor pragmatic; it is constantly fed by *Gnosis*. This doctrine does not make a difference between oneself and one's neighbour. In fact, it becomes compassion (*Karuṇā*) which is different from the concept of love in Christianity. Tagore says "It (initial sacrifice, more or less under compassion) is like plucking fruit when it is unripe, you have to tear it and bruise the branch. But when a man loves, giving becomes a matter of joy to him like the tree's surrender of the ripe fruit".[4] In an essay entitled "The Religion of the Forest"[5] Tagore argues that we in the West have built much of our civilization guided by the assumption that there is dichotomy between man and the natural world, a dichotomy often construed in terms of hostility and antipathy. Man has the task of mastering and subduing the natural world and its creatures, harnessing them to his ends of promoting his own well-being and minimizing disease, poverty, and the upheavals in nature which frequently shatter his aspirations and happiness. While the West seeks to dominate nature, the East attempts to structure life in a way that expresses the unity of man and the world. In my opinion, this tendency of thought based on the kinship between man and the world of nature has a different orientation to love and is far from being rational or ethical (in the *ordinary* sense of the term). Tagore's maxim has a metaphysical foundation. To work for all is based on the recognition of the metaphysical unity of all and implies living in the infinite realm of infinite joy. Tagore calls it Realization in Action and Realization in Love and both of them, being essentially the same, lift man beyond his ego to the path towards the realization of the Infinite.

Tagore is much influenced by Vaisnavism. He calls Reality *advaitam* (non-dual) in which love plays a dominant role. But like a true Vaisnava Advaitin, Tagore maintains that Love is backed by *gnosis*. Love, therefore, leads the seeker to merging in the Absolute. By this process the *Jīva* becomes absolutely one with the supreme person. Religion, for Tagore, is the liberation of individuality in the universal person or the realization of 'I am' in the 'infinite I am'. This is the *mukti* which is a complete deliverance from the net of *māyā*, of appearance which springs from *avidyā*. Love accomplishes this task as it does not know any opposition. Intellect sets us apart from the things to be known, but love knows its object by fusion. Through the dynamics of love, our souls can become Brahman. In love all the contradictions of existence merge themselves and are lost. Only in love are unity and duality not at variance. Love must be one and two, at one and the same time. Only in love are motion and rest one. A heart is restless till it finds love, and there it has its rest. But this rest itself is an intense form of activity where utter quiescence and unceasing energy meet at the same point in love.

It might appear that Tagore places love above knowledge, but at a closer analysis love is not without knowledge. In fact, Tagore says that God can be known by joy, by love. For joy is knowledge in its completeness; it is knowing through the whole being. Such knowledge is immediate and admits of no doubt. Love is the perfection of consciousness. It is through the heightening of our consciousness into love, and extending it all over the world, that we can attain *Brahmavihāra*, communion with the infinite joy. Love, for Tagore, accomplishes the same goal as knowledge does. Both aim at identity by transcending the world of duality. Love, in this sense, is meditative and intuitive. It is neither rational nor ethical.

By calling Love non-rational and unethical, I am not suggesting that it is other-worldly as it is commonly understood in the western world. The highest wisdom, according to Tagore, does not throw away the world nor does it utilize the world for any special material purpose. It simply transforms the nature of the world by sanctifying the motive behind it. It implies that Love, so purified, raises the seeker above the perplexities and anxieties of life. The so-called morality or ethics, in the form in which we experience it is due to the lack of love in a total sense, resulting in the isolation of the experience from its basis, i.e., God. The task of love lies in installing the forgotten basis of the universe not by isolating the world from its basis or renouncing it but by the removal of the ignorance through the realization of unity through love. In fact, it is a reaction against any negative philosophy or religion. When the soteriological love removes ignorance, the latter is cancelled as such (*bādha*) by which Tagore implies that it is transformed—its 'bluff' is called, and pure love that underlies the Truth itself, illuminating it, emerges. The life of activism, thus derived, becomes the expression of the spiritual order which takes precedence over all petty considerations. There is no question of shifting the world from being something to being nothing as that shifting is impossible by any logic. What is to be shifted is the attitude towards the world and all the activities associated with it. This means that man is involved with the world even before the dawn of love and after its dawn, but the way he *was* involved or *is* involved is different. In the lack of love, his involvement reflected a sense of 'I-ness'. In the state of Love, his involvement is meaningless in the sense that his 'I-ness' is meaningless. The whole process is simultaneously attendant on the realization of Reality, thus making Love spontaneous and motiveless. At this stage, the individual as well as the world are sanctified; what was so far artificial becomes spontaneous. By disowning oneself, one owns the whole world. Tagore was here influenced by Buddhism, Christianity and the Vedanta.

Swami Vivekananda, like his teacher Ramkrishna Paramahamsa, does not make much difference between cosmic and acosmic Brahman. The most important point for us to note in understanding his view of Reality is its identification with spirituality. If the original Truth somehow assumes various states—determinate or indeterminate, creator or non-creator, there is nothing within the structure of the human mind which can comprehend it. It is within the freedom of the Reality itself. Truth is God's Truth and hence one Truth, although it may appear differently. Metaphysically speaking Reality is absolute Brahman, but the same reality viewed from the religious point of view is God. That is why he emphasizes the all-pervasive nature of the Truth which is present everywhere and in everything. Through his control the sky expands, through his control the air breathes, through his control the sun shines and through his control all live. He is the Reality in nature. He is the soul of your soul. He says that the Absolute is that ocean, while you and I, the sun and stars, and everything else are various waves of the ocean. And what makes the waves varied? Only the form and that form is time, space and causation, all entirely dependent on the wave! The differences in approaches to Reality in various religions arise on account of ignorance or our fragmentary way of apprehension. Real knowledge through meditation and encounter with the Truth cancels such differences.

In a sense, this interpretation seems in harmony with the Christian Gospel which confirms God as the highest Truth, but at a closer analysis it is not. The West conceives of knowledge in a manner which is ultimately personal. The illusion born of the personal form of language in which God is expressed does not exactly correspond to the form in which the Truth is expressed in contemporary Indian thought. In Hindu thought, language has to be impersonal; in western, it is ultimately personal. In sharp contrast to the cyclic view stands the western assumption of what language is and does.[6] While acknowledging the merit of the western approach, it appears to me that any attempt to translate the Truth as something different from itself in terms of language or concepts, keeps man away from a direct and essentially intuitive experience of the Truth. What we are left with is the concept or idea of Truth, whereas in the East arguments can be put forward for the adventitious things (*āgantuka*) and not for what is presupposed in all proofs and disproofs. Western philosophers, with a few exceptions, have largely mistaken the Truth for *prameya* (object of Truth) and tried to prove it, ignoring the fact that Truth is not an object. A long history of such thinking produced a series of shocks in the domain of the western religious consciousness and reduced God to the status of a mere intellectual belief, perhaps an 'hypothesis' but of no importance in the practical handling of our affairs. In Hindu thought, Truth cannot speak and there is none else to speak the ultimate Truth; so speech and concept are simply names and forms and belong to the phenomenal world. Brahman is Being (*Sat*), Consciousness (*Chit*) and bliss (*ānanda*) which are its own signs (*Svarūpalaksana*). These are called *own-signs* because they are not logical attributes and because they *are* the essence. In Western religious thought in which the linear phenomenology dominates, any assertion of Being presupposes the assertion of the phenomenal world which is dominated by some 'natural cause'. This belief that all events are due to natural causes, though it does not intend to prosecute God, at least theoretically, leads us in a different direction. I am not suggesting that contemporary Indian religious thought is completely free from this error, but the central thrust of it lies in the relentless search for the Truth itself. Phenomenal reality is accepted but its relation to the Truth cannot be called either real or unreal but indefinable (*nāsadāsaddhyam anirvacariyam*). No relationship is assumed between names and essence, for there is only one Essence that is transcendent. Let me make it clear here that this approach is not other-worldly nor is it this-worldly, for the basis of Indian thought is not dualism. Hinduism accommodates and finds place for all assertions as partial illustrations of its Truth. Truth as such is beyond sacred and secular distinctions; as it is totally beyond phenomena and history. Everything else is because of it and therefore it is prior to all categories.

Swami Vivekananda and Mahatma Gandhi both have discarded any rational approach to God. Nothing that is said about God affects His nature. Both of them conceive the cosmos more or less in Śaṃkara's way and try to exclude the presence of causal laws, space and time in the Absolute which becomes personal God. Since the role of meditation lies in transcendence and cessation of all faculties of thought, the Truth is basically indescribable. Its indescribability does not imply its absence because it is the Truth that makes everything explicit. Truth is like the sun emanating light—producing the lights that conform to it. The same Truth, viewed from the spatio-temporal point of view—a point of view based on the *Saṃsakāras* (past impression) and *Vāsanās* (desires), gives rise to everything, but when freed from such hindrances, it reveals itself to itself. That is precisely the meaning of liberation (*mukti*).

Vivekananda and Gandhi both assert that the Truth is not only God but Love. Love, like God and Truth, is all-inclusive and transcends the sensuous and intellectual. True love must be universal. In its initial analysis, the doctrine of love looks similar to that of the Christian virtue of *agápe*, but I think that the concept in contemporary Indian thought is of a different nature. Love is the form in which the identity between the seeker and Truth is established in essence. The identity of one into the one (Truth) is the source and foundation of Love. In fact, properly speaking, Love is not the result of the unity-in-diversity nor has it any outside motive; it is the experience of pure identity with the Essence which in itself is Love. It is the underlying unity of Being that gives rise to the unity of feeling, as the eternal Truth is joy and bliss which is the own-sign (*svarūpalakshnan*) of Brahman. Love, being impersonal, assumes a spontaneous nature and does not have the slightest trace of individuality. By making individuality simply provisional, the Indian view of spirituality transcends the limitations of egoism (*ahaṁkāra*). Here the consciousness of obligations as sheer joy still continues, but there is no awareness whatsoever of one's rights. Once the conflict between rights and duties disappears, love does not function at the plane of common morality. When this love arises, it breaks down all objections of common reasoning and the empirical viewpoint. This can be appropriately called *samyag-dar-shana* or *Satya-drishti* as opposed to the ordinary mode of thought (*Vyavahāradrishti*). To assert it is to assert our true selves. It should not mean that the above thinkers believe in the annihilation of the individual soul. But our finite soul is not the Truth in an ontological sense. The realization of it by intuition and meditation alone frees the self from its finitude and asserts the true self which is God Himself. That is what is meant by statements like (*mahāvākyas*), *That Thou art* or *Ahaṁ Brahmāsmi*.

In the light of what we have presented above, it is possible to see that contemporary Indian thought has an approach to the question of God and spirituality, but it constitutes a particular sphere of spirit. The realization of the hollowness of the ego or individuality is central to it. To the average Christian this is a bitter medicine and few would even attempt to take it, but for the Hindus there is no salvation without this realization. The aim of spirituality lies primarily in experience, rather than in exposition, in personal liberation rather than in scripture, in enjoying religious life rather than in glorifying religion and in taking delight in the world rather than in shaping its history. The answer to the problem, therefore, lies in the acceptance or rejection of the above position.

In the light of what we have discussed, we can come to the following conclusion regarding the question of God and spirituality in contemporary Indian thought. First, spirituality as the central goal of religion has been approached in terms of tranquillity, peace, serenity and inwardness. Its realization is primarily meditative. Secondly, although it has been equated with Truth and God, the concept is different from that of Christianity. Truth is not a one and undivided concept; it is multi-dimensional and can be approached from various angles. Love is one of the ways to approach the Truth but it is neither an ethical nor a logical concept. Thirdly, since the essence of spirituality lies in *gnosis*, meditation or yoga, it belongs to a different realm of existence. Science, modernity or rationality have no access to it; it is neither created nor taken away by anything. Fourthly, all discussions about the Reality are purely theoretical; its basis lies within. Philosophy or religion can clarify the concept, but this theorizing is not a substitute for life. Spirituality and God are not ideologies; they are a way of life. Fifthly, the contribution of science and technology is regarded as significant by contemporary Indian thinkers, but these do not affect the core of spirituality either positively or negatively. They belong to the realm of *Karma-saṁsāra* and are significant in a lower way. The higher realm of spirit is untouched by all the concepts of it as it is not a concept. All categories of thought are relational and as such are not applicable to something unconditioned and non-rational. Viewed in this way, contemporary Indian thought approaches spirituality in its own way. The Indian view of God and spirituality proceeds along lines different from those of western Christianity; therefore, its contributions or limitations should be looked at accordingly.

FOOTNOTES

1 For details, see B.K. Lal, *Contemporary Indian Philosophy* (Delhi: Motilal Banarsidass, 1978), pp. XII-XIII.

2 Huston Smith, *The Religions of Man* (New York: Harper & Row, 1965), p. 71.

3 For details, see Kapil N. Tiwari, *Dimensions of Renunciation in Advaita Vedānta* (Delhi: Motilal Banarsidass, 1978), pp. 73-76.

4 Rabindranath Tagore, *Sadhana* (Tucson: Omen Press, 1972), p. 77.

5 Rabindranath Tagore, *Creative Unity* (London: Macmillan, 1950), pp. 55-56.

6 For details, see J.G. Arapura, *Religion as Anxiety and Tranquillity* (The Hague: Mouton, 1972), pp. 55-56.

The Identity of God and the *Crucifixus*

Robert P. Scharlemann

Das primär für den Glauben und nur für ihn Offenbare und als Offenbarung den Glauben allererst zeitigende Seiende ist für den christlichen Glauben der gekreuzigte Gott.

—*Heidegger*

What kind of thinking is it that makes an identity between the meaning of the name "God" and the historical reality of the crucified Jesus? And what kind of being is the being involved in this identity? It is not enough of an answer to say that these are the "thinking" done by faith (instead of, say, by scientia) and the "being" that belongs to the object of faith (rather than to an empirical or a metaphysical object). On the contrary, these questions demand a reflection on how theology thinks at all. Picht's work toward a thinking that is a thanking,[1] Jüngel's effort to rehabilitate the doctrine of analogy,[2] and Ricoeur's investigations of metaphor all recognize this demand.

The present essay presents a conception of theological thinking that, while differing from the three mentioned, undertakes to follow the same general direction. The direction is indicated by how the being with which they are concerned is a certain unity of being and not being, and also by how the being of God appears in the midst of the being of the world. In this essay, I shall propose, first, that the being of God is not a "being like" (as in Ricoeur's explication of metaphor) but a "being...as," in which what follows the "as" serves as an ostensive definition of God by showing where (or, better, when) in the world God is and also *as* Deity is when it is. The differences set off against each other—between an analogical or metaphorical "being like" and an ostensive "being...as"—within theology are not finally exclusive of each other but are related to each other in a dialectical whole.

Second, I shall propose that the identity between God and the crucified Jesus is not only a matter of "being...as" but also that it is a "being...as" that overturns the thinking of being so that the thought of this identity is a μετανοειν, an afterthinking, and its object is being in the sense of "being other," or in having the free appearance of being that Picht describes as a hovering over the abyss of nothing. Hence, the thought of God as the crucified is a "being...as" that is simultaneously a "being other": "God is God as the crucified Jesus," or, expressed analogically, "God 'comes to' being-there as Jesus is-not there" (this latter a paraphrase intended to express Jüngel's rehabilitated analogia entis), and this "being... as" is the being of God when God is not being God. In order to explicate this, it will be helpful to recall what is meant by the terms "thinking" and "being" in the first place.

1. The being of thinking, which appears in language as logos, is the unity of showing and defining (naming and predicating).

The word "thinking" designates a mental activity that is to be contrasted with prethinking, or dreaming, and also with mechanical performance. It is not thinking, but a prethinking state, when we dreamily gaze out the window and our eye tracks the movement of a falling leaf; it is not thinking, but mechanical performance, when we are reading words from a book while our minds are elsewhere or when we repeat conventional opinions without appropriating them through efforts of our own. It *is* a matter of thinking, however, when, with our attention upon an object, we form the thought "This is X." ("That is a tree." "This is a dog.") Thinking involves holding something before our minds and directing attention to it so that the mind shapes itself in accord with how the thing shows itself. It is the conscious activity in which "I" (that is, any self in the power of what is expressed through the first person singular pronoun) relate myself as a subject to another as an object by reference to the being of the object. "Being," here, refers just to the connection, indicated by the "is" of judgments, between singular ("this") and universal ("dog"), that is, between the percept and the notion of the object. Being appears upon a physical object as the union of what is perceived and what is cognized. To think of something is, thus, to present its being—not its physical appearance, as when we see or recall how it looks, or its abstract notion, as when we define what we see, but the connection between the two—to mind. One way of doing so is through a transcendental image (as Kant called it) or through an intuition of essence (in Husserl's language), as when we mentally picture some generalized tree which contains a schema of all trees without being a replica of any particular one. But there are other ways of doing so too; for the being of things is given not only to the intellect in an image but also to will and feeling. Hence, "thinking," as used here, includes activities of planning, willing, hoping, feeling, and the like, as well as of conceptualization. Each of them, as an activation of thought, may intend a connection between singular and universal. But the focus of attention here will be upon being and thinking in relation to intellectual faculties.

This definition of thinking is reflexive; it results from an activity of thinking about thinking, in which the process of thinking itself is made the object of the activity of thinking. In reflexive thought we direct ourselves to the being of thinking, that is, to being as it appears in the process of thinking itself. But since thinking is not a physical object, we cannot present its being to mind by forming a transcendental image, as may be done with physical objects. Instead, the being of thinking is manifest in language, and manifest as the unity of showing and interpreting, or of naming and defining. The unity of sensation and cognition, which is the being of physical objects, does not appear in the process of thinking—there is nothing to perceive, but only something to be inwardly aware of as we engage in the activity, and there is therefore nothing to cognize through perception. How then can the invisible process of thinking be thought at all? How can the being of thinking be presented to mind? How can we say what thinking is? We can do so to the extent that the being which appears upon objects in the synthesis of sensation and cognition ("This is a tree; a tree is a woody perennial plant, etc.") appears to thinking itself in the synthesis of the words that show their referent with the words that interpret or define what is shown, a synthesis that appears in words that are less deictic than names and more deictic than abstract rules. I would take Tillich's use of what he called the metaphor "ground of being" to be an example of such a synthesis in words; for the term is less ostensive, or deictic, than the name "God" but more deictic than the abstract notion of being-itself, and it contains a schema for the name "God" as well as for the rule of thinking that the concept of being-itself implies.

Thus, whereas we can think of the being of a tree because we can form a general image that is both an abstraction from particular details of perception and also a concretion of the abstract notion, we can think of the being of thinking because we can form a metalanguage which is both less ostensive than the language of nouns and more ostensive than the language of abstract rules; and in this metalanguage the being of thinking becomes manifest. That is to say, the being of thinking appears in a synthesis of language with itself rather than, as with objects, in a synthesis of sensation and cognition.

All thinking is synthetic. To think of something is always to think of it *as* what it is, to present it to mind *as* it presents itself in reality. But just this synthetic character is what provides a distinction in the kinds of thinking that are possible. For we can think of thinking (that is, present the being of thinking to mind) in different ways by rearranging the elements that constitute it. These possibilities are the following:

> a. We can think of thinking *as such*; we can think of it as thinking.
> b. We can think of thinking *as other* than itself; we can think of it as being, that is, as the being of the world or as Dasein (the self-reflective being manifest in human being).
> c. We can think of thinking *as other* than itself and as other than ts own other (being); we can think of it as the being of God.

It is clear that in (a) we have the idea of a critical logic; in (b) is the idea of ontology, from which both physical science and the analytics of Dasein are derived; and in (c), the idea of theology, when the word "God" signifies something or someone other than the unity of thinking and the structure of the thinking of being. Physical science is based upon the identity of the forms of thought with the appearances of the physical world, just as the interpretation of Dasein is based upon the identity of what one is with how one thinks; both of them presuppose the identity between thinking and being which is expressed in the reflexive thought that thinking is being and being is thinking. Science, therefore, represents a certain inversion of thinking, for it thinks of thinking not as thinking (that is, as our activity of making the synthesis) but as being (that is, as the synthesis taking place or existing independently of our thought). This is the thought of the being of the world. Furthermore, when thinking and being are one and the same, as they are in reflexivity (thinking of thinking), we have the idea of our being, the being of Dasein; for when we think, we are, and what we are is the same as how we think. In Dasein, unlike the case of physical objects, being appears not as the connection of a perceptible singular ("this") with an abstract universal ("tree") but as the thinking which enables the universal "I" to be united with a particular embodiment ("this person here")—that is the sense of *cogito ergo sum*. Existential self-understanding, therefore, also represents an inversion of thinking, for it too is based upon a thinking of thinking as being. Science and self-understanding both presuppose the ontological idea of thinking as being; and, accordingly, this first inversion of thought constitutes the structure of the thinking of being.

The second inversion—which is, in effect, the conversion of thinking to afterthinking, of νοειν to μετανοειν—comes with the idea of the being of God, when "God" means what is wholly other than our thinking and other than the being of the world or of Dasein. This idea is formed by thinking of thinking as other than both itself (in the thinking of being) and its own other (being). To form the idea is to think of thinking as other than the constitution of the ontological structure. For this inversion, the word "God" names what is not-I and not-this. Yet thinking is always done by an "I" and is always about a "this." Hence, the idea of God, as the idea of one who is wholly other, cannot be formed as a conception at all. Instead, to grasp the conception, we must break with thinking by thinking of our thinking as wholly other than itself; that is to say, we must think of it not as our thinking of being but as the being of God. This is not a thinking, but a conversion of thinking, the real metanoia of thought; for when we think of our own thinking not as thinking (which ontically it is) nor as our being (which, ontologically, it uniquely is in human being) or the being of the world (which it is in the objects that we think and know as such) but as the being of God, that is, as the thinking which is other than our thinking (because it is of God) and the being which is other than our being and the being of the world (because it is not the object of our thinking), then thought is turned inside out. To "think" thus is to afterthink.

The conversion to afterthinking is made with the thought of thinking as other than itself, as the being of God. But this transition is only an abstract possibility, without real import, if it is not brought about by something real. Thinking can make the transition on its own, to be sure. Indeed, if the question is asked how afterthinking is possible at all, one answer is to say that the possibility lies in the freedom of thinking itself—the power to form a thought is also the power to invert the elements of thought so as to form an afterthought of the same. With the aid of language, the mind just *can* think of thinking as other than itself; it has the freedom and the power to do so—through thinking it can transcend the whole thinking of being. In a limited way, this freedom is there even in the thought of physically present objects. A person viewing a tree must normally think of it as it presents itself in reality, namely, as a tree; one cannot think of it as a stone if one is to think of *it* as it shows itself. Yet the same person can think that the tree, if cut into lumber, provides material for a house, and in that way the mind thinks of the present tree as other than it presents itself, as potentially other than how it actually shows itself, although, in this case, the potential other is still a physical reality. But such inversions remain mere possibilities as long as their origin lies only in the act of the mind itself and not in a response to reality. Hence, something else, something besides the freedom of thinking, is needed in order to make afterthinking a mode of apprehending—an after*thinking* instead of a complete break with reality. This other requirement is the existence of a language which enables thought to make the turn to afterthought as a response to reality, a language that gives the reality to thinking in a "donation" that is, for the thinking of thinking, the same as what a sense "datum" is for the thinking of physical objects. What language is it, then, that "donates" the reality corresponding to the afterthought "Our thinking is (not thinking but) the being of God"? It is the declaration that "God is not God," the declaration that the essence of God's freedom is to be there as other than deity.

The two sides of the matter can now be put together. From the side of the freedom of thought, the transition to afterthinking occurs when we think of the activity of thinking as other than itself. From the side of the donation of reality, the transition occurs when it can be said to us, by our own or by another person, that God is not God, that is to say, when the being of God is presented to mind as other than deity. "Thinking is not thinking" and "God is not God" correspond to each other, the one formulating the freedom that is a power of thinking on its own, and the other formulating the freedom of God (the freedom to be or not to be deity) that is the real donation to which the thought corresponds.

To *think* that thinking is other than thinking, and to do so in correspondence with the giving of deity in freedom, is to join thinking and afterthinking as well as being and being-other. This juncture serves as the basis of the correspondence between after-thinking and being-other so that afterthinking does not replace thinking, as an alternative to and substitute for the whole of think-ing, but is actually joined to it, enabling thinking to be completed in afterthinking or to be "in the world" without being "of the world"; μετανοειν does not do away with νοειν but adds a dimension to it. The combination of the two—of the whole of thinking and being with the other of that whole—is contained in the two propositions:

a) "Thinking is thinking as other than itself" and
b) "God is God as other than God."

These two propositions express the thought and the afterthought of the relation of thinking to afterthinking and of God to non-God, or, in more traditional terminology, of the transcendence to the immanence of God. The first proposition (a) formulates the nature of thinking in its own freedom; the second (b), understood as donating speech, formulates the divine freedom existing as grace. For to think of thinking is to think that thinking is something; and to combine thinking and afterthinking is to form the thought "Thinking is thinking as other than itself." Moreover, if this thought corresponds to reality, then what it corresponds to is something of someone; to combine being with being-there is to say "God is God as other than God." Here, I would suggest, we have the analogy upon which theology rests:

God's transcendence (God's being) : immanence (being-there) :: thinking : afterthinking

in which the point of comparison is the openness of each member of each side to the other member, and of each side to the other side. The analogy can be read as saying, "God is God as other than God when thinking is thinking as other than thinking." This amounts to saying that what corresponds to the conversion of thinking to afterthinking is the nondeification of deity. It is not an analogy of being in which we say that God is to divine being as we are to human being (where the concept of being is common to both sides of the relation), but it is the analogy of otherness, according to which the openness of thinking that is executed in afterthinking is "the same as" (not "like") the openness of God that happens when deity appears as nondeity.

2. The being of God in the world is a "being...as."

Tillich formulated the basic theological proposition, which combines the realm of symbols with the realm of concepts, as the statement "God is being-itself," which asserts that what the symbol "God" presents is the same as what the concept "being-itself" endeavors to grasp. Without such a proposition to join the two realms, the symbolic and the conceptual would coexist as equally complete, equally total, and yet as totally opposed ways of thinking and modes of being. Barth, similarly, adopted from Anselm the basic proposition "God is that *quo majus cogitari nequit*," a definition which combines the name of God, as given to faith, with the rule of thinking contained in the phrase "than which nothing greater can be thought." Neither of these two formulations, however, expresses the unity of being and nonbeing that is the character of the freedom or grace of being and that is recognized in more recent interests in metaphor and analogy.[3] These more recent interests in a being that is "being like" chart a direction to follow in order to arrive at a being that is "being . . . as."

By way of preparation, we might recall some remarks made by Picht about the nature of the metaphysical idea of God incorporated in Christian theology in the West. In this metaphysics, the synthesizing activity of thought is considered to be a positing, an activity that places an object within a whole of ordered relations so that true thought is determined by the necessity imposed upon thinking by how being presents itself in objects. Being, positivity, and affirmation go together. To judge "This is a tree" is to affirm it; to do something else—such as cut it into firewood —is to negate it. To this kind of positing thought, Picht contraposes, by following suggestions of Heidegger, a form of thinking that is a "thanking" or "marveling"; and he has contended that this latter is the thinking theology requires. The difference between the two can be illustrated by how the ontological question is answered. The "age of metaphysics," Picht writes (512), tried to answer the question by referring thinking to a final ground of being. This ultimate ground was absolute being, which had to be thought of as be-ing, otherwise it could not sustain all other entities; and the concept which expressed the being of this *summum ens* was "substance." Metaphysics considered as true all those propositions which could be reduced to the truth of this absolute ground and which accordingly could show what it is that gives every entity its stability and inner consistency. But how else can we understand the sense of being, metaphysically, if not as positivity? Picht replies by calling attention to the "experience of thanking," an experience in which something is affirmed without being posited or held fast as so posited; in gratitude, we experience being not as "firmly grounded positivity" but as "groundless hovering in time" (513). Such affirmations do not allow us to "assert" anything or to express ourselves with them, but they are affirmations.

This way of affirming, as Picht recounts it, has something in common with metaphorical and analogical thinking, for he adds that the "hermeneutics of the basic experience of thanking makes the opposition between doubt and faith disappear" (514). That is to say, it is a thinking of being in which there is a unity of the positive and the negative, a unity of what is otherwise understood as the opposition between being and not being. Doubt contradicts positivity and is always bothersome to thinking when thinking is positing. But for the assent which is expressed in thanks and which uncovers the wonder of creation—or the freedom of being—doubt is the very condition of its possibility.

What is involved here is the following contrast. To "posit" X as X is to place and to fix it on a basis; to "thank" X as X is to marvel at what shows itself in the midst of nothing or of other possibilities. Each of them is a way of thinking—that is, of presenting being to mind. In the context of sense perception, the judgment "This is a tree" is a matter of positing, but in the context of sport or, generally, of playing, an affirmation—e.g., "That was a real game!"—is a matter of thanking or marveling. In the first case, being appears as a positive ground of what is there, the under-standing (*substans*) unity of the perceptible and the cognizable in the object; in the second case, being appears as what shows itself despite the fact that things could just as well have worked out otherwise. Judging is a response to the positivity of being, whereas thanking (which may be expressed in what looks like a judgment) is a response to the grace of being. Positing suggests building on a foundation. To support judgments is to lead them back to their ground, to give a basis for them, and the ultimate basis is that of absolute substance, which just is. Marveling, or thanking, suggests letting something hover in mid-air. To support thankful affirmations is always to grant their improbability, to doubt them, but to point out that that is how, marvelously and nonetheless, things show themselves. If thinking is positing, then doubt is answered by referring to disclosures or events (in the etymological sense of e-vent). The pattern of positing is illustrated by "S is mortal because S is a man and all men are mortal," which cites a necessary and sufficient ground for the judgment. The pattern of thanking is illustrated by "S is mortal not for any hidden reason, such as the mortality of all human beings but because—and 'because' is not strictly correct here—that is just how, luckily, he shows himself freely to be." Positing always has the character: "X is X because, given the ground or reason, it must be so and could not be otherwise," whereas thanking has the character: "X is X though it need not be so and could always also have been otherwise." The being of X in the latter case appears as a fortunate coming together of the opposites that it unites (particular and universal, sensation and thought, activity and result). Its only basis is freedom or felicity; there is no necessary substance upon which it is founded.

I would take the formulations offered above to be in accord with the direction indicated by Picht's remarks. I would also understand those formulations—"God is God as other than God," "Thinking is thinking as other than thinking"—as in accord with the intention of Tillich's method of correlation and of Barth's statement "God is who he is in the deed of his revelation"[4] as well as with the intention of the doctrine of analogy, even though the formulations involve a certain correction of the analogy—"God is God as other than God" instead of "God is like something (namely, man) that is other than God." The difference in wording has some bearing on how we understand the function of parables too. The parables of the Kingdom of God, which do, of course, use the phrase "is like" (and not "is . . . as"), are cases in which the sense is, nonetheless, that the Kingdom of God *is* the Kingdom of God *as* what occurs in the parable. It is not that the Kingdom of God has something about it that the content of the parable resembles but rather that the existence of the Kingdom of God is contemporaneous with the events of the parable. The difference between the two becomes clear if one contrasts the statement "Richard is Richard as Hamlet" (understood to mean that Richard comes to be himself in the role of Hamlet) with the statement "Richard is like Hamlet."

From this point of view, I think I would have to disagree with part of what Jüngel says of the parables of the Kingdom of God. He argues that they do not, in any case, say what the Kingdom of God *is*; instead, they say that "mit der Gottesherrschaft *verhält es sich—wie mit* [e.g.] einem Schatz im Acker" (402, italics in text) —with the Kingdom of God, matters are as they are with a treasure in a field. It is not that the Kingdom of God *is*, for example, a costly pearl or this treasure in a field; it is rather that, as things go with a pearl or a treasure in a field, so they go with the Kingdom of God. Thereupon follows the telling of the story of how things do go. With a treasure in a field, it is so that a man, finding the treasure, sells everything he has and buys the field where he has found it (Mt. 13:44 f.). The Kingdom of God has a character of such a kind that the relation told of in the parable corresponds to it: "Die weltlich unbekannte und aus der Welt allein auch schlechterdings nicht erkennbare Gottesherrschaft (x) setzt sich von sich aus in ein Verhältnis zur Welt (a), das in der Welt dem entspricht, wie es sich mit der Geschichte vom Schatz im Acker verhält: x→a = b:c" (403)—the Kingdom of God, unknown and unknowable from within the world, places itself in a relation to the world (x→a), a relation that, in the world, corresponds to how matters are with the treasure in the field (b:c). But other remarks that Jüngel makes in this context come closer to what I am proposing here. For he also adds: "Und *während* diese Geschichte erzählt wird, wird der Hörende eingestellt auf die Pointe.... Und mit der Pointe kommt dann die Gottesherrschaft im Gleichnis selber beim Hörer an, wenn dieser sich auf das Gleichnis einlässt und sich durch dieses in dieses versammeln lässt" (402, italics in text). And, in all of this, he emphasizes that the first part of the analogy (ᵃ→b) means that God comes into language: "Gott *kommt* zur Sprache. Er *kommt* zum Wort" (403). Indeed, it is only the "analogical power" of the Gospel that "even brings about" (rather than supposes) "this special proximity of things which, in principle, are different [viz., God and world]" (404 n.25). Hence, a parable does "in truth and really (*eigentlich*)" speak of God even while it uses "the language of the world" (403).

The question in these latter remarks is only what formulation might best express that "proximity," or identity, of the difference that is brought about in the effective presentation of a word, as in a parable. For this, again, it seems to me that the most accurate rendering is to say that God *is* God *as* .... What follows the "as" then points out when, where, and as what, God is the deity God is.

In a literal sense, according to our judgment, the happening, the word, or the story that thus points out the being of God in the world is not God. This is so of the parables of the Kingdom of heaven, as it is of the existence and career of Jesus. The events in which a man sells all he has in order to buy a field where he has found a treasure are not of themselves the Kingdom of God. But, at the right time, such events can become the place in the world at which the Kingdom is what it in truth is. And when that happens, one can say, "The Kingdom of God is the Kingdom of God as what happens here." (As an incidental observation, it might be added that the tense of the declaration should perhaps always be the past—the Kingdom of God *was* just there when this occurred, and it can come again; or: God *was* in Christ reconciling the world; and so on. Although this matter of tense is hardly negligible, it is part of the theme from which I am ruthlessly prescinding in the present essay.) The Kingdom of God is what it is concretely as this particular occurrence. In this formulation, both the difference between God and non-God and their identity in time are asserted. The worldly entity or event is the concretion of the being of God, showing when, where, and as what God is really God. And in the whole thought and afterthought that it expresses, there is a combination of necessity and freedom (which Jüngel calls "nothing else than the essence of analogy" [399]) since the necessary thought of the entity or event as the entity or event it is is combined with the afterthought of this entity or event in relation to the free existence of God—the being of God when God is other than God.

These considerations can be applied, now, to the identity between God and the crucified Jesus. The assertion that in the death of Jesus God shows himself as God is the assertion of the identity between God and the death of the man Jesus. It is, in Christian theology, the basic assertion of the way in which God is in the world and of the time when God was in the world. Abstractly viewed, the identity is an identity between God and not-God. The crucifixion of the man Jesus is the extreme opposite of the living God. The opposition is not only that between deity and humanity—an opposition pervading the biblical tradition, though not necessarily characteristic of other religious traditions, and an opposition that Spinoza expressed sharply in a letter in which he remarked that to speak of God as having taken on a human nature is as nonsensical as to speak of a circle as having taken on the nature of a square (quoted in Jüngel: 382)—but also that between life and death, the living of deity and the suffering death of a man. If this assertion of identity is intended as the judgment or the thought "God is Jesus and Jesus is God," in which the predicate defines and interprets what the subject names and shows, then it is indeed as nonsensical as any assertion of a contradiction. It can make sense only if it is further interpreted to mean that there is a common basis, a ground, with reference to which one can see both the similarity and the difference between the being God and the being of Jesus, just as we can make sense of such a contradiction as "an oak is a maple" (when to be a maple means to be not an oak) only by referring both terms to a concept of "tree" as their ground—an oak is a maple because both of them are trees although they are different trees. So, too, we might explain that God is Jesus in the sense that both are deity though they are different persons of the deity: "God" is deity as present to the mind in a word and an image (the first persona), and "Jesus" is deity as present in actual existence (the second persona).

The deficiency of this interpretation is that it must overlook the sheer incompatibility between what the word and image "God" present to mind (e.g., the meaning not-I, and the image of power and activity) and what the actual existence of Jesus is (the appearance of powerless suffering in one who is the "I am"). Christian theology has never really succeeded in showing how there can be an identity of the difference in a way other than the way that thinking must always follow—that is, through a reference to some ground of the difference and similarity. But this deficiency can be eliminated if we understand the identity of the living God with the having-died of Jesus as the point at which the freedom of thinking, executed in its turn to afterthinking, and the freedom of God, embodied in being other than God, correspond to each other. In its turn to afterthinking, it thinks of the death of Jesus as other than what it is; and in the freedom to be, God shows himself as other than God. In such a case, we understand the identity between God and Jesus to be the identity and difference expressed in the proposition:

c) "God is God as the man Jesus,"

a proposition which neither confers deity as a predicate upon Jesus nor denies the actual being of God in the world, at a definite time and in a definite way.

FOOTNOTES

1 Georg Picht and Enno Rudolf, eds., *Theologie—Was ist das?* (Stuttgart: Kreuz-Verlag, 1977).

2 Eberhard Jüngel, *Gott als Geheimnis der Welt* (Tübingen: J.C.B. Mohr, 1977).

3 Karl Daub comes closer in his formulation that being as thinking is the essence of God and thinking as being is the existence of God. Karl Daub, *Philosophische und theologische Vorlesungen* (Berlin: Verlag von Duncker und Humblot, 1841), vol. 6, p. 63.

4 *Kirchliche Dogmatik* II/1:288.

The Attributes of God:
An Islamic Point of View
Gaafar Sheikh Idris

$\mathbf{P}$rior to the modern age very few people disputed the fact that the world has a creator. This fact was for them as obvious as a logical truth or an observed phenomenon. They only differed about the nature of this creator and about the appropriate attitude people should have towards Him. But now the very existence of a creator is disputed. Why? This is not an easy question to answer. However, I tend to agree with those contemporary writers who trace the origins of modern atheism to the ideas of some influential western philosophers, some of whom were themselves believers. Nonetheless, they argued in such a way as to make people at least doubt, if not reject, some of the facts belief in whose truth used to be considered by earlier thinkers to belong to the essence of being rational. Good reasons for believing in the creator, whether they be rational arguments or otherwise, were related in one way or the other to belief in the truth of those facts. Belief in God was based on the fact that there was something in our nature and in the nature of the world which points to a transcendent creator whom we should worship. The heart of the new thinking was the view that our world is in every respect a closed system which cannot therefore point to anything outside itself. The first step toward this separation of heaven and earth was perhaps Descartes' mechanistic conception of the world which claimed that it was possible to explain natural phenomena by reference to matter and motion and their laws. Hume widened the distance between heaven and earth by claiming that the causal principle by which we make such explanations of natural phenomena was nothing but observed regular succession. God cannot therefore be a cause since He lies outside the world of experience. The world cannot be His creation or effect, since it is not observed to occur after Him. Kant took the final step by arguing that the concept of causation cannot apply to anything outside the world of our experience. This atheist philosophy then became, as it were, the official philosophy of science. And since ordinary people and even many scientists do not see the distinction between the facts which science establishes and the philosophies which scientists adopt, especially when such philosophies become popular among great scientists, this atheistic philosophy was believed by the public to be the philosophy which science demands or even the philosophy whose truth it has established.

Many believers accepted the atheistic assumptions of this philosophy but nevertheless maintained their belief in God hoping to find a place for Him in the realms which science could not yet conquer. But the atheists argued, with some strength, that since science was rapidly progressing in giving us 'rational' explanations of phenomena which we used to believe to be the works of God, it was only a matter of time before everything would be so explained, thus driving God completely out of our world.

The severance of the relation between God and the world was thus, on the one hand, a result of a new conception of the nature of our world. But on the other hand it led some believers to a new conception of the nature of God. God as a result of this new thinking became more and more an abstract idea rather than a living person. But this in its turn strengthened the atheistic trend. Who is interested in a God that is a mere idea, who has no active role to play either on the level of our intellects and behaviour or on the level of nature?

But the idea that our world is a closed system, that it does not point to a transcendent creator, has received a serious blow from the steady state theory, which is being more and more accepted by scientists as the most plausible scientific cosmological theory. According to this theory our natural world had a definite beginning. And if so it would not be illegitimate to ask: Who started it? But this means that the world is itself telling us that it is not self-sufficient, i.e., it is pointing to something beyond itself. But this fact, as we said earlier, was taken for granted by early thinkers. They did not have to wait for a twentieth-century scientific theory to prove it. Almost everything around them pointed to the fact that our world had a beginning, and could not therefore be self-sufficient.

I think that it will soon be obvious that those who denied the existence of a creator cannot support their claim by any scientific facts. But mere belief in the existence of a creator is not of much consequence. We need to know who this creator is so that we can establish appropriate relations with Him, relations that would make a difference in our life.

It is to this end that thinking believers should henceforth direct their energies. We must overcome the pre-steady state complex which induced many of us to think of God as an abstract idea, and start expounding and defending the ordinary believer's conception of Him as a living and loving Person.

I believe that there is much in the writings of early Muslim theologians, especially those of the Sunnite School, from which we can benefit in this respect. And it is towards this end that I am writing the rest of this paper. I shall attempt to give contemporary believers an idea about the way early Muslim theologians thought about an issue in which we are still interested, namely, the nature of God and His attributes.

There are three major views concerning the nature of divine attributes among Muslim believers. These are the views of the *mujassima* or anthropomorphists, *mu'attila* or negators, and the *muthbita* or affirmers:

(a) The physicalistic or anthropomorphistic view thinks of God as a huge human being, and thus attributes to Him things like hearing, seeing, speaking, having eyes, etc., in a humanistic sense. The difference between Him and ordinary human beings, according to this view, is not of kind but of degree. Only a few influential people held such a view in the history of Islam, and they were immediately condemned as idol worshippers. Since this view is no longer taken seriously by any contemporary believers, it need not detain us. The only important point to mention here, because it relates to the two following views, is the reason behind such a view, i.e., the assumption that only physical things exist, and since God exists He must be physical and have the attributes of physical things.

(b) The negators' view assumes that all the attributes we express in the Arabic language or any other human language are attributes of physical existents. But God is not physical. When He attributes to himself, in the Qur'an, things like hearing, seeing, being above this world, having hands or eyes, etc., He is addressing us in the only language we can understand, but He is not using words describing these qualities in any real sense. What are we then to understand by such words and expressions when we use them?

Nothing, according to the extreme advocates of this view. This view, though it was not known until about the third century of Islam, soon became, especially in its milder forms, very influential and popular among many theologians and educated Muslims. It is sometimes wrongly assumed to be the only alternative to the first view.

(c) The affirmers' view says that when God describes Himself as being capable of seeing, hearing, etc., He is using these words in a real sense, because God really sees and hears. He has a real face and real hands. Since "nothing is like Him", His attributes, though real, are not like the attributes of human beings or any other created things. This is the view of the early generations of Muslims and of all the great Sunnite 'ulama' (learned men) who followed in their footsteps. It is, I believe, the view of all believers in their hours of worship. But it is no longer popular among theologians and "modernist" believers. One reason for this, as I have said, is that it is confused with the anthropomorphistic view, which is obviously untenable. It is this view which I am going to briefly expound and defend against the second view.

Does God exist? The extremist advocates of the second view would refuse to answer in the affirmative, because existence in the real sense is ascribed, in their view, to natural things only. Since God is not like them we cannot even describe Him as existent. What is He then? We cannot say anything positive about Him, they say: we can only say what He is not. Against this view, the affirmer view asserts that by refusing to liken Him to any physical existent, you end up likening Him to non-existents because it is only non-existents about which we cannot say anything positive.

A contemporary philosopher might think that what the negators are saying is that it is a category mistake to describe God as existent and therefore it would be equally wrong to describe Him as non-existent. The affirmers may respond that: we did not say that negators liken God to non-existents merely because they refused to describe Him as existent, but because of their argument for doing so, namely, that nothing positive can be said about God. Our claim is that this description applies only to non-existents. Moreover, the affirmers might continue, the claim that a category mistake is being committed must be supported by showing that the nature of the thing to which a certain attribute is wrongly applied is different in at least one relevant aspect from the things to which this attribute is rightly applied, i.e., that they belong to different categories. But to claim that two things belong to different categories you must know something positive about each one of them. If the only thing you know about one of them is that nothing which applies to anything applies to it in a real sense, you are saying that it belongs to the category of nothingness. That is why the famous Imam Ahmad said in replying to the *Jahmiyyah*, a very influential school of negators, that a thing which is not like anything else is not a thing at all.[1] Admittedly, there is a verse in the Qur'an which says that "Nothing is like Him".[2] The *Jahmiyyah* took this to be strong Qur'anic support for their negativist view, but this verse does not say that nothing which is said of other things can be said of God, in any real sense. That is why after saying that "Nothing is Like Him", it goes on to say "He is the All-Hearing, All-Seeing". All that the verse is saying is that God is not to be likened to His creatures. But you do not liken Him to them by merely saying that He exists and they exist, or that He knows and some of His creatures know. You do so only if you take His existence to be as ephemeral and dependent as the existence of His creatures and His knowledge to be as limited as theirs is limited.

The affirmers' second objection to the negator refusal to describe God as existent is that anyone who takes such a belief seriously cannot really worship God. How can one worship, love, fear, turn for guidance to, depend on, or pray to something about which he cannot say, even to himself, that it exists? This is not to say that they do not actually worship God; many of them do, but only at the expense of their theoretical standpoint.

The third objection is that since as Muslims you read the Qur'an and believe in its divine source, what do you understand by expressions which attribute to God things like knowing, hearing, acting, creating, speaking, seeing, etc.? Some negators would say that since God is completely different from anything we know, His real attributes cannot be couched in human language because human languages are necessarily confined to things which fall within our sense experience. But since this language is the only one we understand, God is using it to give us a glimpse of something which is really beyond our comprehension. The question is how our human language can succeed in giving us even such a glimpse. If the words and expressions of our language do not apply to God in any real sense, then they cannot convey to us anything about Him. And in that case, God would be revealing to us a mere string of words which have no meaning. But no one who really believes in God would attribute to Him such a folly. On the other hand, if they do convey to us even a glimpse, there must be a relationship between them and the real attributes of God.

Other negators would acknowledge the existence of such a relation, but would say that the words used in their metaphorical and not in their real sense. For example, when it is said in the Qur'an that God sees or hears, what is meant is that He knows,[3] because seeing and hearing in their real senses apply to animals only. There are three objections to this view.

(a) It can easily be shown that to see is linguistically different from to hear, and both are different from, though related to, knowing.[4]

(b) If it is claimed that all the words of our language are used in the metaphorical sense when they apply to God, this would lead either to an infinite regress or an impasse. If every word or expression in our language had a metaphorical sense, then once a word, say X, is used in a sacred book to describe God, we must look for its metaphorical sense, but that metaphorical sense must be expressed in yet other words whose metaphorical senses are expressed in X^2 and so on, *ad infinitum*. If, however, some words have no metaphorical senses, then if we take them on their face value, we violate our principle.

(c) If the claim is that this applies to some and not all words and expressions describing God, then no one would object to it in principle, because this is true even of expressions describing human beings. But each particular claim that a certain expression is used metaphorically must be supported by linguistic as well as textual evidence, and cannot depend on the supposition that since God is different from other things, our human language cannot be used in any real sense to describe Him.

***

This leads us to a milder version of negationism. Propounders of this milder version are ready to attribute to God things like existence, knowledge, life, power, will, seeing and hearing in their real sense, but would take as metaphorical attributes such as love, pleasure, anger and hate. The reply to a person who makes such a distinction between these two classes of attributes—affirming the former and denying the latter—is to say "there is no difference between what you affirmed and what you denied. What applies to one of them does indeed apply to the other. If you say that His will is like the will of human beings, so also would be His love and pleasure. But this is anthropomorphism. But if you say that He has a will that suits Him just as a human being has a will that suits him, it will be said to you: He also has a love that suits Him, and an anger that suits Him; and the human being has an anger that suits him."[5] "If one interprets things like love, hate and anger in an anthropomorphistic way, we say that the same can be said about will, knowledge and power".[6]

People like Ibn Taymiyyah, the author of the above quotations, are often mistakenly described by their opponents and by some modern scholars as being literalists, or even worse, anthropomorphists. Those who say this assume that the only alternative to negationism or allegoricalism is literalism or anthropomorphism. But it is clear from Ibn Taymiyyah's statement that when he affirms that God loves or hates in a real sense and not in a metaphorical sense, he is not, thereby, likening Him to human beings. He rejects the view that language cannot be used in a real sense except when it applies to created things. He thinks that some descriptive words have general meanings which as abstract meanings do not apply to anything in particular, whether it be human or divine. But when they are used to describe a particular, then they describe something which is peculiar to the particular in question.[7] For example, if we describe two persons, X and Y, as "learned", the connotation of "learned" when it applies to X is not the same as its connotation when it applies to Y. Does this mean that all words are equivocal? No, by no means. Ibn Taymiyyah thinks that though the referents are different, the word has an abstract meaning that is common to both referents. This, he thinks, applies even in the case of God.

When we describe Him as loving, for example, we are not likening Him to human beings, i.e., we are not saying that He loves in the same way as humans; we are not using the word "loving" in an equivocal way. There is a common meaning which applies to both God and the human being and which, therefore, justifies the use of the word to describe both.[8] It is wrong, he insists, to think that the real meanings of such words are their meanings when they apply to human beings. Descriptive words, as such, are neutral. They take their specific meanings from the particulars which they describe. And just as there are differences between particular created things, there are differences—and greater ones—between God and the world of created things.

***

How do we know about the attributes of God? According to the school of *Ahl as-Sunnah*, who are also called the people of affirmation, some of the divine attributes can be known by reason alone, though most of them are known by revelation also. Other attributes of God are not known except through the medium of divine revelation to God's chosen prophets or messengers. Those which can be known by reason alone may be divided into three categories: God's attributes as an existent, His attributes as a living being, and His attributes as a creator and the object of our worship.

It is of paramount importance to see the difference between the attributes of something as an existent and its attributes under other descriptions or headings. Failure to see this has led both believers and atheists into confusion about their conceptions of God. The mistake starts when either the theist or the atheist assumes that all the attributes of the physical are limited to its attributes under this physical description. Once this mistake is committed, it is easy to argue from it that since God is not physical, nothing which is said of physical things can be said of Him in any real sense. Thus, Lenin, seeing that the progress of science was creating havoc for the materialists' conception of matter, thought of defining the latter in a way which no scientific discovery could render obsolete. He came to the conclusion that the material was anything that existed objectively, i.e., outside our mind.[9] But, this is not a definition of the material; it is a necessary condition of every existent. If Communists took Lenin's definition seriously, the difference between them and the believers would be only verbal, i.e., whether it is proper to say of God that He is material or not. But they do not take their own view seriously. In fact, they insist on having their cake and eating it. Thus, if you tell them that you are ready to say that God is material according to their definition of this word, because you believe that He exists objectively, they would react by asking you to show Him to them, thus reverting back to an earlier definition of the material.

Because material things exist objectively, and God is not material, then His existence must be only subjective. It seems that Lenin argued in this way. Some theistic theologians argued in a manner that is rather similar to this. In their attempt to exalt God above all material things, they ended up depriving Him of the very necessary attributes of the existent thus making Him a mere word that designates nothing. The *Ahl as-Sunnah* were very much against this trend, and they dubbed the people who followed it *mu'attila*, i.e., negators. In contrast the *Ahl as-Sunnah* called themselves the people of *ithbat*, i.e., affirmation. The negators talk of God only in negative terms: all they say about God is that He does not have the attributes that material things have. The affirmers, on the other hand, believe that the basic attributes of God are positive ones. The negative attributes are only the negations of these positive attributes and what is logically implied by these negations. They think that as a creator, God must exist and exist objectively. To exist objectively God must have all the attributes of objective existents. God must therefore be in a particular 'place' and cannot thus be everywhere. Why not? Because to be everywhere is to fail to be distinguished from other existents and thus not to have a special identity. To believe that He is everywhere leads, moreover, to yet other absurdities. If God was everywhere before He created anything, then where did He create His creatures? To say that He created them inside Himself is absurd. To say that He created them outside Himself contradicts the statement that He is everywhere. To say that God shrank to leave some space for them is absurd. At least it contradicts the assumption that He is infinite. It also leads to the absurdity that whenever a new thing comes into existence, God shrinks to give way to this new thing, and whenever anything passes out of existence God extends Himself to fill the empty space.

Where is God then? The *Ahl as-Sunnah* do not hesitate to answer that He is above His throne in heaven. Does this mean that He is limited? If by this is meant His person, then the answer is yes. But although His person is confined to a particular "region", His power, knowledge and other attributes are not so limited. God is in heaven, but His power and knowledge are everywhere. He cannot in this sense, therefore, be said to be limited.

The negators believe that God cannot at all be known by the five senses because they thought that to be thus known is to be physical. The affirmers agreed that He cannot be observed by us while we are in this world. But this is not because it is in His nature not to be observed; it is rather because of our own present nature. There are verses in the Qur'an and the authentic sayings of the Prophet Muhammad which affirm that believers shall behold God in the Hereafter. In fact, beholding Him would be their greatest joy. They would be able to behold Him because their nature would be different from what it is now.

The affirmers do not depend on this religious argument alone. They also believe that it is a contradiction in terms to say that something exists objectively and yet cannot in principle be observed. It is only non-existents which cannot in principle be observed, or as al-Dārimi says, "a thing which cannot be observed, *yudrak*, by any of the senses, is nothing."[10] As an existent, then, God must exist outside our minds, i.e., He cannot be a mere idea or an abstract concept. Secondly, He must have some defining qualities.[11] Thirdly, He must exist in a "place", that is distinct from places occupied by other existents.[12] Otherwise, He would be one with them and hence could not be anything in His own right. Fourthly, He must be in principle observable.

God is not only an existent, He is a Living existent. And as a Living existent He must have the attributes of willing, knowing, seeing, hearing, etc. In short, God must have all the attributes which living things have *qua* living things and not because of their materiality or animality.

But God is the Creator of everything. As such He must be eternal and hence self-sufficient, unique and perfect. All the other attributes that He has must be seen in the light of these basic attributes. Thus if we say that He knows, His knowledge must be different from that of any of His creatures in that it must be knowledge of everything. It must be knowledge of the past, present and the future. It must be knowledge which is not preceded by ignorance and thus acquired through the senses or any other means. And so on. The same must be said of all the other attributes. That is why it is one of the pillars of the Muslim faith to believe that God is unique in His person as well as in His attributes. Just as none of His creatures resemble Him, so none of their attributes resemble His attributes. And so while we know the meanings of the divine attributes, we do not know their modality or the form which they take when they apply to His unique person.

Some of the attributes of God we cannot know except through His own words revealed to chosen prophets. In Islam, these words are confined to the Qur'an and the Sunnah, the sayings of the Prophet Muhammad. These sources attribute to God things like being above His Throne, having hands, smiling, etc. The negators take all these attributes to be metaphorical, but the *Ahl as-Sunnah*'s position is to affirm about God whatever He affirms about Himself in the Qur'an or through His prophet without *tashbih*, i.e., likening Him to created things, or *ta'til*, i.e., explaining away His attributes as metaphorical. We understand them, affirmers say, in the light of the principle stated in the verse "Nothing is like Him, the All-hearing, the All-seeing."[13]

Let me end this paper by quoting some famous Qur'anic verses about God's attributes which every practicing Muslim knows by heart and repeats on many occasions as an expression of his devotion to God:

> Say: He is God, one God the Everlasting Refuge, Who has not begotten, and has not been begotten, and equal to Him is not any one.[14]

> God, there is not God but He, the Living, the Everlasting, slumber seizes Him not, neither sleep; to Him belongs all that is in the Heavens and the earth. Who is there that shall intercede with Him save by His leave? He knows what lies before them and what lies after them, and they comprehend not anything of His knowledge

save such as He wills. His throne comprises the heavens and the earth; the preserving of them oppresses Him not; He is the All-High, the All-Glorious.[15]

FOOTNOTES

1 Imam Ahmad, *ar-rad 'ala-az-zamadigati wa-l-jahmiyyah*, p. 68.

2 The Qur'an *ayah* (verse) *11: Surah* (chapter) 42.

3 See Ibn Qutayba, *Kitab al-ikhtilaf fi'l-lafz ar-rad 'ala'-l-jahmiyya Wa-l-mushab-biha*, in the collection, *Aqa'id as-salaf*, ed. Ali Sami Nashshar and 'Ammar Jam'i Talibi (Alexandria, 1971), p. 233.

4 *Ibid.*, p. 233.

5 Ibn Taymiyyah, *op. cit.*, p. 21.

6 *Ibid.*, p. 22.

7 *Ibid.*, p. 80.

8 *Ibid.*, p. 79.

9 V.I. Lenin, *Materialism and Empiro-Criticism* (Moscow: Foreign Languages Publ. House, n.d.), pp. 269-70.

10 Abu Sa'id Ad-Dārimi, *Kitab al-rad 'ala-l-jahmiyyah, Aqa'idus-Salaf* and *Kitab ar-radi-l-Imami-d-Dārimi, 'Uthman Ibn Sa'id ala-l-marisil-'anid*, p. 570.

11 *Ibid.*, p. 508.

12 *Ibid.*, p. 249.

13 The Qur'an *ayah* 11: *Surah* 42.

14 Chapter CXII of the Qur'an, trans. Arthur J. Arberry, *The Qur'an Interpreted* (Oxford Univ. Press, 1964), p. 667.

15 *Ibid.*, trans. verse 255, chapter 11, p. 37.

Experience and the Justification of Religious Belief

Eugene Thomas Long

Perhaps you have heard the story of the philosopher who fell off the edge of a cliff and was hanging by the limb of a tree. After calling for help for some time he heard a voice from the heavens saying, "I am here." The philosopher explained his dilemma and then asked, "Can you help me?" The voice replied, "Do you believe in me?" to which the philosopher without hesitation, given the circumstances, said, "Yes, of course." The voice came back, "Then, let go." There was silence and some moments passed before the philosopher somewhat meekly replied, "Lord, I know that this is not the best time and place for a discussion, but you know how philosophers are, and you do seem to be asking a good bit of me. I know that many of your followers in recent times would agree that I should let go, but I have this feeling that they may be confusing the doctrine of salvation by faith alone with an epistemological doctrine that faith is a commitment that requires no justification. Could we talk about this? And, in the meantime, I hope you will not be offended if I ask, 'Is there anyone else up there?'"[1]

This story seems to me to depict the situation in which many philosophers of religion find themselves today. Many twentieth century studies have stressed the role of experience and commitment in religion and this may be understood as a corrective to those who would place primary emphasis on the role of argument. The role of experience and faith, however, has been taken too far at times with the result that we seem to have reached an impasse which was described well by Basil Mitchell when he wrote: "Either God is at best an inferred hypothesis and faith in God is no more than the acceptance of an hypothesis; or God is an experienced reality about which rational doubt is, at least, for the one who experiences, impossible."[2]

For now, I must leave the philosopher suspended from the side of the cliff. I do want, however, to propose a scheme of work for the construction of a rope which may assist the philosopher and help us escape from the impasse which Mitchell has described. Philosophers of religion who have placed primary emphasis on the role of argument in religion have to face the widespread belief that none of the traditional arguments for the existence of God can be accepted as valid proofs. More importantly, perhaps, even if one were to hold that there were arguments which could prove that infinite Being exists, one would still have to face the chasm that exists between the object of such arguments and the object of religious faith. How, for example, can one bridge the gap between the object of a purely intellectual enterprise and the object of religious faith which is believed to be the source of a new mode of existence for man: This problem is suggested at the end of Norman Malcolm's well known essay on the ontological argument. After arguing for the validity of one version of the argument, Malcolm concludes "At a deeper level I suspect that the argument can be thoroughly understood only by one who has a view of that human 'form of life' that gives rise to the idea of an infinitely great being, who views it from the *inside* not from the outside and who has, therefore, at least some inclination to *partake* in that religious form of life."[3] Although formulated in different ways, it is this problem which stands in the background of many of those persons who follow Schleiermacher in emphasizing the role of experience in religion and in expressing a distaste for or skepticism about religious arguments of a purely intellectual nature separated from experience.

From the preceding, it is probably clear that I am sympathetic with those who have argued that we do not have available proofs in any strict sense for the existence of God and with those who are skeptical of arguments of a purely intellectual nature separated from experience in religion. One need not conclude from this, however, that arguments have no place in discussions of religious faith or that the only remaining option is one of a variety of recent fideistic views of religion. When religious faith is reduced to commitment in the absence of understanding, an essential ingredient of religion is lost. Religious faith is not merely a way of looking at the world; it claims in some sense to be an insight into or discernment of the way things are, and the truth of beliefs about the way things are cannot be read immediately from the experience itself. The scheme of work that I wish to propose is concerned with an empirical approach which would not ignore the role of reason and argument in religious knowledge.

If we are to be successful in developing an empirical approach to the philosophy of religion which has some hope of getting beyond the impasse described by Mitchell, we will need initially to make progress towards the development of an adequate theory of experience, one which avoids the claim that experiences are merely subjective. John Smith seems to me to be on the mark when he suggests "that no appeal to experience is naive, for every such appeal carries with it a theory of experience, some principle indicating what experience is and how much it is supposed to contain."[4] The prevailing theory of experience in classical empiricism was one in which experience was essentially equated with subjective mental events; and disclaimers and intentions to the contrary this theory of experience seems to lurk in many corners of contemporary discussions of religion. This theory of experience is, however, being challenged from a variety of traditions. Indeed, efforts to get beyond the tendency to equate experiences with subjective mental events may provide the most fundamental common ground between philosophers of religion working in traditions which otherwise differ in many ways. Subjectivist theories of experience conflict with ordinary notions of experience in which experiences are said to intend or refer to what is experienced. Experience in religion as in other dimensions of life, it can be argued, takes place in a context in which one is already related to persons and things in the world and because of this it cannot without misunderstanding be divorced from one's history or tradition. One cannot, it would seem, without considerable effort, arrive at an understanding of experience as a closed circle of mental events.

In many twentieth century efforts to take seriously the place of experience within religion there has been a tendency to turn in greater and lesser degrees to religious experience and revelation as self-authenticating, and at the root of this move is, I suspect, a commitment, recognized or not, to a subjectivist theory of experience. If, however, a theory of experience can be developed which shows it to be the product of the interaction between persons and things in the world, we might be able to give proper recognition to the role of experience in religion without having to turn aside questions concerning the justification of religious belief. It is the belief that reality is manifested in some interaction with the world that allows us to judge experiences as appropriate or inappropriate, rational or anti-rational. I cannot make of experience what I will. There is some sense in which it is given. Yet it is not given independently of some set of beliefs which I bring with me in my encounters in the world. There is, one might say, a reciprocal relationship between me and what is given requiring an interpretative act on my part, and it is in this that efforts to understand and interpret are rooted. Understanding and interpreting are not activities independent of experience in this case but are part and parcel of efforts to articulate encounters with persons and things in the world. In this sense experience may be said to have a social dimension for it is in interpreting that I encounter others, interact with them and compare judgments. In this view experience cannot be held to be self-authenticating; it is always subject to misinterpretation. As I will suggest later in this paper, however, this need not result in pure relativism.

If an adequate theory of experience along the lines suggested can be developed, we will have taken an important initial step towards laying the groundwork for the development of an adequate empirical approach to the philosophy of religion. This should provide the basis for an empirical approach to religion which avoids the problems associated with immediate experience on the one hand and inference on the other hand. Nevertheless, experience understood in terms of encounter is not without its difficulties, and some of these difficulties become greater when we are concerned with what is referred to variously as religious experience or the religious dimension of experience, what I will refer to here as the transcendent dimension of experience. By "transcendent dimension of experience," I refer to those experiences of ultimacy or mystery which seem to bring one up against the limits of what can be accounted for in ordinary terms.

Perhaps the most significant of these experiences is called the experience of contingency. I call this the most significant because it appears to be the most widely recognized aspect of what I am calling the transcendent dimension of experience. It is this experience which is often associated with the question—why things are rather than are not, a question which I take to be more than a merely abstract philosophical question. Contemporary philosophers as diverse as Wittgenstein, J.J.C. Smart, and Heidegger, as well as religious thinkers, give testimony to this dimension of experience, although of course there are significant differences regarding what claims can be made for this experience.

Closely related to the experience of contingency and not easily distinguished from it is what we might call the experience of the numinous. I have reference here to what Schleiermacher called the feeling of absolute dependence and what Otto described as the *mysterium tremendum et fascinans*. Heidegger seems to be speaking of a similar experience in his talk of the Holy. A third transcendent dimension of experience is suggested in moral experience. John Baillie, for example, argues that in our relations with others we encounter in them the embodiment of a right set over against our otherwise uninhibited desires, a right which the other cannot confer upon himself. In our relations with others we are said to encounter "something greater than themselves, an intrinsic right and a universal good. My relations with my fellows have the significance of reality for me only because and insofar as they mediate this greater reality."[5]

I will mention one additional example, one most typically associated with some existentialist approaches to understanding human existence. Karl Jaspers makes reference to boundary or limit situations, experiences in which ordinary ways of understanding one's self in the world are no longer adequate. In such experiences we may become aware, argues Jaspers, that our being is not fully chosen by us but is in some sense a gift from beyond the world of persons and things. "*Existenz* can grasp itself in its own freedom only if at the same time, and in the same act, it will perceive something other than itself.... For my self-realization I depend on a fulfillment that comes to me.... The test of the possibility of my *existenz* is the knowledge that it rests upon transcendence."[6]

Reports of a transcendent dimension of experience are, of course, notoriously difficult to handle. Even if we limit ourselves to persons who admit of such experiences, we have to be aware of the different ways in which these persons have responded. Some claim intuitive certainty of the Divine; others claim that a basis is provided for a proof of the existence of God; other persons report such experiences without assigning any religious significance to them. Problems of understanding and interpreting are more difficult in this case than in sense or even aesthetic experience because many of the checking procedures available to us in other dimensions of experiences are not available to us here.

How then can we proceed to deal with reports of a transcendent dimension of experience? If experience and interpretation are connected in the way suggested, we cannot in the strict sense get to uninterpreted experience. The idea of an uninterpreted experience is a purely artificial one. Experiences are always *someone's* experiences, and that someone is never free from what he brings with him. We can, however, make an effort to describe the transcendent dimension of experience without reference to any specifically religious interpretation, and in this effort we may be able to discover contact points between different religions as well as between religious and non-religious views of reality.

Experiences do not come to us independently of the language and interpretations in which they are enclosed, but this need not result in our having to say that no distinction can be drawn between descriptions and interpretations of experience. We need, at this point, a distinction somewhat like the one that Ninian Smart draws between descriptions of experience which range from the highly ramified to the relatively unramified.[7] That is, we need to distinguish between those descriptions of experience which are relatively independent of a set of doctrines or beliefs which make up one's world view and those interpretations which consciously attempt to provide an interpretive framework within which the experience can be understood. Description of experience in the sense understood here is basically an effort to focus on the phenomenon itself independently of theory laden interpretations which may tend to distort or conceal it. It is something like this that Heidegger had in mind when he wrote that phenomenology means "to let that which shows itself be seen from itself in the very way in which it shows itself from itself."[8]

Careful analytic descriptions of the transcendent dimension of experience may help us see more clearly what is being referred to and help us distinguish between related kinds of experience as well as identify characteristics which are shared in the experiences of persons bringing different cultural and philosophical commitments to experience. The tasks of providing detailed descriptions and judging their adequacy are, of course, not easy ones. To some extent we are dependent upon persons looking in the same direction in an effort to see things as they are given, but we are not without any kinds of tests. Paul Tillich was at least pointing in the direction of a testing procedure when he wrote that "The test of a phenomenological description is that the picture given by it be convincing, that it can be seen by anyone who is willing to look in the same direction, that the description illuminates other related ideas, and that it makes the reality which these ideas are supposed to reflect understandable."[9]

Assuming that we are able to provide detailed descriptions of these experiences, does this mean that we are presented with neutral descriptions which may at will be interpreted in a religious or a non-religious way? To put this in another way, is the difference between the theist and the atheist or the Christian and the Hindu merely a matter of the same experience understood under two or more interpretations? I have in mind H.D. Lewis' objection to Ronald Hepburn on this point and Lewis' claim that the theistic experience of the numinous differs significantly from the non-theistic experience and that whatever further interpretation is in order, the question whether God exists or not is not left open by the experience.[10] The issue between Lewis and Hepburn at this point is an important one and is not easily resolved. Lewis argues forcefully that the experience of the numinous is not just some neutral experience to which may be appended a variety of interpretations. The essential point is that experiences are experiences by someone and cannot be detached from the contexts in which they occur. However, Lewis seems to take this too far—to the point where experiences of the numinous appear to be independent of interpretative disagreements. As I have suggested elsewhere, we need in some way to be able to account for the person who has experienced what he believed to be the presence of the Divine but who now believes that he misinterpreted his experience. If experiences of the transcendent are understood to be mediated through our encounter with persons and things in the world, it is difficult to see how we can avoid questions of judgment in our interpretative efforts. But this need not result in our having to say that interpretation is not integral to experience or that experience is merely a neutral event to which is appended an interpretation. It would be more profitable to argue, I believe, that experiences are understood in some preliminary way by the person having the experience and that his preliminary understanding may be developed, corrected, or perhaps even abandoned, as he proceeds to articulate that experience. This is the import of Dilthey's well known saying that "Interpretation would be impossible if expressions of life were completely strange. It would be unnecessary if nothing strange were in them. It lies, therefore, between these two extremes."[11]

Interpretation understood in this sense is in the language of Heidegger a "relatedness backward or forward," a relating back and forth between our preliminary and our articulated understanding.[12] Interpretation has a dialectical character. However we formulate our interpretation, it should always be referred back to the experience in relation to which it may be subject to alteration or correction. It is this which accounts in part for our ongoing efforts to reinterpret doctrinal formulations, and, if this is forgotten, doctrinal formulations will tend to supplant the experiential basis of religion, and religious faith will become little more than intellectual assent to a set of propositions.

The theist and the atheist may grant, it seems to me, that interpretation is integral to experience. They may also share much in their descriptions of what I have called the transcendent dimension of experience, but they may disagree regarding whether or not the experience is of God. In order to deal with this disagreement we turn to interpretation proper, that is, to efforts to provide a map or interpretative scheme by which we account for such experiences. With reference to what I have called the transcendent dimension of experience, there are presumably a number of alternatives open at this point. One might, for example, provide a reductionist account which rules out references to transcendent reality in the name of an imaginary parent substitute; one might provide an interpretation along the lines of Heidegger which requires reference to Being, or one might provide a more strictly theistic interpretation. To admit, however, that there are competing interpretations or even that no particular interpretation is required by the data of experience does not necessarily lead in the direction of relativism where we merely admit to different ways of looking at the world. What is at stake here is, in the words of James Richmond, "whether a religious or a non-religious interpretation of the world is the most satisfying, the most rational and the most illuminating."[13] To the extent that these interpretations claim to give an account of the data of experience, we may judge between those more and less adequate interpretations in accordance with their ability to account without distortion for the data of experience.

Those schemes for interpreting what I have called the transcendent dimension of experience by reference to Being or greater Reality and which understand Being to be in some sense fulfilling of life or the ground of belief in the worth of our existence might be called religious, and I believe that we are in error if we draw too sharp a distinction between those interpretations of the experience of Being within the general dimensions of experience and the particular concrete experiences of God which arise within the context of a particular community of faith. To put this in another way, we need to recognize a distinction between philosophical reflection on the transcendent dimension of experience and religious faith, but we should not draw too much of a line between the so-called God of the philosophers and the God of faith. Philosophy does not out of its own resources generate the idea of God, but philosophers may make claims regarding the character of Reality or Being, and the religious believer can hardly without schizophrenia avoid efforts to relate or harmonize what philosophers and theologians are saying about Reality.

Implicit in what I am saying is the suggestion that we seek an approach to the relation between philosophical and theological reflection on experience which avoids the position of some writers who seem to make philosophical reflection dependent on extra philosophical norms of religious faith and the popular twentieth century position which restricts the role of philosophical reflection to asking questions of ultimate concern which independently of historical revelation and a particular faith are held to end in confessions of ignorance. I am suggesting that we should maintain a distinction between philosophical reflection on the general characteristics of experience and reflection from within the particularities of a concrete historical faith, but that we should also recognize that the philosopher and the theologian are both making claims concerning Reality. This opens up the possibility that philosophical reflection may provide a metaphysics by means of which the religious believer may better understand and communicate his faith and that faith may provide insights into the dimensions of experience which should be taken into account by any metaphysical theory.

It is probably the case that no one becomes religious merely as the result of an argument. Religious believers are more likely to report the impact of the Divine upon their lives as being the foundation of their faith. It is also the case that religious faith involves a commitment that differs from merely accepting or rejecting some hypothesis on an experimental basis. But neither of these factors lends support to the view that experience and argument should be divorced from each other in discussions of religion. In describing and interpreting our experiences, we are already engaging in arguments of a sort as we try to link one bit of data with another.

It is here that we may find the contact point between philosophical interpretations of the general dimensions of experience and theological interpretations of the experience of a particular historical community. The particular experiences within a religious community may be taken as contributing to an understanding of one's being in the world, but will do so ultimately only as they are systematically related to interpretations of the general dimensions of our experience. It is in this sense that the theologian may look to the various metaphysical theories or perhaps better the interpretive schemes which purport to give accounts of the various dimensions of experience. In this activity the theist moves beyond the more immediate experiences of the particular historical community in an effort to fill out and correct what is implicit in his speaking about God and in an effort to find confirmation for his faith in an independent realm of understanding. In this way the theist recognizes that God is both Being in whom one finds fulfillment and that which accounts for things being the way they are.

In appealing to interpretive schemes as a way of filling out and confirming the sense of the presence of God which is testified to in his act of faith, the religious believer may be said to be engaging in argumentation of a sort. The kind of argumentation that is relevant at this point may not have the form of proofs but may be related to the kind of argumentation that we encounter in many of the humanistic disciplines. Genuine disputes may arise, for example, in the interpretation of literary or historical texts, and we may appeal to factual data in attempting to settle such disputes. Literary critics may quickly agree that some interpretations are of little or no merit, but it is not always easy to decide on the best interpretation. Indeed, we may decide in some cases that the interpretations differ as the result of the different foci brought to the text and that some of the interpretations complement rather than contradict each other. I do not want to suggest that it is always clear what is taking place in disputes within this area of studies. I do want to suggest, however, that some kind of argument is going on or at least that reasons are being given and that many literary critics will argue that they are trying to give an account of all of the data without ignoring or distorting it. Something similar seems to be operating in discussions of religious faith. Beginning from the experience of the presence of the Divine, the believer may go on to provide an interpretative scheme which, to use the language of Peter Donovan, is intended to answer the question, "How else do you explain this phenomenon?" and to evoke a recognition of the presence of God in the world of persons and things as the ground of their existence.[14] The ultimate test of this interpretative scheme will be its adequacy in lighting up what is being talked about, in its letting us see it for what it is, and in accounting for the full range of our experience, linking the personal and the scientific aspects of life.

The position that I am here describing is one which would give primacy to experience but look to an interpretative scheme or metaphysics as part of the process of understanding and justifying. An interpretative scheme should be understood to be an extension of the primary experience, and such schemes are understood to help one see patterns in experience that one might otherwise overlook. At times persons who proceed in this manner ultimately give primacy to the interpretive scheme, saying that it must validate the experiences interpreted by it. I am suggesting, however, that there should be a dialectic between experience and the interpretive scheme and that in religion the experience of faith is primary. This means that in addition to ordinary tests of consistency, etc., any proposed interpretive scheme will have to be judged adequate to religious faith where the emphasis is more practical than theoretical, more concerned with the understanding of the self in relation to the Divine than with speculative theory. It should be noted, however, that if metaphysics is understood in the way suggested here, the distinction between the practical and the theoretical is not as sharp as it is sometimes thought to be.

It is probably the case that no one interpretive scheme is sufficiently comprehensive to be fully adequate to experience. Indeed even within the limits of Christian faith there appear to be a multiplicity of interpretive schemes, and when we turn our vision beyond the limits of this tradition the options are even greater. Seen together these schemes often overlap, complement or even contradict each other. In time, and with further analysis, perhaps the number of live options may diminish, but if the existentialists have taught us nothing else, they have taught us of our finiteness and historicity which set limits to our efforts to arrive at one final comprehensive interpretive scheme. The metaphysician, as understood here, extends himself beyond the provable in any strict sense of the word and this extension brings with it an ever present sense of risk and commitment. It seems more likely that in one's efforts to provide a comprehensive interpretation of experience, one will appeal to more than one interpretive scheme and that these may derive from different cultural and historical points of view.

In describing and interpreting the transcendent dimension of experience, one may be said to be giving expression to religion in language, and those authors who have emphasized the metaphorical character of religious language have done a service in focusing attention on the experiential foundation of religious faith. However, approaches which emphasize the metaphorical character of religious language have often failed to give adequate accounts of the empirical anchorage of religious language. Some views, for example, so emphasize the otherness of the Divine and the evocative character of religious language, that content is assigned to religious faith only by appeal to a self-authenticating experience or the authority of tradition. Others give up altogether the effort to assign any positive content to religion and either look to religious language as evocative of that which is other than what appears in the world of persons and things, or turn to silence. In each of these cases there is a failure to take seriously the claim that the Divine is encountered in the world of persons and things. To the extent that God is held to be transcendent to particular entities, one cannot say of a particular property that it is identical with God. To the extent, however, that God is also understood as the condition for there being entities and properties of entities at all, and to the extent that God is understood to be manifest in one's experience of persons and things, it would seem more reasonable to suggest some kinship between God and world than the contrary. The transcendent may be more than the finite, but if it is merely beyond or other than the finite, it is not clear that anything of significance can be conveyed about it.

It is, of course, one thing to say that there is this kinship and another to say in what it consists, and this task cannot be adequately undertaken here. However, a clue to the problem may be suggested in the kind of relationship that exists between persons and their language and behavior. Although persons may be said to transcend their expressions of themselves, there is a sense in which we encounter them and come to understand them through their language and behavior. A person, it may be argued, is not identical with his language and behavior, but neither is he completely other. Perhaps one might say that the language and behavior which mediate the presence of God are related to God in a way analogous to the way in which the language and behavior which mediate the presence of persons are related to them.

It is important to keep in mind that the forms of expression that one uses in this case refer ultimately to what is experienced and that in this connection an analysis of the meaning of religious expressions is intended to direct us to the experience of the Divine. One gives expression to one's experiences of God, and analyses of the meaning and truth of this language lead eventually to these and other experiences of God which tend to confirm or deny these expressions in much the same way that encounters with persons tend to confirm or deny the accuracy of talk about them.

This leads to a final point. When a religious person refers to God as the "Almighty Father," he may be said to be giving expression to patterns in experience in which the Divine is encountered. When we forget this, when we take such images to be separable from experience, we lapse into dogmatism and idolatry. Such images are intended to draw attention to some features of experience which may otherwise be overlooked, and the full significance of such images may be said to be grasped when they are seen to open the way into the disclosure of the presence of God.

Images or symbols of this kind play a vital role in religion but they are not adequate in and of themselves. Such language is far from being universally understood and seems to be dependent on the interpretive framework of a particular historical tradition. Further, such language does not seem sufficient to sustain the experience of religion amidst critical discussions. Because of this one needs to look beyond the imagery of a particular religious tradition to a more conceptual or, better perhaps, to a more universally intelligible language. This is to say neither that symbolic language should be replaced by a more conceptual language nor that the symbolic language of a religious tradition is merely evocative in character. It is to say that there should be a dialectical relationship between the imagery of a particular religion and the more conceptual language of a metaphysics or interpretive scheme. In the language of John Macquarrie, "The particular symbols are illuminated by the language of existence and being, but these concrete symbols become in turn illuminating for relatively abstract statements of an existential or ontological character."[15] To put this in another way, the imagery lights up levels of meaning which more conceptual language cannot reach. Yet without the conceptual elucidation of imagery the meaning of images would lapse into obscurity.

I am not claiming in this paper to have provided either a fully developed theory of experience or a justification for this understanding of experience and its place in the philosophy of religion. I am suggesting that an empirical approach to the philosophy of religion, somewhat along the lines that I have sketched, may provide an avenue beyond the impasse described by Mitchell. As for the philosopher hanging off the side of the cliff, perhaps there is yet someone else up there.

FOOTNOTES

1 This essay also appears in *Religious Studies*, vol. 17, no. 4 (Dec. 1981), and is reprinted by permission of the author and the publisher, Cambridge University Press.

2 Basil Mitchell, *The Justification of Religious Belief* (New York: Macmillan, 1973), p. 112.

3 Norman Malcolm, "Anselm's Ontological Arguments," *The Existence of God*, ed. John Hick (London: Collier-Macmillan, 1969), p. 67.

4 John Smith, *Experience and God* (London: Oxford Univ. Press, 1968), p. 22.

5 John Baillie, *The Sense of the Presence of God* (London: Oxford Univ. Press, 1962), p. 36.

6 Karl Jaspers, *Philosophy*, trans. E.B. Ashton (Chicago: Univ. of Chicago Press, 1971), vol. 3, pp. 5-6.

7 Ninian Smart, "Interpretation and Mystical Experience," *Religious Studies*, vol. I (1965), p. 79.

8 Martin Heidegger, *Being and Time*, trans. John Macquarrie and Edward Robinson (New York: Harper & Row, 1962), p. 58.

9 Paul Tillich, *Systematic Theology* (Chicago: Univ. of Chicago Press, 1951), vol. I, p. 106.

10 H.D. Lewis, *Our Experience of God* (London: George Allen, 1959), p. 102. See my "Experience, raison et croyance religieuse d'apres H.D. Lewis," *Archives de Philosophie*, Tome 43, Cahier 3 (1980). A revised version of this article appeared in *The Review of Metaphysics* (Sept. 1981).

11 W. Dilthey, *Meaning in History*, ed. H.P. Rickman (London: George Allen and Unwin, 1961), p. 77.

12 Heidegger, *Being and Time*, p. 28.

13 James Richmond, *Theology and Metaphysics* (London: S.C.M. Press, 1970), p. 89.

14 Peter Donovan, *Interpreting Religious Experience* (London: Sheldon Press, 1979), pp. 89ff.

15 John Macquarrie, *Principles of Christian Theology*, 2nd ed. (New York: Scribner's, 1977), p. 137.

God Is Now

Closer

Young Oon Kim

A few years ago Dorothee Sölle, a well-known German political theologian,[1] published an article in *Concilium* describing how the mainline denominations differ from Christian sects and fringe groups because the latter experience "Christianity as joy."[2] Sects and Christian fringe groups "attempt to build an island of new life in the midst of the sea of the old." Although only a small minority, tiny, despised and persecuted, these new groups proclaim all-embracing love in the power of the Spirit. For them the Christian faith can be described as an infinite passion, a passion for life. Their happiness possesses the boundlessness of an ocean; their hearts swim in pleasure because they literally *delight* in God. Members of Christian minority groups thus experience unity with the whole which produces greater vulnerability as well as intenser joy. As Professor Sölle and her colleague conclude, "It can be shown that in all sects the mood of joy and unity prevails over that of guilt and fear" because for one thing, paradise and the kingdom of God are not just a vague memory and a distant promise but a pattern for daily life and a guide to action. Secondly, a person's self-identity is not isolated from others nor is its exercise indefinitely postponed. Rather, one's personality is brought out into the open and fulfilled, because whereas older, established religions tend to adopt a pessimistic view of individuals and people, the new religious groups possess an optimistic trust in ordinary people and in the creative power of the Spirit.

Dr. Sölle proves her point by referring to the Franciscan Spirituals, Hussites, Anabaptists of the Reformation period and several Christian activist groups of our day. She characterizes minority groups as experiencing intense, life-transforming joy. I have been brought up spiritually in such minority groups all my life. The Unification Church is the third group I have been associated with. It is true, as Sölle indicates, that in all three groups there were feelings of solidarity, vitality, love, and above all great inner joy which enabled me to overcome other people's misunderstanding and all kinds of criticism.

Where did this vitality and joy spring from? They came simply because I discovered God. Before I found God, I had struggled to find some purpose for my life. That purpose and direction became clear. From then, I experienced vitality, certainty and joy in my work.

Gordon Kaufman, among others, points out how difficult it is to come into the presence of God. God has no visible body, no hands or feet.[3] So our contact is somewhat limited to His presence as an immaterial and infinite Spirit. Most mystics and psychics would agree. We cannot see God face to face.

The Judeo-Christian tradition emphasizes the personal nature of God. But it is not as easy to get to know Him as it is to know a person seated next to us. We know another human by looking at him as he talks. However, the Old Testament reports that no man can look upon God and live, so great is the blinding radiance of His face. Similarly in the New Testament we read that no man has seen God at any time. Even Moses was only allowed to view God's back.

On the other hand, the Bible teaches that all of creation is to some extent a revelation of the divine nature. "The heavens declare the glory of God and the earth shows forth His handiwork," says the Psalmist. Also Genesis records that man and woman are made in the image and likeness of God. Thus, in creation as a whole we can discover at least "vestiges" of the divine, and in each individual person we have an even clearer sign of God's nature and attributes. In spite of Barthian insistence that the creation reveals nothing but the hidden God and the sinfulness of fallen mankind completely veils God's nature,[4] the majority of Christians have always held that nature and humankind do manifest God's power and wisdom. All of Teilhard de Chardin's writings testify to the revelatory character of nature and humanity. Much to the same point is the following brief statement from a twentieth century Yale biologist: "The highest expression of man's life—the climax of the evolutionary process and still a biological fact—is his spirit, the inner, questing, desiring, aspiring part of him.... The human spirit is a bridge to the Divine. Man's spirit, rooted in life, may actually be part of the Universal Spirit, emerging from it and returning to it again."[5]

Testifying to what the Bible says, Rev. Moon likewise teaches that the essential nature of God can be learned from His creation and particularly from the creation of humankind. Lots of people talk about God. Theologians have been expounding the nature of God for years. Why is it then that Rev. Moon's ideas have created a new church? What is there to explain why he has attracted so many people in such a short period? Because of him they found God.

Since God has created man and woman in His likeness, God must have both male and female characteristics. That is quite a simple statement, yet that simple statement teaches us many important lessons about God. 1) God is personal. That means God has heart and sensations of feeling, mind and understanding, will and purpose. 2) For man and woman the most treasured experience is that of love. Their ultmate goal is to achieve mutual happiness, satisfaction and joy. Therefore the most important thing in God must also be love. The purpose of creation, providence, and all His endeavors must be to give Him divine satisfaction, happiness and enjoyment. 3) The most significant function of a person's nature is seen in his pursuit of love. Man and woman are united by love in marriage. Thereby there exist interdependence and interaction between them. When the male and female become harmoniously united, they experience maximum joy. Likewise, in God the masculine and feminine aspects must be perfectly united and harmonized. In other words, God's heart and mind perfectly interact. 4) A human being is healthy, wholesome and happy when his body and spirit are wholly united. Then his will and purposes can be achieved. Likewise, when God and mankind (His external manifestation) have harmonious interaction, His goal can be achieved. 5) Humankind is selfish as well as altruistic. People love themselves, yet they find great value and enjoyment in serving, helping and working for others. By doing so, their wisdom is multiplied and happiness is increased. In loving and serving others, people can contribute to the building of a better world while simultaneously they learn that their self-love is exalted. If this is human nature and it is derived from God, God Himself must be far more loving, self-giving and serving. 6) We are imperfect as finite creatures and fallible as sinners. Humans are not always good and loving; they hurt one another, damage one another and are destructive of one another. Consequently we find ourselves estranged from God, and the only way to reunite with Him is to correct ourselves and forgive others. Thus we can be forgiven by God. So from this experience we learn God's merciful, patient and forgiving nature. 7) Now it becomes clear how our doctrine of divine polarity is derived. Simply by observing human nature and relationships, we learn what God is like. Since polarity exists in humans and in nature in general, it also exists in God.

Several critics have charged that *Divine Principle* borrows from Oriental philosophy. Let us compare the idea of polarity espoused in Unification theology with that in Chinese thought. The original core of the *I Ching* must have been received from an unknown Chinese sage long before Lao-tzu and Confucius who transmitted it to their followers. Yin/Yang philosophy became part of traditional Korean culture many centuries ago.[6]

What does Yin/Yang theory teach? The basic clue to the ontological structure of creation is seen in the relationship between Yin and Yang: earth and heaven, moon and sun, shade and light, cold and hot, wet and dry, wood and fire, left and right, female and male. There exists the Supreme Ultimate from which the Yin and Yang principles are derived. Through the interaction of Yin and Yang, all things are created and these reflect the two principles.

Yin/Yang philosophy is not dualistic, as some mistakenly assume. Rather it is a basic metaphysics of relatedness and a philosophy of mutuality. Yin/Yang is not a matter of opposites, not either/or but both/and. Yin does not contradict Yang; and the female is not fundamentally antithetical to the male principle. They are like two sides of a coin or two wings of a butterfly. Yin/Yang complement each other and are fulfilled in a relationship of harmony.

Nor are Yin and Yang to be understood as inferior and superior, lower and higher. This is another common mistake. Sunshine and rain, night and day are equally valuable depending on the circumstances. As the Chinese used to say, a gentleman is both a Confucian and a Taoist. He is a Confucianist exercising Yang as a public official. He is a Taoist following Yin at home in his study when he is composing poetry or playing his lute.

Y.P. Mei of Yenching University summarizes East Asian metaphysics as follows:

1) Both the universe and man's life are real.
2) The nature of reality is dynamic and relational rather than static

or absolute.

3) All changes result from the interaction of Yin and Yang, between which there should be balance and harmony.

4) These changes supplement and alternate with one another, usually in a cyclical or a spiral way.

5) The universe is a macrocosm and man is a microcosm.[7]

Yin/Yang philosophy illustrates the mutuality of internal and external, female and male, in man, nature and God. However, there is a major difference between *Divine Principle* and Yin/Yang theory. In Chinese philosophy the Supreme Ultimate (Tai-Chi) is not interpreted as a personal God who has a loving heart or a conscious will, but as the Tao, a cosmic law.

Moreover, in Christian thinking, God created two human individuals as the crown of creation, whereas in Yin/Yang philosophy the Tao creates two impersonal natural principles. For Christianity, the creation of Adam and Eve was of central importance in God's providence, while Yin/Yang theory does not emphasize man's crucial role and does not give a strong impression of a man-centered creation. Nevertheless, the ancient Yin/Yang philosophy does adequately explain the relationship between God and creation, God and man, male and female.

Some scholars think *Divine Principle* is nothing but neo-classical theism. Let us compare the *Divine Principle* doctrine of God with that of Whitehead and the process theologians. There is much similarity between process thought and Unification theology. Both espouse dipolar theism. Both reject the exclusively masculine definition of God. Both emphasize divine sensitivity. Both raise questions about God's omnipotence. And both teach the importance of man's free will and the need of his cooperation if God's ultimate purpose is to be realized.[8]

Considerable differences should also be noted. Unification theology talks about God's heart and body or internal nature and external form rather than the primordial and consequent natures of God. By "heart" or "internal nature" we include God's affectionate qualities, His rational mind and His conscious will. By "body" or "external form" we do not mean that God is material or corporeal: we believe God is infinite Spirit. God's body refers to the whole creation and particularly humankind, both in the spirit world and on earth through whom God expresses Himself in varied degrees by means of His divine energy.

Divine Principle talks about universal prime energy and heart (which is really a combination of heart and mind). Traditionally Christians call God the source of life. What does this mean? My understanding is that everything in nature is made up of patterns of energy which originate with God.

There is another aspect to polarity in *Divine Principle*: the masculine and feminine elements in the Godhead. As the process theologians maintain, God's character is not exclusively masculine but also possesses feminine qualities.[9] Furthermore, for Unificationism the interaction between these two sides of God's nature generates the prime energy needed to bring about creation. Thus, the work of creation is a continuing process, as the Whiteheadians maintain. Since *Divine Principle* interprets polarity as a mutual relationship between heart and body, there is constant interaction between them, much as process theology affirms continous interaction between God's primordial and consequent natures.

As Moltmann complains, in the past theologians asserted that God is completely impassive.[10] Copying Aristotle, they said that God is the Unmoved Mover and First Cause. But this philosophic Absolute of the Greeks is not at all the concerned, involved, loving God of the Bible. Here process theology and Unification theology are very close.

Since God is the God of heart, He is very sensitive to everything that goes on in the world. Process thinkers say that God is as much affected by events happening in the world as the world is affected and influenced by God.

Unificationists declare that God rejoiced at the creation of Adam and Eve. He grieved at their fall and expulsion from Eden. In Noah's day God became angry when He saw men's sins and wickedness. He heard the cry of the enslaved Hebrews in Egypt and was happy to lead them to the Promised Land.

In later times, Isaiah received the word of the Lord, saying:

> I have nourished and brought up children, and they have rebelled against me. The ox knoweth its owner and the ass its master's crib.

But Israel doth not know, my people doth not consider.... (Is. 1:2b-3)

Similarly Hosea used his own experience with a faithless wife to illustrate how broken-hearted God felt when Israel betrayed His trust and love.

In the parable of the prodigal son, Jesus described vividly how God awaits the return of His wayward child. No matter how much a parent hates the sinful action of his child, how much it hurts or how bad it is, he cannot ever cut the bond of love between them. This fact teaches the foundation for God's saving providence. He cannot cut the bond of love. If God could cut His ties to man and give him up, He would be unable to carry out His saving will.

Finally, when God's anointed, His own Son, was crucified by faithless and wicked hands, God stood by the cross, grieving and suffering with Jesus Christ. These are not just stories from the past. Up to the present time, God has been with his loved ones everywhere, sharing their joy and sorrow, strengthening the weak, comforting the lonely, inspiring the seeking. Thus, we Unificationists believe that God is very personal, the God of passionate love and tender-hearted affection.

Now then, how can the Infinite Spirit, the cosmic Creator, affect every individual and be affected by them? For process theologians, the world affects God's consequent nature because everything that happens is part of His own body or internal environment.[11] God is affected by the events in the world exactly as we are affected by a cut, a bruise, a sensation of pleasure or pain in our body. This means God is everywhere and close to us at all times, "the Fellow-sufferer who understands."[12]

I would look at this matter a little differently. How can the infinite God be related to each and every individual? Let us think of God in terms of divine love and wisdom, usually symbolized by warmth and light. As the diagram shows, God is at the center which is the hottest and brightest spot. He appears like the sun around which exist many concentric circles. Those near to the center are warm and bright, while those farther from the center are cooler and dim, with those at the outer edge even cold and dark.

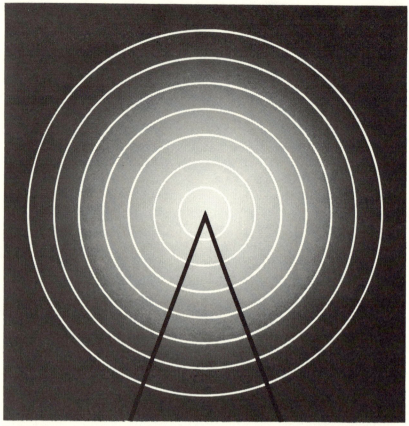

In this diagram, the concentric circles revolve around a center which symbolizes God. God is the cosmic center of love radiating outward. The two straight lines meeting at the center indicate the upward path to God at the highest point of truth.

People already gone to the spirit world and people still on earth dwell somewhere in those concentric circles, depending upon their spiritual growth and maturity. By spiritual growth I mean how much they understand God's truth, perceive God's love and manifest them in their lives. How can they advance closer to the center which is God? Only by serving others and helping other people through teaching and guidance, thus ministering to them and to God.

So around God are many people willing and eager to serve Him and their fellows. God can never directly reach those in the far distant circles. For one thing, it is painful for God to come in contact with men who are so unlike Him, and it would be destructive to those souls who are used to life in an outer circle. Similarly, for the same reason a soul on the outer edge finds it impossible to reach so far up to God. Hence the only means of communication for both God and the spirits at various levels is through intermediaries who serve as God's mouth, hands and feet.

Recall how Jesus said (Matt. 18:10), "See that you don't despise any of these little ones. Their angels in heaven, I tell you, are always in the presence of my Father in heaven." This means that you are never alone; you are always with some spirits and angels who function as ministering intermediaries between you and God.

Since we are not dealing with Christology I shall not go into any detail, but it is necessary to mention the unique role of the Messiah as a mediator. God intended to have Adam and Eve as His first representatives. When Adam failed to fulfill that position, God sent another Son to replace him. Therefore if Jesus had fulfilled his mission He would have become God's first representative forever. People can never see God face to face, but through Christ they see the Father.

Communication between God and any soul is instantaneous, like the way the nerve system works in our bodies. So all sincere prayers are heard, whether spoken or unspoken. And the distance between you and God at the center is determined by the degree and intensity of your love for Him. You can shorten the distance if you so desire, of course; if you earnestly and intensely long to love God and others. Only by love, in love, through love can you hasten your course. Thus you see how sensitive God is. Because He is the God of love He must be supersensitive, far greater than anyone can imagine.

Process theologians claim that God is not omnipotent because mankind has free will and the entire creation possesses a measure of indeterminacy.[13] This is to deny that an omnipotent and omniscient God predetermined everything before creation. If God is all-knowing and almighty, He knew the Fall would take place and allowed it to occur, knew Jesus would die on the cross and permits everything that ever happens.

We agree with most of this process criticism. But we look at the problem rather differently. For Unificationists, God's omnipotence is qualified at this stage because man is under Satan's dominion and is Satan's ally. God is therefore unable to exercise complete freedom. However, when His sovereignty is fully reestablished on earth and the majority of mankind allies itself with God, He will become freer and mightier than now. It is really people and their fallen condition which bind God and limit His power.

There are still other important differences between Whiteheadian theism and *Divine Principle*'s teaching about God. Unificationists believe in the reality of a personal Satan and his present dominion over mankind. We affirm that God created a single couple as the parents of the entire human race. Adam and Eve were seduced by Satan, sexually fell and were expelled from the Garden of Eden. The effects of their original sin are transmitted to all their descendants, alienating them from God. Hence a Messiah is needed to remove original sin and establish the kingdom of God on earth. God has been working throughout history to realize the original plan for creation, to restore man to his true status and to reestablish the divine sovereignty. Thus, we do not believe history is open-ended but rather that history has a definite goal consummating in a new heaven and a new earth.

There are striking similarities between *Divine Principle* and Swedenborg's idea of God, so some wonder if Rev. Moon was influenced by Swedenborg's teachings. When I heard Divine Principle lectures for the first time in Korea twenty-seven years ago, I immediately noted their closeness. Both *Divine Principle* and Swedenborgianism are revealed theology; therefore, it is impossible not to combine revealed and natural theologies in my discussion.

Swedenborg describes God's essence as a union of divine love and divine wisdom.[14] Love is the underlying substance of God, and wisdom is God's form. A man has two faculties—understanding and will—so does God. God is the source of man's wisdom, and His love is the cause of our will toward goodness. What does it mean to say God is love? 1) God loves others out of Himself. 2) God desires to become one with humanity. 3) God makes people supremely happy. He longs to give them the blessings of eternal life and unending delight. By making divine love and wisdom the starting point for his theology, Swedenborg corrects many features of traditional Christian thought.

He teaches that man is a representative image of wisdom, and woman is a representative image of love, so they naturally form a reciprocal relationship. This is like Unification theology's emphasis upon the balance of man and woman and their interaction.

To emphasize the mysterious supernatural power of God, many Christians have said that God created the universe *ex nihilo*. Swedenborg disagreed, as *Divine Principle* does. It is impossible for anything to be made out of nothing. God created the universe out of Himself. As God was the only substance prior to creation, from His being were derived all things that exist. The created universe is not God, yet comes from God. Creation is so full of divine love and wisdom, it could be called their image, Swedenborg wrote.

Man and the universe are microcosm and macrocosm. There is a correspondence of all things in the universe with all things in man. Like man, all animals possess desires or affections. Like man, all vegetables have a will to live and grow. And like man, the mineral kingdom has a lastingness and stability which resemble our concern to be related to the ultmate. So when we see spiritually, the created world is an image which is "representative of God-man."

There are two worlds, the spiritual and the natural. These are distinct yet similar. Spirit world has trees, mountains, cities and societies, just as does the natural world. The only difference is that each thing in one world is spiritual, whereas its counterpart in the other world is natural. Here too there is a striking agreement between Swedenborg and Unification theology.

Why did God create the world? Swedenborg teaches that its universal purpose is that there might be an eternal conjunction of the Creator and His creation. God wants men and women to be His habitations, so every created thing is finally designed for the sake of man and woman. Creation is in continual progression toward an ultimate end. God expects men to elevate themselves to their Creator and conjoin themselves with Him.

After creation, God's government by love and wisdom is called His providence. He did not create the universe for its own sake but for the sake of humankind. Providence therefore refers to God's means by which man can be turned from hell and led to heaven. Again Unification theology and Swedenborg are in general agreement.

Holy marriage is one of the most important doctrines for Swedenborg.[15] Men and women are inclined for "conjunction into one" as part of God's plan for creation. However, there are two kinds of marriage: the natural or biological kind and the spiritual. Swedenborg stresses the significance of the higher type. Man was created by God to understand truth, while woman was created to be "an affection of good." Spiritual marriage then refers to the masculine understanding of truth wed to female goodness. The male represents the wisdom of love while the female symbolizes the love of wisdom. The holiness of marriage is derived from the union of these two embodied virtues.

As man is born intellectual and woman is created affectional, when male and female become one, their union signifies humanity in its fullness. To use Swedenborg's language, when earthly marriages come from love of goodness and truth, the kingdom of God on earth corresponds to the kingdom in heaven. Marriage originates with God, fills humans with heavenly love, and makes them in the image of the Lord. Such marriages are therefore eternal.

There are a great many resemblances between Swedenborgianism and Divine Principle: Infinite Spirit is personal and contains two aspects, masculine and feminine, wisdom and love. There exist regular correspondence and communication between the two worlds. God's highest blessing comes with the union of a man and woman whose marriage is the image of the conjunction of divine wisdom and love. The purpose of creation for God and humanity is to experience the greatest joy and delight; therefore, its final goal is a kingdom of ecstatic bliss. Accordingly, our ultimate destiny in the spirit world will be a state where both God and all humans experience perfect conjugal love and unity.

Now is there any difference between *Divine Principle* and Swedenborg's teachings, specifically in their doctrines about God?

Here we must keep two things in mind: First, Swedenborg lived about two hundred and forty years before Rev. Moon. We must assume that important spiritual developments have taken place since the eighteenth century. Secondly, each claimed a special and different mission in revealing the hidden truths about God. Swedenborg's unique mission was to instruct and enlighten mankind through his writings, namely, by revealing the inner spiritual meaning of the Word of God. By doing so he displayed remarkable insight, yet, like Origen, sometimes went too far in his allegorical exegesis. Like Swedenborg, Rev. Moon believes that certain important scriptural passages have to be decoded to see their true meaning, but he does not use the allegorical method as frequently and extensively. Yet both men proclaim teachings which are as rational as liberal theology at its best and quite revolutionary in the light of their environments.

On the other hand, Rev. Moon's unique mission is not only to instruct mankind but to carry out God's will in our special time. Even though their doctrines of God are very close, *Divine Principle* is more specific and concrete and reveals more determined readiness to act. There is also an urgency in Rev. Moon's sense of mission which is missing from the rather philosophic, abstract tone of Swedenborg.

Another point of difference is that Rev. Moon interprets the beginning and end of human history from the perspective of the establishment of God's kingdom on earth, whereas Swedenborg explains the creation of man and the consummation of history from the perspective of the most ancient church and its renewals. Adam and Eve represented the most ancient church which has been corrupted and repeatedly restored through God's successive dispensations. At last God will establish a new church and New Jerusalem with the revealed truth at the consummation of history.

Some critics of Unificationism allege that we lack a sense of God's holiness. To relate Creator and creation as intimately as we do destroys God's utter transcendence, it is said. Earlier I compared God to a center of heat and light, absolute love and wisdom, so hot and so bright that it is not possible to come close to Him. In the Old Testament period Jews therefore spoke of God's holiness as unapproachable, like a consuming fire.

As numerous mystics testify, when one sees God's radiance —even only a stream of light or ray of divine heat—he feels ecstatic joy and tremendous vitality, enlightenment and inspiration. He also experiences being cleansed and the satisfying comfort of forgiveness and total bliss. Rudolf Otto describes this state as the "mysterium tremendum."[16] When God appears, we tremble, shudder and become transported into ecstasy. We are utterly fascinated, exalted, literally possessed by the divine and filled with ineffable joy. Therefore Otto describes this as the highest, strongest, best, loveliest and dearest experience that men can think of. At such moments, man feels utter dependence upon God, which I suppose is why Schleiermacher defined religion as the feeling of absolute dependence. Out of such elation and adoration one feels a sense of complete release and liberation. You express yourself, sometimes in laughter like the Shakers, in singing, or even in dancing as King David did bringing the ark to Jerusalem.

On the basis of such experiences of the sacred, I can understand how theologies of play and joy, a dancing God and a feast of fools are produced.[17] People outside, on-lookers, may criticize such worshippers for lack of holiness, reverence and proper solemnity. But is that really a fair allegation? Such critics have never witnessed the seriousness, sanctity and holiness of our hours of meditation and prayer but have only seen our light, humorous mood and sociability.

Here I would like to refer to Eliade.[18] Talking about the primordial religions, he explains that the holy and secular need not and should not be sharply contrasted. For the religious person, the sacred exists to transform the world. The holy transcends this world but manifests itself in and through the world, sanctifying it and making it more real. Life has a sacred origin and human existence realizes its potentialities as it becomes permeated with the divine spirit. An experience of God opens up man to the world. For him the whole of life becomes capable of being sanctified. All vital experiences—whether eating or loving, work or play—are sacralized.

Hence religious experience is not designed to separate people from the ordinary world, to turn them into contemplative monks. Jesus and his disciples went from the mountaintop experience of the Transfiguration back into the valley to continue their ministry of teaching and healing. The same was true of William Booth. After his conversion, he immediately moved into the London slums to minister to the outcast, the forgotten, the rejected dregs of society. Gripped by God's love, Booth set forth to save the world. With the same spirit, Kagawa in Japan lived with and worked for people in the slums with the love of Christ. These illustrate how the sacred can permeate the secular to transform it. Such a relationship between the sacred and profane is derived from a profound understanding of God. God's range of feelings and breadth of concern are limitless. He feels the most exuberant joy and heart-rending sorrow.

Rev. Moon teaches us to experience a deep and wide scope of feelings and to achieve harmony with many different types of people. This is why we try not only to embrace all kinds of persons but to engage in a wide variety of activities to enrich our spirituality as well as to build a multi-dimensional kingdom of God. So sometimes we may look quite secular and not at all religious. But a precious experience with the Almighty is always deeply treasured and becomes the source of and the motivation for all one's external activities.

If I ended here, I would be no different from those who merely read theology and hand down that knowledge to others. Religion must be based on first-hand experience. Through your own feelings you have to perceive God's life-giving power and love. Therefore as my conclusion I should like to explain how one can have a personal encounter with God. Of course, this has nothing to do with a detached, apathetic state of mind.

First you must have a fervent desire and overwhelming yearning for God. This urge must be so intense, so predominant in your mind, that you cannot think of anything else until it is satisfied. Your prayer must be desperate and passionate. And this attitude should not last only a week or a month but continue until God responds to you. To use Tillich's phrase, you have to be in a boundary situation, between life and death, so to speak, as in the lives of Sadhu Sundar Singh, St. Francis, Therese of the Little Flower, Ann Lee of the Shakers, Joseph Smith and John Wesley who sought God fervently and desperately until their cry finally reached Him. (I only mention familiar names, but I personally know many others who had the same experience).

Kierkegaard said and Barth agreed that every age is equidistant from God.[19] We are not any closer to God than Abraham or St. Paul. They are mistaken. Spiritually we are now living in an unprecedented time. Due to God's providential accomplishments and mankind's spiritual growth, we are much closer to God than ever before.

You can be close to God or God will come close to you in many ways, not just in your times of prayer and meditation. He may come when you struggle to get at the truth about certain problems. Or He may come when you engage in a lifetime vocation of service to humanity, like Mother Theresa, loving small abandoned children, feeling they are her own brothers and sisters, seeing God in their dirty faces, providing them with food and shelter, for the sake of God's love. That kind of loving service and action has the same effect as prayer to attract God's attention.

In conclusion let me quote one of my favorite poems by Tagore:

Have you not heard His silent steps?
He comes, comes, ever comes.
Every moment and every age, every day and every night
He comes, comes, ever comes...
In sorrow after sorrow, it is His steps
    that press upon my heart
And it is the golden touch of His feet
    that makes my joy to shine.[20]

FOOTNOTES

1 She wrote this with her husband, sociologist Fulbert Steffensky.

2 J.B. Metz and J. Jossua, *Theology of Joy* (1974), pp. 113-25.

3 G.D. Kaufman, *God the Problem* (1972), pp. 84-85.

4 K. Barth, *Nein* (E.T. 1946); cf. H. Von Balthasar, *The Theology of Karl Barth* (1972), pp. 48-69.

5 E.W. Sinnott, *The Biology of the Spirit* (1955), p. 164.

6 A. Forke, *The World-Conception of the Chinese* (1975), pp. 163-226.

7 C.A. Moore, ed., *The Chinese Mind* (1967), p. 150.

8 J. Cobb and D. Griffin, *Process Theology* (1976), pp. 8-10.

9 *Ibid.*, pp. 61-62.

10 Cf. M.D. Meeks, *Origins of the Theology of Hope* (1974), pp. 80-86.

11 C. Hartshorne, *Man's Vision of God* (1964), pp. 174-205.

12 A.N. Whitehead, *Process and Reality* (1929), p 413.

13 D. Brown *et al.*, *Process Philosophy and Christian Thought* (1971), p. 79.

14 E. Swedenborg, *Divine Providence* (1764) and *Divine Love and Wisdom* (1763).

15 E. Swedenborg, *Conjugal Love* (1768).

16 R. Otto, *The Idea of the Holy* (1970).

17 Cf. books by Moltmann, S. Keen and H. Cox with these titles.

18 M. Eliade, *The Sacred and the Profane* (1959), pp. 167-68, 201-13.

19 D.D. Williams, *God's Grace and Man's Hope* (1949), pp. 123-26.

20 R. Tagore, *Gitanjali* (1971), pp. 58-59.

God and Prayer

Shlomo Biderman

I

Prayer is commonly held to be one of man's most noble and profound ways of expression. To many, it seems that in prayer man not only gives voice to innermost desires, feelings and experiences, but articulates the very essence of his experience as a human being. Consider, for example, the impassioned cry, "Oh, Lord, not will you reject me", found in an ancient Babylonian prayer dedicated to Marduk. One cannot remain unmoved by the emotional depth of this entreaty. In turning to his God in prayer, man expresses, perhaps above all else, his feeling of absolute dependence; standing before the sublime, man subordinates his existence to that of the divine Being. This profound feeling of total dependence is expressed in many diverse prayers in different religions at different times. A Hindu devotional hymn, for example, written in the tenth century A.D., begins with the words:

> God of my clan,
> I shall not place my feet
> but where your feet
> have stood before:
> I have no feet
> of my own.[1]

However, prayer is not only a profound mode of expression for the individual believer. Prayer, in one form or another, can be found in almost all historical religions. Being a universal element of living religions, prayer must be considered an essential element of religious phenomena as such. William James wrote, in this vein, that

> Prayer...is the very soul and essence of religion.... Prayer is religion in act; that is, prayer is real religion. It is prayer that distinguishes the religious phenomenon from such similar or neighboring phenomena as purely moral or aesthetic sentiment.[2]

The purpose of the present article is to present an analysis of the religious phenomenon of prayer in which the psychological background and personal aspects of prayer will play no significant role. Focusing our attention on the elements of prayer within public, institutional religion, the view will be defended that what characterizes prayer should be phrased in terms of its content, a function of which is to maximize the participation of the members of the religious community in what the religion takes to be its history.

II

According to one prevailing conception, prayer is to be understood as a specific form of communication. One proponent of this view defines prayer as "an act of communication by man with the sacred or holy—God, the gods, the transcendent realm, or supernatural power".[3]

This definition of prayer as communication raises various sorts of difficulties. First, it raises an empirical difficulty: How, exactly, does the conversation between man and God take place? To what extent is God involved in the process of communication? Second, it raises theological difficulties. One may ask, for example, what point is there to man's petitioning God with prayer, if God is held to be omniscient, good and beneficent? Moreover, there exists a conceptual difficulty that bears on the very *meaning* of the concept of prayer as an act of communication. What does it mean to talk with God or with a supernatural being? Doesn't the notion of prayer as communication completely distort the original meaning of the notion of communication? To put it more bluntly, is not the believer who prays in fact talking to himself?

One philosopher for whom this conceptual issue is especially important is D.Z. Phillips. In his book, *The Concept of Prayer*,[4] Phillips, a follower of the later Wittgenstein, adopts Wittgenstein's dictum that philosophy "leaves everything as it is": the task of philosophy is "to put everything before us and neither explain nor deduce anything".[5] Phillips holds, accordingly, that an appropriate philosophical treatment of the concept of prayer must avoid explanations and theories, and restrict itself to giving an account of prayer. Such an account can be given if we understand prayer 'from the inside', through the eyes of the believers themselves. In so doing, close attention must be paid not only to the surface grammar of the believers' speech-acts, but also their depth grammar, which is dependent on the context of the religious utterances. Phillips attempts, by means of this form of observation, to clarify the conceptual framework necessary for understanding prayer.

Phillips starts from the premise that prayer is an act of communication. He claims that although "not all prayers can be described as talking to God ... they are nevertheless claimed to be meetings with the supernatural or encounters with the divine".[6] Here the question I posed earlier arises again: Is it not the case that the believer who prays is actually talking to himself?

Phillips devotes a large part of his book to this problem. His solution to the problem may be summed up as follows: The meaning of prayer depends on a wider body of religious beliefs and practices. The question of whether or not in praying one speaks with the divine is identical with the question of whether or not one prays. This question is an essentially religious one, and can be decided only by appealing to the criterion of prayer as it finds expression within the religious community. On the one hand, prayer cannot be regarded as a dialogue the believer conducts with himself: "A conviction that one is talking to oneself is the death of prayer";[7] but on the other hand, prayer is not to be identified with talks and conversations one conducts in everyday life. There are crucial differences between talking with God and talking with a human being. God, as opposed to human beings, does not participate in the conversation. Phillips thus concludes that prayer is not conversation, for "When God is reported to have said something, it does not make sense to suppose that anyone else can say directly what God has said".[8] Therefore, "God does not participate *in* any language, but He *is* to be found in the language people learn when they come to learn about religion".[9]

In prayer, man's address to God is unlike that to anyone else. For example, the believer does not tell God anything that God does not already know. Accordingly, Phillips maintains that through prayer man attains deeper knowledge of himself. He quotes Kierkegaard in this connection:

> The prayer does not change God, but it changes the one who offers it...Not God, but you, the maker of the confession, get to know something by your act of confession.[10]

Phillips concludes that "God is told nothing, but in the telling, the person who confesses is told something about the state of his soul".[11]

It is not my intention here to analyse Phillips' position in detail. I only wish to make one further point. Phillips devotes a chapter of his book to the relation between prayer and the "concept of community", but this chapter does not add much to what he says about prayer on the part of the individual. As he puts it, "in talking to God, the members of the community are also talking to each other, in so far as what they tell God tells them something about each other at the same time".[12] Just as prayer reveals to man something about himself, so too the members of the community employ it to learn something about each other.

III

Phillips' understanding of the concept of prayer develops, it seems to me, in a rather odd manner. At the outset of his analysis Phillips expressly adheres to the 'Wittgensteinian' method. However, as his analysis progresses, he gradually drifts away from this method, and introduces in its place a series of psychological postulations. Indeed, many attempts have been made to analyse and explain prayer in terms of the psychology of the believer. These attempts all assume that prayer reflects some psychological need or other of the believer, or, to put it more generally, that the need to pray stems from the individual's mental make-up. Those who thus 'psychologize' prayer maintain that some people have a greater need for praying while others can easily do without it. Those who pray are seen as having the type of personality for which prayer is an important means for expressing the individual's inner instincts and needs.

It is very difficult to make a definitive judgement concerning the adequacy of a psychological interpretation of prayer. If we understand the concept of a 'psychological need' in its everyday sense, then the claim that prayer meets a psychological need becomes trivial. Any form of human behaviour can, directly or indirectly, be interpreted as serving some psychological need or other. In order to escape the trap of triviality, the psychological interpretation of prayer must anchor itself in a satisfactory *theory* of the nature of psychological needs and their relation to human behaviour. Once such a theory is produced, the psychological interpretation of prayer then stands or falls by it. Should a candidate theory be produced, the philosopher of religion would be obliged to follow a policy of restraint, and refrain from taking a position on the meaning of prayer until the issue of the conceptual status of the psychological theory in question has been resolved—a long and complex undertaking.

However, philosophy of religion is not obliged to await the verdict upon any psychological theory. It may view religion, not as a matter of individual psychology, but as a social institution. According to this conception, philosophy of religion will not dwell upon phenomena of private religious experience but rather focus its attention on the system of rules, norms and ways of behaviour which constitute a given society. Its aim will be to give an adequate account of the system of rules, norms and ways of behaviour which constitute religion as a social institution. Thus, prayer is to be understood as a sub-institution of religion.

Prayer, considered in a social context, is often called 'liturgical prayer'. Liturgical prayer is distinguished from the personal, spontaneous prayer of the individual by its being organized within the framework of the religious institution. This framework varies, of course, from religion to religion, and there is no need to go into the differences here. Suffice it to say that the religious rules and regulations may apply to diverse aspects of prayer (such as the very obligation to pray, the set times for prayer, the places where prayer is allowed or prohibited, the quorum required to conduct prayer, authorized and binding texts for prayer, the behaviour of the worshipper during prayer, and so forth). In addition to such rules and regulations, most religions embrace a larger framework of norms the aim of which is to link up prayer with other life-directing patterns of religion.

Thus, the philosophical analysis of prayer must not take as its subject the prayer that a man whispers to himself in times of crisis and distress, or when he is spiritually elated. I do not mean to belittle such experiences, but it seems to me that preoccupation with them will blur the boundaries between religion and other fields of human thought and action. Furthermore, in order to account for such experiences we would need to have a satisfactory psychological theory, as I have pointed out before.

Returning now to Phillips, we see that there are two mutually exclusive alternative approaches to the subject of prayer. The first is to accept Phillips' pre-theoretical psychological determinations as a basis for explaining the concept of prayer. This would mean focusing our attention on understanding "the state of man's soul" (as Phillips puts it). Phillips speaks of man's limitations, and of his feeling of dependence; as followers of Phillips' approach we would have to propose a theoretical model that would interpret the terms 'limitation' and 'dependence'. This would, of course, mean disregarding Wittgenstein's approach according to which philosophy must "leave everything as it is". The other alternative is to account for prayer as something constituted by a framework of rules, norms and modes of behaviour embedded in institutional religion. On this alternative we set ourselves the more modest task of 'drawing a picture' of prayer. We must remain descriptively faithful to the ways in which prayer is characterized *within* religion, and to the place it occupies in the thoughts and behaviour of the members of the religious community. I believe this alternative to be the more fruitful for an understanding of the concept of prayer. In what follows I shall adumbrate an analysis of liturgical prayer along these lines.

IV

An obvious starting point for our descriptive task would seem to be the 'addressee' of prayer—God, the divine being, or the supernatural realm (this was, as you may recall, Phillips' point of departure). However, if our aim is to describe prayer from the point of view of institutional religion, with its rules and norms, we cannot begin with God. This is because God's status as the one who receives prayers will depend on the specific character of the framework of religious rules. Accordingly, the status of God as the 'addressee' of prayer may differ greatly from one religion to the other. With regard to some monotheistic religions, one may speak of God as independent of man's worship of him, whereas with regard to other monotheistic religions (Judaism being, in my opinion, a case in point), the notion of God is conceptually dependent upon the notion of 'the worship of God'—that is, there is no point in developing a 'neutral' theology that would be independent of the religious obligation to worship God. Another possibility is that of a religion which holds liturgical prayer as one of its tenets and, at one and the same time, holds a purely atheistic viewpoint (such a religion is presented, for example, by the Hindu *Mīmāmsā* school).[13] There are, of course, many other ways in which the concept of God may be related to the concept of prayer. Therefore, I would suggest that we refrain from using God as a starting point in our descriptive task, since our aim is to give as general a description as possible of prayer in religion.

There is, however, another possible point of departure: the *content* of prayer. It is obviously not my intention to belabour the reader with a detailed and elaborate comparison of prayer-texts of various religions, but rather to dwell upon the basic common characteristics of the content of prayers in religions. Adopting such a procedure will result, it seems to me, in a three-fold typology of liturgical prayer:

1. Prayers concerning the past. These prayers relate to what has already occurred, either in the life of the believer, or in the history of the religious community of which he is part and member. Prayers of thanksgiving belong to this category; through these prayers the individual or the community offer thanks for a past event. Prayers of confession also belong to this category; through these prayers the individual or the community confess to past deeds.

2. Prayers concerning the future. These prayers contain descriptions of future states-of-affairs desired by the individual or the community. Foremost in this category are, of course, petitionary prayers. These prayers may express the desire for individual benefits (such as good health, long life, material goods and prosperity, the achievement of personal goals, etc.), as well as an expression of craving for the attainment of future material or rather spiritual ideals concerning the community. In certain cases these prayers may contain descriptions of an ultimate ideal future, along the lines of "the wolf shall live with the sheep".

3. Prayers that relate to no definite time. These prayers relate to what may be called (if I may be allowed to use a theological usage) the 'eternal present'. Prayers of such a kind express adoration of the objects the religion holds to be divine or sacred (God, Buddha, holy sages, and the like). They may as well express praise of objects held divine, that is, praise not contingent upon the wants and desires either of the individual or the community.

Earlier I maintained that there can be no religion without prayer. Now I wish to claim that every institutional religion must relate to the three types of prayer mentioned above. My claim is not that every religion must actually contain prayers of each type, but that in cases where prayers of one type are missing, the absence should be accounted for explicitly by the religion in question. In other words, the content of prayer embraces these three types —past, future, and 'eternal present'—and whenever a religion omits one or more of the three types, it should include a specific justification concerning the omission. For example, Jainism explains the absence of future-related (petitionary) prayers in terms of its rigorously deterministic outlook, according to which it is pointless to try changing the future. Jainism thus expressly places the future beyond the pale of prayer; it does allow, however, for prayers that do not relate to future events.

My view, implicit in my previous remarks, is that the function of prayer in institutional religion is to maximize the participation of the members of the religious community in what the religion considers as its *history*. Obviously, religion does not aim at presenting a scientific, 'objective' historical document; rather it aims at an evaluation of history in terms of its *religious* significance. In prayer, religious significance is attached to past, future, and to what is beyond them.

In most cases, the scriptures of a religion provide the foundations of its history. Prayer, together with other rituals and ceremonies, stems directly from these common foundations. When the believer accepts the obligation of prayer, with all its exacting requirements, he accepts thereby a religious evaluation concerning his own personal history, as regards to the believer's past and future alike. Likewise, through prayer the believer assumes his place among a community which has a collective history (such as significant past events, places that have become sacred, dates that have special religious importance, and the like). The same is true with regard to the future; through prayer each individual expresses his resolve to maintain and preserve the religious values of the community. For the believer it means that religious values take priority over all other values that may conflict with them. The religious past and the religious future are jointly bound to what I called the 'eternal present'. The 'eternal present' in prayer serves as the distinguishing mark that sets religion apart from all other social institutions that have histories and values of their own. Its aim is to attach a religious perspective to past and future. If the religion in question is a theistic one, then God will feature prominently in all three types of its prayers. In non-theistic religions, however, God's status within prayer will be less prominent. Atheistic religions will, of course, present prayers in which God, as the 'addressee' of prayer, plays no role. The notion of God is not, therefore, one which determines the meaning of the concept of prayer. To the contrary, the very concept of prayer determines the meaning and the status of the notion of God.

FOOTNOTES

1 *Speaking of Siva*, trans. A.K. Ramanujan (London: Penguin, 1973), p. 106.

2 William James, *The Varieties of Religious Experience* (Toronto: Collier, 1961), lecture 19, p. 361.

3 A.G. Hamman, "Prayer", *Encyclopaedia Britannica: Macropaedia*, 1974 ed., vol. 14, p. 948.

4 D.Z. Phillips, *The Concept of Prayer* (London: Routledge & Kegan Paul, 1965).

5 See L. Wittgenstein, *Philosophical Investigations*, I:123, 126.

6 Phillips, *The Concept of Prayer*, p. 30.

7 *Ibid.*, p. 41.

8 *Ibid.*, p. 49.

9 *Ibid.*, pp. 50-51.

10 S. Kierkegaard, *Purity of Heart*, as quoted in Phillips, *The Concept of Prayer*, p. 56.

11 Phillips, *The Concept of Prayer*, p. 59.

12 *Ibid.*, p. 132.

13 Although *Mīmāṃsā* rejects monotheism, that is, God, it requires at least some version of polytheism. The gods it accepts are not the creators or legislators of the cosmic order (*rita*) but, like man, are subject to it, and the rules of the Vedas apply to them just as they apply to mankind. They act, not freely, but in accord with a fixed causal principle, so that human ritual can obligate the gods to act for the benefit of human beings.

Against Despair

John Roth

In his book, *Legends of Our Time*, the Jewish survivor-author, Elie Wiesel, remarks: "At Auschwitz, not only man died, but also the idea of man.... It was its own heart the world incinerated at Auschwitz."[1] Part of what Wiesel is alluding to with that imagery, I believe, can be discerned by tracing how various senses of human identity are influenced as one confronts the catastrophe that befell the Jews of Europe under Hitler forty years ago. The more one studies the Holocaust, the clearer it becomes that the destruction process enlisted and encompassed the support of diverse human energies and occupations. Thus, as we contemplate our own identities today, we may find that purity and innocence are not easy to come by.

Let me illustrate what I mean. We often identify ourselves by the kind of work we do or plan to do. Some of us are teachers and writers. Others are lawyers, physicians, business executives, or artists. Insofar as such professions link us with a human tradition, and they do, an encounter with the Holocaust reminds us that none of these vocations permits us to stand by smugly and assert that our ways of work had nothing to do with Auschwitz. Teachers and writers helped to till the soil in which Hitler's virulent antisemitism took root. Lawyers helped to draft and enforce the laws that isolated Jews and set them up for the kill. Physicians were among the first to experiment with the gassing of men, women, and children that would become so much a way of life—and death—at Treblinka and Sobibor. Scientists performed research and tested their racial theories on Jewish guinea pigs who had already been branded as subhuman by German science. Business executives found that Nazi concentration camps could provide cost-effective labor: they worked people to death. And artists, such as the filmmaker Leni Riefenstahl, helped advance the propaganda that made Hitler's policies persuasive to so many.

The list could go on and on, for genocide on this scale requires the complicity of countless people and talents. It took many nationalities, too, and American identity must be included in the roster.

Not only did Hitler get his ideas about concentration and extermination of Jews partly from America's dealing with Indians, but also American foreign policy during the 1930s and 1940s was certainly less than completely favorable toward Jewish plight. That fact was due in part to the reality of antisemitism in the United States, a reality that is still very much alive.

The boundaries of the problem expand still further. For example, religious and non-religious outlooks are also implicated. The Holocaust is simply unthinkable without a centuries-old anti-Jewish tradition spawned by Christianity. But if that fact moves one to abjure Christianity for seemingly more enlightened secular philosophies, the slate on that latter side is not as clean as could be wished either. Antisemitism takes many forms, and the religious is only one of them. It has economic, racial, and cultural versions that touched and were expressed by secular minds of great repute. It is true, after all, that the Holocaust broke out within one of the highest cultures human history has witnessed.

Obviously the analysis I have developed thus far focuses on issues of identity that might be regarded as pertaining more to Gentiles than to Jews. That fact, however, does not mean that Auschwitz creates no identity problems for Jewish men and women. To the contrary, the issue of what it means and does not mean, what it must mean and must not mean, to be a Jew today, is in large measure a post-Holocaust question that touches a range of feeling going from pride to fear and from despair to the conviction, "Never again!"

To sum up what I have been driving at thus far, the deeper one plunges into a study of the Holocaust, the more one becomes convinced that a boundary of possibility has been crossed. Auschwitz tells us that virtually everything is permitted, and in doing so, it says that no one is blessed with some cosmic insurance policy that can keep us totally assured that we will not commit, condone, or suffer the wasting of human life. Such an outcome is not a happy one, nor does it seem like an auspicious context in which to think about God. And yet I think it is well to do so in just this situation.

The reasons for doing so, I hasten to add, have very little to do with providing convincing answers about why the Holocaust took place. As a matter of fact, I quite agree with Elie Wiesel when he says that the Holocaust is inexplicable *with* God. Indeed, there may even be a sense in which the Holocaust is easier to take without God's being considered at all. Historical analysis can draw together factors such as centuries of antisemitism, a World War that the Germans lost, economic collapse in the Weimar Republic, the rise of a fascist state, advances in technology, and in doing so the Holocaust reveals a logic that is not without sense. But I also agree with Elie Wiesel when he argues that the Holocaust cannot be understood *without* God either.

At the very least that claim is true in the sense that human beliefs about God figured centrally into the historical events that brought the Holocaust about. More than that, however, the Holocaust stands as a major event in our time as far as human hope and faith are concerned. "How is one to believe?" asks Elie Wiesel. And he counters that question with another: "How is one not to believe?"[2]

As Wiesel poses both of those questions, I think he is suggesting how the Holocaust produces feelings of forlornness, grief, and rage, but also perhaps wonder, yearning, and defiance that may thrust the question of God upon us and even move us to confront God anew. If God cannot be easily accepted on the old traditional terms after Auschwitz, a refusal to let God go might be one way —not the only, but a significant way—of testifying that the human heart was not incinerated completely at Asuchwitz. Likewise, such refusal might be one way of helping us to know who we are and what we ought to be.

Exploring these possibilities, the position I shall go on to sketch revolves around the theme of *protest*. As it does so, the point of view is informed by two further motifs from Elie Wiesel, whom I regard as one of the most profound religious voices of our time. First, Wiesel has been heard to say: If I told you I believed in God, I would be lying; if I told you I did not believe in God, I would also be lying. What he means by holding those opposites together may be clarified by his recent novel, *The Testament*. In this book, Wiesel explores the fate of a Jewish poet, one of hundreds of Jewish intellectuals condemned to death by Stalin in 1952. Wiesel's poet, Paltiel Kossover, writes a letter to his son, Grisha, not certain that the boy will ever read it but hoping nonetheless that a father's words will not be lost forever. As Wiesel pens Kossover's letter, the poet reflects for a time on God. What God "requires is affirmation," says the father, "and there I draw the line." And yet Kossover prefaces that comment by writing that "as a source of questioning I would gladly accept Him," as if to suggest that God provides an approach for the right questions, for questions that keep a man or a woman intensely human so long as they are asked and searched.[3]

What follows, then, I offer not as a definitive argument, nor do I regard this outlook as somehow obviously better than others that can be held authentically. My hope is only that by sharing some of my own searching in the light of the Holocaust, I may raise a few of the right questions and sound a few of the protests that can fight against despair. In doing so, I will speak from within my Christian tradition, quarreling against it as a way of identifying with it, just as I shall try to be for God and for humankind partly by being against God. This spiritual style, such as it is, I have learned largely from Jewish teachers encountered as I am trying to come to terms with my own sense of identity in a post-Holocaust age.

Before going further, let me clarify how I shall use some important terms. *Evil* is one of them. That word often functions as a noun, suggesting that evil is an entity. In fact, evil is *activity*, sometimes *inactivity*, and thus it is a manifestation of power. Evil power displays are those that *waste*. That is, evil happens whenever power ruins or squanders, or whenever it fails to forestall those results. Moreover, evil comes in many shapes and sizes. The kind that concerns us here ignores and violates the sanctity of individual persons. Everyone inflicts that sort of pain, and yet some individuals and societies are far more perverse than others. The measure is taken by the degree to which one's actions waste human life.

Seventy million human beings have been uprooted, enslaved, or killed in the twentieth century alone. Albert Camus made that estimate when he published *The Rebel* in 1951. What the figure should be today, God only knows. Truly, "the problem of evil" does exist, and as philosophers and theologians often reflect on such aspects of human life, they are prone to do so in terms of what is called *theodicy*. That term, brought into vogue by Leibniz and Voltaire long ago, derives from the two Greek words meaning "deity" and "justice." Usually, then, theodicy refers to human attempts to justify the goodness of God in the face of the manifold evil present in the world. Human apologies on God's behalf, however, are rarely completely convincing, Indeed, in the wake of the Holocaust such apologies may be demonic. That possibility, it seems to me, makes it appropriate to consider what I call *a theodicy of protest*. Jewish spirituality is already familiar with this stance, but Christians are less so, and they can learn from their Jewish brothers and sisters.

In developing a theodicy of protest, one of the problems is that most people want a totally good God or none at all. In religious circles, then, it has not been too popular to put God on trial. For centuries human beings have taken themselves to task in order to protect God's innocence and not without reason. Even at the price of an unwarranted guilt-trip, the desire runs strong to separate good and evil neatly. Life is simpler that way, and so theology puts God in the right and God's children in the wrong. A protesting theodicy, however, finds both of those views wanting because Camus is correct: "Man is not entirely to blame; it was not he who started history."[4]

It is irresponsible to assign responsibility inequitably. If God exists, God must bear a fair share. God's responsibility would be located in the fact that God is the one who ultimately sets the boundaries in which we live and move and have our being. True, since we are thrown into history at our birth, we appear in social settings made by human hands, but ultimately those hands cannot account for themselves. To the extent that they are born with the potential and the power to be dirty, credit for that fact belongs elsewhere. 'Elsewhere' is God's address.

Do not take lightly what God's responsibility entails. It means: In the beginning... Auschwitz, Hiroshima, and the words of a nine-year-old girl, one of the current Vietnamese refugees, who was heard to say, "I prayed that my death would be quick and merciful."[5] The point is not that God predestined or caused such events directly. Some theodicies have taken that position, but not this one. It rejects such conclusions because it assumes the reality of human freedom. At the same time, that freedom—much as some thinkers would like—does not remove God from the dock.

Richard L. Rubenstein's penetrating study of the Holocaust, *The Cunning of History*, makes the following observation: "Until ethical theorists and theologians are prepared to face without senti-mentality the kind of action it is possible freely to perpetrate under conditions of utter respectability in an advanced, contemporary society, none of their assertions about the existence of moral norms will have much credibility."[6] The inference I want to draw from Rubenstein's assertion is this: Human freedom has been used as God's defense; in fact, it is as crucial in his offense.

Using freedom as a defense for God is a well-known strategy. Moving from the idea that freedom is a good, the argument has usually been that God gave freedom to human life in innocence. The gift, to be sure, did include a capacity for self-perversion. God knew that fact and perhaps even that liberty would be abused. Still, the apology continues, God's gift is justified. Only with the freedom we were given can men and women truly be the children of God. Moveover, where sin infests us, God's own freedom is gracious enough to offer forgiveness and love that can both release us to try again and ultimately rectify every wrong. On all counts, apparently, God's benevolence is validated even as humanity's is not.

This so-called "free will defense" for God, I submit, should no longer be credible after Auschwitz. The reason why is that human freedom is both too much and too little; it is far more an occasion for waste than a defense of God's total goodness can reconcile. The Holocaust illustrates both sides of that coin, for when the fury of the death camps was unleashed, the destructive powers of human freedom were so deeply entrenched that none of humanity's coun-tervailing energy, individual or collective, could halt them before millions perished.

To think of millions, however, may not make the point sharp enough. Consider, therefore, *Sophie's Choice*. Sophie Zawistowska is a Polish survivor of Auschwitz. As William Styron tells her story, his brilliant and controversial novel becomes a commentary on the powerlessness of individual freedom as it faces overwhelming forces of social domination. For a time, Sophie has been a privileged prisoner, assigned to secretarial duties in the house of Rudolf Hoess, the commandant of Auschwitz. Urged to use her position to assist the underground resistance movement, Sophie will try to steal a radio from Hoess's house.

Sophie knows where one can be found, a small portable that

belongs to Hoess's daughter, Emmi. She passes the girl's room every day on her way upstairs to the office where Hoess does his work. Once she tries for the radio, but Emmi catches her, and Sophie is nearly undone. Her sense of failure runs deep, only less so than the realization that she will never regain her courage to steal the radio again. Sophie knows "how, among its other attributes, absolute evil paralyzes absolutely."[7]

She knows the frailty of freedom not simply because of the incident with the radio, but because of the setting that surrounds it. And nothing is more important in that setting than her children, Jan and Eva. Jan is alive somewhere in the children's camp at Auschwitz. Hoess has promised that Sophie can see him, and her attempted theft took place with the knowledge that she would jeopardize her chance to embrace the boy whose life gives hers a reason for going on. Sophie is not without courage, far from that, but once is enough. She cannot put the radio ahead of her need for Jan.

Who could blame Sophie, especially when Eva is remembered? Eva is gone, gassed. And Sophie's freedom, or the lack of it, shows how pathetic a "free-will defense" for God can be. Eva's life was lost because Sophie was left free to choose. As she disembarked from the stifling train that brought her and the children from Warsaw to Auschwitz, a selection took place. An SS official—Styron calls him Dr. Jemand von Niemand—decided to make freedom real, dreadfully so, by forcing Sophie's choice. Instead of losing both Jan and Eva to the gas, which was the fate of most young children there, Sophie could pick one of hers to live. "*'Ich kann nicht wählen!'* she screamed."[8] I cannot choose... and then so as not to lose them both, Sophie let Eva go. Sophie's choice stayed with her. She experienced liberation in 1945, but only fully in 1947 when she gave up her own life—also by choice.

It is only a story. But there is truth in it because paralysis and untimely death are results of freedom that is allowed, like Sophie's, to be too little. Of course there was heroism in Auschwitz, hers not least of all, and ultimately the death camps died. The price, however, was horrible, and even to suggest that there could be no adequate display of human virtue—or no sufficient glory in heaven—without such testing odds... well, that proposition mocks the victims far more than it honors them. Sophie's choice accuses God and rightly so.

The matter does not end there, however, because the freedom God gives us is also too much and too soon. That fact follows as a corollary from what has gone before. The Holocaust shows that human beings can and will do anything to each other. We have more power, more freedom, than is good for us. Perhaps there was an Eden where all the factors of freedom were in healthy equilibrium. In present history, however, that dream is a myth at best.

Freedom's defense for God looks more and more like a ploy by the devil's advocate. That defense cannot avoid saying: Only if freedom has the potential to be what it has become can there be a chance for the highest goods. But can the end justify the means? —that is the question. A protesting theodicy is skeptical because it will not forget futile cries. No good that it can envision, on earth or beyond, is worth the freedom—enfeebled and empowered—that wastes so much life.

Perhaps Stendhal was right: God's only excuse is that he does not exist. Not so, suggest some contemporary voices. God, they say, has been mistakenly viewed as all-powerful. In fact, his creative activity reveals limitations in his existence, and thus the claim that he is totally benevolent can be preserved. In effect, then, this God's excuse is that he always does the best he can. Originally, he brought order out of chaos—uncreated, primordial, resistant—and fashioned a world of beauty and richness. Within that setting, he lured humanity into existence, endowed with freedom to choose. But if God's authority can minimize the confusion that we produce with our liberty, it is also true that he cannot both intervene directly and still retain the integrity of free human creatures. This God holds his breath, as it were, while we act . . . and then the best he can do is to pick up the pieces so that survivors can try again.

Such a view would be fine if the pieces were not so many and so bloody. This God of weakness may indeed be excused, not least because he is hardly worth bothering about. He is simply too ineffectual to forestall waste decisively, unless of course one holds that he has some heretofore unwitnessed potential for eschatological power. On what ground, however, could such a claim be based? Most versions of Jewish and Christian faith would locate that ground in historical events: the Exodus or the Resurrection, for example. History testifies, however, that any God with power to lead people out of bondage or to raise persons from death is *not always* doing the best he can, for his saving acts in the world are too few and far between.

Things are not going very well. A protesting theodicy denies that God's love presently controls the world completely, and it disagrees that there is any good sense in claims that find this world to be the best one possible. Thus, it must reckon with despair.

To despair is to lose or give up hope. For our purposes two dimensions of that experience are of special significance. First, this theodicy of protest despairs over the hope that history is evolving toward a Kingdom of God on earth. That claim does not deny that there is progress, which one writer defines as "a condition that is better by far than what it replaces after accounting for any side effects."[9] What it affirms, however, is that all progress is cunning, and so one can agree when Rubenstein states: "the Holocaust bears witness to *the advance of civilization*."[10] Far from assuming that things will get better and better if only we work well enough together, this outlook supposes that human life is always under siege. All gains are precarious, periodic, and problematic. Many of them are killing.

And yet the human prospect is not hopeless, nor is it without reasons for joy and thanksgiving. In fact, that prospect can be enhanced to the degree that the widespread experience of despair is turned on itself to yield a spirit of dissent. The logic of this reversal makes a straightforward appeal, namely, that once we realize how strong the good reasons for despair really are, then short of abdicating to waste there is little left to do but to turn and fight. Such responses have no utopian illusions. They stand instead with this conviction: Unjustifiable waste is everlasting, but it deserves no more victories.

Second, this theodicy of protest despairs over the hope that there will be any future good "so great as to render acceptable, in retrospect, the whole human experience, with all its wickedness and suffering as well as all its sanctity and happiness."[11] Put another way: No matter what happens, God is going to be much less than perfectly justified. But wait, someone may say, even if it is true that we cannot now fathom how God could possibly salvage this mess in a way that justifies him perfectly, surely that task can be fulfilled. Indeed the biblical claim that with God all things are possible would seem to demand such an option. People can believe in that optimistic outcome if they wish, but dissenters demur and the reason is simply history itself. The irretrievable waste of the past robs God of a perfect alibi. Only if he obliterates truth by wiping out the memory of victims can a protesting "Why?" be stilled forever. So long as that question can sound, the whole human experience stands as less than acceptable.

And yet the human prospect is not hopeless, nor is it without reasons for joy and thanksgiving. Life can be less unacceptable. We know that to be true because from time to time there are works of love that people do. Those realities, linked with despair that finds love not enough, may lead us to affirm life by refusing to give despair the final say. In those experiences. one may discover that the issue of whether God is without any justification depends on what he does with the future, his and ours.

Most theodicies have a fatal flaw: they legitimate evil. In recent literature, that point is revealed most clearly in Elie Wiesel's drama *The Trial of God*. The play is set in the village of Shamgorod at the time of Purim, a joyous festival replete with masks and reenactments that celebrate a moment in Jewish history when oppressors were outmaneuvered and Jews were saved. Three Jewish actors have lost their way, and they have arrived at the village. Here they discover that Shamgorod is hardly a place for festivity. Two years before, a murderous pogrom ravaged this place. Only two Jews survived. Berish the innkeeper escaped, but he had to watch while his daughter was unspeakably abused on her wedding night. She now lives, mercifully, out of touch with the world.

In the region of Shamgorod, anti-Jewish hatred is festering once again, and it is not unthinkable that a new pogrom may break out and finish the work previously left undone. Purim, however, cannot be Purim without a play, and so a *Purimspiel* will be given, but with a difference urged by Berish: This time the play will enact the trial of God. As the characters in Wiesel's drama begin to organize their play-within-a-play, one problem looms large. The Defendant, God, is silent, and on this Purim night nobody in Shamgorod wants to speak for him. Unnoticed, however, a stranger has entered the inn, and just when it seems that the defense attorney's role will go unfilled, the newcomer—his name is Sam—volunteers to act the part. Apparently Maria, Berish's Gentile housekeeper, has seen this man before. Have nothing to do with him, she warns, but the show begins nonetheless.

Berish prosecutes. God, he says, "could use His might to save the victims, but He doesn't! So—on whose side is He? Could the killer kill without His blessing—without His complicity?"[12] Apologies for God do not sit well with this Jewish patriarch. "If I am given the choice of feeling sorry for Him or for human beings," exclaims Berish, "I choose the latter anytime. He is big enough, strong enough to take care of Himself; man is not."[13] Still, Berish will not let God go. His protest is real, and thus it does not deny God's reality but affirms it in calling God to account.

Sam's style is different. He has an answer for every charge, and he warns that emotion is no substitute for evidence. In a word, he defends God brilliantly. Sam's performance impresses the visiting actors who have formed the court. Who is he, they wonder. Sam will not say, but his identity and the verdict implicit in *The Trial of God* turn out not to be moot. As the play's final scene unfolds, a mob approaches to ravage the inn at Shamgorod once more. Sensing that the end is near, the Jewish actors choose to die with their Purim masks in place. Sam dons one, too, and as he does so, Maria's premonitions are vindicated. Sam's mask is worthy of his namesake, Samael. Both signify Satan, and as a final candle is extinguished and the inn's door opens to the sound of deafening and murderous roars, Satan's laughter is among them.

Elie Wiesel witnessed a trial of God in Auschwitz, and he reports that fact in his introduction to this play, which is set three centuries earlier. What Wiesel did not record in the introduction, but has indicated on another occasion, is that when the three rabbis who conducted the Auschwitz trial had finished and found God guilty, these erudite and pious men noted that it was time for their customary prayers, and so they bowed their heads and prayed.[14]

Apologies for God may be demonic. Thus, there is a sense in which a theodicy of protest must be anti-theodicy. That is, it must be wary of any answers that justify God too much. On the other hand, Wiesel's testimony about the rabbis in Auschwitz also warns us to avoid a trap that may lie in insistence that God is guilty and even without apology for apparent refusal to change his worldly ways in the foreseeable future. Without caution that outlook could become just another form of scapegoating, one that places a premium on blaming God, leaving the impression as it does so that there is really not very much that human beings can do.

We do face great odds. Still, there is much that we can do. Indeed we shall have to act or there will be too little action on humanity's behalf. The world—too much no doubt—is in our hands. For if God listens and answers, it is usually in silence. If he is judge or ally, it is less by intervention that metes out justice in total equity and more by letting events fall as they may to reveal the corrupt absurdity, as well as the grandeur, of what we do together. The future is more open than it ought to be. We have all that we can do and then some, and if we fail to act well, the waste will only increase.

"'My God, my God, why have you deserted me?'" (Matt. 27:46)[15] Jesus' ancient Jewish question is contemporary. It evokes others: Can we learn not to blame God as a way of covering over our responsibilities? Can we learn to be boldly honest with God and with ourselves as a means to deepen compassion? A theodicy of protest must keep raising those questions about itself. It must also keep struggling to answer them affirmatively.

As William James summed up *The Varieties of Religious Experience*, he observed that "no two of us have identical difficulties, nor should we be expected to work out identical solutions." A few sentences later, he went on to say: "The divine can mean no single quality, it must mean a group of qualities, by being champions of which in alternation, different men may all find worthy missions."[16] Such wisdom informs all sound theodicies. Human religious needs are diverse. No single response can encompass them all or nourish every spirit. Thus, every good theodicy will be, in part, an anti-theodicy. It will disclaim the full adequacy of its own outlook and that of every other as well.

Imperfect as it is, the theodicy explored here does originate in felt needs. Two are fundamental: a sense that human affairs are far worse than any good reason can justify or than our powers alone can alter; and, second, a yearning that refuses to settle for despair that the first feeling generates. A God encountered in Jewish and Christian experience makes possible an option that keeps hope from dying, without making the dreary facts unreal. But this God offers little tranquillity because he defers rescue. He allows us—and thereby participates in—our own undoing.

Tragedy, pain, injustice, death—all of these and more waste us away. No explanation seems quite able to still our anger, hostility, and sadness. A theodicy of protest believes not only that such emotions are profoundly real, but also that they are in many cases justified. Any religious perspective that fails to give them expression diminishes the human spirit. Whether unintentionally or by design, the Christian emphasis on God's love has had a repressive effect in this regard. It strains to make everything fit the care of a Father who is love itself. For some persons that strain is too much. There may be others for whom an open admission of that fact would bring healthy release. Although the faith of us Christians would not be rendered easier, it would be quickened by quarreling with the claim that "God is love," even as we refuse to let it go. (I John 4:8)[17]

Annie Dillard's poetic book, *Holy the Firm*, is a meditation prompted by the crash of a small airplane. Miraculously no one was killed. But Julie Norwich, a seven-year-old flying with her father, has had her face burnt beyond recognition.

There is a small church in the Puget Sound country where Annie Dillard lives. She believes that its minister, a Congregationalist, knows God. "Once," she writes, "in the middle of the long pastoral prayer of intercession for the whole world—for the gift of wisdom to its leaders, for hope and mercy to the grieving and pained, succor to the oppressed, and God's grace to all—in the middle of this he stopped, and burst out, 'Lord, we bring you these same petitions every week.' After a shocked pause, he continued reading the prayer." For this protest, Annie Dillard adds, "I like him very much."[18] Dillard's vignette suggests that a theodicy of protest has a place in Christian life.

William James distinguished between outlooks that are healthy-minded and sick-souled. The former find that, at worst, evil is instrumental; disagreement drives the latter. The late twentieth century is a time for sick souls. If there are those who can look evil in the eye and still be healthy-minded . . . well, that possibility may be a sign of hope in itself. But healthy minds are not for everybody. The theodicy outlined here is one for sick souls who know that their sickness cannot—must not—be cured, and who likewise refuse to acquiesce because to do so would accomplish nothing.

Long ago a Jewish family was expelled from Spain. Plagued at every turn, they could find no refuge, except that sleep turned into death for them, one by one. At last only the father was left, and he spoke to God:

> Master of the Universe, I know what You want—I understand what You are doing. You want despair to overwhelm me. You want me to cease believing in You, to cease praying to You, to cease invoking Your name to glorify and sanctify it. Well, I tell You: No, no—a thousand times no! You shall not succeed! In spite of me and in spite of You, I shall shout the Kaddish, which is a song of faith, for You and against You. This song You shall not still, God of Israel![19]

That Jewish story summarizes well one strand of a protesting theodicy. An ageless dialogue sounds out another. God's creation is at stake. It is far from perfect, and thus . . .

> "Could you have done better?"
> "Yes, I think so."
> "You could have done better? Then what are you waiting for? You don't have a minute to waste, go ahead, start working!"[20]

If the world did incinerate its own heart at Auschwitz, perhaps it did not do so completely. So what are we waiting for? We have few minutes to waste. The battle against despair depends on human identities that can provoke a spirit that says, "go ahead, start working." The struggle depends, too, on human identities that respond by refusing to let silence and indifference prevail. Auschwitz leaves us on trial. We all have something important to say about what the verdict of that trial shall be.

FOOTNOTES

1 Elie Wiesel, *Legends of Our Time*, trans. Steven Donadia (New York: Avon Books, 1972), p. 230.

2 Elie Wiesel, *Ani Maamin*, trans. Marion Wiesel (New York: Random House, 1973), p. 25.

3 Elie Wiesel, *The Testament*, trans. Marion Wiesel (New York: Summit Books, 1981), p. 20.

4 Albert Camus, *The Rebel*, trans. Anthony Bower (New York: Vintage Books, 1956), p. 297.

5 I quote from an article by Paul Dean, "Coming to the Aid of the Boat People," *Los Angeles Times*, 23 July 1979, IV, 1, 4, 5.

6 Richard L. Rubenstein, *The Cunning of History* (New York: Harper Colophon Books, 1978), p. 67.

7 William Styron, *Sophie's Choice* (New York: Random House, 1979), p. 392.

8 *Ibid.*, p. 483.

9 Ben J. Wattenberg, *The Real America* (Garden City: Doubleday, 1974), p. 9.

10 Rubenstein, *The Cunning of History*, p. 91 (Rubenstein's emphasis).

11 John Hick, *Evil and the God of Love*, rev. ed. (New York: Harper & Row, 1978), p. 386.

12 Elie Wiesel, *The Trial of God*, trans. Marion Wiesel (New York: Random House, 1979), p. 129.

13 *Ibid.*, p. 133.

14 Robert McAfee Brown notes this anecdote in his article, "Wiesel's Case Against God," *The Christian Century*, 30 Jan. 1980, pp. 109-12.

15 Quoted from the Jerusalem Bible. See also Ps. 22:1.

16 The sentences quoted in this paragraph can be found in *The Varieties of Religious Experience* (Garden City, N.Y.: Doubleday Image Books, 1978), p. 470.

17 Quoted from the Revised Standard Version.

18 Annie Dillard, *Holy the Firm* (New York: Bantam Books, 1979), pp. 58-59.

19 Elie Wiesel, *A Jew Today*, trans. Marion Wiesel (New York: Random House, 1978), p. 136.

20 Elie Wiesel, *Messengers of God*, trans. Marion Wiesel (New York: Random House, 1976), pp. 35-36.

The Experience of God in Christian Apophatic Mysticism

William Johnston, S.J.

Christian mysticism may be broadly divided into the two categories of *apophatic* and *kataphatic* mysticism.

Kataphatic mysticism (taking its name from the Greek *kataphasis* meaning affirmation) is the mysticism of light. It affirms that we can know and experience God. Apophatic mysticism (taking its name from the Greek *apophasis* meaning negation) is the mysticism of darkness. It asserts that we know more about what God is *not* than about what he is. This apophatic mysticism is often traced back to Gregory of Nyssa (335-395) who has been called the father of Christian mysticism. From Gregory it passes to the pseudo-Dionysius in the sixth century, then on to the Rhineland mystics (Eckhart, Tauler and Suso), on to the English mystics (particularly the anonymous author of *The Cloud of Unknowing*), reaching a climax with St. John of the Cross in sixteenth century Spain. In more recent times, the early Merton was greatly influenced by St. John of the Cross, as also was T.S. Eliot in *Four Quartets* and in his later plays. As for the kataphatic stream, it is well represented by St. Bernard of Clairvaux, St. Teresa of Avila and St. Ignatius Loyola. This latter speaks of clear vision of the three persons of the Trinity, using language which is in striking contrast with that of St. John of the Cross who speaks of a dark vision in the night of faith.

I have divided Christian mysticism into apophatic and kataphatic. It should be noted, however, that the dividing line between these two types of mysticism is by no means clear. No Christian mysticism is totally apophatic. Even the most radical apophatic mystic asserts the existence of a transcendent God, claiming that we know *that* he is even when we do not know clearly *what* he is. *The Cloud of Unknowing* states the position well when it says that God can be loved but that he cannot be conceptually known. The English author then nuances this statement by stating that God can be known *as he is in creatures* but cannot be known *as he is in himself*. In modern terminology we might say that God cannot be known by science but that he can be known by metaphysics and (and here is the point of *The Cloud*) he can be known by love.[1]

And as apophatic mysticism has its kataphatic dimension, so kataphatic mysticism has its apophatic dimension. Even the most radical kataphatic mystic acknowledges that we know little about God, that God is the mystery of mysteries and that (as the Fourth Gsopel, harking back to *Exodus*, affirms) "No one has ever seen God..." (Jn 1:18).

In short, while there are different traditions, there is no Christian mysticism which confines itself to negation; and there is no Christian mysticism which confines itself to affirmation.

What I have said about affirmation and negation is no mere theory. It tallies with, and comes out of, the very practical experience of innumerable Christian mystics. These assert that at the beginning of the mystical life they are drawn by love into a cloud of unknowing. That is to say, they leave behind clear-cut imagery; they leave behind reasoning and thinking; they enter into a state (symbolized by the cloud) in which they are aware of what they call an *obscure sense of presence*. At first this sense of presence may engender deep joy and sensible consolation, to such an extent that the contemplative cannot doubt about the existence of a God with whom he or she is united and who is close at hand. But as the experience deepens, it may become dry and arid; and the sense of presence may give way to a sense of absence or a sense of abandonment. Yet there may be moments of great illumination, as in the following words from *The Cloud*:

> Then perhaps God may touch you with a ray of his divine light which will pierce the *cloud of unknowing* between you and him. He will let you glimpse something of the ineffable secrets of his divine wisdom and your affection will seem on fire with his love. I am at a loss to say more, for the experience is beyond words.[2]

Here is an example of a kataphatic flash in the apophatic experience.

Gregory of Nyssa and the apophatic mystics who follow his inspiration constantly appeal to a mystical interpretation of the *Book of Exodus*. Assuredly *Exodus* has a strongly kataphatic dimension. It is filled with the presence of God who leads his people with the cloud by day and the pillar of fire by night. It even speaks of Moses who meets God face to face: "Thus the Lord used to speak to Moses face to face, as a man speaks with his friend" (Ex 33:11). And commenting on these words, mystical theologians asked if Moses had received the beatific vision ordinarily reserved for the elect. Nevertheless the same *Book of Exodus* tells us that Moses could not see God; and it paints a graphic picture of Moses wending his way up the mountain to enter the cloud of thick darkness.

The apophatic mystics seize upon the image of Moses entering the darkness of the cloud. "What does it mean that Moses entered the darkness and then saw God in it?" asks Gregory. And he answers his own question by telling us that "as the mind progresses and, through an ever greater and more perfect diligence, comes to apprehend reality, as it approaches more nearly to contemplation, it sees more clearly what of the divine nature is uncontemplated."[3] There then follows a passage which was to have considerable influence on subsequent mystical theology:

> For leaving behind everything that is observed, not only what sense comprehends but also what the intelligence thinks it sees, it keeps on penetrating deeper until by the intelligence's yearning for understanding it gains access to the invisible and the incomprehensible, and there it sees God. This is the true knowledge of what is sought; this is the seeing that consists of not seeing, because that which is sought transcends all knowledge, being separated on all sides by incomprehensibility as by a kind of darkness. Wherefore, John the sublime, who penetrated into the luminous darkness, says, *No one has ever seen God*, thus asserting that knowledge of the divine essence is unattainable not only by men but also by every intelligent creature.[4]

In this neoplatonic interpretation of *Exodus* Gregory claims that in the mystical life the mind travels beyond all sensible seeing, all imaginative seeing, all understanding and all reasoning. It goes into the darkness and there (paradox of paradoxes) it sees God. This dark seeing, this seeing which is not seeing, this knowledge which is ignorance, this way of darkness—all this influences the subsequent tradition of mystical theology of which St. John of the Cross is the most sophisticated exponent.

For St. John of the Cross, the darkness which fills the mind when it goes beyond the sensible and the intellectual is faith. This is pure faith, naked faith, the faith which guides, the faith which is a dark vision of God. But let me say briefly what the Spanish mystic means by faith.

In the apophatic tradition the mystical life begins when a blind stirring of love (the terminology is from *The Cloud*) arises in the heart. This stirring of love is blind or naked because it is not "clothed" in thoughts or concepts. But it is also a light which gives wonderful knowledge. And this knowledge is sometimes called wisdom or *sapientia* while at other times (as in the case of St. John of the Cross) it is called faith. It is a dark vision of God. Here are the words of the great Spaniard:

> For the likeness between faith and God is so close that no other difference exists than that between believing in God and seeing Him. Just as God is infinite, faith proposes Him to us as infinite; as there are Three Persons in One God, it presents Him to us in this way; and as God is darkness to our intellect, so does faith dazzle and blind us. Only by means of faith, in divine light exceeding all understanding, does God manifest Himself to the soul. The more intense a person's faith, the closer is his union with God.[5]

From this it is clear that faith is knowledge of God. But it is dark knowledge. Moreover, as I have said, it is knowledge which transcends everything sensible or intellectual. So much so, that it is only when the senses and the intellect are plunged in darkness that the light of faith can reach perfection. Or, more concretely, when the natural faculties are plunged in doubt faith reaches its highest point. For faith is belief in God for God. If my faith is authentic, I do not believe because I feel sensibly the presence of God; I do not believe because my intellect is convinced by proofs; I believe because I believe.

And like Gregory, St. John of the Cross appeals to *Exodus*. "Faith," he tells us, "was foreshadowed in that cloud which separated the children of Israel, just before their entry into the Red Sea, from the Egyptians (Ex 14:19-20). Scripture says of the cloud: *Erat nubes tenebrosa et illuminans noctem* (The cloud was dark, and illuminative in the night) (Ex 14:20)."[6] And then he goes on:

> How wonderful it was—a cloud, dark in itself, could illumine the night! This was related to illustrate how faith, a dark and obscure cloud to man is also a night in that it blinds into the darkness of his soul by means of its own darkness.[7]

Here again the mystic's point is that the senses and the intelligence must be plunged into darkness and doubt if faith is to reach its purest form. This explains his extraordinary, even frightening, asceticism, the aim of which is to "annihilate" the natural faculties in order that the light of faith may shine brightly in the human heart. "As for God," he writes, "who will stop Him from accomplishing his desires in the soul that is resigned, annihilated and despoiled?"[8] His use of words like "annihilate" are unfortunate and have disturbed more than one theologian. But a careful reading of the text shows that the Spanish mystic is not out to annihilate the faculties but to transform them.[9] Besides he is not speaking to beginners but only to those with ears to hear:

> Observing how we annihilate the faculties in their operations, it will perhaps seem that we are tearing down rather than building up the way of spiritual exercise. This would be true if our doctrine here were destined merely for beginners, who have to prepare themselves through these discursive apprehensions.[10]

In short the meaning of St. John of the Cross is that as the light of faith becomes stronger and stronger it blinds the natural faculties, plunging them into darkness. And the mystic, far from fighting against this darkness should embrace it since in this way he or she will have a dark vision of God. For the darkness is good and the night is beautiful; and the mystic sings ecstatically:

> O guiding night!
> O night more lovely than the dawn!
> O night that has united
> The lover with His beloved
> Transforming the beloved in her Lover.[11]

I have spoken about the mystical interpretation of *Exodus* and about Moses the mystic. And now my reader may wonder about the specifically Christian dimension of this apophatic experience. How does Christ fit into the mysticism of darkness?

And in answer to this I would first say that in the New Testament Jesus Christ is the new Moses, the second Moses. Take, for example, the Gospel of Matthew. As Moses climbs the mountain to receive and to promulgate the old law, so Jesus climbs the mount of beatitudes to promulgate the new law. "You have heard that it was said to the men of old.... But I say to you..." (Mt 5:21). Or again the Epistle to the Hebrews tells us that "Moses was faithful in all God's house as a servant...but Christ was faithful over God's house as a son" (Heb. 3:5). And then there is that powerful scene on Mount Tabor when Jesus is transfigured in the presence of his disciples, while Moses and Elias are seen talking to him.

Now the apophatic mystics do not pray *to* Moses; they imitate him. And in the same way the apophatic mystics (while engaged in this kind of contemplation) do not pray *to* Jesus; they identify with Jesus. They become Jesus. He speaks through them and cries out: "Abba, Father!" With him they are nailed to the cross (so said St. Paul) and in the night of the soul they call out: *"Eli, Eli, lama sabachthani'* (Mt 27: 46). And with Jesus they rise from the dead. Their experience is Trinitarian: one with Jesus and filled with the Spirit they cry out to the Father. In this sense the experience of the mystic like St. John of the Cross is truly penetrated with the presence of, and the person of, Christ.

I have said that apophatic mystical theology is no mere theory but fits the experience of thousands of Christian mystics. Now let me cite briefly the example of Therese of Lisieux, a young French girl who entered the Carmelite order and died in 1897 at the age of twenty-four.

Born into a pious Christian family, Therese had no doubts that she would one day leave earth to live forever with God in heaven. "Just as the genius of Christopher Columbus gave him a presentiment of a new world when nobody had even thought of such a thing, so also I felt that another land would one day serve me as a permanent dwelling place."[12] But this clear belief in another world began to fade as she entered into the cloud of unknowing and, finally, into the dark night of faith. Here are her words:

Then suddenly the fog which surrounds me becomes more dense;

it penetrates my soul and envelops it in such a way that it is impossible to discover within it the sweet image of my Father-land; everything has disappeared! When I want to rest my heart fatigued by the darkness which surrounds it by the memory of the luminous country after which I aspire, my torment redoubles; it seems to me that the darkness, borrowing the voice of sinners, says mockingly to me: "You are dreaming about the light, about a fatherland embalmed in the sweetest perfumes; you are dreaming about the eternal possession of the Creator of all these marvels; you believe that one day you will walk out of this fog which surrounds you! Advance, advance; rejoice in death which will give you not what you hope for but a night still more profound, the night of nothingness".[13]

The fog is, of course, the cloud of unknowing. But how dark it has become! It is no longer a luminous cloud but a thick night. And Therese continues to write to her Superior: "Dear Mother, the image I wanted to give you of the darkness that obscures my soul is as imperfect as a sketch is to the model; however, I don't want to write any longer about it; I fear I might blaspheme; I fear even that I have already said too much."[14]

In spite of all this darkness, Therese continues to write and speak enthusiastically about the love of God and about its mercy. But she herself confesses:

When I sing of the happiness of heaven and the eternal possession of God, I feel no joy in this, for I sing simply of what *I want to believe*. It is true that at times a very small ray of the sun comes to illumine the darkness, and then the trial ceases *for an instant*, but afterwards the memory of this ray, instead of causing me joy, makes my darkness even more dense.[15]

The italics are not mine, but hers. She felt that she no longer believed in eternal life or in a transcendent God. She felt, that while she wanted to believe, she did not in fact believe; she felt that at heart she was an atheist. All this fits with the doctrine of St. John of the Cross. And, I might add, Therese read the works of St. John of the Cross again and again. No doubt his teaching helped her to support this apparent lack of faith and to see it as a dark vision of God.

From all that has been said it will be clear that apophatic mysticism is eminently relevant for our times. It is a mysticism which the atheist can understand; it is a mysticism which has caught the imagination of not a few existentialist philosophers. Moreover, it is a mysticism which has much in common with Zen. In both cases we have the emptiness, the nothingness, the darkness and the cloud of unknowing. Yet we should not be too quick to assume that the two experiences are the same. One great difference is that in spite of the emptiness in sense of and intellect, the apophatic mystics never cease to assert the existence of a transcendent God who can be loved even when he cannot be known. And the last words of Therese of Lisieux were: "My God . . . I love you."[16] Perhaps at this moment her dark vision was becoming bright in preparation for resurrection. For St. John of the Cross divides his dark night into three parts: "The first part, the night of the senses, resembles early evening, that time of twilight when things begin to fade from sight. The second part, faith, is completely dark, like midnight. The third part, representing God, is like the very early dawn just before the break of day."[17]

FOOTNOTES

1 The author of *The Cloud* writes: "Thought cannot comprehend God. And so, I prefer to abandon all I can know, choosing rather to love him when I cannot know. Though we cannot know him we can love him. By love he may be touched and embraced, never by thought." *The Cloud of Unknowing*, ed. William Johnston (New York: Doubleday Image Books, 1973), p. 54.

2 *The Cloud*, p. 84.

3 Gregory of Nyssa, *The Life of Moses*, trans. Abraham Malherbe and Everett Ferguson (New York: Paulist Press, 1978), p. 95.

4 *Ibid.*

5 *The Collected Works of St. John of the Cross*, trans. Kieran Kavanaugh and Otilio Rodriguez (Washington, D.C.: ICS Publications, 1979), p. 129.

6 *Ibid.*, p. 111.

7 *Ibid.*

8 *Ibid.*, p. 112.

9 I have written extensively about this in my book *The Mirror Mind* (San Francisco: Harper & Row, 1981).

10 *Collected Works*, p. 214.

11 *The Dark Night*, stanza 5.

12 *Story of a Soul: The Autobiography of St. Therese of Lisieux,* trans. John Clarke (Washington, D.C.: ICS Publications, 1976), p. 213.

13 *Ibid.*

14 *Ibid.*

15 *Ibid.*, p. 214.

16 *St. Therese of Lisieux: Her Last Conversations*, trans. John Clarke (Washington, D.C.: ICS Publications, 1977), p. 206.

17 *Collected Works*, p. 75.

God as a Problem in the Dialogue between Zen and Christianity

Kakichi Kadowaki

Elements of the question.

Is it possible that Zen and Christianity, which are so heterogeneous one from the other, could carry out a true dialogue,[1] even though the former seems to deny God and the latter believes in God? This is the first problem we have to face. If a dialogue is possible then it should be about God that the Christian should want to discourse with the Zenist. In what sense could Zen recognize God? This is the second question we should be confronted with.

Regarding the first question, the Catholic experts on the matter have reached a common opinion that in the current stage of dialogue a discussion on the level of dogma or doctrine would seem to be useless or meaningless. As the Christian and the Zenist each has a different cultural background and an alien mentality and stands on an entirely diverse horizon, they do not have a common ground in doctrine, although they do have similar ideas and concepts here and there. Where could they find a common ground for a true dialogue? I would say with Professor Dumoulin that a common ground for such a dialogue can be found—in religious experience.[2] In fact today many Christians, even priests and sisters, are making great efforts to receive Zen training under the direction of Zen masters. This effort itself, no matter how they do or do not intend it, is a sort of true dialogue with Zen.

In this paper I would like to find an answer to the above-mentioned question, by listening to Zen experts in the spirit of a Zen disciple, reflecting on my own experience of both Zen and Christian kinds, and re-thinking this experience in the light of current Catholic theology.

Fortunately, Dr. Taisetsu Suzuki and Dr. Kitaro Nishida, both well-known scholars of Zen or of Zen inspiration, have prepared a route for our discussion, and Professor Ryumin Akizuki has followed it to make clear in what sense the Zenist can recognize God. In the second section of this paper I will carefully listen to them "without trying to make them conform to my own self-centered viewpoint", as Master Dogen taught, in "Points to watch in Buddhist training".[3] This will give us preparatory knowledge and viewpoints for further steps in the dialogue. In the third section I will get an insight from Karl Rahner's theology in order to be able to reach a theologically probable sentence or opinion on the theological character of Zen enlightenment.

In what sense can the Zenist recognize God?

It is said that Dr. Taisetsu Suzuki in his later years said to Professor Ryumin Akizuki[4], "There is not in the least any inconvenience for Zen to approve God". It is, however, often said that Zen Buddhism is "atheism". This is especially maintained by Professor Shin'ichi Hisamatsu—that Zen is "atheism".[5] Although there is not enough space to discuss Professor Hisamatsu's view in detail here, I believe that atheism in his view does not have its ordinary sense, but that it is, as Professor Katsumi Takizawa[6] and Seiichi Yagi[7] say, a view which may be admitted by those who know the true God. In the light of my close experience in Zen, it can be said that the Zen expression "When you encounter Buddha, kill Buddha" which apparently sounds as if one is denying Buddha (the absolute) is, as will be mentioned later in this paper, a living phrase which will bring the Zen practitioner to the "event" where the true Ultimate Being manifests itself.

Zen is nothing other than the self-realization of what the Rinzai calls "one rankless true man embodied in a lump of red flesh" and the life lived in this self-realization.[8] This "one rankless true man" is called the "formless self" (by Shin'ichi Hisamatsu), the "true self" (by Kitaro Nishida) and the "Trans-individual's individual" (by Taisetsu Suzuki).

"The lump of red flesh" is our concrete living body. "One rankless true man" is the real existence (original life, Buddha's life) which transcends all ranks and limitations. This "true man" is the "Trans-individual" in the terminology of Dr. Taisetsu Suzuki. This "Trans-individual" is not regarded as existing apart from us who exist with living bodies. The Zenist is always in the "event" where this "true man" is making the self (the individual) that is at this moment at this place, living and working; the Zenist performs acts from there and returns there. In this "event" the "Trans-individual" and the "individual" cannot be separated from each other, but are dynamically one in their function and exist operating totally as the "Trans-individual's individual". One who is in this "event" realizes that this living self is immediately the individual made to live by the "Trans-individual" (the "Trans-individual's individual").[9] It can be said that it is the self-realization by the subject who has become dynamically one with the Ultimate Being. This is the event called the spiritual awakening (satori).

Professor Nishida says, "In the self-realization, we return to the origin of our selves. It is, therefore, nothing other than entering into the origin of the formation of the world. When the self begins, the world begins. When the world begins, the self begins."[10] If that is the case, then the "event" mentioned above turns out to be the "first moment of the creation of the world."[11] The Zenist participates in this "first moment of the creation of the world" with his body and mind unified, realizes that he is the "Trans-individual's individual", and performs acts from there and returns there. In this "first moment", the "Trans-individual" and the "individual" are dynamically one, the mind and body one, the world and the self one. The "Trans-individual" is the dynamic power which unifies all things and makes them work as one.

What should be especially noted is the fact that in this "event", the "Trans-individual" and the "individual" are distinguished absolutely and yet at the same time they are immediately one. If one objectifies the "Trans-individual" in perceiving it, the unifying dynamism of the "Trans-individual's individual" is immediately destroyed and degrades from the "first moment of the creation" into the dimension of recognition by human reason.

Rinzai teaches us "When you encounter Buddha, kill Buddha" and Professor Shin'ichi Hisamatsu also expounds "atheism" simply because they intend to make us transcend the objectification of the "Trans-individual" (Buddha, God), to make us participate in the very "first moment of creation", stay there, and keep on performing acts from there. In that sense, it can be called the manifestation of the Bodhisattva's mind.

Incidentally, according to Professor Akizuki, if man keeps on living in the "event" and being always "one rankless man", then there is absolutely no place for Zen to admit such a useless idea as "God".[12] I also admit this, since it is clearly evident from what I have explained thus far. I would, however, like to go one step further and question on the point that this might include some kind of "experience of God" or some such experience no matter whether the person involved in it is conscious of it or not. In the third section of this paper, I would like to pursue this question according to my own experience in Zen and Christianity.

Professor Akizuki continues as follows. In fact it is absolutely difficult to be always a true man, ceaselessly. Therefore when one recognizes the contradiction between the "true self" one should properly be, and one's actual self, one comes to recognize "shame". Goso Hoen said, "After twenty years of my life in Zen Buddhism, I just came to realize shame", which is indeed the way a genuine Zenist should be. At this point, it cannot be helped that "God" should matter in Zen, because it is an actual existential fact that in this existential agony of "shame", the "Trans-individual" and the "individual" should be confronted with each other.[13] Professor Akizuki criticizes Professor Hismatsu's "atheism" as neglecting this point, but I will not go into this problem.

Zen Enlightenment and the Pauline Christ-experience.

After we have discussed Zen experience rather theoretically, we now come to reflect on it experientially.

Ordinary people may think in the following way. In doing Zen one must be in a "thought-less, image-less" state, and there must be no "object" of meditation or worship. On the other hand, Christian prayer, being offered to God, involves an object and content of meditation and of worship as well. In this way Zen and Christian prayer seem to present irreconcilable contrasts. So the following doubt arises with regard to what I said in my book: *Zen and the Bible* about my experience:[14] how can a Christian deepen his Christian prayer in doing Zen?

Ordinarily, it is thought that the objective in Zen is to attain the state of "no-mind". In fact for a long time I myself thought this was so. However, having done Zen to some extent, I had come to realize that such a general opinion is mistaken. Moreover, from reading Zen texts I have come to see that Zen does not aim at the so-called "thought-less, image-less" state. There are many texts to illustrate this, but let me just quote one Rinzai text on this point.

> The Patriarchs say, "If you settle your mind and perceive tranquility, take your mind and let it shine outwards, gather your mind and let it brighten inwards, concentrate the mind and enter *samadhi*, such a state is all but of artifice (i.e., delusion)".[15]

What then does Zen aim at? Again borrowing the words of Rinzai, it is "total, all-embracing activation".[16] The True Self comes to operate and dynamically to be activated in my living body in a total and all-embracing manner. The Zen Master Takuan himself expresses this from his own experience when he says that the state of "no-mind" is not to become as a blockhead, like a stone or a tree, but rather to be of a mind that pervades the whole body without lingering in any one particular place.

In actual fact, if one is well versed in the practices of Zen, it is not difficult to attain the state of "no-thought". However, one must not linger in this "thought-less, image-less" state. Mustering up all the energy of one's body-mind totality, exhausting all one's spiritual vitality, one must sit in Zen. The Zen Master under whom I am training and receiving direction constantly instructs his disciples in this way.

In this way, if one is able to sit exhausting one's spiritual vitality to the full, one will come to an awareness of dynamic energy and wisdom gushing forth. But the enlightenment experience that Zen aims at is not just that. A person training in Zen must transcend such a state, and completely and totally die to himself. "The Great Death, bringing forth New Life" is rightly the state which characterizes one who has come to this attainment. Dying the Great Death, the Original Self (the Life of the Enlightened) comes to be activated totally and in an all-embracing way in *this* living body. At this point, since the Life of the Enlightened (Buddha) becomes fully manifested and activated in my living body and I become aware of it as such, I become aware, in Zen Master Hakuin's words, that "this living body is itself the Buddha". This awareness is what Zen is aiming at.

The Christian experience is supposed to be heterogeneous to the Zen experience. I also had thought this was so before starting my Zen training. Since I have gotten some Zen experience, I have realized that the deeper the Christian experience is, the more similar it becomes to the Zen experience.

Surely in the early stages of Christian prayer, it is entirely different from Zazen, but as one comes to progress into deeper stages it comes to a very close similarity with what is aimed at in Zen. Many may think that Christian prayer is only turning to God to speak to Him, to ask for something as a petition, or to give thanks for some grace given. But as one comes to progress in prayer, one comes to know that God is not one who "stands vis-à-vis" oneself, but is One much more intimate that this. Moreover, as one's prayer deepens even further one comes to know that God dwells in oneself. In this way, God becomes not one who stands vis-à-vis me, as it were "confronting me", but one who lives and works within me. Further, God is not one "close by my side", but as Augustine said, one "more intimate to me than I am to myself".

Furthermore, this divine immanence in me is not a passive, static state as many Christians may tend to think, but in a surprising way very dynamic. Even for those who have made some progress in prayer, even those have experienced God's intimacy to some extent, there are many who think of God's immanent presence within the self in a static way. But the God that the scriptures proclaim is not a static God. He is a God who continues in his work of creation of the whole universe and who continues to operate in the whole of history. And what is more, "God so loved the world as to send his only-begotten Son" (John 3:16), and even right now loves me absolutely and infinitely. Then, He sends his Spirit, the spring and source of Love, to enable us to love God totally and wholeheartedly.

If this is the case, Christian prayer is something that must become more dynamic. "Strip off the old man, put on the new" as Paul says to this effect. The German mystic Meister Eckhart, who taught that, similar to Zen, one must strip off all thought, and conceptions and die with Christ, did so with the same point in mind. And the Zen practitioner experiences the "Great Death, bringing forth New Life", so the Christian dies with Christ and lives with him in the newness of life. Thus the dynamic life of Christ overflows in abundance, "out of the overflowing richness we received grace upon grace" (John 1:16), and one comes to the awareness of just this. Then "It is no longer I that lives, but Christ in me" (Gal. 2:20), as the Christian can say with Paul. That experience of Paul is something many Zen Masters have come to recognize.

From the foregoing reflection we may conclude that Zen enlightenment and the Pauline experience of Christ-living-in-me are similar to each other. We cannot maintain, however, at least so far, that they are the same or similar in their contents. It has been shown just that they are isomorphic. But we should pay special attention to the similarity in that they are penetrated by the dynamic existential principle: The Great Death, Bringing forth New Life.

A further step in the dialogue with the help of Karl Rahner's theology.

In this section I would like to make the dialogue move a step forwards by means of Rahner's theology. As it is a Catholic theology, no matter how great, the next step of the dialogue will be taken from a Catholic point of view.

"According to the Catholic understanding of the faith, as is clearly expressed in the Second Vatican Council, there can be no doubt that someone who has no concrete, historical contact with the explicit preaching of Christianity can nevertheless be a justified person who lives in the grace of Christ. He then possesses God's supernatural self-communication in grace not only as an offer, not only as an existential of his existence; he has also accepted this offer and so he has really accepted what is essential in what Christianity wants to mediate to him: his salvation in that grace which objectively is the grace of Jesus Christ",[17] though he may not be aware of it. With Rahner we can call such a person an "anonymous Christian".

It seems to me that the genuine Zenist comes under Rahner's classification. There are two reasons for my assertion. First because the Zen Enlightenment, as we have seen in the second section, is a self-awareness of dynamic oneness with the Ultimate Being. Entering into "the first moment of creation" the person realizes that his living body is "the Trans-individual's individual". In order to reach such a realization he must die the Great Death to live the New Life, as a Christian must die to the old man to live the Life of Christ. Secondly, as the Zen experience, as seen in the third section, is similar to the Pauline experience: "Christ is living in me", it is a natural inference that Christian salvation comes true in a genuine Zenist.

"What do we mean by God's self-communication more precisely? To explain this we must look once again to the essence of man which becomes present basically and originally in transcendental experience".[18] The transcendental experience is the subjective unthematic consciousness of both the knowing, free and responsible subject and his openness to the unlimited expanse of all possible reality. It is prior to and permeates every objective experience of particular things. In other words man experiences himself by means of knowing particular objects as transcending being, as a subject who transcends all particular objects, and at the same time is conscious of the term of transcendence as nameless undefinable mystery. By the fact that the term of transcendence extends beyond our reach and thus offers to knowledge the space for its individual objects of knowledge and love, this term is essentially distinct from anything which appears within it as an object.[19]

"Here man experiences himself as a finite, categorical existent as established in his difference from God by absolute being, and at the same time as an existent coming from absolute being and grounded in absolute mystery. The fact that he has his origin permanently in God and the fact that he is radically different from God are in their unity and mutually conditioning relationship fundamental existentials of man".[20]

"The term 'self-communication' is really intended to signify that God in his own most proper reality makes himself the innermost constitutive element of man".[21] If it is seen from man's side, "man is the event of God's absolute self-communication".[22] If looked back on to the transcendental experience of man, it is originally oriented toward God's absolute self-communication, in which the transcendental desire of man is fulfilled completely and "supra quam speravimus". In the event of God's self-communication "the term of transcendence and its object coincide in a way which subsumes both and their difference into a more original and ultimate unity which can no longer be distinguished conceptually".[23] Here God "is present in the mode of closeness and not only in the mode of distant presence as the term of transcendence, a closeness in which God does not become a categorical and individual being, but he is nevertheless really present as one communicating himself".[24] In self-communication God does not cease to be infinite reality and absolute mystery and man does not cease to be a finite existent different from God, who remains the absolutely nameless and ineffable One.[25] If you recall what was said about Zen experience, you would take notice of a similarity between "the Trans-individual's individual" and the event of God's self-communication. For in the act of "the Trans-individual's individual" as well as in the event of God's self-communication, the Trans-individual (God), no matter how different he is from the individual (man), becomes the innermost constitutive element of the individual (man), but still remains the absolutely nameless and ineffable.

From the above consideration we may conclude that the genuine Zen experience would be structurally similar to what Rahner explains in "man is the event of God's self-communication". If my judgment that a genuine Zenist is an anonymous Christian may be true, the above conclusion would seem to be highly probable.

FOOTNOTES

1 For "A true dialogue", cf. Kakichi Kadowaki, "Ways of Knowing: A Buddhist-Thomist Dialogue", *International Philosophical Quarterly*, vol. VI, no. 4 (Dec. 1966), pp. 574-75.

2 H. Dumoulin, *Christianity Meets Buddhism* (LaSalle, Ill.: Open Court, 1974), pp. 42, 77-80.

3 Y. Yokoi, *Zen Master Dōgen* (Tokyo: Weatherhill, 1976), p. 54.

4 K. Takizawa, S. Yagi, and R. Akizuki, *Where Can God Be Found?* (Jap.), (Sanichi Shobō, 1977), p. 284.

5 S. Hisamatsu, *The Absolute-Subject-Way* (Jap.), (Risōsha, 1972), pp. 53-93.

6 K. Takizawa, *Buddhism and Christianity* (Jap.), (Hōzōkan, 1964), pp. 22-32.

7 K. Takizawa, *Where Can God Be Found?*, p. 238; S. Yagi and S. Hisamatsu, *The Religion of Kaku* (Jap.), (Shunjūsha, 1981).

8 S. Ōmori, *An Introduction to Zazen* (Jap.), (Shunjūsha, 1980), pp. 13-15.

9 R. Akizuki, *Suzuki-Zengaku to Nishida-Tetsugaku*, (Shunjūsha, 1971), p. 58.

10 Nishida Kitarō Zenshū, *Iwanami Shoten*, vol. 11 (1965), p. 137.

11 R. Akizuki, *Auzuki-Zengaku to Nishida-Tetsugaku*, p. 57.

12 K. Takizawa, *Where Can God Be Found?*, pp. 285-86.

13 *Ibid.*, pp. 289, 296-97.

14 K. Kadowaki, *Zen and the Bible* (London: Routledge & Kegan Paul, 1980).

15 Rinzairoku (Jap.), *Iwanami Shoten* (1967), p. 71.

16 *Ibid.*, p.125.

17 K. Rahner, *Foundations of Christian Faith* (New York: Crossroad, 1978), p. 176.

18 *Ibid.*, p. 119.

19 *Ibid.*, pp. 52-55, 57-65.

20 *Ibid.*, p. 119.

21 *Ibid.*

22 *Ibid.*

23 *Ibid.*

24 *Ibid.*

25 *Ibid.*, p. 200.

Transcendental Humanism

A Paper About God

and Humanity

Ninian Smart

If in the West there is a prevailing world view which guides political, economic and educational thinking, it is scientific humanism. It is therefore no surprise that two prominent topics of philosophy these days are the nature of scientific method and the problems of utilitarianism. For the doctrine that we should aim so far as possible at the greatest happiness of the greatest number and the least suffering of the least number is the mostly unstated assumption of Western social policy and of its humanist ideology. And the doctrine that all that can be known can only be known through the application of scientific method is the mostly unstated ideology of most of our educated people and technocrats. The bridge between the two is technology, indeed; it is science brought to bear in the service of happiness and the elimination of suffering. Technology is secular magic.

Traditional religion has a rather differing vision. Happiness is not seen in conventional and worldly terms; and some kind of revelation or transcendental insight is seen as a source of knowledge over and above sense-experience and scientific exploration. Nevertheless, recent philosophy of religion in the West has had to take seriously the prevailing scientific and humanist context. The result is to soften the basis of religious knowledge. I want in this paper to consider a creative way to deal with this "softening", relating a new version of humanism, a transcendental humanism, to the nature of God.

When I say that there has been a softening of the basis of religious knowledge (actually, knowledge is not an appropriate word, but more of that later), I refer to the following ideas, themselves varying responses to the challenge of scientism—that is, the doctrine that all knowledge is in principle scientific knowledge.

There is the idea that a religious scheme of belief amounts in effect to a way of seeing the world, or of experiencing it: this is the picture we get from Wisdom through to Hick.

There is the idea that science deals with what is "objective", while religion deals with relationships which are subjective and personal: this is the existential personalism of Buber and Bultmann among others.

There is the idea that religious belief derives from a special kind of experience or intuition: this is the intuitionism of Otto through to H.D. Lewis.

About "experiencing as": here there is as it were a choice. We are not forced to see the world *sub specie aeternitatis*. About the "I-Thou" encounter: all may experience this with other humans, but only some seem to have such an encounter with the supreme Person. Likewise with the sense of the numinous and the intuition of the Transcendent.

But all that is fair enough, is it not? For the fact is that people are seriously divided in their apprehensions of the world. Many fine and not so fine people fail to believe in God; and many fine or not so fine people believe in God; there are others again who would not call the Transcendent, "God". Beliefs indeed abound, and world views are various. It is an ideologically and religiously plural world which we live in. This we knew already. So is it not reasonable for the epistemology of religion to take the basis of a belief system to be rather soft? It is this softness which explains how it is that some—beguiled by faith and a way of seeing things—are sure of their vision, and others do not seem to see the same thing at all.

There is in parallel with such philosophical and rather "soft" epistemologies the appeal to revealed authority. For many Christians the truth is known biblically and the Bible is seen as "given", as the revealed word of God. Even here some softenings can occur. Thus for the followers of Barth and some others, revelation is what the Bible is about; it is not the statements themselves. So we soften the text, as it were (doubting this and doubting that, as historical probings turn up problems about the statements), and—while making revelation transcendental—give yet a more ambiguous air to what is revealed. But even if we take a "hard" stance, we are bound to notice that problems arise in a different direction. Or rather, in two directions. In one direction we notice different conclusions being drawn from the same "hard" text: the Bible is one, but interpreters are many. This is the problem of hermeneutical scattering. In another direction there is the question of what is to be done when some statements taken in a "hard" way conflict with what the present state of science suggests is the case. It is out of this that the famous debate between science and religion in the West has chiefly stemmed. It is the primary reason why so-called "liberal" theologians have been unable to take a "hard" line.

Now if softening is just a matter of exigency, if it is just a matter of bending to the wind, then it loses credibility. Yet it seems that in the milieu of an increasingly scientifically trained world and in the context of a modern world view, it is impossible to avoid some degree of epistemological softening. But, as I shall argue, this softness is not something external to the religious situation: it is intrinsic to it, and—to put it more concretely—it is something arising from the very nature of the Transcendent.

I use here the word "Transcendent" partly out of recognition that there are profound religions, notably Buddhism, which do not accept the terminology of God, or indeed the doctrine of God as understood in the Western traditions. To simplify my discussion, however, I shall refer just to God, and here I mean to refer to the Being who is central to the faith of the Christian tradition and some others. Similar arguments as I shall here use apply in the case of Buddhism and Advaita Vedānta and other apparently not fully theistic faiths; but I shall not here deploy them. I shall keep the discussion within the context of God.

Further, the question of how to think about God is not just a problem in how to defend religious belief. It is not something to be defended. The issue is whether religion has something to offer, whether it helps in living, whether it provides insight. These fruits of religion are what is important. So the truth of religion is not something which so to speak has to be defended, perhaps by strategic withdrawals here and there in the face of the rampaging advances of the armies of scientific humanism. I want therefore at first, perhaps a little dogmatically, to present some ideas which, to me at least, indicate the relevance of religion to the world of today and to the context of scientific humanism.

First, the "breakthroughs" in the understanding of God have been chiefly, in the Western theistic traditions, through prophets. This prophetic side of religion is in essence challenging. So insofar as the prophet expresses God, he or she shows forth a God who challenges, who is dynamic, who impinges from "beyond" into our world. In the case of Jesus, the God he showed forth was both challenging and enigmatic, cutting through many of our assumptions. The challenging parable was the principal genre for Jesus to delineate the nature of the divine Being. God is not so much an exclamation mark as a question, a mysterious questioner. To pun: a cross-questioner.

A theology of such a God should then be an *interrogative* theology. It should also express divine creativity and dynamism. God is mystery, imagination, interrogation. This notion can perhaps be summed up by thinking of revelation as like an aphorism: an aphorism is original, and it is an imaginative and challenging way of saying something, and can, because of its brevity, give forth an air of mystery. I shall return to these points a little later.

Second, a religion indeed makes us experience the world *as*: experience it in a certain way. Part at least of the function of religion is to give us an overall vision of the world as we experience it. There is a divide here of a sort between science and religion: science is theoretical, quantitative, experimental. Religion sees the same world, but sees it in a contemplative rather than a theoretical mode. If it is experimental it is so in a very loose sense: it represents an experiment or a series of differing experiments in *living*. It is a mode of orientation for daily life.

Both science and religion go beyond common sense experience: the one by revealing curious unseen depths among the molecules and atoms and beyond the blue sky above; and the other by showing that the true world is a transfigured world, one seen in the light of eternity. It is not that science is irrelevant to these visions; but science is in the business of understanding, while the religious vision is concerned with significance. The one is analytic; the other in its way synthetic. The one is dispassionate and beyond value-judgments; the other turns values around and makes them more intense. So religion, to put it briefly, is *contemplative* rather than theoretical. The world, however, which it contemplates is also seen under one aspect through the theoretical lenses of scientific enquiry.

Third, theism involves (obviously) belief in a Being who is transcendent. But transcendence needs to be understood: it has an experiential as well as an ontological significance. In fact the two go together. For in saying that God is transcendent we are saying he is "beyond" the cosmos. But what is beyond here? It is not a literal spatial location. It means God is not in cosmic space. It means that he is independent of the cosmos—for it might go and he would still be; but he could not go without the cosmos going too, which means in addition that the cosmos is dependent. But if dependent, it is dependent everywhere and everywhen—here and now and continuously. So God is not just "beyond": he is everywhere present. So we can always feel that this is so: our vision of the world includes an experiment in living in the constant presence of God. So we might say that theism involves not just seeing the cosmos in a certain light, but seeing it as having depth, so that there is something beyond it and within it. This implies that religion differs from science not just in being contemplative rather than theoretical, but also in proposing an extra dimension of existence.

There is in science and in the open society which nourishes science as well as other forms of creativity—something which corresponds to theism's aphoristic and interrogative quality: it is the fact that science is a matter of imagination, criticism, testing. Truth is not taken upon authority: it is subject to testing and therefore ultimately to criticism. This Popperite insight is of central importance, and is often neglected in that science is so often presented in a dogmatic fashion. Science is in effect a kind of dialogue with nature in which new ideas are constantly being put forward awaiting nature's replies. The process of sifting and discarding theories requires a constant open-mindedness as well as the imaginative powers required for creating new theories to try out. So if theology is interrogative, science is critical.

(Yet, it will be said, this is not how things have often seemed. For has not theology had the reputation of being dogmatic, authoritarian? But in part this has been because in the Christian tradition the community was defined by dogma, and later the state too came to enforce dogma and conformity. But these are products of a particular kind of communal and social order.)

There is in the sphere of "secular" knowledge something too which corresponds to the contemplative nature of religion. For much of our scientific as well indeed as humanistic and social concerns are to do with beings who have consciousness. This consciousness can be by-passed, but in a most unsatisfactory manner, by behavioristic ways of exploring the living. As Bergson points out, if consciousness really plays no role in evolution, how did it come to be such a pervasive feature of the higher animals? So science itself is presented with consciousness as a reality. We are of course far from understanding how conscious beings operate. But whatever happens, we shall be left with the fact that nature, through us, is blue and green and red, and so forth; through us it twinkles and thunders; through us it has aromas and feels. Through us, and in some degree through the animals and fishes, even maybe through some crustaceans. Primarily, though, through us. And in a sense what we are left with, once we have dealt with the ways in which perception can issue in action and consciousness in decisions, is the experiencing of the cosmos and the experiencing of one another. In short: there is already in daily life a way in which we lead a contemplative existence, savoring the world around us and within.

There may be projects to unify psychology, biology and physics and to see experiences as brain processes; there may be desires to evolve a truly behavioristic or physicalistic way of understanding human beings. But such projects are just proposals. What we have are conscious beings. And both scientific and humanistic enquiry must connect this up as best they can with the world of electrons and galaxies. There is a contemplative side to nature. To adapt and go beyond Spinoza: the cosmos is *contemplatio sive natura.*

There is something in science, thirdly, which corresponds to the transcendental nature of theism. For science too subverts common sense. It goes behind the cosmos as revealed to contemplation or at least to the contemplations of everday life such as we have been pointing to. It has been a great intellectual and even emotional struggle to break away from earlier thoughts about the cosmos and come to see it in its electrical complexity and enormous scale. Today's theories doubtless will come to be questioned and greatly adapted before we are through: indeed, is there a state of "being through"? Perhaps the scientific quest is indefinite. Beneath the atom, the particle; beneath that the quark; beneath the quark maybe something else; and beneath that? Do the boxes within boxes go on forever? So there is a sense in which science is paradoxical: it tends to go on to conflict with received opinion. It builds on past paradoxes now become orthodoxies, and goes on to new paradoxes.

In brief, science is critical, and it is paradoxical; and it has to take account of experience as the contemplative side of nature.

But if we now turn to the humanistic side of the ideology of scientific humanism, we find certain questions begin to arise. First, there is the problem of the definition of happiness; conversely, there is also the question of the right attitude to suffering. Second, there is the question of the nature of the person, the human being, who according to the humanist is the ultimate bearer of values in the cosmos.

The notion of happiness is complex. One can be happy for a moment, but for the most part happiness is a dispositional concept. But it also typically has an object: one is happy because of some event or whatever. I am happy, let us say, because I see that my children are happy. And they are happy in their jobs and marriages and circumstances. But people may be happy at a shallow level: their goals may be shallow ones, so the happiness gained in achieving them may turn out too to be shallow. There is always a way in which happiness can thus be criticized: "Should you be happy like this?" "Is that true happiness?" And it is at this point that the question of a world view comes in. For what we value is in part to do with the way we arrange our values in a framework which sees our place in reality as a whole. Often we may not have thought out our world views very systematically. They tend in any case to be rather like collages: pieces of insight and knowledge here cobbled together with pieces drawn from other sources. But we do have such a framework: and this itself is open to criticism. In religious terms, conversion is what happens when one way of viewing the world is replaced by another way.

This gives a new role to religion. In traditional societies religion was often a means of conserving values. Religion was dogmatic because challenges to the existing world view were regarded as subversive. But now religion, itself open deeply to question, can no longer, because of the softness of its epistemology, dogmatize about human life. It can, however, question it. Religion comes in now as challenger and as cross-questioner.

It does so in part because it has a transcendental perspective. It asks whether true happiness is "of this world": that is, is true happiness to be found in secular experience? Often that experience is looked at in a shallow way: the consumerist society, for all its lovely achievements and its sense of respect often for the consumer, the human being, nevertheless can trivialize life. In being saved from poverty we often move into a very shallow prosperity. Life becomes devoted to fun. Fun is fine. But there is also life beyond fun.

Thus for theism there is a transcendental critique of secular humanism. This is where the aphoristic interrogation of the Beyond is a challenge to the values which we have from day to day.

A similar remark may be made in regard to the person. Why should the person be the ultimate bearer of values? Religion gives a new perspective on this question. The human being is seen as bearing the stamp of the divine Being, and like the latter, worthy of reverence. In the last resort our behavior towards one another roots respect in performative acts: the way we express our love and concern for others through acts and gestures—symbolically, so to say. The person gains his dignity from the rituals of life. Religion roots those rituals in a higher ritual: of worship of the divine Being.

In a world beset by the fragility of human rights and human courtesies, where so many humans are sacrificed on behalf of abstract and national causes, where people are tortured so other people can stay in power—in such a world, religion comes from Beyond as a challenge to these blasphemies against our brothers and sisters. This is not to say that the humanist cannot share these concerns: indeed humanism has often been a pioneer of them, over against dogmatic and unfeeling religion. But the transcendental gaze brings the person into the light of eternity.

Scientific humanism, when it brings into its own fabric the critique from Beyond, becomes what I call *transcendental humanism*. And because of the analogies which I have sketched between the scientific and religious outlooks, there is no great strain in holding a transcendental humanist viewpoint. One is not compelled to, because of the softness of the epistemology to which I earlier referred. But it is quite "natural", for both science in its paradoxicality and humanism in its reverence for persons can easily be seen in the light, as I say, of eternity.

Because of the critical character of theology, as I have sketched it, faith takes on a slightly different air, compared at any rate with some of the ways it has been viewed in the past. If we are not compelled to see the world in a theistic way—but this is as it were only one option in vision, one kind of experiencing *as*—then living by faith becomes indeed hazardous. It is a particular experiment in living. It is a way of trying out the vision in practice. See the world in the light of God and of eternity and then act thus and thus: see how you get on. See if your life genuinely gains significance. See if the life of others gains significance. There can be no question of absolute *knowledge*. I may commune with God: I may say "I know that my redeemer liveth", but this is not knowledge which can be shared outside of experimental faith. I can propose my vision to others. There is no question of proof.

I may think that the Bible is the word of God, but that is my choice. If I feel certitude in reading the Bible, this is because I have in effect seen the Bible as authoritative and revelatory. There can be no proof of this. So the Bible itself, unproved, cannot of course prove. The softness of the premises must carry over into the softness of conclusions. This means then that fundamentalism is itself an option for living. It is not compelling, save to those for whom it is compelling: and they are tragically mistaken if they think that the compulsion arises from anywhere but the nature of the transaction they are involved in.

That is to say that the softness is not just a matter of "this-worldly" epistemology, though it does arise from our end too. It arises because there are differing "revelations" and accounts of the Transcendent. It arises because of the hermeneutical scatter to which I earlier referred. There is a sort of relativism inherent in the epistemology of religion and world views, looked at from the human and this-worldly end. But there is also a softness which arises from the nature of God. The notion that God is transcendent includes the idea that she is different from the cosmos. It is true that some systems of thought argue that the cosmos is so to speak God's body. This is well worked out by Ramanuja for instance. But even here there is the notion that God as soul is different from cosmos as body. The attraction of the analogy is this: that God uses the cosmos, or events within the cosmos, to express herself. If we define a body as that which is under the control of a soul, then the cosmos is utterly within the control of its divine Soul. In fact it makes little difference whether we use the image of the cosmos as the divine body or see it as the expression of her creative will. But however much we may think of everything as under the control of God, yet the cosmos necessarily is a kind of veil. The imagery of revelation of course already suggests this: that the world is a veil which here and there, so to speak, is removed so that God can be seen through it. God unveils herself.

Indeed, it seems to be a consequence of the relative independence of the cosmos that it should veil its Creator. To be independent means to have independent existence: and this means in effect that the events of the cosmos should on the whole be regular, so that the cosmos has a pattern. If there were no regularities, there would be utter chaos and no cosmos. Utter chaos is equivalent to not existing as a separate something. So the cosmos has to have its own patterns to exist. So though it may express the divine Will, when looked at properly (from the theistic perspective), it nevertheless has its own non-divine nature.

So if God is to unveil herself, this unveiling has to be rather partial, through certain events or experiences which are more intensely revelatory of her than most "regular" events of the cosmos. Thus if I see with the eyes of faith I may see God in grains of sand, in the hair of dogs, in the grain of wood, yet there is little necessity in the experience itself to say "Lo, here is God". So even if there are events where God is much more evident—say in the dramatic experience of a prophet—they as cosmic events still have a place in the regular patterns of independent existence, and so even these are to some degree ambiguous and obscure. God may as it were smile at us through self-revelations, but there are ambiguities in the smile. Perhaps for us as for her, there is a sense of frustration: What lies behind the smile? Do we not wish somehow to penetrate beyond expression to the very being of the Beloved?

To put these things in different language, wherever there is divine input there is also always some human or worldly input. Every revelation meets at the interface between the eternal and the human, between the unchanging and the interpretative, between the certain and the fallible.

When we meet what is eternal we seem to gain a piece of it, to gain a certain unchanging something. We have encountered what cannot decay, and think therefore that we can translate divine into human words which themselves will have unchanging validity. But already in being put into human words interpretation has happened, and we are liable once again to the problem of hermeneutical scatter.

Not only this. If we are made in the image of God, we too are creators. If God wishes us to be creative—in human relations, in families, in science, in the arts, in technologies, in experiments in living, in visionary dynamism—then she must stir creativity in us. Such stirring is not done by handing down stereotypes of conduct. It is by challenging us. It is not for the Christian surprising, therefore, that Jesus should have taught so freshly and enigmatically, wielding knife-like parables, and acting out in his own life that strange mingling of fun and suffering and majesty and nothingness which led him to his Cross. Thus, revelation has to have a character of strange openness. This in turn leads to even greater hermeneutical scatter.

We may say that revelation is a matter of vision, and the means by which people are brought to vision are various. It is important for the Christian to recognize that doctrines and sacraments and texts are so many differing means towards creating a sense of the divine presence and the power of God in human beings. They are skilful means, to use a Buddhist notion.

It emerges in all this that a theistic world view is a vehicle for stimulating and expressing a vision of God and for bringing forth creativity in living. But we cannot suppose that vision and creativity can be had without at the same time attracting hermeneutical scatter; the world view breaks into many; the central conception and perception have many differing human incarnations in the differing styles of life which flow from them. So pluralism is an inescapable condition for the theist as well as for others. Thus there must be a degree of "softness" in our knowledge of God.

Indeed, "knowledge" may in one respect be the wrong word to use. For knowledge usually implies some degree of public agreement. This cannot be had in any strict way in the case of human interpretations of the vision of the Transcendent and of God. Direct experience can be had: but is this knowledge? Not if we think that knowledge has to be reduced to propositional form. For the web of statements which we make about God are themselves liable to revision and criticism.

If we stick to the vehicles of tradition, it is because we may think that they can help us to live fruitful lives and incorporate some insight into the creative nature of the Divine. We may think that authority can help us as a "skilful means". But if so, we are choosing authority, it is not choosing us.

The result of these reflections must be that the nature of God as challenging us from the Beyond, giving us the security of the eternal yet also stirring us through aphoristic interrogations of our lives, is mysterious, not easily to be captured in agreed statements, forever issuing in a critique of our societies and our ways of thinking and living. So our transcendentalism is necessarily a critical transcendentalism. Our humanism is necessarily pluralistic.

These observations are reinforced by reflecting too upon mysticism—the inward search for the divine and for the true self. Many mystics of East and West have tried in various ways to attain to a purification of consciousness in which outer and worldly thoughts and images are banished. It is as though they wanted to get to that pure something which underlies the experiences through which nature, in us, comes alive. It is the search for the pure version of that contemplative aspect of existence of which I spoke earlier. And it is the common testimony of mystics that that which they reach is beyond words. There is always, for the theist, something which cannot be said in relation to God. It is as though beyond our formulations there is an ineffable Godhead: pure light, indescribable. This is a religious reason why we should tolerate and indeed welcome hermeneutical scatter. Rigidity of propositions is not faithful to the experience of God. So a kind of fundamentalism is misleading. In taking too "hard" a line it fails adequately to represent the mysterious softness of the divine light and the divine night.

So it seems that a proper apprehension of God's nature would lead to an interrogative, transcendental, critical perspective which would also express a vision of the world by which the worldly humanisms of modern life could be judged. It, like science, would be open: but its aim is at experiments in living, in creativity and compassion of conduct in which the freedom of divine love is reflected in us.

And instead of our thinking that by seeing people in the light of the Transcendent their worth and the worth of this world are diminished, we should see that in the light of eternity human sacredness becomes more apparent, and a different kind of happiness is offered for those who wish to see morality in relation to the maximization of happiness and the minimization of suffering. The significance of the world is changed when it is perceived as created by that aphoristic God who cannot tell us all, for fear of causing us and the cosmos to dissolve.

So in this way religion, like science, becomes critical. This is religion within the limits of criticism alone.

Closing Remarks

Arabinda Basu

It is a privilege and a pleasure to be called upon to speak a few words at the close of the conference. From my conversations with many participants, I have discovered, to my satisfaction, that the consensus is that the conference has been a success. The organization, hospitality, the division of the groups, the methodology for the reading and response to the papers, and the comments made on them, have all been satisfactory and beneficial. It was also fitting that quite a number of scholars who have no religious convictions have been invited to contribute to a contemporary discussion on God.

In my concluding remarks, it is not my concern to say anything concerning the truth or otherwise of religious beliefs. Truth of life depends on the truth of being. If reality be only material, our life can only be an effort to enjoy the bounty of Nature. But we are not merely physical bodies, we have what in the absence of a better expression I will call a "vital force" which keeps the body alive and also feeds our minds. Man is primarily a mental being. He constructs systems of thought, paints pictures, sculpts statues, builds temples and synagogues, cathedrals and mosques, composes symphonies and concertos. He feels for his fellows and extends a helping hand to the needy. Many of us sacrifice our own immediate interests for the sake of what we consider to be the good of others. Universal Nature may or may not conserve these values that man cherishes. Nevertheless, man must continue to feel them worthy of realization and even under the threat that they will come to nothing in the last analysis, he must worship his ideals and values, as Bertrand Russell pointed out so eloquently in that magnificent prose poem, "A Free Man's Worship."

On the other hand, if there is a reality whose essence is other than physical, vital or mental, or a combination of these three, if in other words it is a spiritual reality, then our sense of value must undergo a sea-change. A time comes, in the lives of many human beings when the world cannot offer them anything which seems to be finally sustaining and satisfying. Transvaluation of values becomes incumbent upon such people. They reach out for something that has been variously called the Self, God, the Divine Being, the Absolute. Our concern in this conference has been with the problem of ecumenism. While all of the great religions proclaim that there is a unitary Being, who may or may not have many personal manifestations called gods and godesses, there have been diverse expositions of the nature of this Being and his relations to the world and man. There also have been diverse approaches to direct knowledge by immediate experience of God. Given this situation, how should we approach the problem of ecumenism? Many liberal and idealistic voices say that as enlightened people we should acknowledge the validity of the different paths to God and respect the mutual differences between the followers of the great religions even when we seek to find the common grounds of beliefs and practices. While this attitude is welcome and can be very effective, it seems to me that one of the requirements of religious ecumenism is an acknowledgement of the idea that the ultimate spiritual Reality is multi-faceted, that it has many aspects and that, therefore, revelations of that Reality vouched to different sections of mankind, must necessarily be divergent though not basically contradictory of each other. Given the variety of human nature, we must also allow diverse approaches to the Truth. "One Truth, many paths" should be the motto of ecumenism.

We should extend this idea even to those who do not have any religious beliefs or even deny the existence of God. For if God is the source of all existence and life, it stands to reason that he is the source of even those who cannot, for various reasons, bring themselves to believe in his reality. It is my firm conviction that God oversees our thoughts, emotions and volitions, initiates our seekings and aspirations, sustains our efforts and endeavors, assures and consummates our achievements. The inspired sages of illumined sight always see the all-pervasive Deity as an eye extended in heaven, *tad visnoh paraman padam sadā pasyanti surayah divivacaksuratatam.*

CONTRIBUTORS

Arabinda Basu
Professor of Philosophy, Sri Aurobindo International Centre of Education and Director, Sri Aurobindo Research Academy, Pondicherry (India)

Shlomo Biderman
Department of Philosophy, Tel Aviv University Ramat Aviv, Tel Aviv (Israel)

Petro B.T. Bilaniuk
Professor of Theology and Religious Studies, St. Michael's College, University of Toronto, Toronto, Ontario (Canada)

Jotiya D. Dhirasekera
Editor-in-Chief, Encyclopedia of Buddhism Ratmalana (Sri Lanka)

John N. Findlay
Professor of Philosophy, Boston University Boston, Massachusetts (USA)

Christian R. Gaba
Professor, Department of Religious Studies University of Calabar, Calabar (Nigeria)

Vitaliano Gorospe, S.J.
Professor, Departments of Philosophy and Theology, Ateneo de Manila University Quezon City (Philippines)

John H. Hick
H.G. Wood Professor of Theology, Birmingham University (United Kingdom) and Danforth Professor of Religion, Claremont Graduate School Claremont, California (USA)

Gaafar Sheikh Idris
Associate Professor, Research Centre Riyadh (Saudi Arabia)

William Johnston, S.J.
Professor, Sophia University Tokyo (Japan)

Kakichi Kadowaki
Professor of Philosophy, Sophia University Tokyo (Japan)

Young Oon Kim
Professor of Systematic Theology Unification Theological Seminary Barrytown, New York (USA)

Chung Hwan Kwak
Advisor, HSA-UWC and Vice-President International Cultural Foundation New York City (USA)

Eugene T. Long
Professor of Philosophy, University of South Carolina, Columbia, South Carolina (USA)

John Macquarrie	Professor, University of Oxford, Oxford, England (United Kingdom)
Tiruppattur R.V. Murti	Professor Emeritus of Philosophy Banaras Hindu University, Varanasi (India)
Heinrich C. Ott	Professor, University of Basel Basel (Switzerland)
Philip L. Quinn	Professor of Philosophy, Brown University Providence, Rhode Island (USA)
John K. Roth	Russell K. Pitzer Professor of Philosophy Claremont Men's College Claremont, California (USA)
Robert P. Scharlemann	Commonwealth Professor of Religious Studies, University of Virginia, Charlottesville, Virginia (USA)
Ninian Smart	Professor of Religious Studies, University of California at Santa Barbara (USA) and University of Lancaster, England (United Kingdom)
Huston Smith	Professor of Philosophy and Religion Syracuse University, Syracuse, New York (USA)
Kapil N. Tiwari	Senior Lecturer and Head, Department of Religious Studies, Victoria Unversity Wellington (New Zealand)
Theodore R. Vitali	Associate Professor of Philosophy, Bellarmine College, Louisville, Kentucky (USA)

PARTICIPANTS

Masao Abe	Professor of Religion, Claremont Graduate School, Claremont, California (USA)
Mahmoud M. Abu-Saud	Head of Islamic Studies and Research Southwest Missouri State University Springfield, Missouri (USA)
Isma'il R. al-Faruqi	Professor of Islamics, Temple University Philadelphia, Pennsylvania (USA)
Lois L. al-Faruqi	Professor, Dept. of Religion College of Liberal Arts, Temple University Phildelphia, Pennsylvania (USA)
Roy C. Amore	Professor of Religion, University of Windsor Windsor, Ontario (Canada)
Joseph O. Awolalu	Head of Department of Religious Studies University of Ibadan, Ibadan (Nigeria)
Larry E. Axel	Associate Professor of Philosophy Purdue University West Lafayette, Indiana (USA)
Anne M. Bancroft	Author and Lecturer, Dorset (United Kingdom)
Arabinda Basu	Professor of Philosophy, Sri Aurobindo International Centre of Education and Director, Sri Aurobindo Research Academy Pondicherry (India)
Mohamed Ben-Bachir	Faculté des Lettres de Rabat Rabat (Morocco)
Joseph D. Bettis	Professor of Religion Western Washington University Bellingham, Washington (USA)
Agehananda Bharati	Professor of Anthropology Syracuse University, Syracuse, New York (USA)
Shlomo Biderman	Department of Philosophy Tel Aviv University Ramat Aviv, Tel Aviv (Israel)
Petro B.T. Bilaniuk	Professor of Theology and Religious Studies St. Michael's College, University of Toronto Toronto, Ontario (Canada)

Hector Borrat	Professor of Law and Social Sciences Facultad de Ciencias de la Informacion Universidad Autonoma de Barcelona Barcelona (Spain)
Maurice Boutin	Associate Professor of Theology University of Montreal Montreal, Quebec (Canada)
Lawrence B. Briskman	Lecturer in Philosophy, University of Edinburgh, Edinburgh (United Kingdom)
Colin G. Brown	Senior Lecturer in Religious Studies University of Canterbury Christchurch (New Zealand)
Delwin Brown	Professor of Religious Studies, Arizona State University, Tempe, Arizona (USA)
M. Darrol Bryant	Associate Professor of Religion and Culture Renison College, University of Waterloo Waterloo, Ontario (Canada)
Ronald L. Burr	Associate Professor of Philosophy and Religion, University of Southern Mississippi Hattiesburg, Mississippi (USA)
A. Byaruhanga-Akiiki	Head of Department and Dean of Faculty of Arts, Makerere University, Kampala (Uganda)
David W. Chappell	Associate Professor, Religion Department University of Hawaii at Manoa Honolulu, Hawaii (USA)
Margaret Chatterjee	Professor and Head of Department of Philosophy, Delhi University, Delhi (India)
Jose Chaves	Ambassador O.E.I. to the United Nations New York City (USA)
Chung-Ying Cheng	Professor of Philosophy University of Hawaii, Honolulu, Hawaii (USA)
Bowman Clarke	Professor of Philosophy University of Georgia, Athens, Georgia (USA)
Cromwell Crawford	Department of Religion University of Hawaii at Manoa Honolulu, Hawaii (USA)

410

Donald W. Dayton	Librarian and Assistant Professor of Historical Theology, Northern Baptist Theological Seminary, Lombard, Illinois (USA)
Frank P. De Graeve	Professor of Comparative Religion Catholic University, Leuven Heverlee (Belgium)
Padmasiri De Silva	Chairman, Department of Philosophy University of Peradeniya Peradeniya (Sri Lanka)
Guy Deleury	Writer, Neuvy-le-Roi (France)
U. Dhammaratana	Honorary Professor of Pali and Buddhist Philosophy, Mahar Vihara, Nalanda, Bihar (India)
Mariasusai Dhavamony	Professor of History and Philosophy of Religion, Gregorian University, Rome (Italy)
Peter A. Dopamu	Lecturer, Department of Religion University of Ilorin, Ilorin (Nigeria)
Christian Kobla Dovlo	Member, Council of State, Accra (Ghana)
Tom Driver	Professor of Theology and Culture Union Theological Seminary, New York City (USA)
D.J.C. Duraisingh	Assistant Professor in Theology and Ethics Director, Interfaith Dailogue Centre United Theological College, Bangalore (India)
Mose Durst	President, Unification Church of America New York, New York (USA)
Leo J. Elders	Professor of Metaphysics Rolduc, Kerkrade (the Netherlands)
Leonard J. Eslick	Professor of Philosophy St. Louis University, St. Louis, Missouri (USA)
Frederick P. Ferré	Professor of Philosophy and Head of Department, University of Georgia, Athens, Georgia (USA)
John N. Findlay	Professor of Philosophy Boston University, Boston, Massachusetts (USA)
Rainer Flasche	Professor, Department of History of Religions Philipps University, Marburg (West Germany)

Anthony G.N. Flew	Professor of Philosophy and Head of Department, The University, Reading (United Kingdom)
A. Durwood Foster	Professor of Christian Theology Pacific School of Religion and Graduate Theological Union, Berkeley, California (USA)
Helmut Fritzsche	Director, Department of Theology Wilhelm-Pieck-Universität Rostock (East Germany)
Christian R. Gaba	Professor, Department of Religious Studies University of Calabar, Calabar (Nigeria)
Walter Gardini	Professor and Research Fellow, Escuela de Estudios Orientales, Universidad del Salvador Buenos Aires (Argentina)
Lloyd G. Geering	Professor of Religious Studies Victoria University, Wellington (New Zealand)
Erich W. Geldbach	Reader, University of Marburg Consultant, Konfessionskundliches Institut des Evangelischen Bundes, Bensheim (West Germany)
Adolphe P.M.F. Gesche	Professor, Université de Louvain Louvain-La-Neuve (Belgium)
Vitaliano Gorospe S.J.	Professor, Departments of Philosophy and Theology, Ateneo de Manila University Quezon City (Philippines)
Shrivatsa Goswami	Director, Sri Caitanya Prema Sansthana Vrindaban (India)
David R. Griffin	Professor of Philosophy of Religion School of Theology at Claremont Claremont, California (USA)
John H. Hick	H.G. Wood Professor of Theology, Birmingham University (United Kingdom) and Danforth Professor of Religion, Claremont Graduate School, Claremont, California (USA)
William Hill	Associate Professor of Systematic Theology Catholic University of America Washington, D.C. (USA)
A. Masaaki Honda	Professor of Philosophy, School of Medicine University of Occupational and Environmental Health, Kitakyushu (Japan)

412

Ching-Fen Hsiao	President, Tainan Theological College Tainan (Republic of China)
Hubertus G. Hubbeling	Professor, Faculteit der Godgeleerheid Rijksuniversiteit, Groningen (the Netherlands)
Phil-Ho Hwang	Assistant Professor of Philosophy Dongguk University, Seoul (South Korea)
Shohei Ichimura	Kealakekua, Hawaii (USA)
Gaafar Sheikh Idris	Associate Professor, Research Centre Riyadh (Saudia Arabia)
Lawford Ndege Imunde	Lecturer and Head, Department of Religion and Society, St. Paul's United Theological College, Limuru (Kenya)
Alfred E. Jäger	Professor, Kirchliche Hochschule Bielefeld (West Germany)
Theodore E. James	Professor Emeritus of Philosophy Manhattan College, New York City (USA)
Izzat M. Jaradat	Director, General Islamic Congress Amman (Jordan)
Elavinakuzhy C. John	Study Secretary, Evangelisches Missionwerk Stuttgart (West Germany)
William Johnston, S.J.	Professor, Sophia University Tokyo (Japan)
William R. Jones	Director, Black Studies Program Florida State University Tallahassee, Florida (USA)
Lal M. Joshi	Professor and Chairman, Dept. of Religious Ethics, Punjabi University, Patiala (India)
Kakichi Kadowaki	Professor of Philosophy, Sophia University Tokyo (Japan)
David J. Kalupahana	Professor of Philosophy University of Hawaii at Manoa Honolulu, Hawaii (USA)
Asa Kasher	Professor, Department of Philosophy Tel Aviv University, Tel Aviv (Israel)
Ezekiel M. Kasiera	Lecturer, Department of Religious Studies University of Nairobi, Nairobi (Kenya)

M. Wasiullah Khan	Chancellor, East-West University Chicago, Illinois (USA)
Sam G. Kibicho	Head, Department of Religious Studies University of Nairobi, Nairobi (Kenya)
David S.C. Kim	President, Unification Theological Seminary Barrytown, New York (USA)
Young Oon Kim	Professor of Systematic Theology Unification Theological Seminary Barrytown, New York (USA)
Kamuti Kiteme	Associate Professor, Black Studies Department City College, New York City (USA)
T. James Kodera	Chairman and Associate Professor of Religion Department of Religion, Wellesley College Wellesley, Massachusetts (USA)
Richard Kropf	Writer, Johannesburg, Michigan (USA)
Chung Hwan Kwak	Advisor, HSA-UWC Vice-President, International Cultural Foundation, New York City (USA)
Whalen W. Lai	Assistant Professor of Religious Studies University of California at Davis Davis, California (USA)
Basant Lal	Professor and Head of Department of Philosophy, Magadh University, Bodh Gaya (India)
Myrtle S. Langley	Course Leader/Head, Practical Theology and Missiology, Trinity College Bristol (United Kingdom)
Peter D. Latuihamallo	Professor of Social Ethics Graduate School of Theology, Jakarta (Indonesia)
Seung-Kook Lew	Dean of the School of Confucian Studies Sungkyunkwan University, Seoul (South Korea)
Tu Li	Professor and Coordinator, Department of Philosophy, New Asia College The Chinese University of Hong Kong Shatin, N.T. (Hong Kong)
Shu-hsien Liu	Professor of Philosophy, New Asia College The Chinese University of Hong Kong Shatin, N.T. (Hong Kong)

414

Aloysius P. Lobo, S.J.	Professor of Systematic Theology St. Joseph's Regional Seminary Allahabad (India)
David M. Lochhead	Associate Professor of Systematic Theology Vancouver School of Theology Vancouver, British Columbia (Canada)
Eugene T. Long	Professor of Philosophy University of South Carolina Columbia, South Carolina (USA)
Bernard M. Loomer	Retired, El Cerrito, California (USA)
John T. Maniatis	Executive Director of New ERA and Head Librarian, Unification Theological Seminary Barrytown, New York (USA)
Pino Marras	Lecturer, TENRI University Kobe (Japan)
George N. Marshall	Minister/Director, Church of the Larger Fellowship, Unitarian Universalist Boston, Massachusetts (USA)
Peter D. Masefield	Visiting Fellow, Department of Religious Studies, University of Sydney Sydney, New South Wales (Australia)
George I. Mavrodes	Professor of Philosophy, University of Michigan, Ann Arbor, Michigan (USA)
Vincent A. McCarthy	Associate Professor of Philosophy Central Connecticut State College West Hartford, Connecticut (USA)
Malcolm D. McLean	Lecturer in Religious Studies University of Otago, Dunedin (New Zealand)
John C. Meagher	Professor of Theology and Religious Studies St. Michael's College, University of Toronto Toronto, Ontario (Canada)
Leonardo Mercado	President, Divine Word University Tacloban City (Philippines)
Jeremy E. Miller	Professor of Systematics Lutheran School of Theology Chicago, Illinois (USA)
Kewal Mittal	Reader in Buddhist Philosophy Department of Buddhist Studies University of Delhi, Delhi (India)

415

Battista J. Mondin	Dean of Philosophy, Pontifica Universitè Urbaniana, Citta del Vaticano (Italy)
Peter Munz	Professor of History, Victoria University Wellington (New Zealand)
K. Satchidananda Murty	Professor of Philosophy, Andhra University Waltair (India)
Michael Y. Nabofa	Lecturer, Department of Religious Studies University of Ibadan, Ibadan (Nigeria)
James S. Nelson	Associate Professor of Religion/Philosophy North Park College, Chicago, Illinois (USA)
Francis W.R. Nichol	Principal and Professor of Theology Knox College, Dunedin (New Zealand)
Wellington W. Nyangoni	Chairman and Associate Professor, African and Afro-American Studies Department, Brandeis University, Sudbury, Massachusetts (USA)
Anthony O'Hear	Lecturer in Philosophy, University of Surrey Guildford, Surrey (United Kingdom)
Henry Odera Oruka	Professor, Department of Philosophy University of Nairobi, Nairobi (Kenya)
Heinrich C. Ott	Professor, University of Basel Basel (Switzerland)
Govind C. Pande	Professor of Ancient History Centre of Advanced Study, University of Allahabad, Allahabad (India)
R.C. Pandeya	Professor of Philosophy, University of Delhi Delhi (India)
Raimundo Panikkar	Professor, Department of Religious Studies University of California Santa Barbara, California (USA)
Nelson Pike	Professor of Philosophy University of California Irvine, California (USA)
Martin H. Prozesky	Senior Lecturer, Department of Divinity University of Natal Pietermaritzburg (South Africa)
Richard A. Quebedeaux	Author, Berkeley, California (USA)

416

Philip L. Quinn	Professor of Philosophy, Brown University Providence, Rhode Island (USA)
Emerita S. Quito	Department Chairperson and Professorial Chair Holder, Department of Philosophy De La Salle University, Manila (Philippines)
K.L. Seshagiri Rao	Professor of Religious Studies University of Virginia Charlottesville, Virginia (USA)
Gene Reeves	Dean, Chief Executive and Professor Meadville/Lombard Theological School Chicago, Illinois (USA)
Paul A. Rentz	Ph.D. Candidate, Michigan State University East Lansing, Michigan 2(USA)
Herbert W. Richardson	Professor of Theology St. Michael's College, University of Toronto Toronto, Ontario (Canada)
Samdhong L.T. Rinpoche	Principal of the Central Institute of Higher Tibetan Studies, Sarnath (India)
James Deotis Roberts	Professor/President, International Theological Center, Atlanta, Georgia (USA)
James Robinson	Professor of Religion, Claremont Graduate School, Claremont, California (USA)
John K. Roth	Russell K. Pitzer Professor of Philosophy Claremont Men's College Claremont, California (USA)
Betty R. Rubenstein	Arts Journalist and Arts Historian for the *Tallahassee Democrat*, Tallahassee, Florida (USA)
Richard L. Rubenstein	Robert O. Lawton Distinguished Professor of Religion, Florida State University Tallahassee, Florida (USA)
Jörg Salaquarda	Privatdozent (Philosophie) Freie Universität Berlin Berlin (West Germany)
Martin L. Samuels	Executive Director, Church of Scientology Mission of Davis, Sheridan, Oregon (USA)
Andy F. Sanders	Assistant Professor, State University of Groningen, Groningen (the Netherlands)

Osvaldo Santagada	Professor, Catholic University Buenos Aires (Argentina)
Hans M. Sass	Professor, Department of Philosophy Georgetown University, Washington, D.C. (USA)
Robert P. Scharlemann	Commonwealth Professor of Religious Studies, University of Virginia Charlottesville, Virginia (USA)
Michel L.C. Schooyans	Professor, Université de Louvain College Jacques Leclercq, Louvain-La-Neuve (Belgium)
Osborne E. Scott	Professor of Religious Studies City College, New York City (USA)
Leroy Seat	Visiting Professor of Religion William Jewell College Kansas City, Missouri (USA)
Santosh C. Sengupta	Professor of Philosophy, University of Visva-Bharati, West Bengal (India)
Paul Sharkey	Associate Professor of Philosophy and Religion, University of Southern Mississippi Hattiesburg, Mississippi (USA)
Arvind Sharma	Lecturer, Department of Religious Studies University of Sydney Sydney, New South Wales (Australia)
Rachel Shihor	Lecturer, Department of Philosophy Tel Aviv University Ramat Aviv, Tel Aviv (Israel)
Ramakant A. Sinari	Professor of Philosophy and Chairman, Department of Humanities and Social Sciences Indian Institute of Technology, Bombay (India)
Krishna Sivaraman	Professor of Comparative Religion Visva-Bharati University, West Bengal (India)
Ninian Smart	Professor of Religious Studies, University of California at Santa Barbara (USA) and University of Lancaster, England (United Kingdom)
Huston Smith	Professor of Philosophy and Religion Syracuse University, Syracuse, New York (USA)

Frederick Sontag	Professor of Philosophy Claremont Graduate School Claremont, California (USA)
John St. John	Author and Company Director London (United Kingdom)
Wolfgang Stribrny	Professor, Pädagogosche Hochschule Flensburg (West Germany)
S.M. Tewari	Professor of Philosophy University of Gorakhpur, Uttar, Pradesh (India)
James C. Thornton	Senior Lecturer in Philosophy and Religious Studies, University of Canterbury Christchurch (New Zealand)
Gregory Tillett	Executive Editor, Encyclopedia of Religion in Australia, Sydney, New South Wales (Australia)
Kapil N. Tiwari	Senior Lecturer, Department of Religious Studies, Victoria University, Wellington (New Zealand)
Mahesh Tiwary	Professor of Buddhist Studies Delhi University, Delhi (India)
Wolor Topor	Deputy Minister of Justice, Monrovia (Liberia)
Garry W. Trompf	Senior Lecturer and Head, Department of Religious Studies, University of Sydney Sydney, New South Wales (Australia)
Jaganath Upadhyaya	Professor and Dean of Faculty, Shramanvidya Sankaya, Sampurnanand Sanskrit University, Varanasi (India)
C.S. Upasak	Retired Professor and Former Director, Nalanda, Varanasi (India)
Jack Verheyden	Professor of Theology, School of Theology Claremont, California (USA)
Theodore R. Vitali	Associate Professor of Philosophy Bellarmine College, Louisville, Kentucky (USA)
Michael von Brueck	Visiting Professor, Gurukul Lutheran Theological College, Kilpauk, Madras (India)
R.J. Zwi Werblowsky	Professor of Comparative Religion The Hebrew University, Jerusalem (Israel)